The Functions of Arbitral Institutions

International Arbitration Law Library

VOLUME 38

Editor

Professor Julian D.M. Lew QC has been involved with international arbitration for more than 40 years as counsel, as arbitrator and as an academic. He has held the position of Professor and Head of the School on International Arbitration, Centre for Commercial Law studies, Queen Mary University of London since its creation in 1985. He is now an independent arbitrator at 20 Essex Street, London.

Introduction

Since its first volume published in 1993, this authoritative practitioner-oriented series has published in-depth and analytical works on niche aspects of international arbitration, authored by specialists in the field.

Objective

This authoritative and established series covering in-depth analyses of niche areas appeals to both practitioners and academics.

Frequency

A volume is published whenever an interesting topic presents itself.

The titles published in this series are listed at the end of this volume.

The Functions of Arbitral Institutions

Rémy Gerbay

Wolters Kluwer

Published by:
Kluwer Law International B.V.
PO Box 316
2400 AH Alphen aan den Rijn
The Netherlands
Website: www.wklawbusiness.com

Sold and distributed in North, Central and South America by:
Wolters Kluwer Legal & Regulatory U.S.
7201 McKinney Circle
Frederick, MD 21704
United States of America
Email: customer.service@wolterskluwer.com

Sold and distributed in all other countries by:
Turpin Distribution Services Ltd
Stratton Business Park
Pegasus Drive, Biggleswade
Bedfordshire SG18 8TQ
United Kingdom
Email: kluwerlaw@turpin-distribution.com

Printed on acid-free paper.

ISBN 978-90-411-6217-5

Printed in the United Kingdom.

A Blandine, Arnaud, Caroline et Antoine Gerbay.
A ma chère Eileen, ainsi qu'à notre fils qui arrive en juillet!

About the Author

Dr *Rémy Gerbay* is an international arbitration lawyer who divides his time between private practice and academia.

He is *Of Counsel* at Enyo Law LLP in London, and a lecturer (full time/ permanent) at the School of International Arbitration, Queen Mary University of London. Remy also frequently sits as arbitrator. He has been appointed as co-arbitrator, sole arbitrator and Presiding arbitrator in ad hoc and institutional arbitrations.

Remy is qualified as an Attorney (State of New York) and as a Solicitor (England and Wales). He holds a PhD from Queen Mary University of London, an LLM from Georgetown University (Dean's List, Fulbright Scholar), a Masters from the University of Geneva (Graduate Institute), and a French law degree from the University of Lyon (Jean Moulin).

Remy is a co-Chair of the LCIA's Young International Arbitration Group (YIAG). He is a member of the Editorial Board of the *Journal of International Arbitration*. Remy is a former Deputy Registrar of the LCIA and former Registrar pro tem of DIFC-LCIA in Dubai.

Table of Contents

About the Author vii

Foreword xv

Preface xix

List of Figures xxi

List of Tables xxiii

List of Abbreviations xxv

Acknowledgements xxvii

Introduction 1

CHAPTER 1
Understanding the Notion of Arbitral Institution: Definitions and Typologies 5
§1.01 Introduction 5
§1.02 Defining "Institutional Arbitration" 6
[A] Contingent Definitions: Defining Institutional Arbitration by Distinguishing It from Neighbouring Notions 6
[1] Institutional Arbitration Defined by Comparison with ad hoc Arbitration 6
[2] Institutional Arbitration Defined by Comparison with Judicial Mechanisms 8
[B] An Autonomous Definition: Defining Institutional Arbitration by Identifying Its Essential Characteristics 11
[1] Permanent Organization 12

[2] Arbitration Rules 13
[3] The Services 14
§1.03 Defining "Arbitral Institutions" 18
§1.04 Typologies of Arbitral Institutions 19
[A] Legal Status of Arbitral Institutions 19
[B] Self-Standing Independent Institutions versus Institutions Connected to Another Organization or a State 21
[C] Charitable versus For-Profit 23
[D] Types of Cases Handled: Generalist Institutions versus Specialist Ones 24
[E] Domestic versus International 25
[F] Cultural Background and Historical Heritage 26

CHAPTER 2
Institutional Arbitration as a Growing Phenomenon: Quantitative Growth, "Institutionalization" and "Judicialization" 29
§2.01 Increasing Use of Institutional Arbitration: The Quantitative Growth 29
[A] Increase in the Volume of Cases Referred to Institutions 29
[B] Increase in the Number of Institutions 33
[C] The Rationale behind the Growth: The Perceived Benefits of Institutional Arbitration 35
[1] Logistical Support 35
[2] Pre-established Arbitration Rules 36
[3] Authority in the Implementation of the Rules 37
[4] Treatment of Costs 38
[5] Enhanced Enforceability of the Award 39
[6] Lower Costs 39
[7] Confidentiality 41
[D] Popularity of Institutional Arbitration versus Legitimacy of Arbitral Institutions 43
§2.02 Institutionalization of Arbitration? The Alleged Qualitative Growth 47
[A] Institutionalization of Arbitration 47
[B] Institutionalization versus Judicialization 51

CHAPTER 3
An Overview of the Activities of Arbitral Institutions: Institutional Arbitration as a Multifacted Reality 55
§3.01 Introduction 55
§3.02 Non-casework Activities 56
[A] Awareness Raising, Training, Advocacy and Policy 56
[B] Activities Relating to Other Forms of ADR and ad hoc Arbitration 58
§3.03 Casework Activities 59
[A] The Initial Stages (Up to the Constitution of the Tribunal) 60

[1] Receipt and Notification of the Request for Arbitration 60
[2] Which Sets of Rules Apply? 61
[3] Decisions on Language 63
[4] Decisions regarding the Seat or Place of the Arbitration 64
[5] Extension of Deadlines 66
[6] Decisions on Jurisdiction 68
[7] Interim Measures 71
[8] Consolidation of Proceedings 73
[9] Joinder of Third Parties 77
[10] Constitution of the Tribunal: Decision on the Number of Arbitrators 79
[11] Constitution of the Tribunal: Selection of Arbitrators 80
[12] Constitution of the Tribunal: Confirmation of Arbitrators 82
[B] The Proceedings Proper (from the Constitution of the Tribunal to the Award) 84
[1] Approval of Terms of Reference 84
[2] Logistical Support 84
[3] Treatment of Costs 86
[4] Challenges to, and Removal of, Arbitrators 89
[5] General Power of Interpretation of the Rules 92
[6] General Supervision Role 95
[C] The Award and Post-award Phase 100
[1] Scrutiny of Draft Awards 100
[2] Issue of Awards and Assistance with Enforcement 103
§3.04 Different Levels of Institutional Involvement Expressed as A Continuum: The Spectral Representation of Institutional Arbitration 104
[A] Why a Continuum? 104
[B] Caveat: Limitations of the Spectral Representation of Institutional Arbitration 107
[C] First Continuum: From the Filing of a Request for Arbitration to the Constitution of the Tribunal 109
[D] Second Continuum: From the Constitution of the Tribunal to the Award 112
§3.05 Chapter Conclusions 115

CHAPTER 4
The Traditional Representations of the Role of Institutions: A Critical Evaluation 117
§4.01 Chapter Introduction 117
§4.02 First Representation: An Occasional Participant in the Adjudicative Process Which Decisions Are Somehow Immaterial 118
[A] Presentation of the Representation 118

[1] Short Overview 118
[2] Rationale behind the Representation: The Non-applicability of Due Process Requirements, and the Necessity to Preserve the Effectiveness of Institutional Arbitration 123
[3] Origins and Historical Development of the First Representation 125
[a] The *Société Appareils Dragon* Case 126
[b] The *Société Techni Import Professionnel* Case 129
[c] The *Syrian Refineries* Case 130
[d] The *Opinter v. Dacomex* Case 133
[e] The *SCPA* Case 135
[f] The *REDEC* and *Pharaon* Case 137
[g] The *Cubic Defense System* Case 139
[h] The *Guinea v. CAP* Case 142
[i] Recent Decisions 144
[B] Critical Analysis of the First Representation: Rejection of the "Administrative" versus "Jurisdictional" Dichotomy 147
[1] Rejection of the Arguments Based on Material Criteria 148
[a] Argument Based on the Lack of Finality of the Institutional Decisions 149
[b] Argument Based on the Timing of Institutional Decisions 151
[c] Arguments That Institutional Decisions Do Not Decide between Two Conflicting Positions 153
[d] Arguments Based on the Alleged Organizational Character of Institutional Decisions 155
[2] Rejection of the Arguments Based on Organic Criteria 158
[a] Argument That Institutions Are Not Arbitrators 158
[b] Argument That the Parties Have Agreed to Confer a Non-jurisdictional Function to the Institution 160
[c] Arguments Based on an Alleged "Unity of the Adjudicative Mission" of the Arbitrator 163
[C] Conclusions on the First Representation 172
§4.03 Second Representation: A Mere Purveyor of Logistical Services with No Decision-Making Power at All 173
[A] Presentation of the Representation 173
[B] Critical Analysis of the Representation: Institutions Do Have a Measure of Decision-Making Power 175
[C] Conclusions on the Second Representation 182
§4.04 Chapter Conclusions 183

CHAPTER 5
A Realistic Representation of the Role of Institutions: Arbitral Institutions as Ancillary Participants in the Adjudicative Process 185
§5.01 Introduction 185
§5.02 Substance of the Representation 187
[A] Proposition 1: The Decisional Character of Certain Institutional Measures 187
[B] Proposition 2: Ancillary Nature of the Role of the Institution 188
[C] Proposition 3: Materiality of Institutional Decisions 188
[D] Proposition 4: The Rejection of Dichotomic Approaches 196
§5.03 Consequences of the Representation 196
[A] Proposition 5: Desirability of the Application of Due Process by Institutions When They Participate in the Adjudicative Mission 196
[B] Proposition 6: Identification of the Aspects of Due Process That Are Relevant to the Activities of Arbitral Institutions 199
[1] Impartiality and Independence 199
[2] Equal Treatment of the Parties 202
[3] Adversarial Process 204
[4] Reasoning 205
[5] Judicial Review of Institutional Decisions 207
[C] Proposition 7: Materiality of a Decision as a Viable Proxy for Determining to What Extent Due Process Should Be Complied With 209
§5.04 Chapter Conclusions 210

CHAPTER 6
General Conclusions 213

APPENDIX
Template of Questionnaire Sent Out to Arbitral Institutions 217

Bibliography 221

Table of Cases 237

Table of Arbitration Rules Examined 241

Index 247

Foreword

Historically, institutional and ad hoc arbitration appeared to be receiving similar caseloads: anecdotally until the end of the twentieth century, the standard comment of arbitral institutions was that for every institutional arbitration there was at least one ad hoc case. This was perhaps due to the dominance of ad hoc arbitration in traditional international disputes involving carriage of goods by sea. However, in the last twenty years there has been a significant shift. Many major users of arbitration services now appear to clearly prefer institutional arbitration (save perhaps for the shipping industry) and this well-documented shift (not least from a series of Queen Mary University of London arbitration surveys since 2005) can be traced back to a number of reasons.

First, a very large number of general or specialist arbitration institutions have been established, so that nowadays it is impossible to state with any degree of certainty how many arbitral institutions exist: most likely the number of arbitral institutions is in the thousands rather than hundreds and with several jurisdictions now having several hundred institutions, albeit many of them have no real case load or rather only localized and limited activity. Second, given the increased competition amongst institutions, the larger and higher profile arbitral institutions have revised their rules at least twice and have intensified their efforts to promote their rules and their use. The revision of rules was seen as a way of improving the services provided to arbitral users and a way of addressing concerns about efficiency of the arbitral process. This has had a near domino effect not only with bigger institutions revising their rules every ten to fifteen years, but also with emerging institutions producing new versions of their rules every few years and also producing different sets of rules for different types of disputes. Third, many institutions have improved the ways in which they interact with their actual or potential users by introducing users groups, membership structures, task forces and working groups and have also formalized seminars and training courses offered by them. Consequently there is now increased expertise and awareness and even a sense of particular "attachment" or affinity with certain institutions, although it is inevitable that some arbitration experts do have multiple such attachments and affiliations.

As we are experiencing this unprecedented proliferation of domestic, national, regional and international arbitral institutions and arbitral rules, we can also identify an emerging novel fashion in the way arbitral institutions support arbitration, in general, and arbitration proceedings, in particular. The classical representation is that arbitral institutions provide a set of rules and administration in support of arbitration proceedings. Their experience adds value to the process, their knowledge of the market ensures the appointment of more suitable arbitrators when they have to make such appointment or confirmation, and their reputation and cache can contribute to the enforceability of awards. There are also many further "side benefits" to engaging an arbitral institution to provide the context and organization of arbitral proceedings: they can deal with advance of costs relieving arbitrators from potentially unpleasant and mundane communications with disputing parties, they can provide light technical assistance to parties unfamiliar with arbitration, and they can hold funds on behalf of tribunals. Their cost and fee structure is arranged in a fashion that renders most of them not-for-profit institutions and provide their services at cost level only.

The monograph by Dr Remy Gerbay takes the discussion and assessment of the functions of arbitral institutions to an entirely new level. During his extensive research, he identifies a series of questions that have not been adequately addressed in scholarly or practitioner writings and he provides answers and new insights. First, he provides a typology of arbitral institutions as well as an autonomous definition; he focuses his attention on international arbitration institutions and more specifically reviews the rules and practices of more than forty institutions based in and operating in many different jurisdictions. The picture presented is a global one and is not confined to any particular region. He also provides an assessment of institutional arbitration as a growing phenomenon and the collateral effects of increased institutionalization and judicialization. One could perhaps add the finding that the language used in arbitration rules becomes increasingly mandatory, slowly limiting certain aspects of party autonomy, especially in cases where efficiency is to be warranted. Second, he surveys the activities of arbitration institutions and challenges traditional representations. His main finding is that arbitral institutions perform certain functions which are not merely administrative but are effectively decision-making activities; certain of these activities are even material to the outcome of disputes as they are nearly jurisdictional or hybrid in nature. In this respect, it is important to have a clear context of due process according to which such decisions can be made and a due process which has to be observed in the discharge of such functions. Dr Gerbay argues that arbitral institutions are "ancillary participants in the adjudicative process". To support his finding, he masterfully surveys and maps out relevant case law, some of which has never been presented before in the English language.

Dr Gerbay is accurate in the appraisal of the functions of arbitral institutions and correctly points out that not all arbitral institutions perform *quasi*-jurisdictional tasks. He also points out that they are careful in the discharge of such tasks. Still, his proposal is valid; there are clear benefits in introducing due process standards for the performance of hybrid functions which go beyond the "regular" administrative tasks.

I have thoroughly enjoyed reading this book and I am delighted to have an opportunity to introduce it. It is a significant addition to international arbitration scholarship and should be read by academics, practitioners and arbitration institutions. The research is thorough, the writing is unbiased and the conclusions are constructive and useful. No doubt the book deserves much attention, reflection and further discussion. Warm congratulations are due to Dr Gerbay.

Loukas Mistelis
London, July 2016

Preface

While thousands of cross-border disputes are resolved each year through institutional arbitration, there appears to be little understanding of arbitral institutions. In particular, very little academic scholarship has been produced on the nature of the functions exercised by arbitral institutions in the proceedings they administer.

This book seeks to rectify this gap by: (1) identifying in the literature conventional assumptions as to the functions of arbitral institutions in the institutional arbitration process; (2) critically assessing such conventional assumptions; and (3) offering a novel and more realistic representation of the functions of arbitral institutions.

The research behind this book is principally based on a systematic study of the activities performed by over forty international arbitration institutions in their administration of cases. This study also examines court decisions on the nature of the functions exercised by such institutions in some leading civil law and common law jurisdictions.

A finding of my research is that arbitration institutions are conventionally portrayed in the literature in one of two ways: According to a first representation, arbitral institutions are mere administrators with no decision-making power whatsoever. According to another representation, while institutions are occasionally called upon to exercise some measure of decision-making, measures taken by institutions remain immaterial because of their alleged "administrative"/"non-jurisdictional" nature. In both instances, it is conventionally assumed that, contrary to arbitrators, arbitral institutions should not be concerned by due process when they discharge their duties.

In this book, I argue that these two conventional representations are difficult to reconcile with the diverse reality of institutional arbitration. While some institutions have a very limited involvement in the arbitrations conducted under their auspices, others participate more actively in their resolution. The book therefore concludes that arbitral institutions can be more accurately described as ancillary participants in the adjudicative process which decisions, insofar as they may occasionally be outcome-determinative, should call upon the application of some due process standards.

List of Figures

Figure 2.1	Evolution of the Caseload of the ICC (1956-2014)	30
Figure 2.2	Evolution of the Caseload of Other Major Institutions (2000-2014)	31
Figure 3.1	Continuum of Institutional Powers (Pre-appointment Phase)	112
Figure 3.2	Continuum of Institutional Powers (Post-Appointment Phase)	115

List of Tables

Table 3.1	Visual Representation of Institutional Powers (Pre-Appointment Phase) The table below is based on the version of the relevant arbitration rules in force at 8 January 2016.	110
Table 3.2	Visual Representation of Institutional Powers (Post-Appointment Phase)	113

List of Abbreviations

AAA	American Arbitration Association
ACICA	Australian Centre for International Commercial Arbitration
ADR	Alternative Dispute Resolution
ASA	Association Suisse de l'Arbitrage (Swiss Arbitration Association)
BAC	Beijing Arbitration Commission
BCICAC	British Columbia International Commercial Arbitration Centre
CAMEX	Centro de Arbitraje de Mexico (Arbitration Centre of Mexico)
CAMP	Chambre Arbitrale Maritime de Paris (Maritime Arbitral Chambre of Paris)
CIArb	Chartered Institute of Arbitrators
CEDRAC	Cyprus Eurasia Dispute Resolution and Arbitration Center
CEPANI	Belgian Centre for Mediation and Arbitration
CRCICA	Cairo Regional Centre for International Commercial Arbitration
DIA	Danish Institute of Arbitration
DIAC	Dubai International Arbitration Centre
DIS	Deutsche Institution für Schiedsgerichtsbarkeit (German Institution of Arbitration)
ECAFE	Economic Commission for Asia and the Far East (now named Economic and Social Commission for Asia and the Pacific)
FCC	Arbitration Institute of the Finland Chamber of Commerce
FOSFA	Federation of Oils Seeds and Fats Associations
GAFTA	Grain and Feed Trade Association
HKIAC	Hong Kong International Arbitration Centre
ICAC	International Commercial Arbitration Court at the Russian Chamber of Commerce and Industry

ICC	International Chamber of Commerce
ICCA	International Council for Commercial Arbitration
ICDR	International Center for Dispute Resolution
ICJ	International Court of Justice
ICSID	International Centre for Settlement of Investment Disputes
IDRC	International Dispute Resolution Centre
KCAB	Korean Commercial Arbitration Board
KIAC	Kigali International Arbitration Centre
LCIA	London Court of International Arbitration
LMAA	London Maritime Arbitrators Association
MAC	Maritime Arbitration Commission at the Chamber of Commerce and Industry of the Russian Federation
NAI	Nederlands Arbitrage Instituut
PCA	Permanent Court of Arbitration
PCC (Warsaw)	Arbitration Court at the Polish Chamber of Commerce in Warsaw
SCC	Stockholm Chamber of Commerce
UNCC	United Nations Compensation Commission
UNCITRAL	United Nations Commission on International Trade Law
VIAC	Vienna International Arbitration Centre
WIPO	World Intellectual Property Organisation
YAF	Young Arbitrators Forum
YAP	Young Arbitration Practitioners
YAS	Young Arbitrators Sweden (SCC)
YIAG	Young International Arbitration Group

Acknowledgements

This book is based on a doctoral thesis written at the School of International Arbitration, Queen Mary University of London. As such, it would not have been possible without the support and guidance of my supervisor, Professor Loukas Mistelis to whom I am truly indebted.

I also wish to thank my examiners, Professor Carrie Menkel-Meadow (UC Irvine/Georgetown University Law Center) and Professor Phillip Capper (King's College London) for the invaluable advice they gave me, and for their encouragement to publish my thesis.

My eternal gratitude also goes to the colleagues and friends who generously gave so much of their time to review early drafts or help in other ways, in particular: Claire Inder-Charpe, Mohamed Mahayni, Théo Boutruche, James Clanchy, John Ribeiro, Gloria Maria Alvarez, Rutger Metsch and Noor Khadim. Special thanks to my research assistant Arthad Kurlekar for his tireless contribution in the last few months. Any errors that remain are mine alone.

I am grateful to the staff of the many arbitral institutions which have accepted to respond to my survey questionnaire. I am also particularly grateful to Dr Kun Fan, and Dr Emmanuel Jolivet and Wing Shek for their insights, on Chinese arbitration, the ICC and the LCIA respectively.

Finally, I wish to acknowledge the support of the team at Kluwer Law International (and in particular Eleanor Taylor) as well as my law firm Enyo Law LLP[1].

London, March 2016.

1. The views expressed in this book are solely those of the author and do not necessarily reflect those of Enyo Law LLP.

Introduction

"Man knows much more than he understands"
Alfred Adler[2]

The above quote about the different levels of consciousness in psychoanalysis could have very well been written to describe the state of our collective comprehension of the role of "arbitral institutions" in the institutional arbitration process.

While thousands of disputes[3] are resolved each year under the auspices of arbitral institutions[4], and while significant expertise has been gathered by practitioners and arbitrators as to the manner in which such arbitrations ought to be conducted, there appears to be little understanding of the role of arbitral institutions[5].

Much like the user of a computer may operate, with relative success, a machine which he does not fully comprehend, users of institutional arbitration have for many decades resolved their disputes through institutional arbitration without fully understanding the precise nature of the functions[6] of one of the key players of the process,

2. Attributed to Alfred Adler, as quoted in Harold Mosak and Michael Maniacci, *Primer of Adlerian Psychology: The Analytic - Behavioural - Cognitive Psychology of Alfred Adler* (Routledge 1999).
3. See below in Chapter 2 the discussions of the increasing caseload of institutions.
4. Chapter 1 of this book offers a definition of the term "arbitral institution". In this book, the terms "institution", "arbitration centre", and "administrator" are used interchangeably to refer to "arbitral institutions". Further, the notion of "arbitration" is understood as a private mechanism by which the parties to a dispute agree to refer it to one or more neutrals for final and binding determination. In this sense, see Nigel Blackaby and others, *Redfern and Hunter on International Arbitration* (5th edn, Oxford University Press 2009) 1-2. <http://www.kluwerarbitration.com/document.aspx?id=Ch5-ipn26309&query=AND(content%3A%22institution%22,content%3A%22institutional%22)> accessed 10 May 2012. See also Gary Born, *International Commercial Arbitration: Commentary and Materials* (2nd edn, Kluwer Law International 2001) 1.
5. Philipp Habegger, Daniel Hochstrasser and Gabrielle Nater-Bass (eds), *Arbitral Institutions Under Scrutiny* (JurisNet 2013) foreword, p. V. In the same sense see, Juliet Blanch, "Appointment and Confirmation of Arbitrators" in Philipp Habegger, Daniel Hochstrasser and Gabrielle Nater-Bass (eds), *Arbitral Institutions Under Scrutiny* (JurisNet 2013) 72.
6. In this book, the term "function" is used in its common ordinary sense. "Function" and "role" are used as synonyms. Both terms are used to refer to the purpose of a thing or person; the purpose for which a thing is used or exists. See in this sense "Oxford English Dictionary, Online Edition, Available at Http://www.oxforddictionaries.com, Accessed 14 March 2014".; "Merriam-Webster

namely the arbitral institution. This fascinating paradox is the original motivation behind the choice of topic for this book.

Very little academic scholarship has been produced on the nature of the role exercised by arbitral institutions in the proceedings submitted to them. There is certainly no all encompassing "theory of institutional arbitration" explaining systematically the respective roles of, or the interaction between, arbitral tribunals, parties and institutions. Conventionally, arbitral institutions are represented as mere "administrators" who do not participate to the resolution of the disputes that are arbitrated under their auspices[7].

My pre-research hypothesis, which was forged during the years I spent "administering cases"[8] at the Secretariat of the London Court of International Arbitration[9], was that conventional wisdom was difficult to reconcile with the reality of institutional arbitration because institutions seem somehow to participate in the overall adjudication[10] of the disputes they administer. More specifically the five hypotheses of this book were as follows: (1) the functions of institutions vary greatly from one institution to another. (2) some institutions' involvement in proceedings conducted under their rules may encompass some measure of "decision-making"[11] (e.g., seat, language, joinder, consolidation, prima facie jurisdiction, scrutiny); so that, (3) in some forms of institutional arbitration at least, the parties can be said to have agreed implicitly or

Dictionary, Online Edition, Available at Http://www.merriam-Webster.com/dictionary, Accessed 14 March 2014". The role or functions of arbitral institutions thus means the purpose served by institutions in the institutional arbitration process, as it transpires from the tasks performed by institutions when they administer arbitrations.

7. See Alan Uzelac, "Succession of Arbitral Institutions" (1996) 3 Croatian Arbitration Yearbook 71, 72. See also the critical assessment of the two traditional theoretical representations of the functions of institutions in Chapter 4 ("*The traditional representations of the role of institutions: A critical evaluation*"). As discussed in Chapter 4, it is unclear what this so-called mere administrative role means in practice. It seems to denote a lack of participation by arbitral institutions in the overall decision of the case.
8. In this book, the expression to "*administer arbitrations*" is used to refer to the activities conducted by arbitral institutions in respect of the institutional arbitration proceedings which are referred to them. An overview of these activities appears in Chapter 3 below ("*The activities of Arbitral institutions: An overview*"), under section §3.03 ("*Casework activities*"). The expression is used in a neutral way and does not imply that the nature of the activities should be considered as merely "administrative" (whatever this term may mean).
9. Between 2008 to 2012 as Counsel, Senior Counsel and then Deputy Registrar of the LCIA, and then Registrar of DIFC-LCIA.
10. The terms "*adjudication*" and "*adjudicative*" refer to the overall process of deciding an arbitration, of determining the dispute referred to arbitration. In this book, therefore, "adjudication" has a broad/inclusive meaning: It is not limited to decisions on the merits of a case but includes decisions on jurisdiction, procedure, quantum, and costs. More generally, it covers all measures that need to be taken for the purposes of determining the dispute submitted to arbitration. This includes measures that are decisional (i.e., decisions), and measures that are not decisional (e.g., organizational measures). The term "adjudication" is therefore broader than "decision-making". "Decision-making" is understood in this book as the fact of making decisions. A detailed definition of what a decision is, is offered in Chapter 4 below (under "*Critical analysis of the second representation: Institutions do have a measure of decision-making power*"). For present purposes, a decision may be defined as a determination between two or more possible outcomes which carries a binding effect.
11. As indicated previously, "decision-making" refers to the fact of making decisions, in the sense binding determinations.

expressly to a split of the overall adjudicative mission between the arbitrators and the institution, with the bulk of that mission being conferred to the tribunal. (4) Decisions taken by institutions are not entirely immaterial because they may affect the outcome of a case or the enforceability of awards[12]. (5) This in turn raises questions as to the relevance of due process standards for institutions[13]. The above five hypotheses have in part been confirmed by my research.

The research work for this book took three years to complete. It started with a systematic examination of the activities or tasks actually performed by arbitral institutions in their administration of the cases in the form of a detailed analysis of the arbitration rules of over forty-five sets of institutional rules[14] together with a number of internal documents of institutions where available[15]. An exhaustive examination of all arbitral institutions in existence was impossible because there are now hundreds, if not thousands, of them, and new ones are established regularly. Therefore, I identified "major" institutions, based on their caseload of international commercial arbitration cases, but also taking into consideration geographical balance[16]. The institutions

12. The notion of outcome (and outcome-determinative decisions) are examined in some detail in Chapter 5 ("*A realistic representation of the role of institutions: Arbitral institutions as ancillary participants in the adjudicative process*"), under proposition no. 3 ("*Materiality of institutional decisions*").
13. Due process is taken to mean in the present context an "*international minimum standard of procedural safeguards*". Matti Kurkela and Santtu Turunen, *Due Process in International Commercial Arbitration* (2nd edn, Oxford University Press 2010) 3-4. The notion of due process and its relevance to the functions of arbitral institutions is examined in Chapter 5 below, under proposition no. 5 ("*Desirability of the application of due process by institutions when they participate in the adjudicative mission*") and proposition no. 6 ("*Identification of the aspects of due process that are relevant to the activities of arbitral institutions*").
14. As per the bibliography provided at the end of this book, the institutions surveyed include the American Arbitration Association, Australian Centre for International Commercial Arbitration, Beijing Arbitration Centre, British Columbia International Commercial Arbitration Centre, Bulgarian Chamber of Commerce and Industry, Cairo Regional Centre for International Commercial Arbitration, Court of Arbitration for Sport, Centro de Arbitraje de Mexico (Arbitration Centre of Mexico), Chambre Arbitrale Maritime de Paris (Maritime Arbitral Chambre of Paris), China International Economic and Trade Arbitration Commission (CIETAC), Croatian Chamber of Economy (Zagreb), Cyprus Eurasia Dispute Resolution and Arbitration Center, Belgian Centre for Mediation and Arbitration, Cairo Regional Centre for International Commercial Arbitration, Danish Institute of Arbitration, Dubai International Arbitration Centre, Deutsche Institution für Schiedsgerichtsbarkeit (German Institution of Arbitration), Economic Commission for Asia and the Far East (now named Economic and Social Commission for Asia and the Pacific), Arbitration Institute of the Finland Chamber of Commerce, Hong Kong International Arbitration Centre, International Commercial Arbitration Court at the Russian Chamber of Commerce and Industry, International Chamber of Commerce, International Council for Commercial Arbitration, International Centre for Dispute Resolution, JAMS, Korean Commercial Arbitration Board, Kigali International Arbitration Centre, London Court of International Arbitration, LCIA India, DIFC-LCIA, Mauritius International Arbitration Centre, Maritime Arbitration Commission at the Chamber of Commerce and Industry of the Russian Federation, Milan Chamber, Arbitration Court at the Polish Chamber of Commerce in Warsaw, International Arbitration Centre, Stockholm Chamber of Commerce, Swiss Institution, Vienna International Arbitration Centre, and the World Intellectual Property Organisation.
15. Such as the statutes of the "Court" or "Board" of certain institutions, when available.
16. Institutions which only handle a handful of international arbitrations per year were deemed less relevant for present purposes. International arbitration is understood as the arbitration of "cross border disputes". The present book does not focus on institutions handling only domestic arbitrations.

covered include institutions from Europe, Asia, North America, South America, Oceania, and Africa. It should be noted at this stage that the focus of this book lies with international arbitration rather than domestic arbitration, and institutions that deal only in domestic cases have therefore been largely ignored in this study. A second phase of the research involved reviewing the literature produced by individuals who exercised official functions within the institutions studied, to understand better how arbitration rules are actually implemented in practice. In addition, a survey questionnaire[17] was also sent to arbitral institutions in order better to assess their approach to case administration. A review of arbitral awards did not appear immediately relevant because awards rarely address the manner in which the institution administering the proceedings has performed its duties. At best they contain a recital of the appointment process, of challenges or of other decisions made by the institution, e.g., on the appointment of arbitrators, the seat of the arbitration, the language, consolidation, joinder of third parties etc. For the same reasons, domestic statutes and court decisions turned out to be relevant only insofar as they permit to assess how domestic legal systems "represent" the role of arbitral institutions. Our review was thus limited to four jurisdictions, namely France, England & Wales, the United States and Switzerland. These jurisdictions were chosen not only because they represent the two main legal traditions (common law and civil law) but also because they are considered the richest in respect of arbitration law and are most frequently chosen as the seat of arbitrations.[18]

17. A copy of the template questionnaire is reproduced at Annex 1 of this book.
18. Stephan Wilske and Todd Fox, "The Global Competition for the 'Best Place' for International Arbitration – Myth, Prejudice, and Reality Bits" [2009] Austrian Arbitration Yearbook 383. Queen Mary, University of London, "Current and Preferred Practices in the Arbitral Process" (2012) at < http://www.arbitration.qmul.ac.uk/docs/1644483.pdf > accessed 24 December 2015. Queen Mary, University of London, "Improvements and Innovations in International Arbitration" (2015) at < http://www.arbitration.qmul.ac.uk/docs/164761.pdf > accessed 24 December 2015.

CHAPTER 1

Understanding the Notion of Arbitral Institution: Definitions and Typologies

§1.01 INTRODUCTION

Norberto Bobbio is credited for arguing that most academic disagreements boil down to disagreements of a semantic nature, and that much of the distance separating the apparently conflicting views of two scholars can often be reduced by agreeing on clear definitions[19]. In our case, a multitude of partially overlapping terms are used to refer to the object of this book. These include "[...] *arbitration 'court', 'centre', 'association', 'chamber', 'commission', 'bureau', etc.*"[20]. Abiding with the wisdom of the Italian legal theorist, this book therefore starts with a discussion of the meaning of the term "arbitral institution".

Defining the term "arbitral institution" requires first understanding the notion of "institutional arbitration". Sections §1.02 and §1.03 below therefore examine the meaning of the terms "institutional arbitration" and "arbitral institutions".

Definitions alone would not give the full picture of the object of this study. Accordingly, section §1.04 offers a brief presentation of the different types of arbitral institutions in existence.

---

19. David Soldini, "*Présentation*", *in* Norberto Bobbio – De la Structure à la Fonction: Nouveaux Essais de Théorie du Droit, Dalloz, 2012, p. 17.
20. Pierre Lalive, "Problèmes Relatifs À l'Arbitrage International Commercial" (1967) 120 Collected Courses of the Hague Academy of International Law, Martinus Nijhoff Publishers & Brill Academic 664. Translation by the author. In the original language: *"On parle parfois, à leur propos, aussi bien de 'cour' d'arbitrage, de 'centre', d'association', de 'chambre', de 'comité', de 'bureau', etc., sans que ces désignations revêtent une signification juridique précise"*. In this book, the expression *"Translation by the author"* indicates that the relevant citation was translated into English by the author of this book.
    In the same sense, see Michel Gaudet, "La Coopération Des Juridictions Etatiques À l'Arbitrage Institutionnel" (1988) 6 ASA Bulletin, Kluwer Law International 90, 100.

§1.02 DEFINING "INSTITUTIONAL ARBITRATION"

Some authors have sought to define institutional arbitration by distinguishing it from neighbouring notions, thereby defining institutional arbitration by a negative (i.e., describing what it is not, rather than what it is). For example, institutional arbitration may be defined by contrasting it with the notion of ad hoc arbitration. Institutional arbitration may also be defined by way of comparison with court litigation. A more helpful approach however is to offer an autonomous definition based on the identification of essential characteristics of institutional arbitration.

[A] Contingent Definitions: Defining Institutional Arbitration by Distinguishing It from Neighbouring Notions

[1] Institutional Arbitration Defined by Comparison with ad hoc Arbitration

Defining institutional arbitration by contrasting it with ad hoc arbitration entails identifying differences between the two forms of arbitration. Ad hoc arbitration may be defined as a form of arbitration in which the participants include "only" the tribunal and the parties to the disputes (be they claimants or respondents), and where the parties and the tribunal alone are responsible for organizing their procedure. Institutional arbitration, may then be defined by adding one additional "participant" (i.e., the arbitral institution) and, as the case may be, by giving an indication of some of the tasks typically entrusted to the institution. This is the approach taken by some of the leading arbitration manuals. Gary Born, for instance, distinguishes ad hoc and institutional arbitration as follows:

> *Institutional arbitrations are conducted pursuant to institutional arbitration rules, almost always overseen by an administrative authority with responsibility for various aspects relating to constituting the arbitral tribunal, fixing the arbitrators' compensation and similar matters. In contrast, ad hoc arbitrations are conducted without the benefit of an appointing and administrative authority or (generally) pre-existing arbitration rules, subject only to the parties' arbitration agreement and applicable national arbitration legislation*[21].

While such an approach permits quickly to capture the essence of the notion of institutional arbitration, it is of limited utility for the present study because it does not permit to establish the outer limits of the notion of institutional arbitration. It is of little

21. Gary B. Born, *International Commercial Arbitration* (Kluwer Law International, 2014) 168 http://www.kluwerarbitration.com/CommonUI/document.aspx?id=KLI-KA-Born-2014-Ch01. See also, Emmanuel Gaillard and John Savage (eds), *Fouchard, Gaillard, Goldman on International Commercial Arbitration* (Kluwer Law International 1999) 33.
    See also Anne Veronique Schlaepfer and Angelina M. Petti, "Institutional versus Ad Hoc Arbitration" in Elliott Geisinger and Nathalie Voser (eds), *International Arbitration in Switzerland – A Handbook for Practitioners* (Kluwer Law International 2013) 13: "*Ad hoc arbitration is where parties agree to arbitrate a particular contract or dispute without referring to any arbitral institution.*"

assistance in respect of "borderline cases" where some permanent organization has a degree of involvement in the proceedings it administers[22], but where it is not immediately clear whether such involvement is sufficient to talk of "institutional arbitration". A prime example would be arbitration in accordance with the terms of the London Maritime Arbitrators Association (LMAA). The LMAA is a permanent organization which acts as appointing authority when needed. An appointing authority is an entity called upon by the parties to make a default appointment of an arbitrator in the absence of a party-appointment (e.g.,when one party refuses to appoint its arbitrator or when the parties are unable to agree on the appointment of a sole or presiding arbitrator). LMAA arbitration would readily be recognized as a form of ad hoc arbitration because the LMAA does not provide any other services to parties engaged in arbitrations under the LMAA terms[23]. Another example would be arbitrations conducted under the rules of arbitration of the Federation of Oils Seeds and Fats Associations (FOSFA). The FOSFA offers some support to parties arbitrating a dispute under its rules of arbitration, but the very limited support it provides appears to fall short of what is conventionally considered as institutional arbitration[24]. FOSFA, for example, will act as appointing authority when needed, and will generally monitor the proceedings (in the sense that it will ensure that the arbitrators proceed expeditiously to an award). It will not, however, offer the services normally associated with institutional arbitration, like the confirmation of the constitution of the tribunal, determining the costs of the arbitration, despatching awards, making arrangements for hearings, deciding challenges etc. This is a view shared, for example, by Robert Merkin according to whom FOSFA proceedings are a form of ad hoc arbitration[25].

---

22. As previously indicated, the expression to "*administer arbitrations*" is used in this book to refer to the various tasks performed by permanent organizations in respect of the arbitration proceedings referred to them. An overview of these administration services appears in Chapter 3 below ("*The activities of Arbitral institutions: An overview*"), under section §3.03 ("*Casework activities*"). A self-contained definition of the role of institutions in respect of institutional arbitration cannot be given at this stage because it is the very purpose of this book to clarify what this role is. Chapter 5 ("*A realistic representation of the role of institutions: Arbitral institutions as ancillary participants in the adjudicative process*") offers an explanation as to what the role of institutions is in the administration of the cases referred to them.
23. See "Website of the LMAA", accessed 25 February 2013. See also Bruce Harris, "London Maritime Arbitration" (2011) 77 Arbitration 116, 122. Bertie Vigras however refers to the LMAA as an institution, but he seems to use the expression in a loose sense. Bertie Vigras, "The Role of Institutions in Arbitration" in Ronald Bernstein and Derek Wood (eds), *Handbook of Arbitration Practice* (2nd edn, Sweet & Maxwell in conjunction with the Chartered Institute of Arbitrators 1993) 461. Chapter 3 below ("*The Activities of Arbitral Institutions: An Overview*") offers an outline of what case administration by an arbitral institution means.
24. See "Website of the Federation of Oils, Seeds and Fats Associations (FOSFA), Http://www.fosfa .org" (15 February 2016) <http://www.fosfa.org> accessed 15 February 2016.
25. Robert Merkin, *Arbitration Law* (3rd edn, Informa 2004) 36. This being said, one could argue to the contrary that FOSFA's role in the proceedings exceeds that of arbitral institutions in that it sometimes decides appeals made against arbitral awards, a function rarely entrusted to arbitral institutions. A similar view is shared in Stuart Dutson, Andy Moody and Neil Newing, *International Arbitration: A Practical Guide,* 50 (Globe Law and Business 3 January 2013).

    Merkin places Arbitration at the Grain and Feed Trade Association (GAFTA) in the same category as FOSFA and LMAA arbitrations, i.e., as ad hoc arbitration. It should be noted however that the GAFTA's involvement in arbitral proceedings conducted under its rules exceeds that of the FOSFA or the LMAA. The GAFTA, for example, may act as the channel of

[2] Institutional Arbitration Defined by Comparison with Judicial Mechanisms

Looking at the other side of the spectrum, it may be tempting to apprehend the notion of institutional arbitration by distinguishing it from judicial dispute resolution mechanisms. At the domestic level, this means court litigation. At the international level, this suggests "litigation" before the International Court of Justice (ICJ)[26] or other permanent judicial organs such as the International Tribunal for the Law of the Sea (ITLOS)[27]. Institutional arbitration would here be understood as those types of dispute resolution proceedings under the auspices of some permanent organization but which would somehow fall short of constituting "judicial dispute settlement". With this approach, the focus is no longer on the meaning of the word "institutional" in the expression "institutional arbitration", but rather on that of the second term ("arbitration") and on the types of proceedings that it covers[28].

Again, if such an approach captures the flavour of what institutional arbitration is (or rather what it is not), it is of little assistance with borderline cases[29], for example the United Nations Compensation Commission (UNCC)[30] and the Iran-US Claims Tribunal[31], which borrow characteristics both from permanent judicial bodies and from arbitral institutions[32]. The UNCC was created in 1991 to decide disputes relating to losses suffered as a result of the invasion and occupation of Kuwait by Iraq during the Gulf War. The Iran-US Claims Tribunal was established ten years earlier to deal

communication between the parties and their tribunal; it may also make arrangements for hearings and monitor the progress of the proceedings –activities which are not undertaken by the FOSFA or the LMAA.

26. The ICJ describes, in its own literature, its procedures as a judicial dispute settlement system distinct form arbitration. See "Website of the International Court of Justice (ICJ), Http://www.icj-Cij.org" (15 February 2016) <http://www.icj-cij.org> accessed 15 February 2016.
27. The UN Convention on the Law of the Sea of 10 December 1982 provides, at its Article 287, a choice between different dispute settlement mechanisms, including referral to the ICJ, to arbitration and to the ITLOS. The convention therefore draws a distinction between arbitration and judicial dispute resolution mechanisms. In addition, in its own literature the ITLOS refers to itself as an "*independent judicial body*". See "Website of the International Tribunal for the Law of the Sea, http://www.itlos.org" (15 February 2016) <http://www.itlos.org> accessed 15 February 2016.
28. As previously indicated, arbitration is taken in this book to mean a private mechanism by which the parties to a dispute agree to refer it to one or more neutrals for final and binding determination. In this sense, see Blackaby and others (n 4) 1-2. See also Born, *International Commercial Arbitration* (n 4) 1.
29. In the words of Judge Gilbert Guillaume, "[...] *international bodies do not always fit neatly into academic categories; recently, certain new institutions have appeared which are on the fringe; they may or may not be considered as judicial, but they should be mentioned*". Gilbert Guillaume, "The Future of International Judicial Institutions" (1995) 44 International & Comparative Law Quarterly 848, 859.
30. See the "Website of the UN Compensation Commission (UNCC), Http://www.uncc.ch" (15 February 2016) <http://www.uncc.ch> accessed 15 February 2016.
31. "Website of the US-Iran Claims Tribunal, Http://www.iusct.net" (15 February 2016) <http://www.iusct.net> accessed 15 February 2016.
32. For an extensive analysis of the nature of the US-Iran Claims Tribunal, see David D. Caron, "The Nature of the Iran-United States Claims Tribunal and the Evolving Structure of International Dispute Resolution" (1990) 84 American Journal of International Law 104.

with claims arising out of the 1979 hostage crisis at the US Embassy in Tehran, and the freezing by the US of Iranian assets. Because both organizations were habilitated to decide the merits of the claims submitted to them, these bodies cannot easily be categorized as arbitral institutions; the idea being that while a domestic or international judicial body concerns itself with the merits of the case, an arbitral institution does not[33]. Likewise, the fact that these organizations' jurisdiction extends to thousands of cases means that they do not fit well with the traditional representation of arbitral tribunals either, which are typically appointed to decide a single dispute. On the other hand, both the US-Iran Claims Tribunal and the UNCC lack the permanence that characterizes judicial bodies, be it international ones like the ICJ, or domestic courts. Both organs were indeed set up to deal "only" with a finite (if very large) number of claims arising out of specific pre-existing events[34]. They were not set up to deal with a potentially unlimited number of future disputes like the ICJ or other permanent judicial institutions arising out of unknown events. This *post hoc* feature makes it arguably difficult to categorize these bodies as judicial organs, in the traditional sense of the term.

Another borderline case, albeit of historical relevance more than ongoing relevance, is that of the arbitration courts operating under the auspices of various chambers of trade throughout the Soviet bloc until the early 1990s. A similar system of mandatory institutional arbitration before "Economic Contract Arbitration Commissions" was in existence in China in respect of domestic disputes[35]. The difficulty with such institutions resides in the fact that, by contrast to the Western arbitral tradition, they were established by States, had a de facto and sometimes de jure monopoly over certain types of disputes (in particular those involving trade with foreign companies), and were subject to strict rules of procedure akin to civil procedure rules applicable in domestic courts[36]. For Professor Berthold Goldman[37] such institutions should nonetheless be seen as operating within the realm of arbitration rather than that of domestic litigation[38]. The key factor for Professor Goldman seemed to be the consensual nature

33. As explained in Chapter 5 below, under the arbitration rules of all institutions studied for this book, the task of deciding the merits of a case is reserved to the arbitrators.
34. The jurisdiction of the US-Iran Claims Tribunal was limited, in particular, to claims filed by the deadline of 19 January 1982. Likewise, various deadlines were set between 1995 and 1997 for the filing of the various categories of claims over which the UNCC had jurisdiction. The UNCC completed its assessment of the claims in 2005, having reviewed some 2.6 million cases.
35. See Wang Sheng Chang, "CIETAC's Perspective on Arbitration and Conciliation Concerning China", in Albert Jan van den Berg (ed), *New Horizons in International Commercial Arbitration and Beyond* (ICCA Congress Series 27, 28, Kluwer Law International 2005) 12. See also generally Uzelac, "Succession of Arbitral Institutions" 74-75.
36. Goldman, "Les Conflits de Lois dans l'Arbitrage International de Droit Privé" 352-353. See also Kirchner and Marriott, "International Arbitration in the Aftermath of Socialism – The Example of the Berlin Court of Arbitration" 6. See also Fouchard, "Les Institutions Permanentes d'Arbitrage Devant le Juge Etatique (A Propos d'une Jurisprudence Récente)" 225.
37. Relying on the then-recent doctoral book of Professor Philippe Fouchard.
38. In the words of Professor Goldman: *"In concrete terms, the problem arises in respect of the arbitration courts operating under the auspices of the Foreign Trade Chambers of the USSR and of other Socialist Republics and popular democracies.* [...] *Far from being the product, as is the case with the arbitral organisations of Western Europe and America, of the free initiative of professional groups, they have been created by the public authorities for these purposes. Can it,*

of the mechanisms that was offered by these institutions: because party autonomy was the source of the mandate of these institutions, the mechanism they offered was more akin to arbitration than to court litigation[39].

Another difficulty with defining institutional arbitration by reference to neighbouring notions resides in the fact that, as we shall see[40], the role of institutions varies greatly from one institution to the next. Some institutions are more involved in the proceedings they administer than others. Each set of arbitration rules reserves to its institution a more or less extensive field of competence. As a result, an arbitration conducted under the auspices of one institution might resemble proceedings before

---

therefore, be said that we are still in the presence of arbitral organisations?" (Translation by the author). In the original language: "*Concrètement, nous l'avons dit, le problème se pose surtout à propos des Cours d'arbitrage fonctionnant près des Chambres du Commerce extérieur de l'URSS et des autres Républiques socialistes ou de démocratie populaire. Elles ont, on le sait, dans ces pays, le monopole de fait, et quelquefois de droit, de la compétence au regard des litiges relatif aux opérations commerciales internationales; et bien loin d'être issues, comme les organisations arbitrales d'Europe occidentale ou d'Amérique, de la libre initiative de groupements professionnels, elles ont été créées par les pouvoirs publics à cette fin. Peut –on alors dire que l'on est encore en présence d'organismes d'arbitrage?*". Goldman, "Les Conflits de Lois dans l'Arbitrage International de Droit Privé" 352-353.

39. The criterion of consent alone, however, appears to be insufficient. The ICJ's jurisdiction is based on consent. As discussed above, however, because of its permanence and of the fact that it decides the merits of the disputes submitted to it, the ICJ seems to fit more easily within the category of judicial dispute resolution than within arbitration.

    Today, arbitral institutions such as ICAC or MAC in Russia or CIETAC, Beijing Arbitration Commission (BAC) and CMAC in China are occupying the space left vacant by the old Soviet chambers of trade. As the mandate of these modern-day arbitral institutions is based on party autonomy the proceedings they administer qualify as arbitration. This being said, as discussed in Chapter 3 below, these institutions exercise functions which are often reserved to arbitrators under the rules of western institutions (making decisions on jurisdiction in particular). Also they maintain an ambiguous relationship with the State judicial apparatus. For example, it was the Chinese government that established CIETAC (in 1956) following a 1954 decision of the country's highest administrative authority, the "Chinese Administration Council" (now called the "State Council"). See "Website of the China International Economic and Trade Arbitration Commission (CIETAC), http://www.cietac.org", 15 February 2016. The same is true of CMAC. See "Website of the China Maritime Arbitration Commission (CMAC), http://www.cmac-sh.org/en/home.asp", 15 February 2016. In some instances the ambiguous relationship comes from the fact that the status of the institution is regulated by a statutory instrument. See for example the International Commercial Arbitration Court (ICAC) or the Maritime Arbitration Commission (MAC) at the Chamber of Commerce and Industry of the Russian Federation, which are regulated by Annexes 1 and 2 of the Russian Federation Law No. 5338-1 of 7 July 1993 on international commercial arbitration. Roman Khodykin, "International Commercial Arbitration Court (ICAC) and Maritime Arbitration Commission (MAC) at the Russian Federation Chamber of Commerce and Industry" in Loukas A. Mistelis and others (eds), *The World Arbitration Reporter*, vol. 3 (Juris 2010). See also Alexander S. Komarov, "Introduction to the Revision of the Rules of the International Commercial Arbitration Court at the Chamber of Commerce and Industry of the Russian Federation (ICAC)" in Albert Jan van den Berg (ed), *Yearbook Commercial Arbitration* XXXI (Kluwer Law International 2006) 456, 457. The arbitration rules of DIAC have been enacted by a decree of the Ruler of Dubai. See J. Martin H. Hunter, "Dubai International Arbitration Centre (DIAC)" in Loukas A. Mistelis and others (eds), *The World Arbitration Reporter*, vol. 3 (Juris 2010). Similarly, the new (2005) Arbitration Act of Malaysia, which is modeled after the Model Law, makes the KLRCA the default appointing authority in certain circumstances; and the Director of KLRCA is provided with "immunity". Syed Ahmad Idid, "Kuala Lumpur Regional Centre for Arbitration-Impact of the Old and New Arbitration Act" (2006) 2 Asian International Arbitration Journal, Kluwer Law International 97, 98-100.

40. This is the object of Chapter 3 below.

some quasi-judicial bodies, whereas proceedings under the auspices of another institution might appear closer to ad hoc arbitration[41]. On that basis, it may be tempting to define institutional arbitration by reference, not to one, but both of the neighbouring concepts of ad hoc arbitration and judicial dispute resolution. Specifically, "institutional arbitration" might be described as the phenomenon occupying the entire space stretching from the judicial resolution of disputes on one side, to ad hoc arbitration on the other. Such a broad definition is of limited practical value because it is too vague to capture the essence of the notion, and this emphasizes the need for an autonomous definition of institutional arbitration.

[B] An Autonomous Definition: Defining Institutional Arbitration by Identifying Its Essential Characteristics

Providing an autonomous definition of institutional arbitration means identifying its essential characteristics or, in other words, setting out the cumulative criteria of institutional arbitration. A few authors have sought to do so. While, naturally, their respective approaches differ slightly, they converge to identify, at a minimum, three cumulative (and partly inter-related) essential characteristics. These are: (1) a permanent organization; (2) a set of arbitration rules; and (3) some "services" offered by the institution[42]. In the words of a former President of the ICC International Court of Arbitration:

> [...] *it seems that certain minimum legal and practical conditions should be met before an organisation may claim to be an arbitral institution. First, the presence of a permanent organisation. Second, the offering, to the parties, their counsel and the arbitrators some logistical facilities, such as the booking of accommodation, meeting rooms and interpreters, or other secretarial and telecommunications services. Finally, some practical assistance in respect of the implementation of the arbitration rules chosen by the parties* [...] (Translation by the author)[43].

41. See the discussions of the spectral representation of level of interventionism of institutions at the end of Chapter 3.
42. Goldman, "Les Conflits de Lois dans l'Arbitrage International de Droit Privé"; Lalive, "Problèmes Relatifs à l'Arbitrage International Commercial"; Pieter Sanders, "Trends in the Field of International Commercial Arbitration" (1975) 145 Collected Courses of the Hague Academy of International Law, Martinus Nijhoff Publishers & Brill Academic; Fouchard, "Les Institutions Permanentes d'Arbitrage Devant le Juge Etatique (A Propos d'une Jurisprudence Récente)"; Gaudet, "La Coopération des Juridictions Etatiques à l'Arbitrage Institutionnel"; Slate, "International Arbitration: Do Institutions Make a Difference?".
43. In the original language: "[...] *il semble que pour se réclamer de l'arbitrage institutionnel les organismes recensés devraient présenter au moins quelques caractéristiques pratiques et juridiques. En premier lieu, l'existence d'un organe permanent d'accueil et d'information. En deuxième lieu, l'offre aux arbitres, aux parties et à leurs conseils de facilités logistiques, telles que la réservation de logements et de locaux de réunion, le recours à des services linguistiques, de secrétariat et de télécommunications. En troisième lieu, une assistance pratique pour la mise en œuvre des règles adoptées par les parties* [...]". Gaudet, "La Coopération des Juridictions Etatiques à l'Arbitrage Institutionnel" 101.

[1] Permanent Organization

The requirement of a permanent organization simply relates to the presence of some permanent entity whose existence precedes, and outlasts, that of the tribunals constituted to decide particular disputes[44]. The institution, indeed, exists prior to the appointment of the tribunal. In fact, as discussed elsewhere in this book, under the rules of a number of institutions, a tribunal cannot exist until the institution has "constituted" it[45]. This is the case in ICC, LCIA, Swiss Chambers and HKIAC arbitrations for example. Under the rules of these institutions[46], individuals, whether nominated by the parties or selected by the institutions themselves, do not form an arbitral tribunal until such time as the institutions have formally appointed them[47]. The terminology differs slightly from institution to institution: the rules of the ICC, the Swiss Chambers, HKIAC and DIAC, for example, talk of the "*confirmation*" of the constitution of the tribunal, whereas the LCIA rules refer to the "*appointment*", but the concept is the same[48].

44. Diana Droulers, "Institutional Commercial Arbitration from the Inside" in Kaj Hobér and others (eds), *Between East and West: Essays in Honour of Ulf Franke* (Juris 2010) 142.
 As previously indicated these permanent organizations may take various forms in practice. See below in section 1.4 of this Chapter 1 ("*Typologies of institutional arbitration*") the discussions of the various legal forms assumed by arbitral institutions. They may take the form of domestic legal entities or of subjects of international law; at the municipal level, they may assume the form of corporate entities like "companies" in common law countries, or of the less formal "associations" of some civil law jurisdiction; some entities will be privately owned, while some others will have a parastatal character; some will have a lucrative purpose whereas some others will be "not-for-profit" etc.
45. See section §3.03[A][12] in Chapter 3 ("*Constitution of the tribunal: confirmation of arbitrators*").
46. Article 13 of the ICC rules (2012); Article 5 of the LCIA rules (1998); Article 5.7 of the LCIA Rules (2014); Article 5(1) of the Swiss rules (2012); and Article 9 HKIAC rules (2013).
47. On this point, in the context of the ICC, see Fry, "ICC International Court of Arbitration" 6. In the context of the LCIA, see Remy Gerbay, "The London Court of International Arbitration" in Julian D. M. Lew and others (eds), *Arbitration in England. Including Chapters on Scotland and the Republic of Ireland* (Kluwer Law International 2013).
48. Article 5(5) of the LCIA rules (1998) provided: *"The LCIA Court alone is empowered to appoint arbitrators"*. Article 5(7) of the new version of the rules (2014) now provides in clearer terms: *"No party or third person may appoint any arbitrator under the Arbitration Agreement: the LCIA Court alone is empowered to appoint arbitrators (albeit taking into account any written agreement or joint nomination by the parties)"*. Article 9 of the HKIAC rules (2013) provide: "[all designations] *are subject to confirmation by the HKIAC Council, upon which the appointments shall become effective"*. Article 5(1) of the Swiss rules (2012) states: *"All designations of an arbitrator made by the parties or the arbitrators are subject to confirmation by the Court, upon which the appointments shall become effective"*. The terms of Article 13 of the ICC rules (2012) are, admittedly, more ambiguous, but it is well accepted that the institution's confirmation of the tribunal constitutes the starting point of its existence.
 This principle (that the tribunal does not exist as such until the institution has confirmed its appointment) is not present in the ICDR rules. In SCC arbitration, if the system appears on paper to differ, the SCC's actual practice is not dissimilar to that of the other institutions referred to above. It is true that the SCC rules do not contemplate a process of confirmation of the constitution of the Tribunal. By operation of the SCC rules, a party nomination therefore suffices. Nonetheless, the practice of the SCC Secretariat is to "refer the case to the tribunal" once the advances on costs have been paid in full. This "referring of the case" to the tribunal fulfils a function similar to that of "confirmation of appointment" with the other institutions in the sense that it marks the point where the tribunal may start its work. For former Deputy Secretary

Likewise, unlike arbitral tribunals, arbitral institutions do not cease to exist following the termination of the proceedings. In fact, institutions sometimes play an important role in the phase that follows the termination of the proceedings, such as assisting the parties with any formalities for the enforcement of the award[49], for example by providing certified copies of the award, or confirming to the satisfaction of a foreign court the bona fide nature of a particular arbitral award (i.e., confirming the fact that the arbitral award has actually been issued by an arbitral tribunal appointed under the rules of the institution, and that the enforcement action is thus not fraudulent). This is not to say that the concept of *functus officio* cannot apply to arbitral institutions. Once an arbitration has ended, there comes a point where the institution's involvement with the case ceases but, at that point, the institution does not cease to exist as an entity. Rather the institution closes the file corresponding to the case at hand.

[2] Arbitration Rules

The existence of arbitration rules is often mentioned as a defining element of institutional arbitration[50]. Redfern and Hunter, for example, define institutional arbitration as "*one that is administered by a specialist arbitral institution, under its own rules of arbitration*"[51]. When they are not mentioned expressly as an element of the definition of institutional arbitration, arbitration rules are instead assumed to be intrinsic to the very notion of institutional arbitration, as in the following excerpt from a leading arbitration manual:

> *It is becoming increasingly rare for the parties to choose their arbitrators and organize their procedure directly. Instead, permanent arbitral institutions have been set up throughout the world and now handle the vast majority of international commercial arbitrations. The existence of an institution and the application of its procedural rules may lead to greater efficiency* [...][52].

In our view, it does not matter whether the rules in question are that of the institution, or whether they are a set of stand-alone rules like the UNCITRAL arbitration rules. Indeed, if a good number of institutions have their own rules, a great deal more do not[53]. When this is the case, institutions often administer proceedings using the

---

General Annette Magnusson: "*Up until this point, the responsibility of planning and moving the process forward has rested with counsel of the SCC secretariat. When referring the case to the tribunal, however, this responsibility is shifted to the chairman of the same*". Annette Magnusson, "The Practice of the Arbitration Institute of the Stockholm Chamber of Commerce – An Inside View" (2001) 2001 Stockholm Arbitration Report 45, 53.

49. See the discussions on the post-award activities of institutions in Chapter 3 below.
50. Blackaby, Partasides, Hunter, and Redfern, *Redfern and Hunter on International Arbitration* 54; Christian Buhring-Uhle, Lars Kirchhof, and Gabriele Scherer, *Arbitration and Mediation in International Business* (2nd Revised edn, Panel Publishers 2006) 33. See also Droulers, "Institutional Commercial Arbitration from the Inside" 142.
51. Blackaby, Partasides, Hunter, and Redfern, *Redfern and Hunter on International Arbitration* 54.
52. Gaillard and Savage, *Fouchard, Gaillard, Goldman on International Commercial Arbitration* 33.
53. Pendell, "The Rise and Rise of the Arbitration Institution". Incidentally, it is noteworthy that certain institutions that have published their own rules of arbitration, have inspired themselves

UNCITRAL arbitration rules. One such example is the Cairo Regional Centre for International Commercial Arbitration ("CRCICA"), which long applied the rules of arbitration published by the UNCITRAL in 1976[54]. The notion of institutional arbitration does not necessarily exclude arbitration proceedings conducted under standalone rules, as long as the proceedings meet the other two criteria discussed here (namely that: (1) they are administered by (2) a permanent organization)[55].

Interestingly, some institutions which have published their own rules of arbitration also agree to administer, from time to time, arbitrations governed by the UNCITRAL arbitration rules (i.e., to say not applying their own rules to these proceedings). Institutions that are known to do so include, for example, the LCIA, SIAC or ICDR[56]. This is also the case of DIS, the German Arbitration Institution, although a difference is that DIS have "adapted" the UNCITRAL rules for the purposes of facilitating the role of DIS in UNCITRAL rules arbitration administered by them[57]. Likewise, while the HKIAC administers arbitrations under its own rules, it also administers arbitrations under the UNCITRAL rules (with some amendments). In that case it applies procedures set out in a document entitled "*Procedure for the Administration of International Arbitration*" of 2005. We are of the view that these UNCITRAL-rules arbitrations, administered by institutions which otherwise apply their own arbitration rules, can potentially constitute "institutional arbitration", if the other two criteria discussed in this section are also met. As discussed below, much will depend on the precise services which the parties have agreed the institution should offer.

[3] The Services

Numerous authors, when defining institutional arbitration, emphasize the administration services provided by the arbitral institution as the main criterion[58]. For a former President and CEO of the American Arbitration Association (AAA): "[i]*nstitutional*

from the UNCITRAL rules, so that it is not infrequent for institutional rules to bear some resemblance to the UNCITRAL rules. This is the case of the International Commercial Arbitration Court at the Chamber of Commerce and Industry of the Russian Federation (ICAC). See Komarov, "Introduction to the Revision of the Rules of the International Commercial Arbitration Court at the Chamber of Commerce and Industry of the Russian Federation (ICAC)" 457.

54. See "Website of the Cairo Regional Centre for International Commercial Arbitration (CRCICA), http://www.crcica.org.eg", 15 February 2016. This being said, CRCICA amended its rules in 1998, 2000, 2002 and 2007 so that, strictly speaking, it may be questioned whether it really applies the UNCITRAL rules.
55. This is the view taken by another leading manual: *"Ad hoc arbitration is where the arbitration mechanism is established specifically for the particular agreement or dispute.* [...] *Institutional arbitration is where parties submit their disputes to an arbitration* procedure, *which is conducted under the auspices of or administered or directed by an existing institution"* (emphasis added). Julian D. M. Lew, Loukas A. Mistelis, and Dr Stefan Kröll, *Comparative International Commercial Arbitration* (Kluwer Law International 2003) 32.
56. See "Website of the London Court of International Arbitration (LCIA), http://www.lcia.org", 2 April 2014. See also SIAC. "Website of the American Arbitration Association (AAA), http://www.adr.org/aaa/faces/home", 15 February 2016.
57. This "DIS version" of the UNCITRAL rules is available on their website. See "Website of the German Institution of Arbitration (DIS), http://www.dis-arb.de/scho/", 12 February 2013.
58. Gaudet, "La Coopération des Juridictions Etatiques à l'Arbitrage Institutionnel" 101.

arbitration is that which is administered by any one of the existing specialist arbitral institutions under its own rules or arbitration"[59]. Or, in the words of Michel Gaudet: "[i]*nstitutional arbitration implies a certain administration of the procedure which may be more or less extensive*" (Translation by the author)[60].

If institutional arbitration requires some measure of "involvement" on the part of the arbitral institution, then it follows that the mere offering by a permanent organization of a set of arbitration rules is not enough for an arbitration to be institutional. This is the view taken, for example, by Professor Sanders according to whom the ECAFE arbitration rules[61] or the ones adopted by the UN Economic Commission for Europe for certain categories of perishable agricultural products, do not give rise to institutional arbitration *stricto sensu* because such rules are not accompanied by some institutional supervision: "[About the ECAFE and the ECE rules] *Here is no question of institutional arbitration. Neither the ECAFE centre in Bangkok nor the ECE in Geneva administer arbitrations. They fall under the category of the so-called ad hoc arbitration*"[62].

But does *any* institutional "involvement" (alongside some arbitration rules) suffice to characterize an arbitration of institutional as opposed to ad hoc? For Professor Fouchard, this question must be answered negatively[63]. In our view, the institution's "involvement" must reach a certain qualitative threshold for there to be institutional arbitration. In the absence of such a qualitative threshold all arbitration proceedings where the parties have agreed on a set of rules and on the involvement of some organization would constitute institutional arbitration even where such arbitrations self-evidently constitute ad hoc arbitration. Here are a few examples:

- An arbitration under the "Paris Arbitration Rules"[64] in which the parties have retained the services of the International Dispute Resolution Centre ("IDRC") in London[65], to offer hearing rooms and ancillary logistical services.

59. Slate, "International Arbitration: Do Institutions Make a Difference?" 34.
60. In the original language: "[...] *l'arbitrage institutionnel implique une administration plus ou moins poussée de la procédure arbitrale par l'organisation*". Gaudet, "La Coopération des Juridictions Etatiques à l'Arbitrage Institutionnel" 102.
61. Adopted under the auspices of the UN Economic Committee for Asia and the Far East in 1966.
62. Sanders, "Trends in the Field of International Commercial Arbitration" 214. In the same sense (i.e., recognizing that the presence of arbitration rules does not *ipso facto* entail "institutional arbitration"), see Vigras, "The Role of Institutions in Arbitration" 469. See also generally Droulers, "Institutional Commercial Arbitration from the Inside" 141.
63. Philippe Fouchard, "Relationships Between the Arbitrator and the Parties and the Arbitral Institution" *The Status of the Arbitrator – ICC Bulletin Special Supplement* (International Chamber of Commerce 1995) para. 38.
64. The Paris Arbitration Rules are a set of stand-alone arbitration rules drafted by the organization "Paris the Home of International Arbitration", and which, like the UNCITRAL rules, can be used without the support of any arbitral institution. See http://www.parisarbitration.com/wp-content/uploads/2014/02/PARIS-ARBITRATION-RULES.pdf, website last consulted 8 January 2016.
65. Not to be confused with the AAA's ICDR, the IDRC offers useful services to parties to arbitration proceedings such as catering, video-conferencing services, general administrative support for the booking of court reporters and interpreters etc., but these services do not relate to the conduct of the proceedings.

- A non-administered UNCITRAL-rules arbitration where the parties have chosen as appointing authority an organization or an individual such as the President of the Law Society of England and Wales, or the Chairman of the English Bar Council[66].
- An arbitration conducted under the UNCITRAL rules in which an arbitral institution, like the ICC or the LCIA, is asked to intervene solely in a capacity as default appointing authority without exercising further supervisory functions.

Saying that the role of an institution must meet a certain qualitative threshold for an ad hoc arbitration to become institutional is one thing; ascertaining what this qualitative threshold is, is another. As previously indicated, the difficulty with any study on the subject of arbitral institutions resides in the sheer number and diversity of arbitration institutions. Some activities (e.g., scrutiny of draft awards, deciding the seat or language of an arbitration, etc.), will fall within the remit of some institutions but not of others. On that basis, it would be illusory to attempt to draw a list of activities which, taken together, would meet the qualitative threshold of institutional arbitration. In fact, because the activities of institutions vary greatly between institutions it may well be conceptually impossible to draw any such list.

If this is so, what makes an arbitration "institutional" may not be the particular activities undertaken by the institution, but rather the manner in which these activities are carried out, or the basis on which they are undertaken. One may argue, for example, that for an arbitration to be institutional, the institution's activities must be undertaken *in application of* or *pursuant to* the relevant arbitration rules. In other words, it would not be enough that some services are offered; such services would need to be offered by operation of the relevant arbitration rules. This is the position which Professor Pierre Lalive seemed to take. According to him, for there to be institutional arbitration it is necessary that the relevant arbitration rules reserve, for the institution, some "competence" in the implementation of the said rules. For Professor Lalive this is the essential criterion that distinguishes institutional arbitration form ad hoc arbitration:

> [what is decisive] *is that the organisation does not limit itself to offer to the parties its procedural rules, its premises, its administrative services, but that it reserves to itself a competence in the implementation of the said procedural rules* (Translation by the author)[67].

66. In England, a number of professional associations or other entities accept from time to time to act as appointing authority, or to propose names of neutrals to parties to arbitration proceedings but the role of these entities falls short of qualifying as institutional arbitration. For one author, such entities as the Institution of Civil Engineers (ICE), the Royal Institute of British Architects (RIBA), the Royal Institution of Chartered Surveyors (RICS), for instance, have a mere "*peripheral involvement*" in arbitration. See Vigras, "The Role of Institutions in Arbitration" 461.
67. In the original language: "[ce qui est décisif, c'est] *que cet organisme ne se contente pas de mettre à la disposition des parties son règlement de procédure, ses locaux, ses services administratifs, mais qu'il se réserve lui-même une compétence dans l'application dudit règlement arbitral*" Lalive, "Problèmes Relatifs à l'Arbitrage International Commercial" 665.

Professor Lalive's idea that there must be a "reservation of competence" implicitly requires that the power conferred on the institution by the parties must extend beyond mere logistical functions (e.g., making catering arrangements for a hearing, booking hearing rooms etc.) to include some measure of decisional authority. We would go further and say that this authority must go beyond that of mere default appointing authority. The role of default appointing authority, even if exercised in application of some arbitration rules like the UNCITRAL rules, is not sufficient and must be accompanied by some other services or activities undertaken in accordance with the relevant rules, for there to be institutional arbitration.

The reservation of competence made by the parties to the benefit of the institution does not necessarily need to be reflected in the relevant arbitration rules. What matters is that the parties have agreed to make such a reservation. Indeed, an arbitration under the UNCITRAL rules, which parties agree should be fully administered by an institution, would readily be recognized as a form of institutional arbitration. This is so because the role of the institution would likely be very similar to its role in arbitrations conducted under its own rules (including, as the case may be, acting as appointing authority, monitoring the proceedings, acting as a channel of communication, offering logistical support, providing assistance regarding the costs of the arbitration, etc.)[68]. The administration of arbitration proceedings governed by the UNCITRAL rules is a role frequently undertaken by the LCIA for example[69]. Some of the services offered by the institution, however, will not necessarily be covered expressly by the terms of the UNCITRAL rules: for instance, the logistical support like arrangements for hearings (booking of hearing rooms, interpreters and court reporters) or more importantly the fixing of the costs of the arbitration on the basis of the institution's own schedule of costs. Therefore, while we agree with the late Professor P. Lalive that there must be a *reservation of competence*[70], what is required is only that such reservation be made by operation of an agreement of the parties (whether in the form of arbitration rules they have agreed to apply, or by a separate agreement express or implied).

As discussed in Chapter 3 below, some other authors draw a distinction between "*supervised*" and "*unsupervised*" institutional arbitration. See Craig, Park, and Paulsson, *International Chamber of Commerce Arbitration* 40-41. See also, Bühler and Webster, *Handbook of ICC arbitration* 4. Similarly, see Jian Zhou, "Arbitration Agreements in China: Battles on Designation of Arbitral Institution and Ad Hoc Arbitration" (2006) 23 Journal of International Arbitration, Kluwer Law International 145, 145-146.

68. In fact, as pointed out by Redfern and Hunter, many of the newly created arbitral institutions base their institutional rules on the UNCITRAL arbitration rules. Blackaby, Partasides, Hunter, and Redfern, *Redfern and Hunter on International Arbitration*, 1-108.

69. As indicated above, a number of institutions administer arbitration proceedings both under their own rules and under the UNCITRAL rules including for example SIAC and DIS.

70. Another term used to describe generally this reservation of competence is "*third-party authority*". See Fabien Gelinas, "Investment Tribunals and the Commercial Arbitration Model: Mixed Procedures and Creeping Institutionalisation" in Mark Gehring and Marie-Claire Cordonier Segger (eds), *Sustainable Development in World Trade Law* (Kluwer Law International 2005) 580.

Exploring the legal nature of such an agreement[71], or discussing the relationship, if any, of that agreement with the parties' arbitration agreement is beyond the scope of this book. However, what matters for present purposes is that the notion of institutional arbitration seems necessarily to imply an agreement by the parties to "submit" to the authority, or some may be tempted to say the jurisdiction, of the institution[72].

In sum, the notion of "institutional arbitration" requires:

(1) a permanent organization;
(2) a set of arbitration rules; and
(3) an agreement by the parties to reserve, to the permanent organization, some decisional authority (a "reservation of competence") beyond the mere task of acting as a default appointing authority[73].

§1.03 DEFINING "ARBITRAL INSTITUTIONS"

Having defined the phenomenon of institutional arbitration, we may now define the actor itself, that is, the arbitral institution. For the purposes of this book, the term "arbitral institution" means a permanent organization to which parties to a dispute reserve some decisional authority in order to facilitate an arbitration conducted in accordance with a set of arbitration rules.

On that basis, organizations such as the IDRC in London, which only offer some logistical support or services, are excluded from the notion of arbitral institution. Are also excluded, organizations, like the LMAA or FOSFA, which offer arbitration rules but services that are so limited that they fall short of that of an institution[74]. On that basis are also excluded organizations that act as appointing authority only, like the Chartered Institute of Arbitrators. Further, judicial bodies such as the ICJ, the ITLOS or panels constituted under the WTO's dispute settlement understanding are also excluded, as they are not concerned with arbitration.

71. And in particular whether or not such an agreement is a contract and, if so what type of contract.
72. This idea that "institutional arbitration" necessarily implies an agreement to submit to the authority of an institution has, on rare occasions, been contemplated by authors, often indirectly. See, for example, Jian Zhou: "[...] *some arbitral institutions also administer proceedings based on ad hoc arbitration agreements. In such cases, the administrative work of the arbitral institution will not change the nature of the ad hoc arbitration because the parties do not surrender jurisdiction to any arbitral institution* [...]". Zhou, "Arbitration Agreements in China: Battles on Designation of Arbitral Institution and Ad Hoc Arbitration" 145-146. See also Schleapfer: *"If one leaves aside the issue whether there is manifestly no agreement to arbitrate* [...], *the other issues that the institution has to address at the beginning of the arbitration are, in fact, unavoidable, If parties choose institutional arbitration, it means that they expect the institution to perform the tasks listed above"* [tasks which, according to the author, involve a measure of decision-making]. Anne Veronique Schlaepfer, "The Role of the Institution at the Commencement of the Proceedings" in Philipp Habegger and others (eds), *Arbitral Institutions Under Scrutiny* (JurisNet 2013), ASA Special Series No. 40, 62.
73. Again, the precise "tasks" will vary greatly from one set of institutional rules to the next. See the overview of the activities of arbitral institutions in section §3.03 ("*Casework activities*") of Chapter 3 below ("*The Activities of Arbitral Institutions: An Overview*").
74. Because such services do not demonstrate a reservation of competence.

The same organization may be involved with both institutional and ad hoc arbitrations, depending on the circumstances. Institutions like the ICC, the LCIA or the SCC, for example, most frequently act in respect of institutional arbitrations conducted under their own rules, but they also sometimes act as appointing authority only in respect of ad hoc arbitrations (whether or not conducted under the UNCITRAL rules)[75]. This book is therefore concerned with those organizations which intervene, at least occasionally, in institutional arbitrations.

§1.04 TYPOLOGIES OF ARBITRAL INSTITUTIONS

The definitions of "institutional arbitration" and "arbitral institutions" given above should not give the impression that these notions are monolithic. To say the least, the terms cover multifaceted realities. Chapter 3 below offers an illustration of the diversity that characterizes the "activities" undertaken by arbitral institutions in the administration of cases, but this diversity characterizes also the manner in which institutions are organized, including, for example, their status in the legal system in which they are incorporated/established, or the way in which they operate (charitable or for-profit), or even the types of disputes they handle. The sections below offer a brief panorama of the institutional arbitration landscape.

[A] Legal Status of Arbitral Institutions

Some (rare) institutions are international organizations set up by treaty. This is the case, for example, of the Permanent Court of Arbitration in The Hague which was established as an intergovernmental organization by the Convention for the Pacific Settlement of International Disputes concluded at The Hague in 1899[76]. Likewise, ICSID was established by the Convention on the Settlement of Investment Disputes between States and Nationals of Other States (the "Washington Convention"). It constitutes one of the five organizations of the World Bank Group[77]. Interestingly Article 18 of the Washington Convention expressly provides that "[the] *Centre shall have full international legal personality*", as is the case of international organizations.

Other arbitral institutions have been established through intergovernmental efforts without these institutions being given the form of an international organization

75. The SCC has long been acting as appointing authority in UNCITRAL arbitrations. See Edwin R. Alley, "International Arbitration: The Alternative of the Stockholm Chamber of Commerce" (1988) 22 International Lawyer 837, 839. So much so that the SCC developed a specific set of procedures for its activities as appointing authority in non SCC-rules cases named "*The SCC Procedures and Services under the UNCITRAL Arbitration rules*". See Öhrström, "The Arbitration Institute of the Stockholm Chamber of Commerce (SCC)" 4.
76. The "Website of the Permanent Court of Arbitration (PCA), http://www.pca-cpa.org", 22 February 2016.
77. Along with the International Bank for Reconstruction and Development (IBRD), the International Development Association (IDA), the International Finance Corporation (IFC), and the Multilateral Investment Guarantee Agency (MIGA). "Website of the International Centre for Settlement of Investment Disputes (ICSID), https://icsid.worldbank.org/ICSID" (17 March 2014) <https://icsid.worldbank.org/ICSID/FrontServlet> accessed 17 March 2014.

with international legal personality. This is the case of both the Cairo and the Kuala Lumpur Regional Centres which were established in 1979 by what is now known as the Asian African Legal Consultative Organisation ("AALCO")[78].

Most arbitral institutions though are set up as domestic law entities. Naturally, the legal form of the institutions that have been set up as domestic law entities varies depending on the law under which they are organized[79]. For one author:

> *the legal status, public or private, corporation or charity, as well as the manner in which these organisations function financially, is very diverse.* [...] *One should note the great diversity of the initiatives that claim to form part of institutional arbitration.* (Translation by the Author).

For example, the "*LCIA Company*" of which the LCIA (in the sense the arbitral institution) is the operational arm, is registered in England as a "company limited by guarantee"[80]. A company limited by guarantee is a corporate form peculiar to common law legal systems, which is primarily used for non-profit ventures that require legal personality. A guarantee company does not have a share capital or shareholders, but instead has members who accept to act as guarantors up to a nominal amount in the event the company were to become insolvent. The LCIA Company, therefore, does not distribute profits amongst its members. HKIAC was also incorporated as a company limited by guarantee, which was granted charitable status in 1985.[81]

The ICC Court of Arbitration is an unincorporated operational branch[82] of a chamber of commerce which, itself, is registered as a foreign "*Association*"[83], a corporate form used for not-for-profit entities in France. But other French institutions take a different legal form. At the domestic level, the Chambre Arbitrale De Cotons and the Chambre Arbitrale des Cafés et Poivres (both based in Le Havre) are organized as "sociétés anonymes" (a legal form normally reserved for medium and large size private companies).[84]

---

78. "Website of the CRCICA, http://www.crcica.org.eg". "Website of the Kuala Lumpur Regional Centre for Arbitration, Http://www.klrca.org" (21 July 2015) <http://www.klrca.org> accessed 15 February 2016.

    The Asian-African Legal Consultative Organization (AALCO), originally known as the Asian Legal Consultative Committee (ALCC) was constituted on 15 November 1956 following the Bandung Conference of April 1955. The organization now comprises forty-seven members including some of the major Asian and African States. See Website of the Asian-African Legal Consultative Organization (AALCO), http://www.aalco.int.
79. In the original language: "*Le statut juridique, public ou privé, société commerciale ou association privée, ainsi que le mode de financement de ces différents organismes sont fort variés.* [...] *Il faut prendre acte de la très grande diversité des initiatives qui se réclament de l'arbitrage institutionnel*". Gaudet, "La Coopération des Juridictions Etatiques à l'Arbitrage Institutionnel" 100-101. In the same sense, see Fouchard, "Les Institutions Permanentes d'Arbitrage Devant le Juge Etatique (A Propos d'une Jurisprudence Récente)" 225.
80. See the website of the LCIA: "Website of the London Court of International Arbitration (LCIA), http://www.lcia.org", under "Organisation".
81. To, "Developments of the Hong Kong International Arbitration Centre," 507.
82. Fouchard, "Les Institutions Permanentes d'Arbitrage Devant le Juge Etatique (A Propos d'une Jurisprudence Récente)" 225.
83. Fouchard, "Les Institutions Permanentes d'Arbitrage Devant Le Juge Etatique (A Propos D'une Jurisprudence Récente)," 225.
84. *Ibid.*

The DIS in Germany is organized as an "*eingetragener verein*", which can be loosely described as a "not-for-profit association"[85]. In Canada, the BCICAC was set up in 1986 as a "*foundation*", that is to say a non-profit organization incorporated under the Society Act of British Columbia[86]. As discussed below, the AAA and ICDR are likewise incorporated as not-for-profit entities under New York law.

[B] Self-Standing Independent Institutions versus Institutions Connected to Another Organization or a State

Some rare institutions are both organically and financially independent, meaning that the entity by which they are organized is not linked to another organization or government and that they do not receive funding from a government. This is the case of the AAA and the ICDR in the United States. The AAA was established in 1926 as a result of the merger of the Arbitration Society of America and the Arbitration Foundation, following the enactment of the New York State Arbitration Law of 1920. It is incorporated in New York under the name "American Arbitration Association, Inc.", and takes the form of a New York law domestic not-for-profit corporation[87]. The ICDR which was established in 1996 by the AAA is likewise incorporated in New York using the same corporate form, under the name "American Arbitration Association/International Centre For Dispute Resolution Foundation, Inc"[88]. The two institutions are not linked to a wider chamber of commerce or State entity, nor do they receive any funding from any government[89].

The same is true of the LCIA. While it was established by the City of London and the London Chamber of Commerce in the late nineteenth century, the entity was re-incorporated in the mid-1980s at which stage it emancipated itself from its two founding bodies. The LCIA thereby also became independent from the Chartered Institute of Arbitrators, which had joined the two founding entities in the supervision of the LCIA in the middle of the 1970s[90].

These two institutions are rare example of organically and financially independent institutions. Many other arbitral institutions are linked to a chamber of commerce.

85. "Website of the DIS, http://www.dis-arb.de/scho/", under "About the DIS". See also Jens Bredow and Isabel Mulder, "Commentary on the Arbitration Rules of the German Institution of Arbitration (DIS Rules), Introduction" in Karl-Heinz Bockstiegel, Dr Stefan Kröll, and Patricia Nacimiento (ed), *Arbitration in Germany: The Model Law in Practice* (Kluwer Law International 2007) 658.
86. Bonita J. Thompson, "Building an Arbitration and Mediation Centre: From International Foundations to Domestic Rooftops': The Establishment of the British Columbia International Commercial Arbitration Centre" in Pieter Sanders (ed), *Arbitration in Settlement of International Commercial Disputes Involving the Far East and Arbitration in Combined Transportation* vol. 4 (Kluwer Law International 1988) 189, 198.
87. See NYS Department of State Division of Corporations, http://www.dos.ny.gov/corps/bus_entity_search.html. Information correct as at 22 July 2015.
88. See NYS Department of State Division of Corporations, http://www.dos.ny.gov/corps/bus_entity_search.html. Information correct as at 22 July 2015.
89. See the financial information presented the annual report of the AAA for the year 2014, available on the AAA's website, http://www.aaa.org, under "About us", and "Annual Reports".
90. See "Website of the London Court of International Arbitration (LCIA), http://www.lcia.org".

This is not surprising because arbitral institutions are often established in part thanks to the efforts of a business community – community which is often organized as a chamber of commerce[91]. Well known examples of institutions linked to a chamber of commerce (whether international or regional) include the ICC, the SCC, the Milan Chamber, or the Swiss Institution. The link to a chamber of commerce presents both advantages and disadvantages for an arbitral institution. For newer institutions, it offers some immediate legitimacy as, in essence, the institution is established by its users, for its users. One possible drawback comes from the fact that an arbitral institution may feel pressured to support financially the non-income generating activities of the wider chamber of commerce, which can in turn create disincentives for the institution to keep its administrative charges as low as possible.

Equally frequent but perhaps more problematic[92] are institutions that are linked to the Government of the jurisdiction where they are based. As previously discussed the link may be an organic one. For instance, it was the Chinese government itself that established CIETAC as a public entity[93] – namely an entity subordinated to a non-governmental social organization[94]. The same is true of CMAC[95]. Without necessarily taking the form of public entities, some institutions have their status regulated by a statutory instrument. This was the case with ICAC or MAC in Russia which are regulated by Annexes 1 and 2 of the Russian Federation Law No. 5338-1 of 7 July 1993 on international commercial arbitration[96]. Similarly, the arbitration rules of DIAC have been enacted by a decree of the Ruler of Dubai[97].

Sometimes the governmental link is more tenuous, and takes the form of a statutory attribution of responsibilities. The new (2005) Arbitration Act of Malaysia for

91. See for HKIAC, Neil Kaplan, "Arbitration in Hong Kong" (1986) 3 Journal of International Arbitration, Kluwer Law International 7, 15; for DIAC see Hunter, "Dubai International Arbitration Centre (DIAC)" 2-3. For BCICAC see, Thompson, "Building an Arbitration and Mediation Centre: From International Foundations to Domestic Rooftops': The Establishment of the British Columbia International Commercial Arbitration Centre" 190-191.
92. For a criticism of the impact of governmental link with an institution see Paulsson, "Moral Hazard in International Dispute Resolution, Inaugural Lecture as Holder of the Michael R. Klein Distinguished Scholar Chair University of Miami School of Law on 29 April 2010" 20. Expressing the view that the absence of apparent link with a government is desirable see Thompson, "Building an Arbitration and Mediation Centre: From International Foundations to Domestic Rooftops': The Establishment of the British Columbia International Commercial Arbitration Centre" 198.
93. See "Website of CIETAC, http://www.cietac.org". CIETAC was established (in 1956) following a 1954 decision of the country's highest administrative authority, the "Chinese Administration Council" (now called the "State Council").
94. Albert Jan van den Berg, "CIETAC Amended Arbitration Rules 2000 Embrace the New Century," in Albert Jan van Den Berg (ed), *Yearbook Commercial Arbitration,* XXVI (Kluwer Law International 2001) 367, http://www.kluwerarbitration.com/print.aspx?ids = ipn22909.
95. See "Website of CMAC, http://www.cmac-sh.org/en/home.asp".
96. Khodykin, "International Commercial Arbitration Court (ICAC) and Maritime Arbitration Commission (MAC) at the Russian Federation Chamber of Commerce and Industry" 2. See also Alexander S. Komarov, "Introduction to the Revision of the Rules of the International Commercial Arbitration Court at the Chamber of Commerce and Industry of the Russian Federation (ICAC)" in Albert Jan van den Berg (ed), *Yearbook Commercial Arbitration*, XXXI (Kluwer Law International 2006) 456, 457.
97. See J. Martin H. Hunter, "Dubai International Arbitration Centre (DIAC)" in Loukas A. Mistelis and others (eds), *The World Arbitration Reporter,* vol. 3 (Juris 2010).

example makes the KLRCA the default appointing authority in ad hoc arbitrations in certain circumstances, and offers immunity to its Director[98]. Likewise, the SIAC in Singapore is designated by the international arbitration act as competent for the certification of awards for enforcement purposes. The act also confers on the Registrar of SIAC the power to proceed to the taxation of the fees of the arbitral tribunal where these have not been agreed between by the parties[99]. Another example is the appointment by the Government of Rwanda of the Kigali International Arbitration Centre as the Government's official advisor on questions of ADR.

But the governmental link may also be a financial one. One extreme example is CIETAC, which financial status resembles that of public establishments in certain civil law countries. According to Jianlong Yu, Chairman of CIETAC, all arbitration institutions in China are required since 2002 to "[...] *hand up their revenues to the Ministry of Finance or its local branches, and to make an annual budget for their expenditures, which has to be submitted to the Ministry or its branches for approval*"[100]. In a different vein, HKIAC, while financially and organically independent today, also benefitted from the strong support of the local authorities in its early days. Not only was the then Attorney General instrumental in the creation of the steering committee which was put in place to consider the creation of what became HKIAC in the early 1980s, but the funding of the centre was ensured in part by the Government which, in addition to making various grants to the HKIAC, also agreed to match every dollar invested by the private sector in the centre[101].

[C] Charitable versus For-Profit

If the vast majority of arbitral institutions operate on a charitable basis[102], some others offer their administrative services with a view to generating a profit for its owners. At the international level, the only institution known to this author to operate on a for-profit basis is JAMS[103]. JAMS, whose name is an acronym for "*Judicial Arbitration and Mediation Services, Inc*" was established by lawyer and former judge, the Hon. H. Warren Knight, in California in 1979 to "market" effective dispute resolution services. Today, JAMS which mostly operates in the field of domestic arbitration in the United States describes itself as "*the largest private alternative dispute resolution (ADR)*

98. Syed Ahmad Idid, "Kuala Lumpur Regional Centre for Arbitration-Impact of the Old and New Arbitration Act" (2006) 2 Asian International Arbitration Journal, Kluwer Law International 97, 98-100.
99. International Arbitration Act, section 21(2).
100. Moser and Jianlong, "CIETAC and its Work – An Interview with Vice Chairman Yu Jianlong" 557.
101. Christopher Wing To, "Developments of the Hong Kong International Arbitration Centre," (2000) 28(11) International Business Lawyer, 507.
102. This is the case of, to mention only a few, ICC, LCIA, ICDR, the Swiss Chamber's Arbitration Institution, the SCC, SIAC, HKIAC, CIETAC, CAS, CRCICA, DIS, KCAB, Milan Chamber of Arbitration, NAI, VIAC and WIPO (Information based on these institutions' responses to the questionnaires sent out by the author).
103. Information based on the institution's responses to the questionnaire sent out by the author.

provider in the world"[104]. At the domestic level in the United States, one may also mention the National Arbitration Forum LLC ("NAF"), a for-profit company established in 1986 and headquartered in Minneapolis. Like JAMS, NAF serves mostly the US domestic arbitration market, but it is not known to offer its services for international arbitrations.

Obviously, the for-profit nature of an institution (or rather of an "ADR provider") may raise doubts as to its capacity to offer neutral and impartial services to its users. It is not illogical to expect a for-profit organization to feel pressured to favour repeat users to the detriment of less frequent ones simply because a larger share of the organization's profits will be attributable to frequent users. This is precisely what was alleged to have happened with the NAF in the mid-2000s where the service provider was said to have favoured systematically companies over consumers. By way of further background, a number of law suits have been filed against the NAF including one in 2008, by the City of San Francisco on behalf of its citizens, and one in 2009 by the Minnesota Attorney General, in which the NAF was accused of unfairly favouring credit card companies in disputes with their customers. This led the NAF in 2009 to stop accepting cases relating to consumer debt collection claims. Some of the allegations were that NAF was giving a preferential treatment to "*famous parties*" (i.e., companies who were inserting NAF arbitration clauses in their contracts) by, *inter alia*, instructing arbitrators to change their decisions when these were adverse to the famous parties, and not reappointing arbitrators who had decided against famous parties[105].

[D] Types of Cases Handled: Generalist Institutions versus Specialist Ones

Another distinction can be made between arbitral institutions on the basis of the types of disputes handled. Some entities focus, more or less strictly, on one particular industry sector while others offer their services across all industries[106]. The Court of Arbitration for Sport ("CAS") in Lausanne, for instance, deals exclusively with sports related disputes. Though, in practice, CAS administers both disputes that are "directly" linked to sports such as disciplinary cases resulting from a decision of a sports organization, as well as disputes that are "indirectly" sports related such as commercial disputes arising out of sponsorship contracts and the like. Another example is the WIPO Arbitration and Mediation Centre, which aims to deal principally with disputes involving intellectual property, such as licensing agreements or other forms of transaction relating to patents, trademarks, copyright or know-how. The WIPO Centre, however, also accepts commercial matters not involving intellectual property[107].

104. Website of JAMS, http://www.jamsadr.com/aboutus.
105. Urs Weber-Stecher, "Principles of Good Governance and Organisation of Arbitral Institutions" in Philipp Habegger and others (eds), *Arbitral Institutions Under Scrutiny* (JurisNet 2013), ASA Special Series No. 40, 41.
106. ICC, LCIA, ICDR, SCC, Swiss Institution, SIAC, HKIAC, SIAC, CRCICA, JAMS, Milan Chamber. Information based on the institutions' responses to the questionnaire sent to them.
107. See website of WIPO, http://www.wipo.int/amc/en/center/background.html.

Worth mentioning is P.R.I.M.E. Finance (whose name stands for the Panel of Recognized International Market Experts in Finance), an institution recently established in the Netherlands that focuses on disputes concerning complex financial transactions.

As previously indicated, certain trade organizations such as the Grain and Feed Trade Association ("GAFTA") or the Federation of Oils, Seeds and Fats Associations ("FOSFA") to name only two, offer arbitration services to their members. Trade associations are industry-specific business associations founded and financed by companies in a particular industry to further the interests of its members. Their key areas of involvement often centre around lobbying, education and standardization of contracts and norms. Dispute resolution services are typically only offered by trade associations in an incidental fashion. A number of trade associations have published their own arbitration rules as is the case with the two organizations mentioned above. Often the cases referred to these forms of commodities arbitration are international in nature. This being said, as previously explained, it is debatable whether these forms of arbitration constitute institutional arbitration as the involvement of the trade association in the administration of the disputes is often limited.

[E] Domestic versus International

Some institutions aim to provide their services globally, whereas others are serving businesses on a regional basis. As previously indicated, the focus of this book lies with international arbitration rather than domestic arbitration, and institutions that deal only in domestic cases have therefore been largely ignored in this study. This being said, few institutions can claim to be thoroughly international. An analysis of the caseload of a large number of arbitral institutions suggests that the majority administer less cross-border disputes than domestic ones. According to one publication the ICC, the LCIA and the ICDR are "*three principal arbitration institutions with the most genuinely international vocation*"[108]. But between these three institutions there are marked differences, with the ICC being by and large the most international institution. For example in 2013, new cases registered at the ICC involved 2,120 parties from across 138 jurisdictions. The percentage of French parties (the equivalent of "local parties" for the ICC, as it is headquartered in Paris) was only 4.8%. The percentage of non-French parties was therefore 95.2%. The same year, the proportion of UK parties at the LCIA was 18.6% and the proportion of non-UK parties was therefore 81.4%. While the same statistics are not publicly available for ICDR, based on the data available, the ICDR's caseload appears much less international. In 2009, for example, the ICDR stated that the number of cases *not* involving *any* US party was sixty-five[109]. The same year the

108. Jan Paulsson and Nigel Rawding (eds), *The Freshfields Guide to Arbitration Clauses in International Contracts* (3rd edn, Kluwer Law International 2010) 62.
109. Martin F. Gusy, James M. Hosking and Franz T. Schwarz, *A Guide to the ICDR International Arbitration Rules* (Oxford University Press 2011) 14. The number had doubled from thirty-two the year before.

total number of cases registered at ICDR was 884, which means that only 7.35% of ICDR had cases with no US parties.

[F] Cultural Background and Historical Heritage

Last but not least, not all arbitral institutions share in the same cultural and historical heritage. Some institutions trace their roots back to the old Soviet chambers of trade (which as discussed elsewhere above used to be strongly linked to the State's judicial apparatus) while some others fall more squarely into the liberal "Western" ADR tradition. The first category of institutions would include Russian and Chinese institutions such as ICAC, MAC, CIETAC, BAC, SHIAC, or CMAC, but also some of the eastern European institutions. The second would encompass such institutions as the ICC, the LCIA, the Swiss Institution, the AAA etc. Conventional wisdom dictates that, in the Western tradition, institutions tend to be created by the joint efforts of the business community and the local authorities. For example, the LCIA was created by the efforts of the Corporation of the City of London with the co-operation of the London Chamber of Commerce[110]. The idea may be summed up as follows: Businessmen, in need of efficient dispute resolution facilities, would lobby for the development of arbitration centres if the domestic courts in their jurisdiction are found to lack in efficiency[111]. As explained previously, by contrast to the Western arbitral tradition, the old Soviet chambers of trade were established by public authorities, had quasi-monopoly over disputes involving trade with foreign companies, and were subject to strict rules of procedure[112]. Consequently, in the Western ADR tradition arbitration is perceived as having developed as a privatized mechanism that was slowly and painfully "carved out" of the jurisdiction of the public courts by its users. In that context the development of arbitration is often primarily perceived as a process of emancipation from the State-run judicial resolution of disputes. In the Soviet tradition arbitration (and therefore arbitral institutions) was more commonly perceived as an integral part of the wider adjudicative apparatus of the State – institutions and courts working in parallel, fulfilling similar social functions.

110. See "Website of the London Court of International Arbitration (LCIA), http://www.lcia.org". See also for HKIAC, Neil Kaplan, "Arbitration in Hong Kong" (1986) 3 Journal of International Arbitration, Kluwer Law International 7, 15; for DIAC see Hunter, "Dubai International Arbitration Centre (DIAC)" 2-3.
111. Conversely, where litigation is considered effective enough, the need to develop alternative facilities including arbitration centres is less pressing. In this sense, see in respect of the creation of BCICAC, Thompson, "Building an Arbitration and Mediation Centre: From International Foundations to Domestic Rooftops': The Establishment of the British Columbia International Commercial Arbitration Centre" 190-191.
112. Goldman, "Les Conflits de Lois dans l'Arbitrage International de Droit Privé" 352-353. See also Kirchner and Marriott, "International Arbitration in the Aftermath of Socialism – The Example of the Berlin Court of Arbitration" 6. See also Fouchard, "Les Institutions Permanentes d'Arbitrage Devant le Juge Etatique (A Propos d'une Jurisprudence Récente)" 225. Similarly one may mention in China the now defunct "Economic Contract Arbitration Commissions" providing for mandatory arbitration of domestic disputes. See Chang, "CIETAC's Perspective on Arbitration and Conciliation Concerning China" 28.

If the above distinctions are noteworthy it is because, on occasion, they shed a light as to why the arbitration rules of a certain institution contains some peculiar provisions which are not widely seen elsewhere. The role of national committees in the appointment process at the ICC, for example, is linked to the fact that the institution is part of a chamber of commerce. More interestingly perhaps the jurisdictional provisions in CIETAC, CMAC or BAC arbitration (discussed in Chapter 3 below) are the result of the fact that these institutions trace their roots back to the old Soviet model of the chambers of trade.

In a sense, the diversity that can be seen in the rules of various institutions, and in the manner in which arbitral institutions approach casework administration[113] reflects the many types of organizations engaged in institutional arbitration.

113. See Chapter 3 below under section §3.04 ("*Different levels of institutional involvement*").

CHAPTER 2

Institutional Arbitration as a Growing Phenomenon: Quantitative Growth, "Institutionalization" and "Judicialization"

Understanding what arbitral institutions do, the nature of their role, and the impact they may have on the arbitration process, raises questions that are pertinent in themselves. But the "intrinsic" relevance of the topic of this book is accentuated by two "extrinsic" factors, namely: (1) the increasing use of institutional arbitration for the resolution of international commercial disputes (quantitative growth of institutional arbitration); and (2) the alleged increased institutionalization of arbitration (qualitative growth of institutional arbitration).

§2.01 INCREASING USE OF INSTITUTIONAL ARBITRATION: THE QUANTITATIVE GROWTH

There are few phenomena in arbitration that are the object of greater consensus than the quantitative growth of institutional arbitration. It is true that a number of indicators lend support to the idea that institutional arbitration is expanding. There is the increase, first, in the volume of cases administered by institutions and, second, in the number of institutions being created.

[A] Increase in the Volume of Cases Referred to Institutions

While most arbitral institutions are not often prolix when it comes to statistical information relating to their caseload[114], a review of the statistics available

114. For Guy Pendell: *"Exactly how many arbitration institutions exist and how many arbitrations they actually administer is unclear. We know the statistics of the major institutions* [...], *but*

demonstrates that the number of cases referred to institutional arbitration has grown tremendously in the past sixty years.

It is difficult to comment on the development of arbitration prior to that because of the scarcity of statistical information available. If figures for the period before 1960 for the ICC are in the public domain, they are not as readily available for the other institutions that were already in existence at the time[115].

Gary Born, reflecting on the "*steadily increasing case-loads at leading arbitral institutions*" explains that "*the number of reported cases* [increased] *between three and five-fold in the past 25 years* [i.e. up to 2009]"[116]. In support of his position, Born refers to the number of Requests for Arbitration[117] filed with the ICC. Born notes that the number of new Requests increased from 32 in 1956, to 210 in 1976, increasing further to 452 in 1997, and to 599 in 2007[118]. In 2014, the total number of new referrals was 801.

Figure 2.1 Evolution of the Caseload of the ICC (1956-2014)

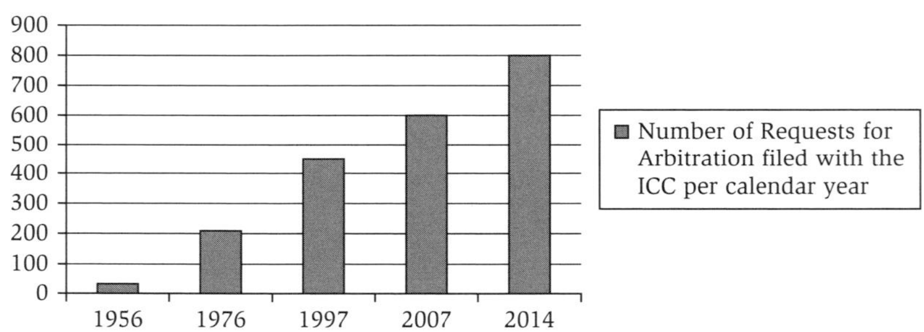

In fact the number was even higher in 2009[119] but figures for the period 2008 to 2010 should be taken with a measure of caution as the global financial crisis, which started in October 2008, appears momentarily to have caused a somewhat "artificial" increase in the volume of cases. Many institutions indeed recorded a significant increase in the number of cases filed in the period immediately following the crisis, and then recorded a drop in the two years that followed. The figures of a number of institutions for 2007

what of all the others?" Guy Pendell, "The Rise and Rise of the Arbitration Institution" (Kluwer Arbitration Blog 30 November 2011).

115. Such as the PCA, the AAA and the LCIA.
116. Gary B. Born, *International Commercial Arbitration* (Kluwer Law International 2009) 68-69; Gary B Born, *International Commercial Arbitration* (Kluwer Law International, 2014) 93 <http://www.kluwerarbitration.com/CommonUI/document.aspx?id=KLI-KA-Born-2014-Ch01>.
117. Hereinafter, "Requests".
118. Born, *International Commercial Arbitration* 70.
119. 817 cases.

(i.e., to say pre-crisis), 2009 (at the height of the crisis) and 2011 (post crisis) show an increase and then a contraction of the number of cases for a number of institutions[120].

Statistical data from other institutions confirms that the number of cases referred to institutional arbitration has continued to grow in recent years[121].

Figure 2.2 Evolution of the Caseload of Other Major Institutions (2000-2014)

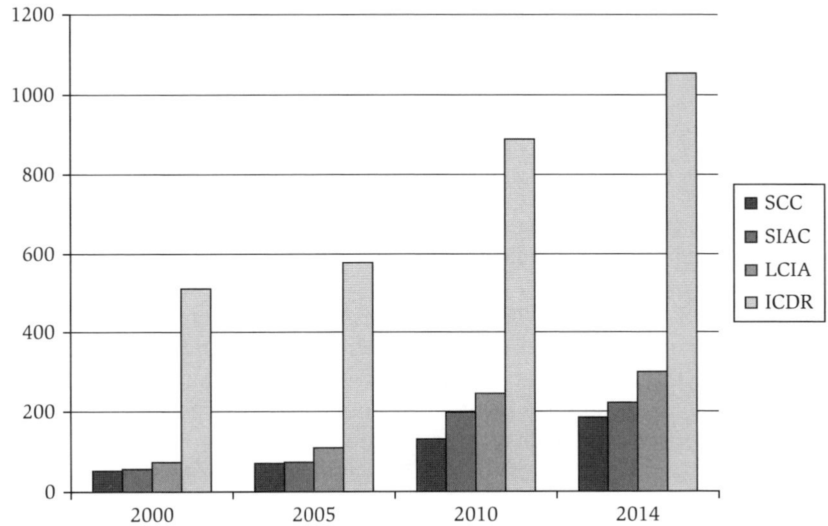

Three observations may be made in relation to the growth of the caseload of arbitral institutions.

First, the growth of institutional referrals is anything but a recent phenomenon. Figure 2.1 above (ICC caseload 1956-2012) demonstrates that the growth was observable as early as the middle of the twentieth century. Some authors were already observing this phenomenon over twenty years ago in respect of the ICC[122].

120. LCIA (137, 272, 224); ICC (599, 817, 796); HKIAC (448, 649, 275), Swiss Chambers (59, 104, 87); KCAB (international cases only) (59, 78, 59), SCC (170, 216, 199). The same, however, is not true of SIAC and ICDR, which both recorded an increase from 2009 to 2011.

121. The numbers for 2000, 2005, 2010 and 2014 are as follows: SCC (53, 73, 131, 183), SIAC (58, 74, 198, 222), LCIA (75, 110, 246, 296), ICDR (510, 580, 888, 1052). For Schlaepfer and Petti "[...] *during the last twenty-five years, the well-established arbitral institutions have witnessed a significant growth in activity* [...]". Schlaepfer and Petti, "Institutional versus Ad Hoc Arbitration" 13. In respect of the SCC specifically see, Marie Öhrström, "The Arbitration Institute of the Stockholm Chamber of Commerce (SCC)" in Loukas A. Mistelis and others (eds), *The World Arbitration Reporter*, vol. 3 (Juris 2010) 1. For the Swiss Chambers specifically, see Anne Veronique Schlaepfer and Philippe Bartsch, "Swiss Chambers' Court of Arbitration and Mediation (Swiss Chambers)" in Loukas A. Mistelis and others (eds), *The World Arbitration Reporter*, vol. 3 (Juris 2010) 19.

122. Michel Gaudet, "La Coopération des Juridictions Etatiques à l'Arbitrage Institutionnel" (1988) 6 ASA Bulletin, Kluwer Law International 90, 99.

Second, it appears that this growth has been a fairly continuous process. Figures 2.1 and 2.2 above suggest that it was not marked by any sustained periods of plateau. As observed by Tila Maria de Hancock:

> [f]*rom its beginning,* [in 1923], *the ICC Court grew steadily until World War II interrupted its work. After 1945 its growth and expansion resumed, and during the past decade the case-load of the ICC Court has dramatically increased.* [...] *The growth trend continues upward and the amounts in dispute have grown enormously*[123].

Third, the growth has accelerated in recent years. Michel Gaudet observed in the late 1980s that:

> [...] *of the 6,130 Requests filed with the ICC in its 65 years existence, as many were registered during the last 11 years (1 January 1977 – 31 December 1987) as in the 54 years before that* (Translation by the author)[124].

As Figures 2.1 and 2.2 above demonstrate, this acceleration has continued after the late 1980s[125]. The pace at which institutional referrals have increased has led some commentators to talk of "*exponential growth*"[126]. This exponential growth seems to concern not only institutions that deal mostly in commercial arbitration cases, but also the ICSID which administers investment arbitrations. It should be noted that, as far as ICSID is concerned, there are specific legal reasons for the dramatic increase in case referrals including *inter alia* the advent of "arbitration without privity"[127].

The increase in the number of cases referred to institutions does not, of itself, prove an increase in the proportion of cases being referred to institutional rather than ad hoc arbitration.

---

123. Tila Maria de Hancock, "The ICC Court of Arbitration: The Institution and its Procedures" (1984) 1 Journal of International Arbitration, Kluwer Law International 21, 21. See also Jason Fry who refers to a *"continuously expanding caseload"*. Jason A. Fry, "ICC International Court of Arbitration" in Loukas A. Mistelis and others (eds), *The World Arbitration Reporter*, vol. 3 (Juris 2010) 3.
124. In the original language: "[...] *des 6130 requêtes enregistrées à la Cour en 65 ans, autant l'ont été pendant les 11 dernières années (1er janvier 1977-31 décembre 1987) que dans les 54 précédentes*" Gaudet, "La Coopération des Juridictions Etatiques à l'Arbitrage Institutionnel" 99.
125. On this point, see also W. Laurence Craig, William W. Park, and Jan Paulsson, *International Chamber of Commerce Arbitration* (3rd edn, Oceana Publications 2000) 2: "[...] *more than two-thirds of all cases brought to ICC arbitration arose in the last 20 years of its 75-year existence*".
126. Karin Calvo Goller, "The 2012 ICC Rules of Arbitration – An Accelerated Procedure and Substantial Changes" (2012) 29 Journal of International Arbitration, Kluwer Law International 323, 340; Mark Mangan, "The Arbitrator and the Arbitration Procedure – Sports Arbitration: Citius Altius Fortius?" in Christian Klausegger, Peter Klein, et al. (eds), *Austrian Yearbook on International Arbitration* (2009) 2011 301, 302; Michel A. Calvo, "The Challenge of the ICC Arbitrators: Theory and Practice International" (1998) 15 Journal of International Arbitration, Kluwer Law International 63, 63.
127. For a discussion of the impact of bilateral investment treaties on the caseload of the ICSID, see Antonio R. Parra, "ICSID and the Rise of Bilateral Investment Treaties: Will ICSID be the Leading Arbitration Institution in the Early 21st Century?" (2000) 94 Proceedings of the 101st Annual Meeting (American Society of International Law) 41-43.

Whether or not the proportion has indeed increased is difficult to establish because, by definition, information on ad hoc arbitration remains scarce[128]. But if actual data is scarce, general statements by practitioners pointing to an increase of the proportion of institutional arbitration vis-à-vis ad hoc arbitration are legion[129]. More generally the private nature of arbitration also explains why data on arbitration, both ad hoc and institutional, remains limited[130]. Be that as it may, the increase in the volume of cases suggests that institutional arbitration is more prevalent today than it has ever been and it therefore underlines the importance of this form of arbitration. This stresses, in turn, the importance of better understanding the role that institutions play in the arbitral process.

[B] Increase in the Number of Institutions

The growing importance of institutional arbitration is also reflected in the increase in the number of arbitral institutions. The multiplication, in recent years, of arbitral institutions is well documented[131]. As early as the 1960s, Professor Goldman commented that:

128. In this sense see, Anne Veronique Schlaepfer and Angelina M. Petti, "Institutional versus Ad Hoc Arbitration" in Elliott Geisinger and Nathalie Voser (eds), *International Arbitration in Switzerland – A Handbook for Practitioners* (Kluwer Law International 2013) 13.
129. See, for example, Michael Hwang, Lawrence Boo, and Yewon Han, "National Report for Singapore (2011)" (2011) Supplement no. 64 Jan Paulsson (ed), International Handbook on Commercial Arbitration, Kluwer Law International 1, 16. See also Bertie Vigras, "The Role of Institutions in Arbitration" in Ronald Bernstein and Derek Wood (eds), *Handbook of Arbitration Practice* (Second Edition. Sweet & Maxwell in conjunction with the Chartered Institute of Arbitrators 1993) 469. For the same point in respect of arbitrations initiated in the United Arab Emirates following the 2008 global financial crisis, see Gordon Blanke and Celine Abi Habib, "Arbitration in Dubai: A Basic Primer" in Christian Klausegger, Peter Klein, et al. (eds), *Austrian Yearbook on International Arbitration* 2011 (2011) 217, 222. Likewise, general statements to the effect that the majority of arbitrations are nowadays institutional rather than ad hoc can be found in the literature. See for example Calvin Chan, "Of Arbitral Institutions and Provisional Determinations on Jurisdiction, Global Gold Case" (2009) 25 Arbitration International, Kluwer Law International 403, 411.
130. See Christopher R. Drahozal, "Arbitration by the Numbers: The State of Empirical Research on International Commercial Arbitration" (2006) 22 Arbitration International, Kluwer Law International 291, 291.
131. Bertold Goldman, "Les Conflits de Lois dans l'Arbitrage International de Droit Privé" (1963) 109 Collected Courses of the Hague Academy of International Law, Martinus Nijhoff Publishers & Brill Academic 352; Pierre Lalive, "Problèmes Relatifs à l'Arbitrage International Commercial" (1967) 120 Collected Courses of the Hague Academy of International Law, Martinus Nijhoff Publishers & Brill Academic 664; William K. Slate, "International Arbitration: Do Institutions Make a Difference?" (1996) 31 Wake Forest Law Review 41, 50; Hans Smit, "The Future of International Commercial Arbitration: A Single Transnational Institution" (1986) 25 Columbia Journal of Transnational Law 9, 12; Toby Landau, "The Effect of the New English Arbitration Act on Institutional Arbitration" (1996) 13 Journal of International Arbitration, Kluwer Law International 113, 114; Gilbert Guillaume, "The Future of International Judicial Institutions" (1995) 44 International & Comparative Law Quarterly 848, 862; Michael Moser and Friven Yeoh, "Choosing an Arbitral Institution Arbitration" (2006) 2 The In-House Perspective 18, 18; Schlaepfer and Petti, "Institutional versus Ad Hoc Arbitration" 13; José M. Alcántara, "An International Panel of Maritime Arbitrators?" (1994) 11 Journal of International Arbitration, Kluwer Law International 117, 117.

> [...] *the increasing number of new national and international organisations offering a permanent framework for arbitral proceedings is a phenomenon that is well known and has often been analysed* (Translation by the author)[132].

Some authors have argued that, similarly to the increase in the caseload of existing institutions, the proliferation of new institutions has accelerated in recent times. For Guy Pendell:

> [...] *the growth of the number of institutions has been exponential. Before 1940 only ten percent of the institutions around today existed. Seventy percent of the institutions have been created in the last thirty years; fifty percent in the last twenty and twenty percent in the last ten years*[133].

The number of arbitral institutions in existence has become almost countless. In China alone there are over 180 institutions entitled to administer both domestic and foreign-related arbitrations[134]. In Latvia alone, a much smaller country than China, there are over 200 institutions[135]. These newly established centres have not all attained the same level of success. Many new centres have, in fact, very limited caseloads and, as previously indicated, those that deal mostly in disputes involving foreign parties are rare[136].

If the rate of creation of new institutions seems to have accelerated, it would be naïve to conclude that institutional arbitration is a new phenomenon. According to Carabiber, if generalist arbitral institutions might have become more frequent in recent times, trade and professional institutions have been around for a long time. For present purposes, it suffices to mention the Chamber of Commerce of New York (founded in 1768), the Chicago Board of Trade, the Milwaukee Grain exchange, the American Seed Trade Association, the Liverpool Cotton Exchange, the London Stock Exchange, the London Corn Association, the Coffee Trade Association, the Baltic Mercantile and Shipping Association, the British Insurance Association, the British Motor Trade Association, all of which were founded in the nineteenth century. Carabiber also mentions, in France, the arbitral chambers organized under the auspices of chambers of commerce in such cities as Marseille, Bordeaux, Strasbourg or Lyon. According to

132. In the original language: *"La création d'un nombre croissant d'organismes, nationaux ou internationaux, qui fournissent des cadres permanents aux procédures d'arbitrage est un phénomène bien connu et maintes fois analyses"*. Goldman, "Les Conflits de Lois dans l'Arbitrage International de Droit Privé" 352.
133. Pendell, "The Rise and Rise of the Arbitration Institution".
134. A survey of the Chinese State Council's Legal Affairs Office numbered 185 such institutions. Survey reported in Michael J. Moser and Yu Jianlong, "CIETAC and its Work — An Interview with Vice Chairman Yu Jianlong" (2007) 24 Journal of International Arbitration, Kluwer Law International 555, 556.
135. Inga Kačevska, "Latvia" *The European, Middle Eastern and African Arbitration Review* (Global Arbitration Review 2014).
136. Jan Paulsson, "Moral Hazard in International Dispute Resolution, Inaugural Lecture as Holder of the Michael R. Klein Distinguished Scholar Chair University of Miami School of Law on 29 April 2010" (2011) 8 Transnational Dispute Management (TDM), 20.

him such institutions were, "*before World War II already resolving tens of thousands of disputes*" (Translation by the author)[137].

[C] The Rationale behind the Growth: The Perceived Benefits of Institutional Arbitration

The growth of institutional arbitration may be tentatively explained by the combination of: (1) the general increase in the use of arbitration as a dispute resolution mechanism[138], and (2) the benefits of institutional arbitration over ad hoc proceedings which should mean, naturally, that a proportion of the increase of arbitrations in general will benefit institutional arbitration.

It is difficult to discuss the advantages of institutional arbitration without giving a "laundry list" of the services offered by institutions. After all, on one view, institutional arbitration consists of outsourcing to an institution certain responsibilities that would otherwise fall onto the parties or the tribunal; responsibilities which, it is expected, the institution is better placed to provide. Rather than give an overview of the services offered to institutions[139] these sections below highlight why some of these services make institutional arbitration more attractive than its ad hoc counterpart.

[1] Logistical Support

A key benefit of institutional arbitration resides in the logistical support offered by arbitration centres[140]. This includes, for example, making arrangements for any hearing. In this respect institutions may, for instance, rent out or otherwise book hearing rooms; offer or book the services of court reporters and interpreters; make catering arrangements for the duration of the hearing; provide video-conferencing or other telecommunications facilities; and make arrangements regarding the accommodation of the tribunal. As pointed out by Redfern and Hunter: "[i]*f an arbitration is not*

137. In the original language: "[ces institutions] *réglaient déjà avant la guerre de 1939/1945 des dizaines de milliers de différends*". Charles Carabiber, "L'Evolution de l'Arbitrage Commercial International" (1960) 99 Collected Courses of the Hague Academy of International Law, Martinus Nijhoff Publishers & Brill Academic 128-133. See also, Frank D. Emerson, "History of Arbitration Practice and Law" (1970) 19 Cleveland State Law Review 156, 156.

138. The phenomenon of the increased use of arbitration in general (i.e., both ad hoc and institutional) is also well documented and often commented upon. The increase of arbitration in general can safely be attributed, at least in part, to the increase in cross-border transactions and the globalization of the economy. To cite only a few leading commentators: Bernard Hanotiau, "International Arbitration in a Global Economy: The Challenges of the Future" (2011) 28 Journal of International Arbitration, Kluwer Law International 89, 90; Smit, "Future of International Commercial Arbitration" 10; Jan Paulsson and Nigel Rawding (eds), *The Freshfields Guide to Arbitration Clauses in International Contracts* (3rd edn, Kluwer Law International 2010) 10; Yves Derains and Eric A. Schwartz, *A Guide to the New ICC Rules of Arbitration* (2nd edn, Kluwer Law International 2005) 3.

139. This is object of Chapter 3.

140. Smit, "Future of International Commercial Arbitration" 15; Sam Aaron, "International Arbitration III: Choosing an Arbitration Institution and a Set of Rules" (1991) 108 South African Law Journal 306, 306; Blackaby, Partasides, Hunter, and Redfern, *Redfern and Hunter on International Arbitration* 55; Schlaepfer and Petti, "Institutional versus Ad Hoc Arbitration" 16.

administered in this way, the work of administration will have to be undertaken by the arbitral tribunal itself—or by a registrar or tribunal secretary appointed by the tribunal for that purpose"[141]. The tribunal may not be well equipped or accustomed to dealing with these issues. In addition, it may be more cost effective to leave these matters with an institution. Whether the fees of the relevant institution are based on an hourly rate[142] or are *ad valorem*[143], these arrangements are likely to be less expensive if made by an institution than by the parties' outside counsel, who can be expected to charge for their time at a comparatively high rate. When making such arrangements, the institution may also benefit from preferential rates that are more advantageous than those available to the parties or their counsel[144].

[2] Pre-established Arbitration Rules

Another benefit resides in the set of arbitration rules offered by the institutions[145]. In ad hoc arbitration it falls on the parties, in the first place, to agree on the procedure to be followed in their arbitration. The parties might have done so by providing some details of the procedure in their arbitration agreement (be it an arbitration clause or a submission agreement), but if this is not the case, then the parties will need to agree on procedure once the arbitration has started. Naturally, in some cases the respondents might not participate in the proceedings at all or be obstructive, refusing to agree even on the most basic points. As explained by Redfern and Hunter:

> *The principal disadvantage of ad hoc arbitration is that it depends for its full effectiveness on cooperation between the parties and their lawyers, backed up by an adequate legal system in the place of arbitration. It is not difficult to delay arbitral proceedings—for instance, by refusing to appoint an arbitrator, so that at the very outset of the proceedings there will be no arbitral tribunal in existence, and no book of rules available to deal with the situation*[146].

Even where the respondent collaborates, the parties may face some genuine disagreements which will need to be resolved. If the tribunal is already in place, this means by way of a decision of the arbitral tribunal on application of a party. Prior to the constitution of the tribunal, it means, in ad hoc arbitration, seeking a decision from the

141. Blackaby, Partasides, Hunter, and Redfern, *Redfern and Hunter on International Arbitration* 56.
142. As in the case of the LCIA.
143. As in the case of the ICC.
144. On this second point, see Nassib G. Ziadé, "Reflections on the Role of Institutional Arbitration between the Present and the Future" (2009) 25 Arbitration International, Kluwer Law International 427, 428.
145. Blackaby, Partasides, Hunter, and Redfern, *Redfern and Hunter on International Arbitration* 55; Born, *International Commercial Arbitration* 150; Smit, "Future of International Commercial Arbitration" 15; Aaron, "International Arbitration III: Choosing an Arbitration Institution and a Set of Rules" Schlaepfer and Petti, "Institutional versus Ad Hoc Arbitration" 20.
146. Blackaby, Partasides, Hunter, and Redfern, *Redfern and Hunter on International Arbitration* 54.

domestic courts[147]. Having to resort to the arbitral tribunal or the domestic courts to decide every procedural disagreement is, obviously, time consuming and costly. The rules of arbitral institutions, insofar, as they cover basic procedural questions, offer a procedural "safety net" which helps save time and money.

As pointed out by professor Hans Smit, theoretically, at least: "[...] *virtually all of the advantages to be gained from institutional arbitration rules can be gained by making appropriate contractual provisions at the time of making the arbitration agreement*"[148]. It is however rare for an ad hoc arbitration agreement to provide as much detail as the rules of procedure offered by institutions. This is probably because doing so would often be both unpractical and disproportionately cumbersome and costly. But even for detailed ad hoc arbitration agreements, their wording may contain ambiguities, or worse, inconsistencies, unlikely to be found in institutional rules. This is so because institutional rules, at least for the older institutions, have been tried and tested over a long period of time. The ICC rules for instance was first enacted in the 1920s, and then amended over the past ninety years. Each revision sought to bring more clarity to the rules on the basis of the experience of the institution acquired in the management of thousands real life cases. For Redfern and Hunter:

> *Rules laid down by the established arbitral institutions (for instance, those of the ICC, the ICDR, ICSID, and the LCIA) will generally have proved to work well in practice; and they will have undergone periodic revision in consultation with experienced practitioners, to take account of new developments in the law and practice of international arbitration*[149].

[3] Authority in the Implementation of the Rules

Equally important is the authority that the institutions reserve to themselves in the application of their arbitration rules[150], which may prove invaluable in case of deadlocks in the phase preceding the constitution of the tribunal. For Michel Gaudet:

> [i]*nstitutional arbitration, especially when the mission of the centre goes as far as that of the ICC, permits to limit the intervention of domestic courts. Whereas, in case of deadlocks in an ad hoc arbitration, a party has no other recourse than going to the domestic courts, thereby adding a multi-layered public procedure to the existing*

147. Paulsson and Rawding, *The Freshfields Guide to Arbitration Clauses in International Contracts* 58.
148. Smit, "Future of International Commercial Arbitration" 15. This is, however, largely theoretical in light of the complexity of drafting workable ad hoc arbitration clauses. On this point see Paulsson and Rawding, *The Freshfields Guide to Arbitration Clauses in International Contracts* 58.
149. Blackaby, Partasides, Hunter, and Redfern, *Redfern and Hunter on International Arbitration* 55.
150. See above the discussion of this authority in the implementation of the arbitration rules as being a defining criteria of institutional arbitration. This "authority" is referred to as the "*management role*" of the institutions by William Slate. Slate, "International Arbitration: Do Institutions Make a Difference?" 55. It is, as discussed above, referred to as a "*reservation of competence*" by Professor P Lalive Lalive, "Problèmes Relatifs à l'Arbitrage International Commercial" 665.

arbitration, the supervision of the proceedings by an experienced arbitral institution may, in the parties' view, save time, legal costs and avoid the publicity that would otherwise be occasioned by additional judicial proceedings (Translation by the author)[151].

[4] Treatment of Costs

Another key advantage[152] of institutional arbitration concerns the role played by institutions in respect of fixing the arbitration costs[153]. This gives a measure of predictability to the parties, avoids any potentially awkward misunderstandings between the parties and the arbitrators[154], and reduces the risk of mistakes in respect of the calculation of these costs[155]. An incidental benefit for the arbitrators, is that, contrary to ad hoc arbitration, they are not required to handle the parties' deposits. This means that they do not have to concern themselves with such issues as the opening of different bank accounts or ledgers for each of their arbitrations, or liaising with the parties with respect to the payment of the advances on cost. In the words of Lew, Mistelis & Kröll, this permits them to "*maintain a certain level of material detachment*"[156].

---

151. In the original language: *"D"autre part, l'arbitrage institutionnel, surtout lorsque la mission et la responsabilité de l'institution d'arbitrage sont poussées aussi loin que dans l'arbitrage CCI, permet de réduire les interventions des juridictions étatiques. Tandis qu'en cas de difficulté ou même de doute dans le déroulement d'un arbitrage ad hoc une partie n'a d'autre recours que de saisir une juridiction étatique, ajoutant ainsi une procédure judiciaire publique à plusieurs étages à la procédure arbitrale en cours, l'information offerte et la surveillance exercée par une institution d'arbitrage expérimentée peuvent constituer aux yeux des parties des garanties suffisantes pour économiser le temps, la publicité et les frais d'une procédure judiciaire additionnelle"*. Gaudet, "La Coopération des Juridictions Etatiques à l'Arbitrage Institutionnel" 505-506.

    In the same sense see N. Ziade: *"Arbitration institutions have an inherent advantage over ad hoc arbitrations in that the institutions have built-in mechanisms that support the arbitral process and offer remedies for procedural deficiencies"* Ziadé, "Reflections on the Role of Institutional Arbitration Between the Present and the Future" 428. For example, institutional arbitration rules provide for mechanisms to ensure the constitution of the arbitral tribunal.
152. Aaron, "International Arbitration III: Choosing an Arbitration Institution and a Set of Rules" 306; Blackaby, Partasides, Hunter, and Redfern, *Redfern and Hunter on International Arbitration* 56; Born, *International Commercial Arbitration* 150; Lew, Mistelis, and Kröll, *Comparative International Commercial Arbitration* 37.
153. See Chapter 3 below for an overview of institutions' role in this respect.
154. For obvious reasons, parties often feel that it is difficult to query the quantum of their arbitrator's fees or expenses.
155. In particular when issues of cross-border VAT come into play. Another benefit, concerning arbitrations where the fees of the tribunal are calculated on the basis of an hourly rate, needs to be mentioned. Where the entire anticipated costs of the arbitration are not covered by advance payments at the beginning of the arbitration, there is a need to monitor regularly, at different stages in the proceedings, the amount of time spent by the tribunal to ensure that the deposits held are always sufficient to pay the arbitrators costs (to avoid work being undertaken by the arbitrators which the funds held will be insufficient to cover). In light of their great experience in the domain, this is a role that is more easily dealt with by the institutions.
156. Lew, Mistelis, and Kröll, *Comparative International Commercial Arbitration* 37.

[5] Enhanced Enforceability of the Award

There is, in some quarters, a perception that the use of a reputable institution may enhance the likelihood of enforcement of the award, should the losing party not comply with its terms voluntarily. For Lew, Mistelis & Kröll for instance:

> *A strongly perceived advantage of institutional arbitration is the cachet behind the name of the institution. Accordingly, especially in countries where there is political interference or where the courts and law are not always arbitration-friendly, parties consider it beneficial when seeking to enforce an award which was issued by, or which carries the name of, an internationally page respected institution*[157].

The rationale may be that, because arbitral institutions monitor the proceedings they administer (and in some instances scrutinize draft awards before they are issued[158]), there is a chance that most procedural defects will have been caught and corrected in time to avoid any difficulties with the enforcement of the award. It is also sometimes argued that the general reputation and standing of certain institutions will, of itself, positively influence the judges that will be called upon to look at the enforcement of the award. According to Aaron, "*the involvement of an institution may afford greater acceptability of the award and facilitate its ultimate enforcement*"[159]. For Gary Born: "[...] *an arbitral institution lends its standing to any award that is rendered, which may enhance the likelihood of voluntary compliance and judicial enforcement*"[160]. The author of this book however is not aware of any empirical study supporting the above assumptions.

[6] Lower Costs

It is often stated that the use of an institution may increase the overall costs of arbitration[161]. The rationale is that the parties to an institutional arbitration are required to pay the administrative fees of the institution – an expense which does not exist in ad hoc arbitration. There are, however, a number of convincing arguments that institutional arbitration often result of costs savings. A first one is that the procedural rules and the authority of the arbitral institution in implementation of these rules will permit to avoid unnecessary recourse to the domestic courts or the arbitral tribunal in cases of deadlocks, and therefore reduce the cost of legal representation[162]. A second

157. *Ibid.*
158. Article 33 ICC Rules (2012). The scrutiny of awards as a function has been discussed in Chapter §3.03[C][1] of this book.
159. Aaron, "International Arbitration III: Choosing an Arbitration Institution and a Set of Rules" 306.
160. Born, *International Commercial Arbitration* 150.
161. Born, *International Commercial Arbitration* 150; Harry L. Arkin, "International Ad Hoc Arbitration: A Practical Alternative" (1987) 15 International Business Lawyer 5-12; Aaron, "International Arbitration III: Choosing an Arbitration Institution and a Set of Rules" 306; Schlaepfer and Petti, "Institutional versus Ad Hoc Arbitration" 20.
162. See Paulsson and Rawding, *The Freshfields Guide to Arbitration Clauses in International Contracts* 59; Schlaepfer and Petti, "Institutional versus Ad Hoc Arbitration" 21.

argument is that the tasks normally performed by the institution (e.g., logistical support) will, in ad hoc arbitration, have to be handled by the parties' outside counsel or by the arbitrators themselves at a higher cost than that charged by the institutions. In this respect it is interesting to note that the administrative fees charged by institutions are often dwarfed by the legal fees of the parties' outside counsel. In a survey of cases that reached a final award in 2003 and 2004 the ICC found that the parties' legal and other costs constituted 82% of the total costs or the arbitration; the tribunal's fees and expenses represented 16%; and the ICC's administrative charges represented a mere 2%[163]. A further argument (which admittedly applies only in the circumstances where the fees of the tribunal are based on an hourly rate), is that certain arbitrators charge higher hourly rates in ad hoc arbitrations than in institutional arbitrations because certain institutions place a (relatively low) cap on hourly rates. This is the case of the LCIA, which Schedule of Arbitration Costs currently provides a maximum hourly rate of GBP 450 per hour[164]. Along the same lines, it has been argued that institutions are, to a certain extent, able to limit the number of hours charged by arbitrators in circumstances where they appear excessive[165]. In fact, the perception that institutions are well placed to exercise such a control was one of the reasons considered by Working Group for the revision of the UNCITRAL rules for extending the role of appointing authorities in respect of costs "[...] *as a precaution to guard against the rare situations where an arbitrator might seek excessive fees*"[166].

Much depends on how cooperative the parties turn out to be once the proceedings are commenced. When a respondent accepts to participate in good faith in the proceedings (which is more likely to be the case where it has a significant counterclaim) the risk of deadlocks is limited and the need to rely on the provisions of a set of institutional rules, or to have recourse to an institution for its decisions, is lower. When a respondent is uncooperative, the situation is different. As a result whether ad hoc or institutional arbitration would have been better for a particular case can only be known with the benefit of hindsight, and that's why, overall, experienced practitioners tend to be of the view that institutional arbitration is safer option than ad hoc arbitration at the drafting stage[167].

163. ICC, "Techniques for Controlling Time and Costs in Arbitration: Report from the ICC Commission on Arbitration", 2007.
164. See the LCIA's Schedule of Arbitration Costs, effective 1 October 2014 available on the "Website of the LCIA, http://www.lcia.org".
165. Christopher Kee, "The Evolving Role of an Appointing Authority" in Stefan Michael Kröll and Loukas A. Mistelis (eds), *International Arbitration and International Commercial Law: Synergy, Convergence and Evolution* (Kluwer Law International 2011) 312.
166. See the *travaux preparatoires* of the 2010 UNCITRAL rules: "Report of the Working Group on Arbitration and Conciliation on the work of its forty-eighth session (New York, 4-8 February 2008), UN Doc. A/CN.9/646" (2008) 20-21.
167. Lew, Mistelis, and Kröll, *Comparative International Commercial Arbitration* 35; see also Slate, "International Arbitration: Do Institutions Make a Difference?" 53; see also Paulsson and Rawding, *The Freshfields Guide to Arbitration Clauses in International Contracts* 57.

[7] *Confidentiality*

It is sometimes perceived that the use of an arbitral institution may negatively affect the confidentiality of the proceedings[168]. The rationale is that institutional arbitration requires the involvement in the proceedings, in addition to the parties and the tribunal, of a "third party" - the institution. Referring a matter to institutional arbitration will mean that the supervisory organs of the chosen institution (e.g., the ICC Court, the LCIA Court, the HKIAC Council, the SCC Board etc.) will necessarily have to become privy to certain basic information relating to the dispute. Less experienced users of the system may have concerns because these supervisory organs tend to comprise private practitioners whose law firms (or their clients) might have some interest in such confidential information. In circumstances, therefore, where the dispute requires an enhanced level of confidentiality, parties might arguably be better off referring a dispute to ad hoc arbitration. However, more often than not, confidentiality will be seen as an advantage of institutional arbitration[169].

The main reason is that ad hoc arbitration (if private) is not necessarily confidential[170]. Much depends on the legal framework applicable to the proceedings. If the parties have not agreed on confidentiality in their arbitration agreement, and if confidentiality is not otherwise required by the law of the seat, it is dubious that the parties and/or the arbitrators will be bound by any duty of confidentiality. While English courts will imply an obligation of confidentiality in any arbitration agreement[171], the same is not true for instance under French law, where the default position for "international" arbitration is that the proceedings are not confidential (unless otherwise agreed by the parties)[172]. The arbitration rules of many institutions, do contain some provisions on confidentiality. This is the case of the rules of HKIAC, the LCIA and the ICC rules to mention only

168. See Born, *International Commercial Arbitration* 150. See also Schlaepfer and Petti, "Institutional versus Ad Hoc Arbitration" 15, referring to the perception that ad hoc arbitration offers "*greater privacy*".
169. See Simon Crookenden, "Who Should Decide Arbitration Confidentiality Issues?" (2009) 25 Arbitration International, Kluwer Law International 603-613.
170. Privacy in respect of arbitration relates to the idea that the hearing of the dispute and the tribunals' deliberations are conducted behind closed doors, "in camera". Privacy of arbitration is recognized in many jurisdictions and is consecrated in various sets of arbitration rules. See for example, Article 25.4 of the 1976 UNCITRAL Rules, Article 28.3 of the UNCITRAL Rules of 2010, Article 21(3) of the 1998 ICC Rules, and the Article 19.4 of the LCIA Rules of 1998. But the concept of confidentiality, in the context of arbitration, goes beyond this and is often expected to mean that nothing from the proceedings may be made available to third parties, including *inter alia:* (1) the evidence and documents produced by the parties, (2) the arbitrators' awards, but also (3) the very existence of the arbitration. On the difference between the two concepts see, for example, Simon Crookenden, "Who Should Decide Arbitration Confidentiality Issues?" (2009) 25(4) Arbitration International, Kluwer Law International 603-613, at 603. On the other hand, on the idea that confidentiality is a necessary corollary to privacy see: Gary B. Born, *International Commercial Arbitration* (Kluwer Law International 2009) 2280, and also M. Young and S. Chapman (n 2) pp. 26-47.
171. *Ali Shipping Corporation v Shipyard Trogir* [1999] 1 WLR 314 (CA). For a historical development of the principle of confidentiality in English case law see, M. Young and S. Chapman (n 2) pp. 26-47.
172. Henri-Jacques Nougein et Romain Dupeyré, Règles et Pratiques du Droit Français de l'Arbitrage, (Gazette du Palais, 2012), pp. 214-216.

a few[173]. While these provisions vary greatly form one institution to the next they offer a basic level of protection which may very well otherwise be absent in purely ad hoc arbitration proceedings[174].

To conclude, there seems to be a marked preference, amongst practitioners and users, for institutional arbitration compared to ad hoc arbitration. For Born: "[...] *most experienced international practitioners fairly decisively prefer the more structured, predictable character of institutional arbitration, and the benefits of institutional rules and appointment mechanisms, at least in the absence of unusual circumstances arguing for an ad hoc approach*"[175]. This preference for institutional arbitration is confirmed by strong empirical evidence. Several successive surveys conducted by Queen Mary, University of London in 2006, 2008 and 2013 show that corporations prefer using institutional arbitration[176]. However, while institutional arbitration has the preference of a majority of practitioners and users, it should be noted that its popularity nonetheless varies from region to region and from industry to industry[177]. It appears that "legal culture" (being region-specific or industry-specific) plays a role in this respect. For example, cultural traditions in Mainland China favour institutional arbitration over ad hoc processes. This preference, which may have been inherited from the Soviet model of trade chambers arbitration[178], is reflected in the statutory prohibition of ad hoc arbitration for China-seated arbitrations[179]. In the shipping

173. For example, Article 42 of the HKIAC rules (2013), Article 22(3) of the ICC Rules (2012), or Article 30 LCIA Rules (2014).
174. It should be noted that the IBA Rules on Taking Evidence (2010) also deal with confidentiality. Article 2(d) specifically requests tribunals to consult the parties on the issue of confidentiality. Article 3(8) makes a provision for confidential documents to be reviewed for sensitivity by the tribunal. Rule 3(13) is even more express in its statement that "*any Document submitted or produced by a Party or non-Party in the arbitration and not otherwise in the public domain shall be kept confidential by the Arbitral Tribunal and the other Parties, and shall be used only in connection with the arbitration*".
175. Born, *International Commercial Arbitration* 151.
176. See Queen Mary, University of London, "Corporate Attitudes and Practices: Recognition and Enforcement of Foreign Awards" (2008); Queen Mary, University of London, "Corporate Attitudes and Practices" (2006); Queen Mary, University of London, "Corporate Choices in International Arbitration: An Industry Approach" (2013).
This is consistent with the Queen Mary survey of 2008 in which 86% of awards rendered were institutional, 14% were ad hoc. See Queen Mary, University of London, "Corporate Attitudes and Practices: Recognition and Enforcement of Foreign Awards".
This is also consistent with the 2006 survey where 76% of participants reported that they opted for institutional arbitration in their clauses. See Queen Mary, University of London, "Corporate Attitudes and Practices".
177. On the idea that different industries have different approaches to arbitration in general, see Toby Landau: "*Rent review arbitration is different from insurance arbitration, which has different needs to construction, commodity or maritime arbitration; so the list continues*". Landau, "The Effect of the New English Arbitration Act on Institutional Arbitration" 117. For empirical evidence of the same, see Queen Mary, University of London, "Corporate Choices in International Arbitration: An Industry Approach".
178. Discussed above in the context of the definition of the notation of institutional arbitration.
179. Article 16 of the Arbitration Law of the PRC requires all arbitrations with a Chinese seat to be administered. Fan Kun, "Prospects of Foreign Arbitration Institutions Administering Arbitration in China" (2011) 28 Journal of International Arbitration, Kluwer Law International 343-353. See also Paul Friedland and Bing Yan, "Negotiating and Drafting Arbitration Agreements with Chinese Parties: Special Considerations of Chinese Law and Practice" (2011)

industry, it is often said that the preference of users is for ad hoc arbitration[180]. On this topic, a past President of the LMAA writes:

> [...] *the fact that London maritime arbitrations are not administered may be one of the reasons why London is found to be attractive. Certainly, the IMAO, an organisation set up some years ago between the ICC and the CMI to provide an international court of maritime arbitration, has been a singular failure. It is plain that shipping parties do not want administered arbitration*[181].

[D] Popularity of Institutional Arbitration versus Legitimacy of Arbitral Institutions

If institutional arbitration enjoys a degree of popularity, it would be naïve to assume that this popularity necessarily extends to arbitral institutions. The statement that institutional arbitration is generally preferred to ad hoc arbitration does not entail that arbitral institutions are perceived as legitimate. In fact, there appears to be, in some quarters, a "mistrust" of arbitral institutions. A number of authors have commented on this phenomenon, but few have expressed this more eloquently than Paulsson[182]:

> *It is difficult to establish, nurture, and maintain permanent organizations able to supervise the arbitral process in a manner perceived to be legitimate.* [...]
>
> *Only a few arbitral institutions can make credible claims to legitimacy. The naïve boasting of a constant stream of new entrants fools no one acquainted with the field. It is easy for resourceful persons to come up with a lustrous governing board comprised of apparently eminent individuals happy to lend their names to what might be a useful venture (and will cost them little if it fails).*
>
> [...]
>
> *My observations of the world of arbitration lead me to believe that many if not most arbitral institutions are empty edifices waiting for someone to bother to dismantle them. Others cannot get away from features of cronyism, which were their raison d'être in the first place. We would hardly entrust the preparation of a penal code to Ali Baba and the 40 thieves*[183].

---

28 Journal of International Arbitration, Kluwer Law International 467, 473-474. See also Chang, "CIETAC's Perspective on Arbitration and Conciliation Concerning China" 34.

180. There may be reasons pertaining to the nature of the disputes in that particular industry or to characteristics of the maritime arbitration bar, which may render the practical benefits of institutional arbitration less salient than in other fields, but this is unfortunately beyond the scope of this book.

181. Harris, "London Maritime Arbitration" 122.

182. A commentator, who, as a former President of LCIA Court, can hardly be classified as an opponent of institutional arbitration. Expressing the idea that lack of transparency may be the cause of the lack of confidence, see Blanch, "Appointment and Confirmation of Arbitrators" 72.

183. Paulsson, "Moral Hazard in International Dispute Resolution, Inaugural Lecture as Holder of the Michael R. Klein Distinguished Scholar Chair University of Miami School of Law on 29 April 2010" 19-20. An example of an "empty edifice" (albeit in the particular context of State-to-State disputes) may be found in the Court for Conciliation and Arbitration of the OSCE, which has, in the two decades since its creation, not administered a single matter. See Aileen Truttmann and Georg von Segesser, "Swiss and Swiss-Based Arbitral Institutions" in

A number of reasons may be advanced to explain this sentiment. According to Professor Fouchard, it may be because arbitral institutions are perceived as weakening the personal relationship (*intuitus personae*) existing between the arbitrator and the parties, while, at the same time, *"failing to offer the guarantees associated with a public and professional justice system"*[184]. According to Professor Fouchard, this alleged mistrust is reflected by the adoption, in 1980, of the then new Article 1451 of the French code of civil procedure, which prevented arbitral institutions from "deciding disputes" themselves (i.e., requiring arbitrators to be individuals rather than legal entities)[185].

Another reason may lie in the perception prevailing within the Western ADR tradition (as opposed to the tradition of former socialist countries), that arbitration is a mechanism which was painstakingly carved out of the jurisdiction of State courts by its users because they were dissatisfied with the overly bureaucratic nature of State litigation. Under this "libertarian" perspective, anything that resembles an attempt to provide more permanence to arbitration is looked at with apprehension.

As a result, it is conventionally assumed that the users of arbitration themselves (i.e., the parties) prefer less interventionist institutions (i.e., to say, institutions which role in the institutional arbitration process remains more limited). When the BCICAC was set up in Western Canada, a conscious choice was made to limit the role of the institution in the proceedings because of that very perception. One author explains in this respect:

> *We opted for "administered" not "supervised" arbitrations. Our Centre would provide assistance to the parties and arbitrators whenever, and to the extent, they wished.* [...] *Administered arbitrations appeared to be the best approach given the*

Nathalie Voser and Elliott Geisinger (eds), *International Arbitration in Switzerland – A Handbook for Practitioners* (Kluwer Law International 2013) 304.

184. In the original language: *"Plus généralement, d'autres réserves ont été émises à l'égard de l'arbitrage organisé: copiant l'institution judiciaire, il ne donne pas pour autant les garanties de la justice publique et de la magistrature professionnelle. Mais il fait cependant disparaître, ou du moins affaiblit, le rapport personnel de confiance qui doit exister entre l'arbitre et les parties, et qui est la meilleure justification de cette justice privée"*. Fouchard (n 36) 227. In the same sense see, Clay, *L'arbitre* para. 695.

185. Fouchard writes: "[...] *article 1451 represents a prohibition imposed on arbitration centres from acting as arbitrators, and a limitation of their powers. This proceeds from a certain mistrust vis-a-vis institutional arbitration, which may also transpires in article 1455 of the same code, and which was perceived as such by the institutions"* (Translation by the author). In the original language: *"En second lieu, l'article 1451 se présente plutôt comme une interdiction faite aux centres d'arbitrage permanents d'être eux-mêmes arbitres, et une limitation de leurs pouvoirs. Il procède d'une certaine méfiance à l'égard de l'arbitrage institutionnel, que l'on retrouve dans l'article 1455 du même Code, et qui a été perçue comme telle par les principaux intéressés"*. Fouchard (n 36) 242-243.

See also Fouchard Gaillard and Goldman, *"The French New Code of Civil Procedure (Art. 1455) therefore sought to limit the role of arbitral institutions in French domestic law, by prohibiting the appointment of an entity or organisation as an arbitrator and by favoring the direct appointment of arbitrators by the parties, even in institutional arbitration"*. Gaillard and Savage (n 21) 32.

> *criticisms we heard from lawyers and businessmen of the cost and delay associated with some systems of supervised arbitrations*[186].

It is, in fact, not uncommon for institutions to advertise their alleged "hands-off" approach to case-administration, on the assumption that this is what their users prefer. This is the case for instance of the HKIAC which, on the occasion of the publication of its latest rules issued a press release emphatically reassuring its users that:

> [t]*he 2013 HKIAC Rules maintain HKIAC's signature "light touch" approach, seeking to facilitate effective institutional involvement within a framework that recognizes the importance of party autonomy*[187].

Conversely, heavy institutional involvement in the proceedings is often described as a negative. In respect of ICAC, for example, one author complains:

> [t]*he involvement of the ICAC goes clearly beyond what is needed to preserve quality standards and to ensure the uninterrupted continuation of arbitration proceedings. It limits party autonomy by imposing on the parties rules for the formation of the Arbitral Tribunal which they can hardly expect or foresee when entering into the ICAC's standard arbitration clause*[188].

---

186. Thompson, "Building an Arbitration and Mediation Centre: From International Foundations to Domestic Rooftops': The Establishment of the British Columbia International Commercial Arbitration Centre" 202-203.
187. Hong Kong International Arbitration Centre, "The 2013 HKIAC Administered Arbitration Rules Unveiled (Press Release)" (12 June 2013). In the same sense, see also Chiann Bao, "Hong Kong International Arbitration Centre" in J. William Rowley (ed), *Arbitration World: Jurisdictional Comparisons* (4th Revised edn, Thomson Reuters 2012), The European Lawyer Reference 58: *"The Rules minimise interference by the Centre, and maximise party autonomy, thereby letting parties focus on essential issues while the Secretariat assists with technical details"*.

    In a similar vein, the Secretary General of the SCC, Annette Magnusson, once described SCC's case management philosophy in the following terms: "[a]*fter the referral, the SCC Institute does not take part in the particulars of the planning and conduct of the proceedings, unless specifically provided for by the SCC Rules or upon request from the tribunal. This model of institutional arbitration differs to some extent from the practice of other international institutions, and has been chosen by the SCC Institute to serve the efficiency of the procedure*". Magnusson, "The Practice of the Arbitration Institute of the Stockholm Chamber of Commerce – An Inside View" 53.

    For the LCIA: " [...] *the LCIA applies a relatively light touch to its casework administration* [...] *it endeavours to intervene only as and when necessary, which will depend to some extent upon the relative sophistication and experience of the parties, their lawyers and the tribunal*". Winstanley, "Review of the London Court of International Arbitration" 3. In respect of the Swiss institution: *"Even though the 2012 revision of the Swiss Rules has strengthened the role of the Swiss Chambers' Arbitration Institution by vesting the Court with additional powers, the 2012 Swiss Rules still provide for a leaner administration of the arbitral proceedings than other institutional arbitration rules, giving the parties and the arbitral tribunal the necessary flexibility to tailor the arbitral proceedings to their needs"*. von Segesser, Jolles, and Stark-Traber, "Swiss Rules of International Arbitration" 195. For another author pointing out that the Swiss rules are less interventionist than that of the ICC see Zuberbühler, Muller, and Habegger, "Introduction to the Swiss Rules" 8.
188. Susan Heger, "The International Commercial Arbitration Court at the Chamber of Commerce and Industry of the Russian Federation: A Short Overview and the New Arbitration Rules" (2008) 2008 Austrian Arbitration Yearbook 283, 297-298.

But are concerns of institutions' legitimacy really legitimate? On one view, there cannot be more of a legitimacy problem with arbitral institutions than with arbitrators. Parties may select their institution, in their arbitration agreement, just like they may select their arbitrators. In fact, one might argue that because institutions are jointly selected by the parties (usually at the contract-drafting stage) they are arguably more legitimate than co-arbitrators nominated unilaterally by one party only[189]. Of course, one difference is that the parties may specifically designate an individual as arbitrator whereas they cannot vet or choose the case-handler or members of the institution's Court or Board that will make decisions on their case. This being said, when it is not the parties that nominate the arbitrators (and this is done by the institution itself acting as appointing authority), then it appears difficult to claim that the institution is less legitimate than the tribunal it has itself appointed. Indeed in a case like this one, the selection of the institution is made by the parties directly, whereas the choice of the arbitrators is indirect only, being made by the institution.

In this context it is interesting to note that empirical evidence suggests that users (i.e., companies resorting to arbitration to resolve their disputes rather than their outside counsel) prefer a hands-on approach to case administration by institutions. The most recent international arbitration survey conducted by Queen Mary University, which focused on the views of in-house counsel exclusively, found that only 4.55% of in-house counsel preferred the so-called *hands-off* approach, while a staggering 70.45% preferred a "*hands-on*" (25% of the respondents stating that they had "no opinion")[190].

If the actual users of arbitration do not seem to share arbitration lawyers' mistrust of institutions, it may be because arbitral institutions fill a "formality gap" by offering a sense of predictability and stability that may otherwise seem lacking in arbitration.

Interestingly, this is a perspective often taken in the field of public international law. In this discipline, institutionalization is less frequently depicted as a negative phenomenon. It is often seen as a positive expression of the increasing sophistication of the international legal order[191].

---

189. Because in that second case only one party (as opposed to all parties to the dispute) has assented to the choice of co-arbitrator.
190. Unpublished statistics collated for the purposes of the 2013 arbitration survey of Queen Mary which gave rise to the publication of the report: Queen Mary, University of London, "Corporate Choices in International Arbitration: An Industry Approach" (2013) referred to previously. It may be the case that outside counsel and arbitrators prefer a lesser degree of institutional involvement but that actual users, i.e., corporations, prefer the opposite.
191. Andrea Schneider, "Not Quite a World Without Trials: Why International Dispute Resolution Is Increasingly Judicialized" (2006) 2006 Journal of Dispute Resolution 119-129.
The idea that institutional arbitration offers a reassuring halfway house between ad hoc proceedings and court litigation is reflected implicitly in Article 1(4)) of the Swiss rules. According to von Segesser et al., this rule, which provides in essence that "[*b*]*y submitting a dispute to arbitration under the 2012 Swiss rules, the parties confer on the Court* [...] *all powers necessary for supervising the arbitral proceedings otherwise vested in the competent judicial authority*", aims at "*ensuring the smooth running of arbitrations by providing for a fall back competence of the Court for any procedural issue that may arise in the course of an arbitration*". Georg von Segesser, Alexander Jolles, and Sonja Stark-Traber, "Swiss rules of International Arbitration" in Karyl Nairn and Patrick Heneghan (eds), *Arbitration World: Institutional & Jurisdictional Comparisons* (4th Revised edn, Thomson Reuters 2012), The European Lawyer

§2.02 INSTITUTIONALIZATION OF ARBITRATION? THE ALLEGED QUALITATIVE GROWTH

One may wonder whether the expansion of institutional arbitration does not also take a "qualitative" form. The idea here is not that institutional arbitration is becoming more frequent ("quantitative" growth), but rather that the process of arbitration has become more "institutionalized" ("qualitative" growth).

[A] Institutionalization of Arbitration

It is indeed sometimes suggested that there has been an "institutionalization" of arbitration[192]. What the idea seems to cover is an increasing sophistication of institutional rules[193] coupled with an increased intervention of the institution in the arbitral process[194]. The idea of institutionalization of arbitration is therefore distinct from that of alleged "judicialization" of arbitration which is discussed briefly elsewhere below[195].

There does seem to be factual evidence of this "institutionalization" of arbitration. The rules of arbitration of a number of institutions, for instance, seem to become incrementally longer and more sophisticated with every successive revision. The number of articles of the ICC arbitration rules has increased overtime as follows: Twenty-six articles in 1975, twenty-six again in 1988, thirty-five in 1998, and forty-one in 2012. The rules are also now accompanied by appendices relating to the statutes and the internal rules of the Court, the schedule of costs, the case management techniques, and the emergency arbitrator which have also inflated over time. The LCIA rules counted twenty articles in 1985 and thirty-two in 1998 and thirty-two again in 2014. The AAA seems to be an exception were the number of articles was thirty-seven articles in 1992 (AAA's international rules), thirty-seven in 2009, and thirty-nine in 2014.

Reference 182. In the same sense see, Habegger (n 187) 274.

192. Gaillard and Savage, *Fouchard, Gaillard, Goldman on International Commercial Arbitration* 32; Hanotiau, "International Arbitration in a Global Economy: The Challenges of the Future" 99-100 Ali Yesilirmak, *Provisional Measures in International Commercial Arbitration* (Kluwer Law International 2005) 16; Iván Szász, "The Value of a Network of Arbitration Institutions" in Pieter Sanders (ed), *New Trends in the Development of International Commercial Arbitration and the Role of Arbitral and Other Institutions* vol. 1 (Kluwer Law International 1982) 26, 26.

193. V.V. Veeder, "Strategic Management in Commencing an Arbitration" (2011) 15 in Albert Jan van den Berg (ed), *Arbitration Advocacy in Changing Times* (Kluwer Law International) 2010 27-34.

194. According to Horacio Grigera Naon, then Secretary General of the Court of the ICC, there are "[...] *trends favouring the adoption of a more pro-active attitude towards the administration of arbitration cases*". Horacio Grigera Naon, "The Powers of the ICC International Court of Arbitration vis-a-vis Parties and Arbitrators" *Arbitration in the Next Decade – ICC Bulletin Special Supplement* (International Chamber of Commerce 1999) 71.

195. As discussed below, the notion of "judicialization" is broader than that of "institutionalization" in the sense that it is not limited to the role of arbitral institutions, but rather relates to the rising formalism of arbitration and its increasing resemblance with litigation.

At the same time, if newly added provisions often contemplate additional responsibilities for the institutions[196], revisions rarely, if ever, seem to result in a reduction of institutions' scope of action. For example, the 1999 revision of the SCC rules transferred from the arbitral tribunal to the SCC itself the responsibility to determine the costs of the arbitration. The previous edition of the rules (1988) provided for the arbitral tribunal to fix these costs[197]. Similarly, the 2012 revision of the CIETAC rules enhanced the responsibilities of the institution by empowering it, *inter alia*, to consolidate proceedings. The 2015 revision of the CIETAC rules still provides for this responsibility under Article 19. For Lu Song, "[t]*he 2012 rules* [...] *demonstrate that the power of CIETAC has increased* [...]"[198]. Likewise, the addition, at Article 42(1) of the 2005 ICAC rules, of a provision on the scrutiny of awards, confers additional responsibilities to that institution[199]. On the other hand, an example of a rule revision which took away from, rather than added to, the powers of an institution, is the adoption of the 4th edition of the SIAC rules in 2010, which transferred the power to decide on the seat of the arbitration from the Registrar to the Tribunal[200].

Some authors[201] see in the increasing complexity of the commencement of arbitration proceedings, an illustration of this phenomenon of institutionalization. Johnny Veeder QC for instance writes:

> *Historically, it used to be so easy, cheap and quick. One ship broker would walk across the floor of the Baltic Exchange in the City of London, with a short telex in his hand (still warm), touch a colleague on his shoulder, and say "we've got a dispute, the owner wants to send his claim to arbitration, so bring your charterer's file and meet you in the pub after work tonight". That was how, traditionally many maritime and commodity arbitrations were commenced in England between*

196. For example, the 2012 Swiss rules grant "*broader institutional powers*" to the newly created "Arbitration Court". Philipp A. Habegger, "The Revised Swiss Rules of International Arbitration: An Overview of the Major Changes" (2012) 30 ASA Bulletin, Kluwer Law International 269, 272 and 307. In the same sense see also, See Von Segesser, Jolles, and Stark-Traber, "Swiss rules of International Arbitration" 181.
197. See Sigvard Jarvin and Briana Young, "A New Arbitration Regime in Sweden – The Swedish Arbitration Act 1999 and the Rules of the Stockholm Chamber of Commerce" (1999) 16 Journal of International Arbitration, Kluwer Law International 89, 103.
198. Lu Song, "The New CIETAC Arbitration Rules of 2012" (2012) 29 Journal of International Arbitration, Kluwer Law International 299, 321.
199. Komarov, "Introduction to the Revision of the Rules of the International Commercial Arbitration Court at the Chamber of Commerce and Industry of the Russian Federation (ICAC)" 460.
200. Gordon Smith, "Commentary on the New Singapore International Arbitration Centre Rules" (2010) 76 Arbitration 727, 738. Rule 18.1 of the SIAC Rules (2013) also continues with the same, the tribunal being given the power to determine seat.
    Another example is the 2005 revision of the rules of the ICAC (Russia). Under the previous rules (the 1994 rules) not only the arbitral tribunal but also the President of the ICAC had the power to order interim relief. This provision has been deleted in the 2005 rules so that this prerogative is now solely that of the tribunal. See Khodykin, "International Commercial Arbitration Court (ICAC) and Maritime Arbitration Commission (MAC) at the Russian Federation Chamber of Commerce and Industry" 9.
201. Veeder, "Strategic Management in Commencing an Arbitration". Hanotiau, "International Arbitration in a Global Economy: The Challenges of the Future" 100.

arbitrator-advocates, until we invented arbitral institutions, three-arbitrator tribunals and slow-track arbitration[202].

What is at the source of this institutionalization of arbitration? Some authors suggest that the globalization of the economy and the increased complexity of disputes that has accompanied it is the main cause[203]. It is true that the growth of multiparty arbitrations, for example, has forced institutions to revise their rules to provide for joinder and consolidation. According to others, it is because arbitration rules are drafted, and revised, by institutions with a view to accommodate the worst scenarios possible, therefore imposing, as a general rule and across the board, overly burdensome procedural requirements. One example of a provision enacted in reaction to a specific "difficulty" is the addition, at Articles 1(2) and 6(2) of the 2012 ICC rules, of provisions stating that the ICC is the only body authorized to administer ICC rules arbitrations. These provisions were adopted as a result of the infamous *Insigma* case in which the Singapore courts held as valid an arbitration clause providing for the administration by one institution of proceedings conducted under the rules of another, which led to an arbitration being administered by SIAC but under the 1998 ICC rules[204].

The institutionalization of arbitration is mostly depicted as a negative development. As previously indicated, some authors[205] suggest that the increased role conferred to institutions, be it normative (with the expansion of institutional rules), or decisional (with the enhanced role in the implementation of institutional rules), raises concerns as to their legitimacy. Another concern with institutionalization is flexibility. At first glance it seems evident that the more regulated arbitration procedure is, and the less room for flexibility there remains. On closer look, however, the inflation of arbitration rules does not, of itself, necessarily entail less flexibility. This is first because most provisions of most institutions' arbitration rules are capable of being displaced or waived by agreement of the parties. There are few provisions that institutions consider as "mandatory", so that parties are still at liberty to tailor their proceedings no matter how detailed the institutional rules they have chosen are. Parties to an LCIA arbitration, for example, are free to modify such things as the default timetable for the written

202. Veeder, "Strategic Management in Commencing an Arbitration" 28. One may wonder, however, whether the view that little formality should be needed to start arbitration proceedings reflects a British conception of arbitration, where the Request for Arbitration is not normally seen as a key pleading, and therefore does not need to be very detailed. This appears to be in contrast with the position in continental Europe where the Request is expected to contain a detailed presentation of the Claimant's case.

203. Hanotiau, "International Arbitration in a Global Economy: The Challenges of the Future" See also Gunther Horvath, "Part I: International Commercial Arbitration, Chapter 13: The Judicialization of International Arbitration: Does the Increasing Introduction of Litigation-Style Practices, Regulations, Norms and Structures into International Arbitration Risk a Denial of Justice in International Business Disputes?" in Stefan Michael Kröll and Loukas A. Mistelis (eds), *International Arbitration and International Commercial Law: Synergy, Convergence and Evolution* (Kluwer Law International 2011) 259.

204. Veeder, "Strategic Management in Commencing an Arbitration". "Insigma Technology Co Ltd v Alstom Technology Ltd, Singapore Court of Appeal, 2 June 2009 (Singapore Law Report, 2009, 3, at p. 24)", Singapore Court of Appeal [2009] 3 SLR(R); Kirby, "Insigma Technology Co. Ltd v. Alstom Technology Ltd SIAC Can Administer Cases under the ICC Rules?".

205. Gelinas, "Investment Tribunals and the Commercial Arbitration Model" 585.

phase of the proceedings, or to agree a bespoke mechanism for the selection of the arbitrators. On the other hand, the LCIA will not accept that the parties waive by agreement the provisions under which the LCIA confirms the constitution of the tribunal, or the provisions under which the LCIA Court is habilitated to fix the arbitration costs. The ICC, likewise, will accept bespoke nomination mechanisms, but will not accept that the parties displace the Court's confirmation of the constitution of the Tribunal, or its authority to fix arbitrator's fees or to scrutinize awards[206].

Likewise, when procedural matters are taken out of the hands of the parties for decision by the institution[207] or by the arbitrators, it does not *ipso facto* reduce "flexibility". Arbitral tribunals and institutions are as much able as the parties to tailor proceedings to the particular circumstances of the case. What is affected, at most, is "party autonomy". The power to make a decision as to what is best for the case is taken away from the parties. That is, in our view, the most tangible objection to institutionalization[208].

If the institutionalization of arbitration might arguably bring about concerns vis-à-vis party autonomy, one may nonetheless wonder whether it does not also have a more positive side. On one view, the phenomenon of institutionalization assists in filling a "formality gap" by offering a sense of predictability and stability that may otherwise seem lacking in arbitration. In this context, increased institutionalization may assist in rendering the arbitral process more acceptable to national legislators in those jurisdictions that are naturally hostile to it[209].

206. Derains and Schwartz, *A Guide to the New ICC Rules of Arbitration* 7-8. See also Bühler and Webster, *Handbook of ICC arbitration* 23. See also Michael Bühler and Sigvard Jarvin, "The Arbitration Rules of the International Chamber of Commerce (ICC)" in Frank-Bernd Weigand (ed), *Practitioner's Handbook on International Commercial Arbitration* (Oxford University Press 2009) 1152. The same may also be said the Swiss Arbitration Institution in relation to its power to confirm the appointment of arbitrators nominated by the parties. See Tobias Zuberbühler, Klaus Muller, and Philipp A. Habegger, "Introduction to the Swiss Rules" in Tobias Zuberbühler and Klaus Muller (eds), *Swiss Rules of International Arbitration: Commentary* (Kluwer Law International 2005) 10.

On this point it is interesting to note that the some institutions do, from time to time, assist parties at the contract drafting stage, in the creation of bespoke dispute resolution mechanisms tailored to the parties' particular needs. This is the case, for example, of the dispute resolution system designed for large scale infrastructure projects such as the Channel Tunnel Rail Link, or the Hong Kong Airport Core Programme. See Anthony Connerty, *"The Role of ADR in the Resolution of International Disputes"*, (1996) 12(1) Arbitration International, 51-53. Bespoke mechanisms of that sort arguably offer ultimate flexibility to the parties. So, in a sense, arbitral institutions can be seen as a factor of flexibility rather than a hindrance to it.

207. For example, selection of the Chairperson in all LCIA India Arbitrations.

208. This being said, the expansion and sophistication of arbitration rules on its own (i.e., not accompanied by an increasing role of the institution) does not affect party autonomy. To the contrary, the choice, made by the parties, to arbitrate under the rules of a particular institution, with its "expanded" rules, is an expression of party autonomy.

209. Fouchard, "Les Institutions Permanentes d'Arbitrage Devant le Juge Etatique (A Propos d'une Jurisprudence Récente)" 226; Born, *International Commercial Arbitration* 57.

The idea that institutional arbitration offers a reassuring halfway house between ad hoc proceedings and court litigation is reflected implicitly in Article 1(4)) of the Swiss rules. According to von Segesser et al., this rule, which provides in essence that "*[b]y submitting a dispute to arbitration under the 2012 Swiss rules, the parties confer on the Court[...] all powers necessary for supervising the arbitral proceedings otherwise vested in the competent judicial*

[B] Institutionalization versus Judicialization

The "institutionalization" of arbitration does not necessarily participate to the alleged phenomenon of "judicialization". As indicated above, the two notions are distinct.

Many practitioners and scholars have commented over the years on the alleged "judicialization" of arbitration[210]. For example, Redfern and Hunter (stressing that the defining features of arbitration have not changed) complain that "[...] *the modern arbitral process has lost its early simplicity. It has become more complex, more legalistic, more institutionalised, more expensive*"[211]. Recent empirical evidence confirms that the same perception exists amongst in-house counsel[212]. At the centre of the notion seems to lay the idea that arbitration resembles litigation more and more[213]. This implies that arbitration has become "procedurally" more complex; that the procedure agreed by

authority", aims at "*ensuring the smooth running of arbitrations by providing for a fall back competence of the Court for any procedural issue that may arise in the course of an arbitration*". Georg von Segesser, Alexander Jolles, and Sonja Stark-Traber, "Swiss rules of International Arbitration" in Karyl Nairn and Patrick Heneghan (eds), *Arbitration World: Institutional & Jurisdictional Comparisons* (4th Revised edn, Thomson Reuters 2012), The European Lawyer Reference 182. In the same sense see, Habegger, "The Revised Swiss Rules of International Arbitration: An Overview of the Major Changes" 274.

One may also wonder if the formality gap that the institutionalization of arbitration fills does not also help make more palatable the autonomous or denationalized theoretical representations of international arbitration -representations which have so far failed to convince on a global scale. For a discussion of these representations see Ashique Rahman, "An Insight into the Application of Arbitral Theory: Arising Judicial Practice" (2011) 7 Asian International Arbitration Journal, Kluwer Law International 97-117.

210. Hanotiau, "International Arbitration in a Global Economy: The Challenges of the Future" 99; Yves Derains, "Synthesis (of the 1993 ICCA Congress in Bahrain)" in Albert Jan van den Berg (ed), *International Arbitration in a Changing World* vol. 6 (Kluwer Law International 1993) 239, 240; Delissa A. Ridgway, "International Arbitration: The Next Growth Industry" (1999) 54 Dispute Resolution Journal 50, 51; Jan Paulsson, "Introduction (to the first volume of Arb. Int.)" (1985) 1 Arbitration International, Kluwer Law International 2, 86; Fali S. Nariman, "The Spirit of Arbitration – The Tenth Annual Goff Lecture" (2000) 16 Arbitration International, Kluwer Law International 261, 262.

211. Blackaby, Partasides, Hunter, and Redfern, *Redfern and Hunter on International Arbitration* 29.

212. The interviews of numerous in-house counsel for Queen Mary University's 2013 International Arbitration Survey confirm that numerous in-house lawyers perceive that arbitration has become more formal: "*Some corporations have expressed concerns over the 'judicialization' of arbitration, citing the increased formality of proceedings and their similarity with litigation proceedings, along with the associated costs and delays involved in these proceedings. This trend is potentially damaging to the overall attractiveness of arbitration as a means of dispute resolution*". Queen Mary, University of London, "Corporate Choices in International Arbitration: An Industry Approach".

213. For Fali Nariman, "[international commercial arbitration] *has become indistinguishable from litigation, which it was at one time intended to supplant*". Nariman, "The Spirit of Arbitration – The Tenth Annual Goff Lecture" 262.

See also Jean-Claude Najar, "Inside Out: A User's Perspective on Challenges in International Arbitration" (2009) 25 Arbitration International, Kluwer Law International 515, 526; Edward R. Leahy and Carlos J. Bianchi, "The Changing Face of International Arbitration" (2000) 17 Journal of International Arbitration, Kluwer Law International 19, 51.

parties and applied by arbitral tribunals is, across the board[214], increasingly based on strict rules or at least on clearly identifiable "best practice"[215].

Different reasons have been advanced for this alleged phenomenon. One is that the parties and their counsel have become more combative in respect of procedural matters in recent years[216]. One illustration of this would be the alleged increase in the number of challenges to arbitrators[217]. Another explanation is that the disputes that are referred to arbitration nowadays are more complex; the increased complexity coming from the number of parties and the increased sophistication of contractual arrangements that give rise to the disputes[218]. Whether the alleged judicialization of arbitration is seen as a consequence of increased complexity of disputes or of more combative advocacy, the fear seems to be that arbitration will become less attractive. For Fali Nariman: "[international commercial arbitration] *as a form of dispute resolution has become so overburdened by its own weight and size, that it is being supplanted by other speedier, more fruitful, more rewarding methods*"[219]. These words, written fifteen years

214. Not just for large disputes for which a tailor-made procedure may be justifiable.
215. A 2012 empirical survey conducted by the School of International Arbitration at Queen Mary, University of London looked into the emergence of this harmonized "best practice" in international arbitration. See Queen Mary, University of London, "Current and Preferred Practices in the Arbitral Process" (2012). See also, Queen Mary, University of London, "Improvements and Innovations in International Arbitration" (2015) at < http://www.arbitration.qmul.ac.uk/docs/164761.pdf> accessed 24 December 2015.
216. It has been suggested that this increased combativeness reflects the increasing participation (and therefore the growing influence of US litigators in arbitration. This may be referred to as the "Americanisation" of international arbitration. See, for example, Hanotiau, "International Arbitration in a Global Economy: The Challenges of the Future" 99; Ridgway, "International Arbitration" 51.

    Some authors have argued that this is not the case. See, for example, John E. Beerbower, "International Arbitration: Can We Realise the Potential?" (2011) 27 Arbitration International, Kluwer Law International 75-90.
217. Nathalie Voser, for instance, points out that the number of challenges to arbitrators at the ICC increased from 37 in 2004 to 57 in 2009. Nathalie Voser, "Removal, Resignation, Dismissal and Replacement of Arbitrators" in Philipp Habegger and others (eds), *Arbitral Institutions Under Scrutiny* (JurisNet 2013), ASA Special Series No. 40, 73. For a comment on the number of challenges at the ICC in the 1980s, see Guillermo Aguilar Alvarez, "The Challenge of Arbitrators" (1990) 6 Arbitration International, Kluwer Law International 203, 205. For the SCC, see Hanna Larsson and Annette Magnusson, "Recent Practice of the Arbitration Institute of the Stockholm Chamber of Commerce: Prima Facie Jurisdiction and Challenges of Arbitrators" (2004) 2004 Stockholm Arbitration Report 47, 48. For a comment that the number of challenges is not growing see Gerbay, Remy, "Is the End Nigh Again? An Empirical Assessment of the "Judicialization" of International Arbitration", (2014) 25(2) American Journal of International Arbitration. Available at SSRN: http://ssrn.com/abstract=2656624.
218. On the idea that arbitration has become more complex see McLean: *"With the astounding growth in the value and volume of transactions over the last thirty years, economic relationships between commercial parties have become far more intricate than before. As disputes substantively grow more complex, involve more stakeholders, and are fought for higher stakes, international arbitration must continue to offer a less time-consuming, more efficient alternative to cross-border litigation"*. David J. McLean, "Toward a New International Dispute Resolution Paradigm: Assessing the congruent evolution of globalization and international arbitration" (2009) 30 University of Pennsylvania Journal of International Economic Law 1087, 1096. See also Born, *International Commercial Arbitration* 2069.
219. Fali S. Nariman, 'The Spirit of Arbitration – The Tenth Annual Goff Lecture' (2011) 16 Arbitration International 261, 265.

ago, at the beginning of a period that saw unprecedented growth in the use of arbitration, might appear a little exaggerated today[220].

It should be noted, however, that the alleged judicialization of arbitration is by no means a twenty-first century phobia. At an ICCA congress nearly twenty years ago a practitioner was already commenting:

> *Over the years we have often talked of arbitration as being less formal, more flexible, speedier and less costly than litigation, but do we really fight hard to keep it that way? Both lawyers and arbitrators have commented on how often arbitrations today are converted into court-like battles by counsel who are used to litigation. Common Law lawyers are undoubtedly the worst offenders in this regard*[221].

Even a decade before that, in 1985, Jan Paulsson, in the editorial introducing the very first volume of *Arbitration International* was already writing:

> *This journal is launched at a time when the international arbitral process shows signs of becoming more formalistic, more court-like; French speakers refer to la juridictionnalisation de l'arbitrage. Litigants become more sophisticated, and come up with more difficult procedural stratagems*[222].

Be that as it may, the relationship between the judicialization of arbitration and arbitral institutions is not immediately clear. It would appear that whether or not the use of institutional arbitration rules brings about judicialization depends on the actual substance of such rules. The presence of institutional rules (or their inflation) does not, of itself, result in more formalism, more complex procedure or more delay. Some rules revision can actually foster increased simplicity. A provision contained in institutional rules imposing an obligation on arbitrators to tailor the procedure to the needs of the case (rather than mindlessly applying "best practices")[223], or to proceed expeditiously with the arbitration[224] is more likely to foster simplicity than engender indiscriminate complexity.

---

220. See in general Gerbay, Remy, "Is the End Nigh Again? An Empirical Assessment of the "Judicialization" of International Arbitration" (2014) 25(2) American Journal of International Arbitration. Available at SSRN: http://ssrn.com/abstract=2656624s.
221. Whitmore Gray, "Is There a Growing International Arbitration Culture?" in Albert Jan van den Berg (ed), *International Dispute Resolution: Towards an International Arbitration Culture* vol. 8 (Kluwer Law International, 1998) Seoul 23, 28.
222. Paulsson, "Introduction (to the first volume of Arb. Int.)" 3.
    Another author taking, in the same volume of Arbitration International, precisely the opposite view is Martin Hunter: *"It is only in the last ten years or so that a modern generation of arbitrators, encouraged by the judiciary, has started to work on making arbitration the more genuine alternative to litigation that it should be; and even now there are practitioners who advocate that arbitration procedure should follow formal court procedures* [...]". J. Martin H. Hunter, "Arbitration Procedure in England: Past, Present and Future" (1985) 1 Arbitration International, Kluwer Law International 82, 86.
223. See for example of Appendix IV (Case Management Techniques) to the 2012 ICC rules which contains *"examples of case management techniques that can be used by the arbitral tribunal and the parties for controlling time and cost"*.
224. See for example Article 22(1) of the ICC rules (2012): *"The arbitral tribunal and the parties shall make every effort to conduct the arbitration in an expeditious and cost-effective manner, having regard to the complexity and value of the dispute"*.

CHAPTER 3

An Overview of the Activities of Arbitral Institutions: Institutional Arbitration as a Multifacted Reality

§3.01 INTRODUCTION

Having defined in the previous chapter the notion of arbitral institution, the present chapter gives an overview of the activities undertaken by arbitral institutions. The aim of this chapter is twofold. First, to illustrate the diversity that exists in the role that institutions assume in respect of the proceedings they administer. This diversity, it is argued, characterizes not only the applicable procedures (e.g., the "mechanics" of appointment, challenges or decisions on costs etc.), but more importantly the level of discretion conferred upon institutions for the purposes of discharging their duties. Second, to provide the background information required to understand the theoretical representations of the "functions" of arbitral institutions that are discussed in the subsequent chapters (Chapters 4 and 5). In particular, this chapter serves to illustrate the fact that, occasionally, institutional "intervention"[225] will materially impact the outcome of arbitral proceedings.

The activities undertaken by arbitral institutions may be grouped in two categories: the administration of arbitral proceedings ("casework activities"), and activities other than the administration of arbitration proceedings ("non-casework activities"). Because the present book concerns the functions of arbitral institutions in the arbitral process, only a few words will be said of non-casework activities.

225. The term "*intervention*", is used in this book as a generic term to describe any action that may be taken by an arbitral institution in respect of proceedings administered by it. Such intervention may take different forms. It can be a decision (e.g., extension of deadline, seat, consolidation, language etc.), or a non-decisional measure (e.g., advice to a tribunal as to how the rules function, drawing the tribunal's attention as to a problem, logistical support etc.).

§3.02 NON-CASEWORK ACTIVITIES

[A] Awareness Raising, Training, Advocacy and Policy

The promotion and development of arbitration as a dispute resolution mechanism has become so indissociable from arbitral institutions, that some authors go as far as considering that this is "*one of the most vital functions of all arbitral institutions*"[226]. It is true that the mandate of many institutions includes, in addition to facilitating the resolution of disputes, supporting the development of international arbitration as a dispute resolution mechanism. For instance, educational events[227], awareness-raising[228] and even advocacy and lobbying[229], form part of the mandate of the three global institutions (i.e., the ICC, the LCIA and ICDR). This also fits the mandate of SIAC, CAS, DIS, CRCICA, KCAB, WIPO, the Milan Chamber, NAI, or VIAC, to name only a few other major institutions[230]. A rare example of an organization which does not consider itself responsible for the development of arbitration is the disputes service provider JAMS International, which operates as a for-profit company[231]. But it appears that even this organization dedicates significant resources to not-for-profit activities conducted in the interest of the larger arbitration community. JAMS has indeed set up a not-for-profit entity, called "JAMS Foundation", with a view to "[...] *offer financial assistance for conflict resolution initiatives with national or international impact and to*

226. Eric A. Schwartz, "The Role of the Arbitral Institution in the New Millennium" (1999) 65 Arbitration 321, 323.
227. Be it conferences, seminars or the like. In recent years, a number of arbitral institutions have set up, for these purposes, young practitioners' groups. Such institutions include *inter alia* the LCIA (with the YIAG), the ICC (YAF), the ICDR (ICDR Young and International), the SCC (YAS), and the DIS (DIS40). Incidentally, other such young practitioners' groups have been created independently from or outside of arbitral institutions, be it under the auspices of some other type of organization or not. This is the case of the YAP, Young ICCA, ASA Below 40, Comité Francais de l'Arbitrage 40, Club Español de Arbitraje 40).
228. Including workshops on arbitration with judges, in-house lawyers or practitioners. Some institutions produce publications on arbitration (whether journals or bulletins). See, for example, the ICC Bulletins, or the LCIA's journal "Arbitration International". Other institutions also include ICDR and the SCC. See, respectively, Mark Appel, "International Centre for Dispute Resolution (ICDR)" in Karyl Nairn and Patrick Heneghan (eds), *Arbitration World: Institutional & Jurisdictional Comparisons* (4th Revised edn, Thomson Reuters 2012), The European Lawyer Reference 74, and Öhrström, "The Arbitration Institute of the Stockholm Chamber of Commerce (SCC)" 7-8.
229. For example meeting with government officials to foster support for arbitration in general.
230. Information based on these institutions' responses to the questionnaires sent out by the author. Even smaller regional institutions recognize seeking to facilitate the development of arbitration: ACICA, CAM, BCICA, the Court of Arbitration at the Bulgarian Chamber of Commerce and Industry, the Arbitration Centre at the Caracas Chamber of Commerce, the Danish Institute of Arbitration, the Arbitration Institute of the Finland Chamber of Commerce, the Vietnam International Arbitration Centre, and the Court of Arbitration at the Polish Chamber of Commerce (Information also based on these institutions' responses to the questionnaires sent out by the author). The Swiss Chambers stated conducting these activities through the Association Suisse de l'Arbitrage (ASA).
231. Information based on the institution's responses to the questionnaires sent out by the author.

share its dispute resolution experience and expertise for the benefit of the public interest"[232].

For a number of institutions, some of these activities (in particular conferences and training seminars) serve as a useful source of revenue[233]. Another benefit for arbitral institutions resides in the publicity derived from such initiatives; publicity which may be expected to translate to an increase in the institutions' caseload. However, the cost of some of these initiatives (in particular awareness-raising, advocacy, and lobbying, as opposed to conferences) often exceeds any revenue that they might generate, even indirectly. In fact, activities advocating the use international arbitration in general (as opposed to under the auspices of one particular institution), will benefit other actors of the arbitration industry (such as arbitrators, counsel, academics and experts) much more directly than it will benefit the institutions themselves. The fact that arbitral institutions concern themselves with resource-intensive activities which serve primarily the interests of the rest of the arbitration industry is interesting. In essence, in doing so, institutions undertake what may be regarded as a "business development" role for the arbitration industry. The fact that institutions have come to assume a role akin to that of a trade association for the whole arbitration services industry seems to be the result of the combination of two factors. First, the not-for-profit nature of many institutions explains how such institutions could come routinely to devote resources to activities that are not directly benefitting them[234]. Second, and more importantly perhaps, the executive organs in charge of deciding the orientation of the activities of many institutions are composed of members from the different sectors of the industry (mostly outside counsel and arbitrators)[235]; sectors that benefit directly from the institutions' business development role. Incidentally, there appears to be no other group or entity better placed to represent the interests of the arbitration industry's various actors. Arguably, the Chartered Institute of Arbitrators (CIArb) fulfils this function in respect of arbitrators; the International Bar

232. "Website of JAMS, http://www.jamsadr.com", 15 February 2016.
233. The 2012 Annual Report of the HKIAC, for example, shows that, for the year 2011, conferences and seminars generated HKD 1,133,269 out of the total incomes of HKD 15,047,294. This represents c.7.5%. In 2010, the figure was 15.7%. See Hong Kong International Arbitration Centre, "Annual Report 2012, available at http://www.hkiac.org/images/stories/hkiac/2012_annual%20report.pdf", 2012 21.
234. As previously indicated, the majority of institutions involved in the administration of arbitration proceedings operate on a not-for-profit basis. This is the case, to mention only a few, of ICC, LCIA, ICDR, the Swiss Chamber's Arbitration Institution, the SCC, SIAC, HKIAC, CIETAC, CAS, CRCICA, DIS, KCAB, Milan Chamber of Arbitration, NAI, VIAC and WIPO (Information based on these institutions' responses to the questionnaires sent out by the author). The only notable exception is JAMS International, which is a for-profit company.
235. For example, the ICC Court, the LCIA Court, the recently created SIAC Court, and the CRCICA's and the DIAC's Board of Trustees, to cite only a few, are principally made up of a mix of arbitration practitioners, arbitrators and academics. See the websites of the respective institutions: "Website of the ICC's International Court of Arbitration, http://www.iccwbo.org/about-icc/organization/dispute-resolution-services/icc-international-court-of-arbitration", 2 April 2014; "Website of the London Court of International Arbitration (LCIA), http://www.lcia.org"; "Website of the Singapore International Arbitration Centre (SIAC), http://www.siac.org.sg", 15 February 2016; "Website of the Dubai International Arbitration Centre (DIAC), http://www.diac.ae/idias", 15 February 2016; "Website of the CRCICA, http://www.crcica.org.eg".

Association could be said to play a similar role for law firms; and the International Federation of Commercial Arbitration Institutions (IFCAI) could potentially fill this role for arbitral institutions, but none of these institutions can claim to represent the industry as a whole. In this context, it is perhaps unsurprising that arbitral institutions would come to be utilized in such a capacity. Be that as it may, these non-casework activities have become an important function of many arbitral institutions.

[B] Activities Relating to Other Forms of ADR and ad hoc Arbitration

In addition to arbitration, certain institutions concern themselves with other forms of ADR such as mediation[236], expert determination, adjudication or disputes boards[237]. Some institutions have also developed mechanisms to deal with specific types of disputes or specific industries, for instance, online domain name dispute resolution[238]. Another successful example may be found in DOCDEX (the ICC's dispute resolution mechanism for documentary credit)[239].

In practice, just like for arbitration, the role of institutions in respect of these forms of ADR may range from merely suggesting names of neutrals when parties to a dispute fail to reach an agreement, to providing full administrative services[240] under a

236. This is the case, for instance, of the LCIA, the HKIAC, the Swiss Chamber's Arbitration Institution and the NAI. This is also the case of the ICC with its Amicable Dispute Resolution rules. It should be noted, however, that it is the ICC's International Centre for ADR (distinct from the ICC's International Court of Arbitration) that oversees disputes under the ADR rules. Likewise, the AAA and the SCC both provide mediation services but under divisions that are distinct from the ICDR and the Arbitration Institute respectively. A major arbitral institution that restricts its activities to arbitration is SIAC. This is because the Singapore government set up a separate entity, the Singapore Mediation Centre, for the purposes of offering mediation services.

237. See, for example, the ICC rules of expertise (effective 1 January 2003), the ICC dispute boards' rules (effective 1 September 2004), the HKIAC adjudication rules (adopted 9 September 2008). The LCIA also appoints experts and adjudicators at the request of parties but it does not have separate rules. See "Website of the London Court of International Arbitration (LCIA), http://www.lcia.org".

238. This is an important function of WIPO for example. WIPO is one of the dispute resolution services provider for domain name disputes under the Uniform Dispute Resolution Policy (UDRP) that have been approved by the Internet Corporation for Assigned Names and Numbers (ICANN). See "Website of the Internet Corporation for Assigned Names and Numbers (ICANN)", 15 February 2016. Other ICANN approved providers include *inter alios*: the Asian Domain Name Dispute Resolution Centre (in Hong Kong), the Czech Arbitration Court (Prague), and the National Arbitration Forum (Minneapolis). Other "generalist" institutions like CIETAC and HKIAC also offer services in relation to domain name disputes. See Chang, "CIETAC's Perspective on Arbitration and Conciliation Concerning China" 36. See "Website of the Hong Kong International Arbitration Centre (HKIAC), http://www.hkiac.org", 15 February 2016.

239. DOCDEX. See website of the ICC: http://www.iccwbo.org/products-and-services/arbitration-and-adr/docdex, accessed 31 July 2013.

240. Including logistical support in respect of hearings or meetings (e.g., making arrangements for rooms, catering, audio-visual etc.), to dealing with the costs of the proceedings (holding advance payments on account of the costs, paying the neutrals' fees etc.).

set of pre-established rules of procedure[241]. Occasionally, some institutions also assist companies with the drafting of dispute resolution clauses or "*compromis*"[242] in the event such companies may wish to use the services of the institution as appointing authority or administrator. This is the case of the LCIA, which "[...] *regularly acts as appointing authority and administrator in such proceedings and* [...] *provide draft clauses for these purposes, and to assist contracting parties with the drafting of such ADR procedures*"[243]. The assistance may also extend to the drafting of detailed bespoke dispute resolution procedures for complex contractual arrangements. SIAC for instance drafted the "*Singapore Bunker Claims Procedure (SBC Terms)*" which was "*codified in 1996 as part of the Singapore Standard Code of Practice for Bunkering by Barges/Tankers ('CP 60')*"[244]. Likewise, the LCIA drafted a bespoke dispute resolution scheme for the construction of the Channel Tunnel Rail Link[245]. Interestingly, this particular role does not appear to be new for institutions. As early as the 1920s, the Arbitration Society of America was setting up bespoke dispute resolution mechanisms, including ones for the then burgeoning US motion picture industry[246]. Yet, the core mandate of arbitral institutions[247] is to provide administrative services in respect of international arbitration proceedings conducted in accordance with the institutions' rules. This is the focus of the remainder of this Chapter 3.

§3.03 CASEWORK ACTIVITIES

An exhaustive comparative analysis of the workings of the major institutional rules available (on such issues as appointments, joinder, consolidation, challenges, costs, etc.) would require a treatise far beyond the scope of this work. The following paragraphs merely aim to offer a brief overview of the types of activities undertaken by institutions in their administration of arbitration proceedings; activities which vary significantly from one institution to the next, notably in terms of the level of discretionary power granted to the institutions, but also in terms of their potential to impact the outcome of proceedings.

For convenience, such activities are described, in the paragraphs below, in a chronological order, from the commencement of an arbitration to the issue of the final

241. A number of institutions have published dedicated mediation rules for example: LCIA Mediation rules (effective 1 July 2012); Hong Kong International Arbitration Centre Mediation rules (effective 1 August 1999), NAI Mediation rules (effective 1 March 2009).
242. In the sense, submission agreement.
243. See "Website of the London Court of International Arbitration (LCIA), http://www.lcia.org". In a similar vein in respect of CIETAC, see Chang, "CIETAC's Perspective on Arbitration and Conciliation Concerning China" 36.
244. Ang Yong Tong, "SIAC: Arbitration in the New Millennium" [2000] Law Gazette (Singapore), 4.
245. Remy Gerbay, "London Court of International Arbitration" in Loukas A. Mistelis and others (eds), *The World Arbitration Reporter*, vol. 3 (Juris 2010) 4. The AAA also frequently design and develop *"alternative dispute resolution (ADR) systems for corporations, unions, government agencies, law firms, and the courts* [...]". "Website of AAA/ICDR, http://www.adr.org/aaa/faces/home".
246. Emerson, "History of Arbitration Practice and Law" 162.
247. At least in the acceptation assigned to the term "arbitral institution" in Chapter 1.

award. Each sub-section (corresponding to a given casework activity) contains a short description of the activity itself including of any discretionary powers granted to institutions; and examines the significance, if any, of such activity in the arbitral process[248].

[A] The Initial Stages (Up to the Constitution of the Tribunal)

[1] Receipt and Notification of the Request for Arbitration

Institutional arbitration proceedings almost invariably start with the filing by the claimant of a Request for Arbitration with the institution (sometimes named Notice of Arbitration or Statement of Claim)[249]. Consequently, the institution is involved in the proceedings from the outset. A notable exception concerns fully administered UNCITRAL-rules proceedings, which are commenced with the service by the claimant of a Notice of Arbitration on the respondent, not the filing of a similar document with the institution[250]. This means in practice that in such administered UNCITRAL arbitrations, the institution may only take cognizance of the existence of the proceedings weeks after the notice was served (often at the expiry of the thirty-day period for the respondent to appoint its arbitrator)[251].

As discussed below in relation to *prima* facie decisions on jurisdiction, the requirement that arbitral proceedings be commenced by filing a Request with the institution often implies a measure of discretion on the part of the institution in deciding whether or not to register a case; and therefore whether and when proceedings have been commenced under the applicable rules. This decision will occasionally take a particular significance when a Request is filed at, or around, the expiry of statutory limitation periods.

Under certain sets of institutional rules, it falls onto the institution to transmit the Request or Notice to all Respondents. This is, for example, the case under the rules of the ICC, VIAC, NAI, the Milan Chamber, CAMEX or under the Swiss rules[252]. To the contrary it is for the claimant to serve the Request onto the respondent under the rules

248. As discussed in this section §3.03 below, some activities are significant in the sense that they have the potential to impact the outcome of cases.
249. Article 4 of the ICC rules (2012); Article 2 ICDR Rules (2014); Article 1 LCIA rules (2014); Article 11 CIETAC rules (2015); Article 3 SIAC rules (2013); Article 8 ICAC rules (2010); Article 4 HKIAC rules (2013); Article 3 Swiss rules (2012); Article 2 SCC rules (2010); Article 5 of the ICSID Rules of Procedure for the Institution of Conciliation and Arbitration Proceedings ("Institution Rules"). See also the ASA survey on institutional arbitration: Simone Hofbauer, Michael Burkart, and Methap Tari, "Survey on Scrutiny of Arbitral Institutions" in Philipp Habegger and others (eds), *Arbitral Institutions Under Scrutiny* (JurisNet 2013), ASA Special Series No. 40, 5.
250. Article 3 UNCITRAL rules (2010).
251. This is because the UNCITRAL rules were drafted originally as ad hoc arbitration rules, and did not therefore contemplate the involvement of arbitral institutions in the administration of the proceedings (other than as default appointing authorities as discussed elsewhere above).
252. Article 4(5) of the ICC rules (2012); Article 3(6) of the Swiss rules (2012); Article 7 of the VIAC rules (2013); Article 7(1) of the NAI rules (2010); Article 9 of the Milan rules (2010); and Article 8 of the CAMEX rules (2009). Under Article 13.2 of the CIETAC rules (2015), after receipt of the

of the LCIA, ICDR, HKIAC, SIAC, WIPO or the CEPANI[253]. This apparently mundane task may, in practice, become critical at the enforcement stage. Under Article V(1)(b) of the New York Convention[254], indeed, recognition and enforcement of an award may be refused if the party against whom the award is invoked was not given proper notice of the proceedings or was otherwise unable to present his case.

[2] Which Sets of Rules Apply?

It is not uncommon for an institution to have more than one set of arbitration rules. For example, an institution may offer general international arbitration rules and rules for expedited or fast-track arbitration[255]. Similarly, some institutions may offer different rules for domestic and international arbitration[256], or for small claims and regular arbitration[257].

When this is the case, the rules themselves will often provide for a clear threshold determining which rules apply in the absence of an agreement of the parties[258]. Occasionally, however, a degree of discretion will be left to the institution to determine

---

Claimant's Request, the centre sends a Notice of Arbitration to both parties enclosing, for the Respondent's benefit, a copy of the Request.

253. Article 1 of the rules of the LCIA (2014); Article 2 of the ICDR rules (2014); Article 4.3(i) of the HKIAC rules (2013); Rule 3.4 of the SIAC rules (2013); Article 6 of the WIPO rules (2002); and Article 3(2) of the CEPANI rules (2013) (Unless otherwise stated, references in this work to the CEPANI rules are references to the rules applying to disputes above EUR 25,000).

254. "Convention on the Recognition and Enforcement of Foreign Arbitral Awards, ('New York Convention')" (1958). See discussions in Chapter 5 below (under "*Proposition 3: Materiality of institutional decisions*").

255. For instance WIPO (see "Website of the World Intellectual Property Organisation, http://www.wipo.int/portal/index.html.en", 17 July 2013); SCC (see "Website of the Arbitration Institute of the Stockholm Chamber of Commerce (SCC), http://www.sccinstitute.com",15 February 2016); ACICA (see "Website of the Australian Centre for International Commercial Arbitration (ACICA), http://acica.org.au", 17 July 2013). The SIAC rules provide for an expedited procedure within its general arbitration rules (see Rule 5 of the SIAC rule s (2013)). The same is true of the Swiss rules (see Article 42 of the Swiss rules (2010)).

256. For example, the AAA/ICDR. "Website of AAA/ICDR, http://www.adr.org/aaa/faces/home" See also JAMS, "Website of JAMS, http://www.jamsadr.com".

257. This is the case of the CEPANI which has two sets of arbitration rules, depending on whether the dispute is for more or less than EUR 25,000. "Website of the Belgian Centre for Arbitration and Mediation (CEPANI), http://www.cepani.be/en/default.aspx", 15 February 2013.

Another, related, problem is that of the inter-temporal application of consecutive editions of the same rules, e.g., the 1985 and 1998 LCIA Arbitration rules, which may require a decision of the arbitral institution as to which sets of rules should apply to a particular arbitration. However, modern sets of institutional rules do resolve this conflict e.g., the ICC rules (2012) provide under Article 6.1: "*[w]here the parties have agreed to submit to arbitration under the Rules, they shall be deemed to have submitted ipso facto to the Rules in effect on the date of commencement of the arbitration, unless they have agreed to submit to the Rules in effect on the date of their arbitration agreement.*" Similarly, the LCIA rules (2014) provide in the preamble, which is part of the rules, that "*the parties thereto shall be taken to have agreed in writing that any arbitration between them shall be conducted in accordance with the LCIA Rules or such amended rules as the LCIA may have adopted hereafter to take effect before the commencement of the arbitration and that such LCIA Rules form part of their agreement.*"

258. The threshold(s) may be monetary (Rule 5.1 of the SIAC rules (2013); Article 42(2) of the Swiss rules (2012)); or based on exceptional urgency (Article 42(2) of the Swiss rules (2012)).

which sets of rules shall apply to the proceedings. The SIAC rules, for example, provide that a party may *"apply to the Registrar in writing for the arbitral proceedings to be conducted in accordance with the Expedited Procedure"*. It is then for SIAC to determine *"after considering the views of the parties, that the arbitral proceedings shall be conducted in accordance with the Expedited Procedure"*[259]. Likewise, the Swiss rules provide that the expedited procedure shall apply under the CHF 1,000,000 threshold *"unless the Court decides otherwise"*[260]. According to Schlaepfer and Bartsch, this provision offers the Swiss Chambers a *"wide discretion"*[261]. Similarly, the ICDR rules provide that they shall apply not only where parties have so agreed but also where they have provided for arbitration by the AAA without designating particular rules but the dispute is "international". It falls on the institution itself to decide the international character of a dispute[262]. The JAMS international arbitration rules follow the same approach[263]. Occasionally the discretion conferred upon the institution to decide which set of rules applies will come from the parties' own arbitration clause, rather than the arbitration rules. For instance, according to Marie Öhrström, it is not uncommon for parties to agree in advance, in their arbitration clause, to entrust the SCC itself with the authority to decide which of the expedited and normal rules shall apply[264].

Decisions on which rules apply to the proceedings are not immaterial in practice[265]. They are determinative of part of the legal framework applicable to the procedure of the arbitration. Such decisions have the capacity to influence such things as the number of submissions to be made by the parties, whether or not there shall be a hearing, or even the powers of the tribunal and the availability of certain remedies. For example, the ICDR rules provide that the tribunal has power to award legal costs[266]. They also contain a waiver of the right to punitive damages[267]. These two items do not appear in the traditional AAA arbitration rules. Accordingly, a decision by the

259. Article 5.1 and 5.2 of the SIAC rules (2013).
260. Article 42(2) of the Swiss rules (2012).
261. Schlaepfer and Bartsch, "Swiss Chambers' Court of Arbitration and Mediation (Swiss Chambers)" 18. A similar procedure exists under the CMAC rules in China. Article 71 of the CMAC rules (2004) contemplates that a "Summary Procedure" apply if the value of the dispute is below CNY 1 million, but that if the claims are not quantified or the parties disagree as to the value of the dispute then it is for the CMAC arbitration commission to decide which rules apply *"considering the complexity of the case, the sum and scope of the interests concerned and other factors* [...]".
262. Article 1 of the ICDR rules (2014).
263. Article 1.1 of the JAMS rules (2011) provides: *"Where parties have agreed in writing to arbitrate disputes under these International Arbitration Rules ('the Rules') or have provided for arbitration of an international dispute by JAMS or JAMS International, the arbitration will take place in accordance with these Rules* [...]".
264. In fact, the SCC offers a model clause contemplating this. See Öhrström, "The Arbitration Institute of the Stockholm Chamber of Commerce (SCC)" 10.
265. According to Anne Veronique Schlaepfer, for instance, a decision of the Swiss institution as to the application of the expedited rules *"is not purely mechanical and* [...] *will have a significant impact on the organisation of the arbitration proceedings"*. Schlaepfer, "The Role of the Institution at the Commencement of the Proceedings" 60.
266. Article 34 ICDR rules (2014).
267. Article 31(5) ICDR rules (2014). See also John Fellas, "AAA/ICDR International Arbitration Rules" in Loukas A. Mistelis (ed), *Concise International Arbitration* (Kluwer Law International 2010) 468.

institution to apply the ICDR or the AAA rules will have for effect to grant, or not to grant, the power to award legal costs and punitive damages to the arbitral tribunal[268]. In this respect, a decision on which sets of rules shall apply to the proceedings may, occasionally impact on the outcome of proceedings[269].

[3] Decisions on Language

In the absence of an agreement between the parties, a question that may arise early-on in the proceedings is that of the language of the arbitration. More often than not it is for the tribunal, once appointed, to decide such a question. This is the position taken by the rules of the ICC, HKIAC, WIPO, ACICA, CRCICA, DIS, CAMEX, NAI and also the Swiss rules and the Milan Chamber's rules[270]. However, the decision is occasionally left to the institution itself. The rules of procedure of the CAS for instance provide that this is a matter for the institution to decide[271]. Likewise, the LCIA rules contemplate that where the arbitration agreement is written in more than one language, the LCIA Court may decide which of those languages shall be the "*initial language*" of the arbitration (unless the arbitration agreement provides that the arbitration proceedings shall be conducted in more than one language)[272]. The 2012 CIETAC rules also conferred on the institution discretion in respect of the choice of language. Under Article 71, in the absence of an agreement between the parties on the subject, "*the language to be used in the proceedings shall be Chinese or any other language designated by CIETAC having regard to the circumstances of the case*"[273].

In addition to the costs implications[274], a decision on language may have a significant impact on the proceedings. This is because a choice of language will affect the choice of the parties in respect of the appointment of arbitrators. First, when the language chosen is a relatively uncommon one, the pool of qualified arbitrators from which the parties can choose will be limited, and the parties may not be able to select

268. Subject to any agreement to the contrary by the parties once the proceedings are commenced.
269. In this sense see Aníbal Sabater, "When Arbitration Begins Without a Seat" (2010) 27 Journal of International Arbitration, Kluwer Law International 443, 458.
270. Article 20 ICC rules (2012); Article 15 HKIAC rules (2013); Article 17.1 Swiss rules (2012); Article 40(a) WIPO rules (2002); Article 20.1 ACICA rules (2011) and Article 24 ACICA rules (2016); Article 19 CRCICA rules (2011); Article 22.1 DIS rules (1998); Article 22.2 CAMEX rules (2009); Article 5.2 Milan rules (2009); and Article 40 NAI rules. Similarly, Article 18 of the ICDR rules (2014) provides that the language of the arbitration shall be that of the documents containing the arbitration agreement, but that the tribunal has discretion to determine otherwise.
271. See Article R29 of the CAS Code (2013).
272. Article 17.1 of the LCIA rules (2014). The words "initial language" indicate that the decision is subject to review by the tribunal once appointed.
273. Article 71 of the CIETAC rules (2012). Article 81(1) of the CIETAC rules (2015) now states "*Where the parties have agreed on the language of arbitration, their agreement shall prevail. In the absence of such agreement, the language of arbitration to be used in the proceedings shall be Chinese. CIETAC may also designate another language as the language of arbitration having regard to the circumstances of the case.*"
274. Any documents that need to be produced as evidence in the arbitration need to be translated into the language of the arbitration. Likewise, any witness testimony at the hearing needs to be translated by live interpreters. These translations come at a cost.

an arbitrator with their precise desired qualifications or characteristics[275]. Second, and more importantly, a choice of language will sometimes mean a de facto choice of the cultural background of the arbitrators. For instance, choosing "Slovene"[276] as the language of the arbitration means that the arbitrators will most likely be Slovenian nationals[277] because the language is not widely spoken by non-nationals[278]. This means in turn that the arbitrators are likely to have a civil law background[279]. The cultural and legal background of arbitrators often has an impact on the manner in which the arbitrators apprehend the case[280]. This includes, for example, the arbitrator's approach to issues of production of documents or standard of proof[281]. As a result, experienced counsels adapt their approach to advocacy depending on the background of the arbitrators[282]. As can be seen, an apparently simple decision on the language of an arbitration may have a significant impact on the proceedings.

[4] Decisions regarding the Seat or Place of the Arbitration

Certain institutional rules also confer on the institution the power to fix the seat or place of the arbitration, in the absence of agreement between the parties. In some instances the decision of the institution will be final. This is the case in ICC, WIPO and Swiss rules proceedings[283]. In others cases the decision will be a provisional one, subject to review

275. For example, an academic versus a practising lawyer; an arbitration specialist versus an industry specialist; a strict "contractualist" versus a business oriented person etc.
276. The official language of Slovenia.
277. Or individuals of Slovenian descent who are not Slovenian nationals.
278. *"Slovene is* [...] *the native language of approximately 2.4 million people: about 1.85 million of them live in the Republic of Slovenia"*. "Website of the Government Communication Office of the Republic of Slovenia, http://www.slovenia.si", 15 February 2016.
279. As Slovenia is a civil law country. The same would not necessarily be true of choosing English as the language. Because English is widely spoken, it is not difficult to find an English-speaking arbitrator who is not from England, the United States or some other common law jurisdiction.
280. For Barbara Steindl: *"The personality and background of an arbitrator strongly influence the way in which arbitrations are conducted and thus have a strong impact on the way in which the parties prepare and present a case"*. Barbara Steindl, "The Development of Due Process under the New York Convention" (2008) 2008 Christian Klausegger, Peter Klein, et al. (eds), Austrian Yearbook on International Arbitration 255, 262.
281. For Philip Capper and Julia Zagonek for instance: "[...] *arbitrators or counsel from England will often bring with them* [in the proceedings] *certain assumptions, perceptions and expectations which stem from their practice as English lawyers practising in the English courts"*. Phillip Capper, "Relevant Aspects of the English Legal System" in Julian D. M. Lew and others (eds), *Arbitration in England. Including Chapters on Scotland and the Republic of Ireland* (Kluwer Law International 2013) 29. See also Eric A. Schwartz, "Is Procedure Really Neutral? The Seat: Does It Matter? (A Tale of More than Two Cities)", A contribution by the ITA Board of Reporters' (2012) 6 Dispute Resolution International, 120.
282. See in this sense Emmanuel Gaillard and Emmanuel Pinsolle, "Advocacy in International Commercial Arbitration: France" in R. Doak Bishop (ed), *The Art of Advocacy in International Arbitration* (1st edn, Juris 2004) 143; and John Beechey, "Advocacy in International Commercial Arbitration: England" in R. Doak Bishop (ed), *The Art of Advocacy in International Arbitration* (1st edn, Juris 2004) 252.
283. Article 18 ICC rules (2012); and Article 39 WIPO rules (2002). Interestingly, Article 16 of the Swiss rules (2012) provide that in the absence of clear agreement between the parties that Court shall determine the seat, but the Court may also request the tribunal to do so. See also Article 14 JAMS rules (2011).

by the tribunal once appointed. This is the case at the ICDR[284]. A common practice is for the rules to specify a default seat whilst, at the same time, granting to the institution, or the tribunal, a measure of discretion to select another seat if the circumstances justify it. The LCIA rules, for example, set London as the default seat subject a contrary decision of the LCIA Court. Likewise, the CIETAC rules provide that the default place of arbitration shall be the domicile of CIETAC or its sub-commission administering the case, subject to a decision to the contrary by the institution[285].

The choice of seat of an arbitration is significant for a number of reasons. First, the seat of the arbitration will often be taken by domestic courts to confer on them jurisdiction over such issues as requests to adopt interim relief, and to assist the tribunal with the taking of evidence[286]. Second, at the end of the process, the seat of the arbitration will have an impact on the legal requirements regarding actions for the setting aside of the award: "[...] *the arbitration laws of the seat usually apply to the proceedings, and an award that is not issued in accordance with them can be nullified or refused enforcement*"[287]. Third, and more fundamentally, whenever the seat of the arbitration is taken by the arbitral tribunal to be determinative of the *lex arbitri*[288], a decision on the seat will regulate the manner in which the tribunal approaches decisions on procedure throughout the arbitration[289]. For Nesbitt, "[a decision on the

284. Article 17.1 ICDR rules (2014).

285. Article 16.1 of the LCIA rules (1998) and (2014). Article 7 CIETAC rules (2012) and (2015). Likewise, Article 4 of the Milan Chamber rules (2010) provides for a default seat of Milan, and grant on the "Arbitral Council" the power to choose another seat.

Article 18.1 of the SIAC rules (2013) provides for a default seat of Singapore but confers on the tribunal rather than the institution the power to decide otherwise. A similar solution may be found in Article 14 of the HKIAC rules (2013).

The CAS code stands out in this respect as it provides for a default seat (Lausanne) but does not contemplate that the seat be changed, whether by agreement, by a decision of the institution or of the tribunal. See rule R28 of the CAS code (2013). ICAC adopts a similar approach (with Moscow as the seat) at Article 22 of its rules (2010).

The ACICA rules adopt a slightly more flexible position, with Sydney as the default seat (Article 19), but with the possibility for the parties to agree otherwise. As pointed out by Simon Greenberg this does create a dis-incentive for parties to cooperate on this issue at the drafting stage because of the knowledge that in case of disagreement the seat will by default be Sydney. Simon Greenberg, "ACICA's New International Arbitration Rules" (2006) 23 Journal of International Arbitration, Kluwer Law International 189, 196.

286. Sabater, "When Arbitration Begins Without a Seat" 443.

287. Sabater, "When Arbitration Begins Without a Seat" 443. Simon Nesbitt, "London Court of International Arbitration (LCIA) Arbitration Rules, 1998" in Loukas A. Mistelis (ed), *Concise International Arbitration* (Kluwer Law International 2010) 431.

288. The *lex arbitri* can be defined as the "*law governing the existence and proceedings of the arbitral tribunal*", as distinguished from "*the law governing the arbitration agreement and the performance of that agreement*" and the one "*governing the substantive issues in dispute*". Blackaby, Partasides, Hunter, and Redfern, *Redfern and Hunter on International Arbitration* 165. Admittedly, there is not a universal agreement as to whether the seat of the arbitration is determinative of the *lex arbitri*. Proponents of the autonomous theory of arbitration for example do not "*attach too much value to the seat of arbitration and its law*". Lew, Mistelis, and Kröll, *Comparative International Commercial Arbitration* 81. See also, Loukas A Mistelis, "Reality Test: Current State of Affairs in Theory and Practice Relating to 'Lex Arbitri'" (2006) 2006 American Review of International Arbitration 155-181.

289. For Fellas, "[t]*he selection of the place of arbitration is significant, as it will determine the lex arbitri, that is the procedural arbitration law that will apply*". Fellas, "AAA/ICDR International

seat] *determines the legal background against which the arbitration takes place* [...]"[290]. Decisions on procedure will shape the parties' presentation of their case, which may in turn affect the outcome of the proceedings[291]. In sum, choosing the seat of an arbitration is a decision which significance should not be underestimated. In the words of Anibal Sabater: "*Along with the choice of the applicable law and rules, and the appointment of the tribunal, the selection of the seat is one of the most critical decisions in any arbitration*"[292].

[5] Extension of Deadlines

On occasion, a party may need to apply, prior to the constitution of the tribunal, to the institution for the extension of a time limit set out in the rules. For example, a respondent may wish to ask for an extension of the time to file its Response or Answer to the Request for Arbitration. Accordingly, a number of institutional rules bestow the administrator with the power to extend such time limits.

In practice this can be done in one of three ways: First, by an express provision of the rules granting to the institution, in generic terms, the power to modify deadlines. An example may be found under the SIAC rules which provide that "[e]*xcept as provided in these Rules, the Registrar may at any time extend or shorten any time limits prescribed under these Rules*"[293]. Naturally, the general power to extend deadlines is often limited to deadlines under the rules[294] or to deadlines fixed by the institution itself[295] (as opposed to deadlines agreed by the parties or set by the tribunal), but this is not always the case[296]. Second, the rules may contain a provision that gives an exhaustive list of provisions under which the institution may extend time limits[297]. Third, and more commonly, some institutional rules proceed on an article-by-article

Arbitration Rules" 482. See also, Blackaby, Partasides, Hunter, and Redfern, *Redfern and Hunter on International Arbitration* 317.

290. Nesbitt, "London Court of International Arbitration (LCIA) Arbitration Rules, 1998" 431.
291. This is why for Sabater: "[t]*he person or entity entrusted with establishing the seat of arbitration should always do so having allowed the parties to express their views, and if needed submit evidence, on the matter*". Sabater, "When Arbitration Begins Without a Seat" 458.
292. Sabater, "When Arbitration Begins Without a Seat" 443 and 458.
293. Article 2.5 of the SIAC rules (2013).
294. That is to say deadlines that are set by the rules themselves. See for instance Article R32 of the CAS Code (2013) which contemplates that the CAS may, prior to the appointment of the panel, extend time limits provided in the Code (with the exception of the time limit for the filing of the statement of appeal).
295. Article 2.3 of the Swiss rules (2012): "[...] *the Court may extend or shorten any time-limit it has fixed or has the authority to fix or amend*".
296. See Article 3.3 of the "*Internal Rules of the Arbitration Center of Mexico*", at Annex I of the CAMEX rules (2009) which reads: "*The Secretary General's functions pursuant to these Rules are* [...] *to extend the procedural time limits when such extension contains benefits for the proceedings and their resolution*". The rules do not explain whether this is limited to time limits set out in the rules themselves or set out by CAMEX, or whether this is intended to extend to ones set by the tribunal, or by the parties' own agreement.
297. An example may be found at Article 4(g) WIPO rules (2002).

basis[298]. An example of this may be found in the ICC rules[299] which contemplate extensions of time for the finalization of the terms of reference[300], the rendering of the award[301], filing of the Answer[302] and of the claimant's response to a counterclaim[303].

Often, however, the rules are silent on the subject[304]. When the rules are silent as to the institution's power to extend deadlines, some institutions take the view that they are unable to extend any time limits[305]. It would appear, however, that where the rules are silent the institution nonetheless retains the power to extend those deadlines that it has set itself[306], for example in relation to payment of advances on costs[307] or when the parties are given an opportunity to comment on a particular issue, such as a challenge to an arbitrator. Some institutions go even further by assuming the power to extend certain deadlines set in the rules (as opposed to ones set by the institution itself) even when the rules are silent as to this power. For example, the SCC accepts to entertain requests to extend the ten-day deadline (at Article 13 of the SCC rules) within which the parties have to agree on a suitable sole arbitrator. Article 10 of the SCC rules, however, simply states that the SCC should make the appointment if the parties cannot agree on a sole arbitrator[308]. In sum, the rules and practices on extension of deadlines

298. They provide for the institution's power to extend certain specific time limits in individual articles.
299. For a detailed description of the role of the ICC in respect of the extension of deadlines see Grigera Naón, "ICC Bulletin Supp., Arbitration in the Next Decade".
300. Extension of the two-month time limit from the transmission of the file to the tribunal. Article 23.2 ICC rules (2012).
301. Extension of the six-month time limit from the terms of reference. Article 30.2 ICC rules (2012). Similar provision may be found at Article 32 of the Milan rules (2010); and Article 41.2(f) of the HKIAC rules (2013).
302. Article 5.2 ICC rules (2012). A similar provision may be found at Article 3.4 of the ICDR rules (2009).
303. Article 5.6 ICC rules (2012). Interestingly, Article 38.2 of the ICC rules (2012) also contemplates that the ICC Court may extend any time limit which has been modified by agreement of the parties (pursuant to Article 38.1) if it is necessary in order for the tribunal and the Court to fulfil their responsibilities under the Rules.
304. See, for example, the 1998 version of the LCIA rules. However, Articles 4.7 and 22(b) of the 1998 LCIA rules did entrust the tribunal with wide powers to extend or abridge deadlines, including ones set out in the parties' arbitration agreement. It must be noted also that the new LCIA rules (2014) at Article 22.5 now empower the institution itself to "[...] *abridge or extend any period of time under the Arbitration Agreement or other agreement of the parties (even where the period of time has expired)*".
305. See, for example, ACICA (Information based on these institutions' responses to the questionnaires sent out by the author). This is also the case of the LCIA, which consistently refuses to extend the thirty-day period for the filing of the Response under Article 2.
306. Interestingly both the Milan rules and the SCC rules contemplate expressly that the institution may extend any time limits that the institution has set. Article 7 SCC rules (2010), and Article 7.2 of the Milan rules (2010). Article 7 of the SCC Rules provide: "*The Board may, on application by either party or on its own motion, extend any time period which has been set for a party to comply with a particular direction*". Presumably this provision is limited to deadlines provided under the SCC rules or deadlines that have been set by the SCC, not by ones set by the arbitral tribunal.
307. This is the case of the CRCICA (Information based on the institution's response to the questionnaire sent out by the author).
308. Johan Sidklev, "Arbitration Institute of the Stockholm Chamber of Commerce (SCC)" in Karyl Nairn and Patrick Heneghan (eds), *Arbitration World: Institutional & Jurisdictional Comparisons* (4th Revised edn, Thomson Reuters 2012), The European Lawyer Reference 171.

vary significantly from one institution to another, in particular in respect of the measure of discretionary power granted, or taken, by institutions.

It is fair to say that institutions' powers in respect of the extension of deadlines appear rather mundane when compared to other institutional powers (like that of deciding challenges for example), which significance might be more immediately evident[309]. This said, decisions on the extension of deadlines have, in practice, given rise to some difficulties at the enforcement stage. As explained by Jan Paulsson in response to Professor Kassis' claim[310] that challenge decisions are somehow more important than decisions on the appointment of arbitrators or the extension of deadlines:

> *Are we to guess that challenge actions are by their nature more controversial or more serious? That would be wrong as a matter of fact. One dispute regarding the bona fides of an extension of deadlines was litigated to the French Court of Cassation; and parties occasionally engage in extensive battles about the confirmation of a party nominated arbitrator*[311].

Losing parties in institutional arbitrations have indeed attempted to prevent the enforcement of arbitral awards on the basis of a decision of the institution to extend deadlines. This was the case, for example, in the *Société Appareils Dragon* case[312] and in the *Techni-Import* case[313], both of which are discussed in some detail in Chapter 4 below[314].

[6] Decisions on Jurisdiction

Under the rules of a majority of institutions it is for the tribunal (not the institution) to decide whether there is a binding agreement between the parties to arbitrate the dispute. This is the principle of Kompetenz-Kompetenz[315]. Exceptionally though,

309. In terms of the impact that that the decision may have overall on the proceedings.
310. The claim was made in Kassis, *Réflexions sur le Règlement d'Arbitrage de la Chambre de Commerce Internationale: les Déviations de l'Arbitrage Institutionnel* 193 et seq.
311. Paulsson, "Vicarious Hypochondria and Institutional Arbitration" 243.
312. "Société Appareils Dragon, Cour de Cassation, 2ieme Chambre Civile, 8 June 1983 (Revue de l'Arbitrage, 1987)", Cour de Cassation, 2ieme Chambre Civile 1987. In this case, the company "Appareils Dragons" was contesting before the Court of Appeal of Paris the decision of the ICC to prolong the six-month period for the issue of the award (provided for at the then Article 18 of the ICC rules), and on that basis was asking for the annulment of the arbitral award.
313. "Société Techni-Import Professionnel v Société Electro Scientific Industries, Cour d'Appel de Paris, 17 May 1983 (Revue de l'Arbitrage, 1987, at p. 309)", Cour d'Appel de Paris 1987. In this case, a company (Techni Import) appealed an exequatur decision before the Court of Appeal of Paris on the grounds, *inter alia*, that the prolongation by the ICC of the six-month period for the award to be rendered was invalid because it was made "*automatically*" and without prior adversarial debates. The appeal was rejected.
314. See section §3.02[A][2] of Chapter 3 ("*The Traditional Representations of the Functions of Institutions: a Critical Evaluation*").
315. Or the "*jurisdiction to decide jurisdiction*". See Born, *International Commercial Arbitration* 200. See also Blackaby, Partasides, Hunter, and Redfern, *Redfern and Hunter on International Arbitration* 347; Gaillard and Savage, *Fouchard, Gaillard, Goldman on International Commercial Arbitration* 396; Audley Sheppard, "Chapter 23 – English Arbitration Act" in Loukas A. Mistelis (ed), *Concise International Arbitration* (Kluwer Law International 2010) 735.

institutional rules will contemplate that any jurisdictional objection is decided by the institution itself. By operation of Article 6 of the CIETAC rules, for instance, the power to decide jurisdictional objection lies with CIETAC. A similar solution may be found in the CMAC rules[316]. Under the CIETAC rules, the institution may choose to delegate such power to the arbitral tribunal. The BAC rules adopt a similar approach[317]. Interestingly, in the case of CIETAC, when a positive decision on jurisdiction has been rendered and a tribunal is therefore constituted, the institution retains the power to make a contrary decision on jurisdiction based on new facts and/or evidence presented before the arbitral tribunal in the course of the proceedings[318]. Admittedly, the approach taken by the CIETAC, CMAC the BAC rules, which confer on the institution instead of the tribunal the power to decide on jurisdiction, is isolated. Nonetheless, these institutions' vast caseloads confer on the Chinese institutions' incongruous stance on jurisdiction a relative importance, which should not be dismissed[319].

Where it is for the tribunal to decide jurisdictional objections, institutions are nonetheless often given the power to decide, on a prima facie basis, whether a binding arbitration agreement referring to the relevant rules exists, subject to review by the tribunal once it has been appointed. This is the case of the ICC rules which contain express provisions on prima facie jurisdiction[320]. Other institutions which rules contemplate prima facie decisions on jurisdiction include *inter alia* the Swiss

316. Article 4 of the CMAC rules (2004) provides that "[t]*he arbitration Commission has the power to decide on the existence, validity or an arbitration agreement and the jurisdiction over an arbitration case*".
317. Article 6 of the BAC Rules (2008). In the case of BAC decisions on jurisdictions made by the institution are in fact made by the case handler in charge of the file! See Fuyong Chen, "Striving for Independence, Competence, and Fairness: A Case Study of the Beijing Arbitration Commission" (2007) 18 American Review of International Arbitration 313-352.
318. Article 6 CIETAC rules (2012). See also Clarisse von Wunschheim and Fan Kun, "Arbitrating in China: The Rules of the Game – Practical Recommendations concerning Arbitration in China" (2008) 26 ASA Bulletin, Kluwer Law International 35, 37-38.
319. In 2012, each BAC and CIETAC received in excess of 1,400 new arbitrations. "Website of Beijing Arbitration Commission, http://www.bjac.org.cn/en", 1 July 2013 (under "*About us*" and then "*Annual Reports*"). "Website of CIETAC, http://www.cietac.org" (under "*Statistics*"). In comparison, the ICC registered 759 cases in 2012.
320. Article 6 of the ICC rules (2012).

    See also the detailed procedure under the Article 7 of the rules of the Arbitration Court at the Bulgarian Chamber of Commerce and Industry. The new CRCICA rules contain a new provision on prima facie jurisdiction at Article 6. Interestingly, it provides that the centre may decide "*not to proceed*" with the arbitration, rather than that the centre may refuse to register a case. This implies that a Request wrongly filed with CRCICA would still have the effect of commencing proceedings, which would then be discontinued by a decision of the centre. See in this sense: Samaa Haridi, Meriam Alrashid, and Amal Bouhabib, "The Cairo Regional Centre for International Commercial Arbitration (CRCICA) Newly Revised Arbitration Rules: Incorporating the New UNCITRAL Model Rules of 2010 and Expanding the Centre's Role as an Appointing Authority" (2011) 8 Transnational Dispute Management, 3; Jalal Abdel Raouf, "New Rules of the Cairo Regional Centre for International Commercial Arbitration (CRCICA)" (2011) 3 International Journal of Arab Arbitration 7, 9.

Institution, the SCC, SIAC, HKIAC, the CAS, the Milan Chamber and the FCC (Helsinki)[321]. Some other established institutional rules remain silent[322].

Even where the applicable rules are silent it is hard to imagine that an institution would not, as a matter of fact, exercise a degree of discretion (and as the case may be refuse to administer a case), where there is manifestly no binding arbitration agreement referring to the rules of the institution[323]. For instance, despite the LCIA rules being silent on the subject, where a Request for Arbitration is sent to the LCIA in respect of a dispute arising out of a contract which either contains no arbitration clause at all, or which clearly provides for arbitration under the rules of another institution (e.g., ICC), the LCIA Secretariat routinely refuses to register the case[324]. The same is true of the ICDR[325], and of WIPO[326]. Institutions that claim not to exercise any such discretion are rare[327].

Negative prima facie decisions on jurisdiction by institutions are admittedly infrequent[328]. Institutions tend to take a liberal approach and leave jurisdictional

321. Article 3(12) Swiss rules (2012); Article 9(1) SCC rules (2010); Article 25 SIAC rules (2013); Article 19.4 HKIAC rules (2013), Article R39 CAS Code (2013); Article 11 Milan rules (2010); Article 14 FCC (2013). The situation at ICSID is a peculiar. Rule 6 of the Institution's Rules give to the Secretary General the power to make prima *facie decisions* on jurisdictions. The difference with the rules of say, the ICC, is that the scope of the jurisdiction of the centre itself (i.e., not the tribunal) is set out in some detail at Article 25 of the convention so that the prima facie decision of the Secretary General forms a rather more tangible barrier than under the auspices of other institutions.
322. There are no provisions on the subject in the LCIA rules (2014), the ICDR rules (2014), or the WIPO rules (2002). It should be noted however that Article 19 of the ICDR Rules contemplate that the institution has the power to proceed despite challenges to jurisdiction of tribunal, prior to its constitution.
323. In this sense, see the ASA survey of institutional arbitration which claims that the "*vast majority of institutions (91%) take a prima facie decision on jurisdiction* [...]". The figure of 91% is based on a sample of 22 institutions. Hofbauer, Burkart, and Tari, "Survey on Scrutiny of Arbitral Institutions" 7.
324. Unless of course the parties are able to agree a variation to their arbitration clause so as to provide for arbitration under the LCIA rules. For confirmation that the LCIA does determine jurisdiction on a prima facie basis, see Adrian Winstanley, "Review of the London Court of International Arbitration" in Horacio A. Grigera Naón and Paul E. Mason (eds), *International Commercial Arbitration Practice: 21st Century Perspectives* (LexisNexis 2010) para. 1.
325. For confirmation that ICDR also determines jurisdiction on a prima facie basis, see Michael F. Hoellering, "AAA Administration of International Arbitration Proceedings" (1998) 13 ICSID Review 51, 53. For confirmation regarding both ICDR and LCIA see Chan, "Of Arbitral Institutions and Provisional Determinations on Jurisdiction, Global Gold Case" 408.
326. Information based on the institution's responses to the questionnaires sent out by the author.
327. This is the case of the DIS, KCAB, and JAMS International. (Information based on these institutions' responses to the questionnaires sent out by the author).
328. In respect of the Swiss rules, see Philipp A. Habegger, "The Revised Swiss Rules of International Arbitration: An Overview of the Major Changes" (2012) 30 ASA Bulletin, Kluwer Law International 269, 275-276. For the SCC see Sidklev, "Arbitration Institute of the Stockholm Chamber of Commerce (SCC)" 173.

    Statistics are scarce but, as reported by Derains and Schwartz, in 1996, the ICC applied the provisions on prima facie jurisdiction (at the time Article 7 of the ICC rules), in less than ten cases out of 433 received. Another author indicates that between 1998 and 2005, negative decisions on prima facie jurisdiction (partially negative of fully negative) were rendered by the ICC in sixty cases. Philippe Mirèze, "Les Pouvoirs de l'Arbitre et de la Cour d'Arbitrage de la CCI relatifs à leur Compétence" (no date) 2006 Revue de l'Arbitrage 591, 610.

objections for an arbitral tribunal to decide unless there is manifestly no valid arbitration clause[329]. The authority to make a prima facie decision on jurisdiction is, in large part, a cost-saving device. Its purpose is to avoid the costs that would otherwise be incurred by having a tribunal appointed only to decide that it lacks jurisdiction[330]. As rare as they may be, negative prima facie decisions on jurisdiction have significant consequences. A claimant faced with the refusal of an institution to administer a case is left with no choice but to commence proceedings before some other forum, which may or may not accept to hear the case. In the words of Derains and Schwartz:

> [...] *if the ICC Court mistakenly refuses to set an arbitration in motion, and there are no courts to which the parties can reliably refer, a party might, as a consequence, be deprived of its only real chance of obtaining effective relief*[331].

In addition, while recourse against the decision of an institution to refuse to register a case is sometimes available in domestic courts[332], such a refusal means that it will be for the courts (rather than an arbitral tribunal) to decide on the validity of the arbitration agreement. As Isabelle Hautot puts it, in effect, a refusal to register a case transfers the competence to decide on the validity of an arbitration agreement from the arbitrators to the domestic courts[333].

[7] Interim Measures

Occasionally, the rules of certain institutions will contemplate that the parties may apply to the institution itself for interim relief prior to the constitution of the arbitral tribunal[334]. Of course, a more common option is for the institution to be entrusted "only" with the nomination, on an urgent basis, of a neutral (whether the actual

329. For the ICC, see Derains and Schwartz, *A Guide to the New ICC Rules of Arbitration* 79-80. For SIAC, see Gordon Smith, "Commentary on the New Singapore International Arbitration Centre Rules" (2010) 76 Arbitration 727, 729. For the SCC, see Hanna Larsson and Annette Magnusson, "Recent Practice of the Arbitration Institute of the Stockholm Chamber of Commerce: Prima Facie Jurisdiction and Challenges of Arbitrators" (2004) 2004 Stockholm Arbitration Report 47, 49.
330. Grierson and Van Hooft, *Arbitrating Under the 2012 ICC Rules. An Introductory User's Guide* 108.
331. Derains and Schwartz, *A Guide to the New ICC Rules of Arbitration* 78. In the same sense, Paulsson argues: "*The stakes involved are often even more significant than those of a challenge action (because, unlike the latter, they put in doubt the very availability of the arbitral mechanism)*". Paulsson, "Vicarious Hypochondria and Institutional Arbitration" 243.
332. Hautot, "Les Pouvoirs de la Cour d'Arbitrage de la C.C.I. de Décider ou Non d'Organiser l'Arbitrage" 26.
333. In the original language: "[...] *la décision de la Cour d'Arbitrage de ne pas organiser l'arbitrage a pour effet de transférer la compétence ratione materiae pour juger de l'existence d'une convention d'arbitrage valable, des arbitres naturellement compétents, à une juridiction étatique dont la compétence ratione loci pourra au surplus être contestée*". Hautot, "Les Pouvoirs de la Cour d'Arbitrage de la C.C.I. de Décider ou Non d'Organiser l'Arbitrage" 26. In the same sense, see Paulsson, "Vicarious Hypochondria and Institutional Arbitration" 245.
334. Ali Yesilirmak, "Provisional Measures" in Loukas A Mistelis and Julian D. M. Lew (eds), *Pervasive Problems in International Arbitration* (Kluwer Law International 2006) 194.

arbitral tribunal[335] or an emergency arbitrator[336]) who will then determine any application for interim measures. Nonetheless in some instances the parties will have the possibility to seek provisional measures from the arbitral institution itself. This is the case under the rules of the Arbitration Court Attached to the Czech Chamber of Commerce[337]; under the procedural rules of the CAS[338]; under the rules of Italian Association for Arbitration[339], and under the rules of the Maritime Arbitration Commission at the Chamber of Commerce and Industry of the Russian Federation (MAC)[340]. Interestingly, this was also the case under the ICAC rules until their 2005 revision. Under section 1(6)) of the 1994 rules, the President of ICAC had indeed the power to order interim relief but this provision was deleted in the 2005 rules so that this prerogative is now solely that of the tribunal[341].

Institutional rules that confer the power to order provisional measures on the institution are admittedly rare. The traditional view that institutions should not deal with the merits of the disputes conducted under their auspices, even on a provisional basis, prevails at the great majority of institutions[342]. However, it would, again, be

335. Article 9A of the LCIA rules (2014) contemplates the expedited formation of the tribunal.
336. Article 29 of the ICC rules (2012), and Appendix II to the SCC rules (2010) both provide for the possibility for a party to seek the appointment of an emergency arbitrator. Another system is that of the ICC's pre-arbitral referee which allows parties, since 1990, to apply to a referee for urgent provisional measures prior to the commencement of arbitration proceedings. See "Website of the ICC's International Court of Arbitration, http://www.iccwbo.org/about-icc/organisation/dispute-resolution-services/icc-international-court-of-arbitration". See also Article 9B of the LCIA rules (2014).
337. Section 13 of the rules of the Arbitration Court Attached to the Czech Chamber of Commerce for instance provides: *"If requested by one of the parties in urgent matters, after the statement of claim has been filed, but before the arbitral tribunal is constituted, the President of the Arbitration Court may provide for conservation of evidence in a manner corresponding to the nature of the evidence and take other suitable measures to this effect"*.
338. Article R37 of the CAS Code (2013) provides, in relevant part: *"The President of the relevant Division, prior to the transfer of the file to the Panel, or thereafter, the Panel may, upon application by a party, make an order for provisional or conservatory measures"*.
339. Article 8 of the rules of arbitration of the Associazione Italiana per l'Arbitrato (AIA) (2012) provides that, before the formation of the arbitral tribunal and in the presence of a request for arbitration validly filed with AIA, any party may apply to the Permanent Committee for any interim measures listed at Article 19. In the original language: *"Prima della costituzione del tribunale arbitra le ed in presenza di una domanda per arbitrato A.I.A., la parte che vi abbia interesse può rivolgere istanza al Comitato permanente d'intervento per l'a dozione dei provvedimenti d'urgenza previsti dall'art. 19"*.
340. Article 3(4) of the arbitration rules of MAC (1994) provide: *"In cases subject to consideration by the MAC the Commission President may, at the request of a party, establish the amount and form of security for the claim, and, in particular, he may make a ruling to attach the other party's vessel or cargo in a Russian port"*.
341. See Khodykin, "International Commercial Arbitration Court (ICAC) and Maritime Arbitration Commission (MAC) at the Russian Federation Chamber of Commerce and Industry" 9. It is unclear why this provision was deleted. It would not be surprising if the ICAC leadership felt that this provision was not in line with international best practice, where (as discussed above) it is more common for the arbitrators to decide applications for interim measures.
342. See Chapter 3 below. Chapter 3 critically assesses the ways in which the functions of institutions have traditionally been depicted (or in other words the *"traditional representations"* of the functions of arbitral institutions). As discussed, in sections §3.02 and §3.03 of Chapter 3, arbitral institutions are either represented as *"a mere administrator with no decision-making power at all"*; or as *"occasional participants in the decision-making process*

incorrect to dismiss examples of institutions deciding applications on provisional measures as mere oddities in an otherwise uniform system. The institutions mentioned above, and in particular ICAC and MAC, are not insignificant institutions both historically and in terms of their annual caseload[343]. As unorthodox as it may seem to the western observer, the practice of institutions deciding provisional measure applications thus forms part of the reality of institutional arbitration.

[8] Consolidation of Proceedings

In light of the increase in the number of multi-party and multi-contract disputes[344], it is perhaps unsurprising that a number of modern institutional rules contemplate the consolidation of proceedings[345]. For present purposes, the term consolidation is understood to mean the merging of several existing arbitration proceedings into a single reference[346]. Consolidation is therefore distinct from the practice of "running

which decisions are immaterial" (because these decisions are said to be "purely administrative"). According to these traditional representations, arbitral institutions should not concern themselves with the merits of the dispute (e.g., issues of jurisdiction, liability, remedies/quantum and costs), and any decision on interim measures are for the arbitrators to take.

343. ICAC registered 241 new cases in 2012. "Website of the International Commercial Arbitration Court at the Chamber of Commerce and Industry of the Russian Federation (ICAC), http://www.tpprf-mkac.ru/en", 4 April 2014. This is comparable to the caseload of other established institutions like the LCIA (265 new cases in 2012), or the SCC (177 new cases in 2012). See, respectively, London Court of International Arbitration, "Registrar's Report (2012), available at http://www.lcia.org//LCIA/Casework_Report.aspx", 2013; Stockholm Chamber of Commerce, "The SCC in Numbers – Statistics 2012, available at http://www.offentligupphandling.se/?id=23696&newsid=44876" (24 January 2013). While MAC is a much smaller institution, it is the oldest arbitration institution in Russia, having been established in 1930. "Website of the Maritime Arbitration Commission at the Chamber of Commerce and Industry of the Russian Federation (MAC), http://www.tpprf-arb.ru/en/mac", 4 April 2014.
344. Nathalie Voser, "Multi-party Disputes and Joinder of Third Parties" in Albert Jan van den Berg (ed), *50 Years of the New York Convention: ICCA International Arbitration Conference in Dublin*, vol. 14 (Kluwer Law International 2009) 343, 343.
345. For Voser there is a trend of including of provisions on the subject in institutional rules. Voser, "Multi-party Disputes and Joinder of Third Parties" 405.
346. The rationale for allowing the consolidation of proceedings is both the promotion of efficiency and the prevention of inconsistent decisions. Significant savings of time and money (in particular in respect of the parties' legal costs) may be achieved when evidence is presented simultaneously to a single tribunal rather than to different tribunals. Likewise, a decision made in a single award eradicates the risk of inconsistent decisions that would otherwise exist absent consolidation. Born, *International Commercial Arbitration* 2069; Bernard Hanotiau, *Complex Arbitrations: Multiparty, Mulicontract Multi-Issue and Class Actions* (Kluwer Law International 2006) 179; Julie Chiu, "Consolidation of Arbitral Proceeding and International Arbitration" (1990) 7 Journal of International Arbitration, Kluwer Law International 53, 55. Difficulties associated with consolidation concern, *inter alia*, the selection of arbitrators, confidentiality and the apportionment of costs. Running proceedings concurrently, without consolidating them, also permits costs and time savings but does not guarantee that there will be no inconsistent decisions because the tribunals could be composed differently in the separate concurrent proceedings.

arbitrations concurrently", which does not require the amalgamation of all proceedings[347].

Consolidation presupposes the existence of more than one arbitration. It also generally presupposes that the arbitration clauses in each of the separate proceedings do not provide for arbitration under the auspices of two different institutions[348]. But beyond these two basic requirements, arbitral institutions' approaches to consolidation vary greatly. Under certain sets of rules, the power to consolidate proceedings belongs solely to the arbitral tribunal[349], whereas under others it is within the remit of the institution[350]. On rare occasions, the rules contemplate that both the institution and the tribunal may order consolidation[351]. More often, however, institutional rules remain silent on the issue[352].

When the applicable rules grant the power to an institution to consolidate proceedings, the requirements for the institution to be able to do so and more importantly the extent of the institution's discretion fluctuate greatly. In some rare instances, the rules provide that the institution may order consolidation but only with the agreement of all parties. This is the case at CIETAC and VIAC for example[353]. In other cases, consolidation may be ordered over the objection of some of the parties. This is the case in ICC, Swiss rules and SCC arbitrations[354]. Institutional rules will also often require one or more of the following conditions to be met:

347. Sheppard, "Chapter 23 – English Arbitration Act" 774. A first difference between the two notions is that, whereas in concurrent arbitrations the separate tribunals that have been appointed in each arbitration, may (theoretically at least) be composed differently, in a consolidated arbitration there is, by definition, only one tribunal. The second difference is that, whereas in concurrent arbitrations the tribunals will have to render separate awards in the different proceedings, albeit sometimes in quasi-identical terms, in a consolidated arbitration the tribunal may (and often will) render a single award against all parties to that arbitration. Born, *International Commercial Arbitration* 2068 footnote 2.
348. Hanotiau, *Complex Arbitrations: Multiparty, Mulicontract Multi-Issue and Class Actions* 179-180. In the context of the ICC see Grierson and Van Hooft, *Arbitrating Under the 2012 ICC Rules. An Introductory User's Guide* 122.
349. Article 22.3 Milan Chamber rules (2010).
350. Article 10 of the ICC rules (2012) contemplates three situations in which the ICC Court may consolidate: first where the different arbitrations are filed under the same arbitration agreement; second when all the parties agree to consolidation and third when the following three cumulative criteria are met: same parties, same legal relationship, compatible arbitration agreements. See also Article 13 CEPANI rules (2013).
351. Article R39 of the CAS Code (2013); Articles 22.1 (ix) & (x) and 22.6 of the new LCIA rules (2014).
352. See, for example, SIAC rules (2013) and DIS rules (1998). See also the 1998 version of the LCIA Rules.
353. Article 19 CIETAC (2015); Article 15.8 VIAC rules (2006); Article 10 CEPANI rules (2013). This requirement is peculiar because where all parties agree to consolidate proceedings it is hard to see how an institution could be said not to have the power to do so. It would appear therefore that a provision that allows consolidation but only with the parties' agreement serves little purpose. Indeed, it remains open to parties to terminate by agreement all existing arbitrations, and for the Claimant(s) to then re-file all claims under one single Request for Arbitration; effectively achieving the same results as consolidation (albeit at a higher cost).
354. As indicated above, Article 10 of the ICC rules (2012) contemplates consolidation not only when all the parties consent to it, but also where the different arbitrations are filed under the same arbitration agreement and when the following three cumulative criteria are met: same

(a) that the parties be identical in the different cases[355];
(b) that the disputes arise out of the same legal relationship[356];
(c) that the arbitration clauses be compatible[357]; and that
(d) a request for consolidation be made by one of the parties[358].

Some institutional rules will also impose some requirements regarding the timing of the application[359] or impose the prior consultation of the parties[360] or the tribunal(s)[361].

Overall, consolidation may be said to be an area where institutions enjoy a relatively significant measure of discretionary authority. This is because, contrary to what happens in other areas such as prima facie jurisdiction or even joinder, institutional decisions on consolidation are not subject to review by the arbitral tribunal once appointed[362]. In practice, this means that once proceedings have been consolidated by

parties, same legal relationship, and compatible arbitration agreements. Consolidation over the objections of a party is also possible under Article 4 of the Swiss rules (2012) and Article 10 of the SCC rules (2010).

This type of scenario, however, remains rare in practice. The ICC Court, for example, has been traditionally *"reluctant to order the joinder of two arbitrations over the objection of one of the parties"*. Hanotiau, *Complex Arbitrations: Multiparty, Mulicontract Multi-Issue and Class Actions* 182. Likewise, for the SCC, see Sidklev, "Arbitration Institute of the Stockholm Chamber of Commerce (SCC)" 167; and Marie Öhrström, "SCC Rules" in Rolf A Schütze (ed), *Institutional Arbitration: Article-by-Article Commentary* (Beck; Hart; Nomos 2013) 826.

355. Under a previous version of the ICC rules, the ICC Court could only consolidate proceedings when there was identity of parties (Article 4.6 ICC rules (1998)). Under the new Article 10 of the ICC rules (2012), the Court can now order consolidation even in case of diversity of parties if the parties have agreed to consolidation or if all of the claims in the arbitrations are made under the same arbitration agreement. Under Article 7 of the CAMEX rules (2009), if the parties are not identical than then agreement of all parties is necessary for consolidation to be ordered.

356. Article 10(C) ICC rules (2012); Article 11 SCC rules (2010); Article 7 CAMEX rules (2009). In the same vein, Article 28 of the HKIAC rules (2013) talks of "*the same transaction or series of transactions*" and of a *"common question of law or fact"*. Article 13 of the CEPANI rules (2013) talk of *"related or indivisible"* arbitrations. Interestingly, while the CAS Code does not require identity of legal relationship, it does require that the second Request for Arbitration be "*related*" both to the "*arbitration agreement*" of the first arbitration and to "*similar facts*". So, in a sense, a degree of convexity is required by the CAS Code. For appeals arbitrations, Article R52 only requires that the second appeal be "*related*" to the first one.

357. Article 10(C) ICC rules (2012); Article 28 HKIAC rules (2013).

358. Article 28 HKIAC (2013); and Article 11 SCC rules (2013). Under the CEPANI rules the institution can order consolidation even in the absence of any request from a party. Interestingly the CEPANI rules also contemplate that a tribunal may request the institution to consolidate proceedings. See Article 13 CEPANI rules (2013).

359. For instance, a requirement that the application for consolidation be made before the terms of reference are finalized. See Article 7 CAMEX rules (2009) (Under these rules consolidation is possible after the terms of reference are finalized but only by order of the tribunal and with the agreement of all parties).

Article 13 of the CEPANI rules (2013) for example provides that the consolidation may not be ordered where a decision has already been rendered with regard to preliminary measures, admissibility or the merits of a claim.

360. Article R39 CAS Code (2013); and Article 6 JAMS rules (2011).

361. Article 13 CEPANI rules (2013); and Article 6 JAMS rules (2011).

362. In this sense in the context of the ICC: Grierson and Van Hooft, *Arbitrating Under the 2012 ICC Rules. An Introductory User's Guide* 122.

an institution, it is no longer open to the arbitral tribunal to "disentangle" the proceedings. In other words, institutions' decisions on consolidation have an irremediable character which does not sit well with the traditional perception of institutions as mere administrators[363].

As indicated above, the measure of discretion conferred upon institutions in respect of consolidation fluctuates greatly from one set of rules to another. Within the spectrum of possibilities, the Swiss rules stand out by the unusually extensive power they confer on the Swiss Chambers. The rules indeed do not restrict the institution's consolidation powers by imposing any of the requirements discussed above (identity of parties; compatible clauses; same legal relationship). Article 4 of the Swiss rules merely requires that the institution consult with the parties and arbitrators and then "*take into account all relevant circumstances, including the links between the cases and the progress already made in the pending arbitral proceedings*".[364] It falls on the Swiss Chamber to decide which "*circumstances*" are "*relevant*", as well as what weight to give to individual "*circumstances*". Similar provisions may be found in the JAMS international arbitration rules[365] and the rules of the Danish Institute of Arbitration[366].

But does this discretionary power of institutions in respect of consolidation really matter in practice? After all, the differences between the way in which the parties put their case forward where proceedings are run concurrently and where they are consolidated are often imperceptible. In that context, it would be easy to conclude that any measure of discretionary power of institutions in respect of consolidation is inconsequential. Nonetheless, the practical consequences of a consolidation should not be underestimated. First, it is conceivable that consolidation may impact the seat of the arbitration. This will be the case when the second set of proceedings were to be conducted at a different seat from the first proceedings[367]. Further, wherever consolidation results in multiple claimants or multiple respondents (as it often does), the side where the parties number more than one will have to agree to make a joint appointment if they want to participate in the constitution of the arbitral tribunal[368]. If they do

363. See Chapters 4 and 5 below. Again, Chapter 4 critically assesses the two traditional representations of the functions of institutions (i.e., institutions as "*a mere administrator with no decision-making power at all*"; or as "*occasional participants in the decision-making process which decisions are immaterial*"). Chapter 5 offers a novel representation of the functions of institutions, which accommodates the adjudicatory powers occasionally exercised by institutions.

364. Article 4 Swiss rules (2012). What is more, Article 4 also provides that in case of consolidation "*the parties to all proceedings shall be deemed to have waived their right to designate an arbitrator, and the Court may revoke the appointment and confirmation of arbitrations* [...]".

365. Article 6.1 JAMS rules (2011).

366. Article 9 DIA rules (2013).

367. Consolidation of the second proceedings into the first one will most likely entail that the seat of the consolidated arbitration will be that of the first proceedings.

368. In the traditional bi-polar model of arbitration there are just two parties (one claimant and one respondent). See Jason A. Fry, Simon Greenberg, and Francesca Mazza, *The Secretariat's Guide to ICC Arbitration* (ICC 2012), 729 93. In such a configuration, where three arbitrators are to be appointed on the basis of party nominations, each party normally appoints an arbitrator, and the third and presiding arbitrator is then appointed either by the parties themselves jointly, or by the two co-arbitrators. When there is more than one party on either side (2 or more claimants or respondents), and when the arbitration clause provides for "*each side*" to

not, the institution will invariably insist on selecting all arbitrators in order not to jeopardize the enforceability of the award, in light of the Dutco jurisprudence[369]. In effect, this means that a decision to consolidate proceedings has the potential to impact on the composition of the arbitral tribunal in a manner that running cases concurrently does not. Naturally, the make-up of the tribunal might in turn affect the outcome of the case[370].

[9] Joinder of Third Parties

Institutional rules may contemplate the joinder of third parties to existing arbitration proceedings[371]. The term "*joinder*" means the addition, as claimant or respondent, of a person or entity that was not originally named as a party to the proceedings[372]. Contrary to consolidation, the majority of institutional rules confer the authority to order joinder on the tribunal[373] rather than on the arbitral institution itself[374]. Apart

nominate one arbitrator, the question arises whether multiple parties should be forced to make a single joint appointment, or whether each individual party should have a right to make its own appointment.

369. "Sociétés BKMI et Siemens v Société Dutco", Cour de Cassation 1992. In this case, the French *Cour de Cassation* annulled an ICC award where the two respondents had been refused the opportunity to make separate nominations (they had ultimately made a joint nomination but under protest) while the claimant was allowed to nominate "its" own arbitrator. The French Court held that the principle of equality of the parties in regards to party nominations was of public policy and that it could only be waived after the proceedings had started (not before through a mere agreement to arbitrate under the ICC rules). The principle established by the *Dutco* case has led institutions to revise their rules so that where the parties on one side number more than one (as a result of joinder or consolidation for example), and all parties on such side do not agree to make a joint nomination, then the institution will select all arbitrators. See Born, *International Commercial Arbitration* 2099; and Chiu, "Consolidation of Arbitral Proceeding and International Arbitration" 58.

    Generally, on the capacity of consolidation decisions by institutions to jeopardize the enforcement of awards, see Schlaepfer, "The Role of the Institution at the Commencement of the Proceedings" 59.

370. Gaillard and Pinsolle, "Advocacy in International Commercial Arbitration: France" 143; Beechey, "Advocacy in International Commercial Arbitration: England" 252; Christopher Seppälä, "Recommended Strategy for Getting the Right International Arbitral Tribunal: A Practitioner's View" (2009) 6 Transnational Dispute Management (TDM), 1-2. As previously indicated, for Barbara Steindl: *"The personality and background of an arbitrator strongly influence the way in which arbitrations are conducted and thus have a strong impact on the way in which the parties prepare and present a case"*. Steindl, "The Development of Due Process under the New York Convention" 262.

371. Rules that are silent on the subject include *inter alia* the ICDR rules (2014); CIETAC rules (2015); DIS rules (1998); KCAB rules (2011); WIPO rules (2002); BCICAC rules (2000); and ACICA rules (2016).

372. Voser, "Multi-party Disputes and Joinder of Third Parties" 347.

373. Article 22.1(viii) LCIA rules; Article 24.1(b) SIAC rules (2013); Article 4.2 Swiss rules (2012); Article 27 HKIAC rules (2013); Article 14 VIAC rules (2013); Article 6.2 JAMS rules (2011); Article 17.6 CRCICA rules (2011); Article 22.5 Milan Chamber rules (2010); Article 41 NAI rules (2010). Interestingly, if the NAI rules contemplate that the decision to order joinder belongs to the tribunal, the application for joinder shall be sent to the centre itself.

374. Article 7 ICC rules (2012); and Article 41 CAS Code (2013). Article 11 CEPANI rules (2013) confers the authority both the tribunal and to the institution to order joinder. Interestingly Article 28 of the ICAC rules (2010) contemplates joinder but does not state whether an

from that, many of the observations made above in respect of consolidation apply *mutatis mutandis* to the question of joinder. In particular, just like for consolidation, sets of rules that do confer to the institution the authority to join a third party are characterized by their diversity. The conditions required for the administrator to be able to order the joinder of a third party (and therefore the extent of the administrator's discretion) fluctuate significantly from one institution to the next. For example, in some instances joinder may only be ordered at the request of an existing party to the proceedings[375], whereas in other cases the third party itself may initiate the process[376]. On occasion, there are restrictions on the timing of joinder applications. For instance, there may be a requirement than any application must be made prior to the appointment or confirmation of tribunal[377] or before the filing of the respondent's statement of defence[378]. Often, there will be a requirement that the third party to be joined either consent to the joinder or otherwise be bound by the arbitration agreement[379].

While a decision made by an institution to join a third party is without prejudice to the tribunal's ability to decide whether or not it has jurisdiction over the third party being joined[380], the practical significance of an institution's power to join third parties is again not to be taken too lightly. A joinder decision alters the identity of the parties to the proceedings, albeit temporarily[381]. By operation of the institution's order, a party is added to the arbitration, pending a decision on jurisdiction by the tribunal. This means, first, that the order for joinder effectively enables the arbitral tribunal to make an award for or against the new party (subject to the tribunal's decision on jurisdiction) who would otherwise have been beyond the reach of the tribunal's decisions. Second, if the joinder of the third party is done prior to the appointment of the arbitrators, it will have the same impact on the constitution of the tribunal as was discussed above in

application is to be made to the institution, the tribunal or both. The same is true of the Zagreb rules (2002) (Article 17). It is to be assumed therefore that a request for joinder could be made to the institution. The question of who has the authority to decide on such a request is not essential in the context of ICAC-rules or Zagreb-rules arbitration because these rules (Article 28 ICAC, and Article 17 Zagreb respectively) request the consent not only of the third party to be joined but also of all the existing parties to the arbitration. In effect, where such unanimous consent is expressly given by all stakeholders, there is little need for the tribunal or the institution to engage in any assessment of a request for joinder; and the institution or tribunal merely have to take note of this unanimous agreement. When, however, the consent of one party is stated to be implied, then there is room for appreciation and the involvement of either the institution of tribunal would appear necessary.

375. See, for example, Article 7 ICC rules (2012).
376. Under Article 11 of the CEPANI rules the application maybe made by a party to the proceedings or by the third party to be joined.
377. Article 7 ICC rules (2012). See also Article 11 of the CEPANI rules under which, once the tribunal is appointed, the joinder requires the agreement of all parties and the third party.
378. Article 28 ICAC rules (2010).
379. Article 27.8 HKIAC rules (2013); Article 41.4 CAS Code (2013). Under Article 11 of the CEPANI rules (2013) there is a requirement that all parties and the third party have agreed to have recourse to arbitration under the CEPANI rules.
380. See, for example, Article 27.8 of the HKIAC rules (2013); Article 7 ICC rules (2012) referring to Article 6.3-6.6 of the rules on jurisdiction; or Article 41.4 CAS Code (2013). In the context of the ICC see Grierson and Van Hooft, *Arbitrating Under the 2012 ICC Rules. An Introductory User's Guide* 100.
381. That is to say pending any decision of the arbitral tribunal that it does not have jurisdiction over the third party being joined by the institution.

respect of consolidation[382]. Again, the make-up of the tribunal might in turn affect the outcome of the case[383].

[10] Constitution of the Tribunal: Decision on the Number of Arbitrators

A first aspect of the constitution of the tribunal with regards to which institutions may be called upon is that of the number of arbitrators. In the absence of an agreement between the parties, certain arbitration rules entrust the institution directly with the authority to decide whether the dispute shall be referred to one or more than one arbitrators. This is the case of the HKIAC and the NAI for instance[384]. A more common scenario is for the relevant rules to set out a default number, normally either one or three, whilst conferring on the institution a measure of discretion to decide otherwise where the circumstances warrant it. This is the case of the ICC rules which provide that:

> [w]*here the parties have not agreed upon the number of arbitrators, the Court shall appoint a sole arbitrator, save where it appears to the Court that the dispute is such as to warrant the appointment of three arbitrators*[385].

On rare occasions, however, the rules set a default number without conferring on the institution any discretion to depart from it, as in the case under the rules of CIETAC, DIS and the Danish Institute[386].

To use the words of Anne-Veronique Schlaepfer, institutional decisions on the number of arbitrators are of "*major importance*"[387]. This is principally for the following reasons. First, such decisions have costs implications, a three-member tribunal being more costly than a sole arbitrator[388]. Second, the decision will determine the manner in which the arbitrator(s) will be selected and therefore, influence the make-up of the tribunal. Indeed, when an institution opts for a sole arbitrator, the arbitrator is statistically more likely to be selected by the institution itself than by the parties jointly. This is because the parties will often fail to agree on a sole arbitrator. On the other hand, if a three-member tribunal is appointed, the parties will often be able to nominate at least two of the three arbitrators. In 2012, for example, only 17.2% of sole arbitrators in ICC arbitrations were appointed jointly by the parties (37 arbitrators out of 215). On

---

382. See the discussions above in relation to the issue of multi-party nominations and the consequences of the *Dutco* decision. See also Born, *International Commercial Arbitration* 2099.
383. Gaillard and Pinsolle, "Advocacy in International Commercial Arbitration: France" 143; Beechey, "Advocacy in International Commercial Arbitration: England" 252; Seppälä, "Recommended Strategy For Getting The Right International Arbitral Tribunal" 1-2; Steindl, "The Development of Due Process under the New York Convention" 262.
384. Article 6.1 of the HKIAC rules (2013) or Article 12 NAI rules (2010).
385. Article 12 of the ICC rules (2012). See also Article 5.4 LCIA Rules (1998); Article 5 ICDR rules (2009); Article 6.1 SIAC rules (2013); Article 6 Swiss rules (2012); Article 10 SCC rules (2010); and Article R40.1 CAS code (2013).
386. Article 23 CIETAC rules (2012); Article 3 DIS rules (1998) and Article 15 DIA (Denmark) rules (2013).
387. Schlaepfer, "The Role of the Institution at the Commencement of the Proceedings" 60.
388. Because the fees of three arbitrators need to be paid instead of only one.

the other hand, 93% of co-arbitrators were nominated by a party (701 out of 751)[389]. The profile of an arbitrator may vary depending on whether his selection is made by an institution or by a party[390]. This is because institutions and parties will seek to achieve different objectives with their nominations of arbitrators. While parties may be expected to try to appoint arbitrators favourably pre-disposed towards their case[391], institutions will be more concerned with such issues as the enforceability of the award or the celerity of the proceedings[392]. The make-up of the tribunal itself will influence the way in which the parties will have to put their case forward[393]. In short, a decision on the number of arbitrators may have some impact on the wider proceedings.

[11] Constitution of the Tribunal: Selection of Arbitrators

One of the key roles of arbitral institutions consists of facilitating the constitution of an arbitral tribunal where the parties are facing a deadlock. In fact, this role has come to be so indissociable from arbitral institutions that during the drafting of the 1976 UNCITRAL rules, it was assumed that the "appointing authority" would necessarily be an arbitral institution[394].

There are a number of variations from one set of institutional rules to the next as to the manner in which arbitrators may be designated in the absence of agreement between the parties. For present purposes, one should note that, in cases of deadlock, institutional rules will almost universally entrust the institution with some authority to

389. International Chamber of Commerce, "2012 Statistical Report" (2013) 24 ICC Bulletin, Bulletin 6, 11.
390. In this sense, albeit implicitly, see Gaillard and Pinsolle, "Advocacy in International Commercial Arbitration: France" 144.
391. Seppälä, "Recommended Strategy For Getting The Right International Arbitral Tribunal" 3; Paulsson, "Moral Hazard in International Dispute Resolution, Inaugural Lecture as Holder of the Michael R. Klein Distinguished Scholar Chair University of Miami School of Law on 29 April 2010" 13; Adrian Winstanley, "Arbitral Appointments at the LCIA" (2013) 1 ABA Newsletter, Section of International Law, International Arbitration Committee 31, 31. In the same sense, albeit implicitly, see Pierre Yves Tschanz, "Advocacy in International Commercial Arbitration: Switzerland" in R. Doak Bishop (ed), *The Art of Advocacy in International Arbitration* (1st edn, Juris 2004) 197. For a practical illustration of the impact of the choice of arbitrator on the outcome of a case see Gaillard and Pinsolle, "Advocacy in International Commercial Arbitration: France" 144-147.
392. Naturally, the profile may also depend on the position of the arbitrator being selected (co-arbitrator, Chair or sole), as different attributes may be perceived, by the parties and the institution, as desirable for these different positions. Institutions will often also seek to achieve a balance of competence on the tribunal as a whole. See Seppälä, "Recommended Strategy For Getting The Right International Arbitral Tribunal" 23; see also Bühler and Webster, *Handbook of ICC arbitration* 142. Other factors that an institution, but not necessarily a party, could look at include achieving a balance in the seniority of arbitrators, and any national and/or cultural characteristics of the parties or the co-arbitrators. See Winstanley, "Arbitral Appointments at the LCIA" 32.
393. Gaillard and Pinsolle, "Advocacy in International Commercial Arbitration: France" 143; Beechey, "Advocacy in International Commercial Arbitration: England" 252.
394. See Christopher Kee, "The Evolving Role of an Appointing Authority" in Stefan Michael Kröll and Loukas A. Mistelis (eds), *International Arbitration and International Commercial Law: Synergy, Convergence and Evolution* (Kluwer Law International 2011) 304.

make default appointments[395]. The possibility to select the decision-maker being considered as one of the key reasons why corporations opt for arbitration instead of court litigation[396], it is not surprising that most institutional rules give great deference to the parties for the constitution of the tribunal. It is, indeed, for the parties in the first place to designate the arbitrators under the rules of a majority of leading institutions including *inter alia* the ICC, CIETAC, HKIAC, SIAC, SCC, Swiss Chambers[397]. However, the level of deference to the parties for the designation of arbitrators varies from one institution to the next. The rules of some institutions, for example, provide that sole arbitrators or Chairs of three-member tribunals be selected by the institution itself, rather than by the parties jointly or by their nominees. In "appeals arbitrations" under the CAS code for instance, it is for the President of the CAS Division to appoint the sole arbitrator or the Chair of the tribunal[398]. This is also the case of Chairmen in arbitrations conducted under the LCIA India rules, which provide that "[i]*n the case of a three-member Arbitral Tribunal, the Chairman (who shall be neither party-nominated, nor nominated by the parties' nominees or by any third party) shall in all cases be selected by the LCIA Court*"[399].

The selection of the arbitrators that will decide a case is an important task. For many commentators it is one of the most important decisions made by a party in an arbitration[400]. This is because, as discussed above, the make-up of an arbitral tribunal

395. Article 12 of the ICC rules (2012); Article 6 ICDR rules (2009) and Article 12 ICDR rules (2014); Articles 24-26 CIETAC rules (2012) and (2015); Articles 7-8 HKIAC rules (2013); Articles 7-8 SIAC rules (2013); Articles 7-8 Swiss rules (2012); and Article 13 SCC rules (2010); Article 21 PCC (Warsaw) rules (2007); Articles 11-12 ACICA rules (2016); Article 14 CAM rules (2009); Articles 17-18 FCC (2013) and Articles 13-14 NAI rules.

396. See in this sense the findings of the 2006 International Arbitration Survey: Queen Mary, University of London, "Corporate Attitudes and Practices" (2006).

397. Article 12 of the ICC rules (2012); Articles 24-26 CIETAC rules (2012); Articles 7-8 HKIAC rules (2013); Articles 7-8 SIAC rules (2013); Articles 7-8 Swiss rules (2012); and Article 13 SCC rules (2010). The LCIA rules, on the other hand, provide that it is for the LCIA Court to make all appointments, unless the parties have agreed otherwise. See Article 5.5 of the LCIA rules (1998). In practice, this means that whenever parties have omitted to provide for party-nominations in their arbitration clause and the parties are not then able to reach an agreement on the same once the dispute has arisen, it is for the LCIA to designate all arbitrators. Whilst the ICDR rules do contain express wording as to party nominations (Article 6 ICDR rules (2009)), the position is similar to that of the LCIA, namely that whenever parties have omitted to provide for party-nominations in their arbitration clause and the parties are not then able to reach an agreement on the same once the dispute has arisen, it is for the institution to designate all arbitrators. The position under Article 14 of the Milan Chamber's rules (2010) is interesting in that it finds itself halfway between the LCIA's and the ICC's approaches: in the absence of an agreement of the parties, the institution has the default power to select a sole arbitrator, but for three-member tribunals, the default is for the parties to make nominations.

398. Article R54 of the CAS code (2013).

399. Article 5.6 of the LCIA India rules (2010).

400. For Juliet Blanch, for instance, "[t]*he choice of arbitrator is one of the most important decisions a party can make in the course of the arbitration*". Blanch, "Appointment and Confirmation of Arbitrators" 65. In the same sense see, Karl-Heinz Bockstiegel, "Commercial and Investment Arbitration: How Different Are They Today?" (2012) 28 Arbitration International, Kluwer Law International 577-590; Jeff Waincymer, *Procedure and Evidence in International Arbitration* (Kluwer Law International 2012) 275; R. Doak Bishop, "Toward a Harmonized Approach to Advocacy in International Arbitration" in R. Doak Bishop (ed), *The Art of Advocacy in International Arbitration* (1st edn, Juris 2004) 457-458.

has the potential of affecting the outcome of the case[401]. From a practical point of view, the decisions of an institution in respect of the selection of arbitrators are thus very significant.

[12] Constitution of the Tribunal: Confirmation of Arbitrators

The rules of a number of institutions provide that any nomination made by a party be subject to confirmation by the institution itself. As discussed above[402], this is the case under the rules of the ICC, LCIA, HKIAC, SIAC and the Swiss rules[403]. This is also the practice at the SCC despite the fact that the rules do not expressly contemplate confirmation of tribunals[404]. Institutions with rules that contain no requirement of "confirmation" are relatively rare. They include the ICDR, ACICA, JAMS, and the PCC (Warsaw) but also ICSID[405].

The aim of a requirement that party-appointed arbitrators be confirmed is twofold: First, it acts as a quality control device for the institutions, in the sense that it gives them an opportunity to ensure that any nominee is adequately qualified[406]. Second, it gives the institutions an opportunity to ensure that arbitrators are impartial and independent of the parties. This is because under the rules of a number of

401. Gaillard and Pinsolle, "Advocacy in International Commercial Arbitration: France" 143; Beechey, "Advocacy in International Commercial Arbitration: England" 252; Seppälä, "Recommended Strategy For Getting The Right International Arbitral Tribunal" 1-2; Steindl, "The Development of Due Process under the New York Convention" 262.
402. See above the paragraphs on the requirement of a "permanent organisation" for the definition of the notion of "institutional arbitration".
403. Article 13 ICC rules (2012); Article 5(5) of the LCIA rules (1998); Article 9 HKIAC rules (2013); Article 6.3 SIAC rules (2013) and Article 5(1) Swiss rules (2012).
404. See Magnusson, "The Practice of the Arbitration Institute of the Stockholm Chamber of Commerce – An Inside View" 53.
405. Though Rule 6 of the ICSID Arbitration Rules contemplates that the constitution of the tribunal only becomes effective upon the notification by the Secretary General to this effect.
406. The institution's "quality control" can extend beyond requirements contained in the parties' arbitration clause. According to Grierson and Van Hooft, the ICC Court could refuse the confirm an arbitrator based on lack of availability. Grierson and Van Hooft, *Arbitrating Under the 2012 ICC Rules. An Introductory User's Guide* 134. Mohamed Abdel-Raouf indicates for instance that under its new rules CRCICA could refuse a nomination on the basis of an arbitrator's past failures to comply with his duties under the CRCICA. Abdel Raouf, "New Rules of the Cairo Regional Centre for International Commercial Arbitration (CRCICA)" 9. Another "quality control" device that achieves a similar result to arbitrators' confirmation is to require any nomination to be made from a roster put together by the institution. In such a case the "vetting" of the arbitrators is done before any nomination is made. CIETAC adopts a hybrid system whereby parties can nominate arbitrators form CIETAC's panel, but if they nominate outside the panel, then confirmation by CIETAC of the nominee is required. Article 24 CIETAC rules (2012). Another example of such a hybrid solution may be found at the maritime arbitral chamber of Paris (Chambre Arbitrale Maritime de Paris). See Emmanuel du Pontavice, "Un centre spécialisé: La chambre arbitrale maritime de Paris" (1990) 1990 Revue de l'Arbitrage 239, 242.

institutions, any nominee is required to provide a statement of acceptance, impartiality and independence[407] before his confirmation by the institution[408].

The task of confirming an arbitrator will often appear rather mechanical. On occasion, however, it may become a complex one, in particular in circumstances where a nominee's statement of independence and impartiality is accompanied by a disclosure. In such a case, the process of confirmation may involve seeking and reviewing submissions from the parties in response to the disclosure. For Schlaepfer and Bartsch, the institution then has to "[...] *make a balance between a party's right to choose an arbitrator, on the one hand, and the necessity to make sure that all arbitrators are impartial and independent, on the other hand*"[409]. Ultimately, deciding whether to confirm the arbitrator means assessing the risk of challenges post-appointment, while keeping in mind the desirability of giving effect to a party's first choice of arbitrator.

In practice, absent a disclosure by the nominee in respect of his independence or impartiality, or an express requirement as to qualifications of arbitrators contained in the parties' agreement, an institution is unlikely to reject a party-nomination[410]. But if refusals to confirm a nominee are likely to be uncommon, it remains that the institution's task of deciding whether or not to confirm an arbitrator is an important one. When confirmation of arbitrators is a requirement of the applicable rules, the parties and their nominees quite simply may not proceed with the arbitration until and unless all arbitrators have been confirmed by the institution. An extreme example is that of the LCIA rules under which, until the LCIA Court has "*appointed*" the tribunal, the arbitrators (whether nominated by the parties, the LCIA Court or someone else) do not constitute an "arbitral tribunal" under the rules, and are therefore unable to make an award. In other words, confirmation in the context of the LCIA rules has for effect to turn "candidate arbitrators"[411] into an arbitral tribunal.

407. Accompanied, as the case may be, with a CV and a disclosure of any circumstances that could give rise to doubts as to the nominee's impartiality or independence.
408. See Article 11 of the ICC rules (2012); Article 5.3 LCIA rules (1998); Article 7 ICDR rules (2009); Article 29 CIETAC rules (2012); Article 14 SCC rules (2010); Article 10.4 SIAC rules (2013). Article 9 Swiss rules (2012) and R33 CAS code (2013) both require that the candidate arbitrators disclose any relevant circumstances but they do not expressly mention the completion of a statement or form to be addressed to the institution.
409. Schlaepfer and Bartsch, "Swiss Chambers' Court of Arbitration and Mediation (Swiss Chambers)" 10.
410. For the SCC, Magnusson, "The Practice of the Arbitration Institute of the Stockholm Chamber of Commerce – An Inside View" 47. Based on the author's own experience, over the period 2009-2011, the LCIA did not reject a single party nomination for reasons other than lack of independence or impartiality or due to an express requirement contained in the relevant arbitration clause. See in the same sense the ASA survey of institutional arbitration which claims that 27% of institutions have had cases where they refused to confirm a nomination. Statistic based on a sample of twenty-two institutions. Hofbauer, Burkart, and Tari, "Survey on Scrutiny of Arbitral Institutions" 11.
411. The term "candidate arbitrators" is the actual term used by the LCIA in correspondence with the parties to refer to any individual selected as arbitrator prior to his or her confirmation by the LCIA Court.

[B] The Proceedings Proper (from the Constitution of the Tribunal to the Award)

Once a tribunal is in place, some institutions become less involved in the arbitration and let the tribunal assume primary responsibility for it[412]. This does not mean that institutions cease to have any responsibility in the proceedings, post-appointment. A number of institutional rules entrust the institution with responsibilities of varying importance in the phase that follows the constitution of the arbitral tribunal. These responsibilities are discussed below.

[1] Approval of Terms of Reference

Where the relevant institutional rules contemplate the entering into of terms of reference after the appointment of the tribunal, it is not uncommon for the rules to entrust the institution with a number of responsibilities in this respect[413]. The ICC for instance has the authority to approve the terms of reference when one party refuses to sign them. In addition, it has the power to extend the two-month deadline for the finalization of the terms of reference[414]. Similar rules may be found in the CAMEX rules in Mexico[415], the KIAC rules in Rwanda[416] or the CEDRAC rules in Cyprus[417]. Interestingly, the CEDRAC rules go further as they also contemplate that the "[...] *arbitral tribunal may request the CEDRAC to prepare with the parties a draft of terms of reference*".

[2] Logistical Support

A useful function of arbitral institutions, post-appointment, is to provide the parties and the tribunal with logistical support[418]. In this respect institutions may, for instance,

412. According to Magnusson the SCC is an example of institution that becomes less involved post appointment. See Magnusson, "The Practice of the Arbitration Institute of the Stockholm Chamber of Commerce - An Inside View" 53. To the contrary, CIETAC remains very involved post appointment. Lu Song, "The New CIETAC Arbitration Rules of 2012" (2012) 29 Journal of International Arbitration, Kluwer Law International 299, 313-314; Xiaobing Xu and George D. Wilson, "One Country, Two-International Commercial Arbitration-Systems" (2000) 17 Journal of International Arbitration, Kluwer Law International 47-106.
413. The Terms of Reference are a document, which is intended to be signed by all parties to an arbitration and the tribunal, recording the details of the arbitral tribunal, the parties and their counsel, and the parties' claims. Terms of reference also record any agreement reached as to procedure that may have been reached at that early stage. Grierson and Van Hooft, *Arbitrating Under the 2012 ICC Rules. An Introductory User's Guide* 147.
414. Two months from the transmission of the file to the tribunal. Article 23.2 ICC rules (2012).
415. Article 29 CAMEX rules (2009).
416. Article 29 KIAC rules (2012).
417. Article 15 CEDRAC rules (2012).
418. Very rare are the institutions that profess not offering any logistical support. One example is the Finish institution, FCC. The institutions that do offer logistical support include *inter alia*, ICC, LCIA, ICDR, CIETAC, HKIAC, SIAC, the Swiss Institution, SCC, CAS, WIPO, CRCICA, KCAB, NAI, CAM, JAMS, Milan Chamber, PCC (Warsaw), DIA, VIAC, ICSID (information based on these institutions' responses to the questionnaires sent out by the author). The PCA also

rent out or book hearing rooms; offer or secure the services of court reporters and interpreters; make catering arrangements for any hearing; provide video-conferencing or other telecommunication facilities; book accommodation for tribunal members, and secure travel visas for any witnesses, counsel or arbitrators[419].

Another aspect of the logistical support of institutions concerns channels of communications[420]. The rules and practices of institutions vary greatly in this respect but most institutions assume some responsibility, whether it is serving of the Request for Arbitration on all respondents at the beginning of the proceedings[421]; notifying awards at the end[422]; channeling all communications between the parties and the arbitrators prior to appointment[423], or simply monitoring communications to ensure that all parties are kept in copy at all times[424]. On a more interventionist side of the spectrum, CIETAC will channel all communications between the parties and the tribunal unless the parties have agreed otherwise. This includes communications exchanged post-appointment of the tribunal[425]. As explained by one author, "[p]*ursuant to the current practice, which has been retained by the 2012 Rules, the CIETAC Secretariat serves as a central hub of exchange of all arbitration documents among the parties and the tribunal, a service most international arbitral institutions do not render*"[426].

As discussed above, the rather routine tasks of channeling communications or of monitoring that there are no breakdowns in communications between the parties and the tribunal may prove invaluable at the enforcement stage. As previously indicated, recognition and enforcement of an award may be refused under Article V(1)(b) of the

---

provides logistical support in the cases it administers. Manuel Indlekofer, *International Arbitration and the Permanent Court of Arbitration* (Wolters Kluwer Law & Business 2013) 340. Sometimes this role is expressly set forth in the rules. For example, Article 9 of the ACICA rules (2016).

419. Information based on institutions' responses to the questionnaires sent out by the author.
420. Sam Aaron, "International Arbitration III: Choosing an Arbitration Institution and a Set of Rules" (1991) 108 South African Law Journal 306, 306.
421. As indicated above this is the case under Article 4(5) of the ICC rules (2012); Article 3(6) of the Swiss rules (2012); Article 7 of the VIAC rules (2013); Article 7(1) of the NAI rules (2010); Article 9 of the Milan rules (2010); and Article 8 of the CAMEX rules (2009).
422. Article 34 of the ICC rules (2012); Article 26.7 LCIA Rules (2014); Article 30.4 ICDR rules (2014). See also the CIETAC rules which are silent on the subject but which implicitly require any award to be sent by the tribunal to the institution, as it states that *"the seal of CIETAC shall be affixed on the arbitral award"*. Article 49.4 CIETAC rules (2015). To the contrary, under Articles 32.6 of the Swiss rules (2012) and 36.4 of the SCC rules (2010) it is for the tribunal to send the award to the parties and the institution.
423. Article 3.3 LCIA rules (2014).
424. For HKIAC see: Neil Kaplan, "HKIAC's Perspective on Arbitration and Conciliation Concerning China" in Albert Jan van den Berg (ed), *New Horizons in International Commercial Arbitration and Beyond*, vol.12 Kluwer Law International 2005) ICCA Congress Series 55, 57.
For the LCIA: Winstanley, "Review of the London Court of International Arbitration" 46.04.
425. Article 20 of the CIETAC (2015).
426. Song, "The New CIETAC Arbitration Rules of 2012" 308.

New York Convention if the party against whom the award is invoked was not given proper notice of the proceedings or was otherwise unable to present his case[427].

[3] Treatment of Costs

Another key function of institutions, post-appointment, concerns the treatment of arbitration costs[428]. The term "arbitration costs" means the tribunal's and the institution's respective fees and expenses, as distinguished from the legal and other costs of the parties.

Institutional rules invariably reserve to the institution some authority in respect of costs. Often this includes the authority to decide the quantum of the tribunal's and/or the institution's fees, as well as approving any expenses[429]. Sometimes this also includes the power to request from the parties the payment, in advance, of sums calculated to cover the anticipated costs of the arbitration ("deposits"); and the ancillary authority to hold and disburse such deposits[430]. In some rare instances, lastly

427. See in this respect the discussions contained in Chapter 5 below (under *"Proposition 3: Materiality of institutional decisions"*), where the impact of notifications on the enforceability of arbitral awards is discussed.

428. Aaron, "International Arbitration III: Choosing an Arbitration Institution and a Set of Rules" 306; Blackaby, Partasides, Hunter, and Redfern, *Redfern and Hunter on International Arbitration* 56; Born, *International Commercial Arbitration* 150.
This is often seen as an advantage of institutional arbitration over ad hoc proceedings. First because the involvement of an institution avoids any potentially awkward misunderstandings or disagreements between the parties and the arbitrators on what can be a sensitive matter (for obvious reasons, parties often feel that it is difficult to query the quantum of the fees or expenses of an individual who is empowered to decide their case.). Second, it reduces the risk of mistakes in respect of the calculation of these arbitration costs. Third, arbitrators do not have to concern themselves with the logistics of handling advances on cost (including such issues as the opening of different bank accounts or ledgers for each of arbitration, or liaising with the parties with respect to the payment of the advances). In the words of Lew and Mistelis, this permits arbitrators to *"maintain a certain level of material detachment"*. See Lew, Mistelis, and Kröll, *Comparative International Commercial Arbitration* 37. On one view, this material detachment is precisely what has led the working group of the UNCITRAL in charge of the 2010 revision of the UNCITRAL rules to confer increased powers on arbitral institutions in relation to costs (new powers under Article 41 to review the basis on which the tribunal's fees are calculated; and power to make adjustments to the tribunal's decision on costs if the fees are manifestly excessive). See Kee, "The Evolving Role of an Appointing Authority" 312.

429. Article 37 ICC rules (2012); Article 28.1 LCIA rules (2014); Article 32 SIAC rules (2013); Article 43.2 SCC rules (2010); Article R64.4 CAS code (2013); and Article 14 of ICAC rules (2010) and ICAC's Schedule of Arbitration Fees and Costs.
If Article 33 of the HKIAC rules (2013) provides that it is for the tribunal to fix the costs including the centre's own charges, the rules in fact contemplate that the tribunal's determination be made *"in accordance with* [the] *Schedule* [of Costs]". The same solution applies under the Swiss rules (Article 39 (2012) rules). This has led some authors to comment that the role of the Swiss institution is limited in respect of costs compared to that of other institutions. Schlaepfer and Bartsch, "Swiss Chambers' Court of Arbitration and Mediation (Swiss Chambers)" 11. Under the ICDR rules, if it is for the tribunal to *"fix the costs of the arbitration"* (which include both the tribunal's and the centre's fees) in the first place, the ICDR nevertheless scrutinizes bills of arbitrators before paying them. Article 34 ICDR rules (2014). See on this point Fellas, "AAA/ICDR International Arbitration Rules" 496.

430. Article 36 ICC rules (2012); Article 24 LCIA rules (2014); Article 30.2 SIAC rules (2013); Article 45 SCC rules (2010); Article 40 HKIAC rules (2013); and Article R64.2 CAS code (2013). Under

this may include the power to decide the apportionment of the parties' own legal and other costs[431].

An exhaustive description of the rules and practices of the major institutions in this respect exceeds the scope of this study. It should be noted for present purposes that what characterizes such rules and practices is, again, their great diversity[432]. In particular, the scope of institutions' powers over arbitration costs varies significantly from one set of institutional rules to another. In ICC arbitrations, for example, the institution takes a leading role vis-à-vis the arbitral tribunal, both in relation to deposits and to the determination of the actual costs. For Jason Fry, "[i]*n ICC arbitration, the Secretariat and the Court manage the entire financial side of the proceedings* [...]"[433]. The opposite may be said of the Swiss Chambers, which rules rely on the tribunal more heavily in respect of costs[434]. As Habegger explains:

> *In contrast to the ICC and other institutional rules, the Swiss Rules vest the arbitral tribunal not the institution with the authority to request the parties to pay deposits, administer the deposits if so requested by the Secretariat, suspend or terminate the proceedings if deposits are not paid, and to render an accounting of the deposits*[435].

A point worthy of attention is that of the authority conferred on some institutions to treat a claim as withdrawn where a party fails to pay a deposit. Under a number of institutional rules, indeed, when a party finds itself in breach of a direction to lodge an advance on the costs of the arbitration, the institution has the authority to decide that the claim of that party shall be treated as having been withdrawn[436]. This is the case at

Article 33 of the ICDR rules (2009) the "*administrator*" only has the power to direct the payment of an initial deposit. Once a tribunal is appointed, further deposits are directed by the tribunal.

431. SIAC's schedule of costs for example contemplates that when a tribunal does not proceed with the assessment of the quantum of the parties' own legal and other costs, the parties may refer such question to the centre. Lawrence Boo, "Singapore International Arbitration Centre" in Loukas A. Mistelis and others (eds), *The World Arbitration Reporter*, vol. 3 (Juris 2010) 36.
432. To mention only a few points: some institutions use an *ad valorem* system while some others apply an hourly rate to quantify the arbitrators' fees and the institution's charges. Some (but few) institutions employ a hybrid system combining the *ad valorem* and the hourly rate systems. Some institutions require all deposits to be paid upfront while some others direct such deposits to be paid at different stages of the proceedings. At the end of the process the arbitration costs are sometimes "determined" by the institution itself. Sometimes it is by the arbitral tribunal. Some institutional rules contain provisions on the apportionment of costs; some others don't, some rules provide for the joint and several liability of the parties regarding the tribunal's and the institution's costs etc.
433. Fry, "ICC International Court of Arbitration" 9.
434. Schlaepfer and Bartsch, "Swiss Chambers' Court of Arbitration and Mediation (Swiss Chambers)" 11.
435. Habegger, "The Revised Swiss Rules of International Arbitration: An Overview of the Major Changes" 283. Likewise see Article 47 of the ACICA rules (2016) and Article 41 Swiss rules (2012).
436. "Sanctions" others than the forced withdrawal of a claim are occasionally found in institutional rules. Article 7.3 of the ICAC rules, for instance, states that if a party appoints as arbitrator a non-Russian resident, that party shall be required to deposit an advance corresponding to the anticipated costs of the participation of such arbitrator in hearings in Russia (travelling expenses, accommodation, visa etc.); if the party concerned fails to pay this additional advance, that party "*shall be deemed to have waived his right to appoint an arbitrator, and the ICAC Presidium shall appoint an arbitrator for the party*". A similar, but not

the ICC, the LCIA, CIETAC, SIAC, SCC, WIPO, VIAC and the CAS[437]. Occasionally it is the arbitral tribunal, rather than the institution which is granted this power[438].

A provision of this sort results in the defaulting party's claim not being considered by the arbitral tribunal. Of course, the decision to treat the claim as withdrawn is without prejudice to the defaulting party's right to initiate new arbitration proceedings, when that party has secured the resources necessary to fund the proceedings. But the practical importance of a decision to treat a claim as withdrawn should not be underestimated. While there are no available statistics on the subject, anecdotal evidence suggests that parties whose claims are treated as withdrawn are then rarely able to gather the resources necessary to fund new proceedings. This means that a decision to treat a claim as withdrawn for failure to lodge a deposit often ends up being the final decision on a matter. This is particularly notable because, occasionally, a claimant's inability to pay a deposit will have been caused by the very actions of the respondent which are the object of the arbitration. When this is the case, institutional provisions which allow a claim to be treated as withdrawn will appear particularly severe for the indigent claimant/counterclaimant. In this context it is unsurprising that the Court of Appeal of Paris recently decided to annul an arbitral award in which an insolvent respondent's counterclaim had been treated by the ICC as withdrawn in application of the then Article 30(2) of the 1998 ICC rules[439]. The decision of the Court

---

identical, provision may be found at Article 82,1 of the CIETAC rules, which reads: *"Where a party has nominated an arbitrator but fails to advance a deposit for such actual costs as the special remuneration, travel and accommodation expenses of the nominated arbitrator within the time period specified by CIETAC, the party shall be deemed not to have nominated the arbitrator"*. It may be the case that under the CIETAC rules, contrary to the ICAC rules, the party concerned may nonetheless make a re-nomination after having paid the required deposit.

Interestingly, Article 72.3 of the 2012 CIETAC rules contains another "sanction": when an oral hearing is to take place elsewhere than at CIETAC, the parties may be requested to pay a deposit to cover the travel and accommodation expenses incurred by the tribunal in relation to the hearing; in the event a party fails to lodge the required deposit, the rules provide that *"the oral hearing shall be held at the domicile of CIETAC or its relevant sub-commission/center"*. A similar provision may be found in Article 82.3 of the 2015 version of the rules.

437. Article 36 ICC rules (2012); Article 24.3 LCIA rules (2014); Article 15.3 CIETAC rules (2012) (for counterclaims only); Article 30.5 SIAC rules (2013); Article 45.4 SCC rules (2010); Article 70(e) WIPO rules (2002); Article 34.3 and 34.4 VIAC rules (2006); Article R64.2 of the CAS code (2013). Interestingly, Article 14 of the ICAC rules does not provide that a claim may be treated as withdrawn but simply provides that the arbitration *"may not proceed"* until the relevant deposit has been paid. On the other hand, Article 7.2 of the ICAC schedule of cost provides that ICAC may *"make performance of any acts in the arbitration of a dispute subject to payment"* of an additional deposit (i.e., a deposit that is due in addition to the "Arbitration Fee"). This provision arguably gives even more power to ICAC than traditional provisions as to the consequences to attach to non-payment of a deposit.

438. Article 36.3 of the ICDR rules (2014). It should be noted however that this provision provides the tribunal with the power to *"order the suspension or termination of the proceedings"*, rather than the withdrawal of a particular claim. It must also be noted that the 2014 ICDR rules confer such a power to the Administrator prior to the appointment of the tribunal. Once the tribunal is appointed the power of termination or suspension is vested with the tribunal. See also, Article 40.4 HKIAC rules (2013); Article 41.4 Swiss rules (2012).

439. "Société Licensing Projects SL v Société Pirelli, Cour d'Appel de Paris, 17 November 2011". See Elie Kleiman and Claire Pauly, "Award Annulled Due to Withdrawn Counterclaims

of Appeal was based on the ground that the respondent was in bankruptcy proceedings at the time, so that the possibility that it may at a later stage introduce a request for arbitration in respect of its counterclaims was purely *"theoretical"*. The decision illustrates the potential materiality of institutional decisions by which a claim is treated as withdrawn[440].

[4] Challenges to, and Removal of, Arbitrators

In light of the allegedly increasing number of challenges to arbitrators[441], an important function of arbitral institutions post-appointment relates to the determination of such challenges[442]. Many institutional rules assign to the institution itself the power to decide such challenges and, incidentally, to remove an arbitrator where a challenge is upheld. This is the case of the ICC, the LCIA, ICDR, CIETAC, SIAC, SCC, the CAS, ICAC WIPO, the Swiss rules, the Milan Chamber rules, the ACICA rules and the CAMEX rules to cite only a few[443]. In some jurisdictions, domestic statutes even reserve to the local arbitral institution (i.e., to the exclusion of the local courts) authority to make decisions on challenges[444]. In fact, it is unusual for a set of arbitration rules not to bestow on the

---

Introduced by Insolvent Defendant" (International Law Office (online commentaries), available at http://www.internationallawoffice.com 12 April 2012).

440. If the decision was then annulled by the Cour de Cassation ("Société Licensing Projects SL v Société Pirelli, Cour de Cassation, 28 mars 2013"), the court nonetheless maintained that in some circumstances the refusal by a tribunal to look at a counterclaim (for lack of payment of the deposit or otherwise) can constitute a breach of due process which would justify refusing the enforcement an award, but only if the counterclaims are in fact *"indissociable from the main claims"* (in effect if they are claims of set off rather than independent counterclaims). In this particular case, the Cour de Cassation found that the Court of Appeal of Paris had failed to establish that the counterclaims were indissociable from the main claims. The principle therefore remains that in some instances a withdrawal of a counterclaim may lead to the non-enforcement of an award.

441. This alleged trend was noted by Aguilar Alvarez as early as the 1990s. See Guillermo Aguilar Alvarez, "The Challenge of Arbitrators" (1990) 6 Arbitration International, Kluwer Law International 203, 205. In the context of the SCC see Larsson and Magnusson, "Recent Practice of the Arbitration Institute of the Stockholm Chamber of Commerce: Prima Facie Jurisdiction and Challenges of Arbitrators" 48.

442. Aaron, "International Arbitration III: Choosing an Arbitration Institution and a Set of Rules" 309-310; Born, *International Commercial Arbitration* 148. The role of institutions in respect of decision on challenges constitutes another advantage of institutional arbitration over ad hoc proceedings. This is because institutional procedures are both quicker and more cost efficient than referring a challenge to the courts and because institutions have particular expertise in dealing with challenges. Mohammed Bedjaoui, "Challenge of Arbitrators" in Albert Jan van den Berg (ed), *International Arbitration in a Changing World* vol. 6 (Kluwer Law International 1993) ICCA Congress Series 85, 98.

443. Articles 14-15 ICC rules (2012); Article 10.2; 10.6 LCIA rules (2014); Articles 13-14 ICDR rules (2014); Article 32 CIETAC rules (2015); Articles 11-13 SIAC rules (2013); Articles 9-11 Swiss rules (2012); Article 15 SCC rules (2010); Article R34 CAS Code (2013); Article 18 ICAC rules (2010); Articles 24-29 WIPO rules (2002); Article 19 Milan Chamber rules (2010); Article 18.4 ACICA rules (2016); and Article 17 CAMEX rules (2009). Interestingly, under Article 14 of the DIA (Denmark) rules (2008), a challenge may be raised not only by a party but also by an arbitrator.

444. The Russian Arbitration Act, for example, provides, in respect of ad hoc arbitrations, that where a challenge is rejected by the arbitral tribunal, a party may appeal the tribunal's

institution the power to make decisions on challenges. When this happens the responsibility tends to be either left to the arbitral tribunal or to the domestic courts[445].

Again, while a comparative analysis of the major institutional rules regarding challenges is beyond the scope of this study, the following observations may be made for present purposes. First, like in other areas, procedures and practices in respect of challenges vary greatly from one institution to the next. Variations concern *inter alia* time limits for challenges to be made, whether proceedings are suspended pending determination of challenges[446], the requirement for a reasoned decision[447], and the possibility for the parties[448], the arbitrator concerned[449] or the other arbitrators[450] to make submissions in response to a challenge. Second, the degree of discretion conferred on institutions as to how they handle challenges also varies from one institution to another. Some institutions have extensive discretion in how to handle

decision to the Presidium of the Russian Chamber of Commerce and Industry (under which auspices ICAC and MAC operate). See Sergey Yuryev and Kantyrev, "Arbitration in Russia" in Torsten Loercher and others (eds), *CMS Guide to Arbitration* (4th edn, CMS Legal Services 2012) 662. See also Khodykin, "International Commercial Arbitration Court (ICAC) and Maritime Arbitration Commission (MAC) at the Russian Federation Chamber of Commerce and Industry" 4-5.

445. The new (2010) rules of the NAI for instance do not contemplate that challenges to an arbitrator be decided by the institution itself. Instead, Article 64 of the NAI rules (2010) states that "*If the place of arbitration is within the Netherlands, the Preliminary Relief Judge of the District Court of Rotterdam shall have jurisdiction in the matters referred to in* [...] *Article 1035(2) CCP with regard to the challenge of an arbitrator* [...]". Under the old rules, (2001) the Executive Board of the NAI had the power to decide challenges (former Article 19.7). Likewise, under Article 18.2 of the DIS rules (1998) it is for the tribunal to determine challenges. Another example may be found in the rules of arbitration of the Court of Arbitration at the Bulgarian Chamber of Commerce and Industry, where a decision on a challenge is to be made by the tribunal. Under Rules 9 of the ICSID Arbitration rules, the other arbitrators are first to seek to agree on a challenge and only in case of disagreement will the matter be referred to the Chairman of the Administrative Council.

446. This is also relatively uncommon. Examples include Article 12.2 SIAC rules (2013); and at Article 27 WIPO rules (2002).

447. The new Article 10.6 of the 2014 LCIA rules require the LCIA to communicate reasons for its challenge decisions. Most institutional rules do not contemplate the issue of reasoned decisions on challenges. Article 11.4 ICC rules (2012); Article 12 Swiss rules (2012); and Article 29 WIPO rules (2002) expressly state that the decisions are not reasoned. Interestingly, Article 30.6 of the CIETAC rules provide both possibilities (decision of CIETAC with or without reasons). In the silence of the rules, the SCC Board has taken the approach of not providing reasons. Öhrström, "SCC Rules" 831. On the other hand, offering reasoned decision is the practice at the SIAC and at the ICC (despite the fact that the rules are silent). In this sense see Hwang, Boo, and Han, "National Report for Singapore (2011)" 18. For the ICC see the communication of the ICC dated 8 October 2015 at http://www.iccwbo.org/News/Articles/2015/ICC-Court-to-communicate-reasons-as-a-new-service-to-users. The same was also the case at the LCIA under the 1998 rules. In this sense see Gerbay, "London Court of International Arbitration" 17. Article 10.6 of the new (2014) rules, however, makes this a requirement for the LCIA. Article 34 CAS Code (2013) contemplates expressly reasoned and published decisions: "*The ICAS Board or ICAS shall give brief reasons for its decision and may decide to publish it*".

448. See, for example, Article 14.3 ICC rules (2012); Article 15.3 SCC rules (2010); Article R34 CAS Code (2013); and Article 26 WIPO rules (2002).

449. See for instance Article 14.3 ICC rules (2012); Article 15.3 SCC rules (2010); and Article R34 CAS Code (2013).

450. This is more uncommon. See Article 14.3 ICC rules (2012); Article 15.3 SCC rules (2010); and Article R34 CAS Code (2013).

what can be described as "proceedings inside the proceedings". For example, some institutions have discretion as to whether to follow the original nomination process when an arbitrator is replaced[451]. Some can decide not to replace an arbitrator that has been successfully challenged and to proceed with a truncated tribunal[452]. On a more practical plane, some institutions have the authority to extend the time limits within which a challenge can be made[453].

Many institutional rules also contemplate the removal, by the institution, of arbitrators absent a challenge by a party – that is to say of their own volition. This is the case of the rules of the ICC, LCIA, CIETAC, SIAC, HKIAC, SCC, WIPO, ICAC, the Swiss rules, the CAS code, and Milan Chamber rules, to cite only a few[454]. In the absence of challenge, the circumstances which will allow the removal of an arbitrator include not only unreasonable delay and the inability of an arbitrator to discharge his duties[455], but also failure to comply with the applicable institutional rules[456]. Not all institutional rules, however, confer on institutions the authority to remove arbitrators *proprio motu*. The ICDR rules, for instance, do not contemplate that the institution may remove an arbitrator outside of challenges or when an arbitrator has passed away. Just like the confirmation of arbitrators nominated by the parties, the power to remove arbitrators *proprio motu* seems to serve as a quality-control function by the institutions. It is a powerful tool which allows the institution to keep control over the proper conduct of the proceedings post-appointment. The mere threat of removal appears as a persuasive incentive for the arbitrator concerned to proceed with the arbitration more expeditiously in cases of undue delay[457]. This power may arguably be seen as a corollary to the power to confirm the appointment of arbitrators[458]. Interestingly, and as discussed above, the ICDR rules do not contain any requirement that arbitrators nominated by

451. Article 15.4 ICC rules (2012); Article 11.1 LCIA rules (2014); Article 12.2 HKIAC rules (2013); Article 17.2 SCC rules (2010).
452. Article 15.5 ICC rules (2012); Article 32 CIETAC rules (2012); Article 13 Swiss rules (2010); Article 20.3 ICAC rules (2010). The SCC can do so even when the challenged arbitrator was nominated by a party. Öhrström, "SCC Rules" 833. The power to decide to proceed with a truncated tribunal is an important one, because it affects the power balance within the tribunal, in particular when the challenged arbitrator is a party-nominee and it can therefore have a real impact on the outcome of the case.
453. This is the case of the ICC. Aguilar Alvarez, "The Challenge of Arbitrators" 206-207.
454. Article 15.2 ICC rules (2012); Article 10 LCIA rules (2014); Article 33.1 CIETAC rules (2015); Article 14.3 SIAC rules; Article 11 HKIAC rules (2013); Article 12 Swiss rules (2012); Article 16 SCC rules (2010); Article R35 CAS code (2013); Article 19 ICAC rules (2010); Article 32 WIPO rules (2002); Article 20 Milan Chamber rules (2010); Article 19 ACICA rules (2016).
455. Nathalie Voser, "Removal, Resignation, Dismissal and Replacement of Arbitrators" in Philipp Habegger and others (eds), *Arbitral Institutions Under Scrutiny* (JurisNet 2013), ASA Special Series No. 40 74.
456. As noted by Voser, the circumstances which can give rise to removal of arbitrators vary from institution to institution. Voser, "Removal, Resignation, Dismissal and Replacement of Arbitrators" 87.
457. Hofbauer, Burkart, and Tari, "Survey on Scrutiny of Arbitral Institutions" 26.
458. Article 14.9 of the DIA (Denmark) rules (2008) illustrates the interrelationship between confirmation and revocation by addressing both issues in the same provision: "[e]*ven in the absence of a challenge* [...], *the chairmanship of Danish Arbitration may decide not to appoint an arbitrator or to revoke his appointment if it finds that there are justifiable doubts as to the impartiality or independence of the arbitrator, or if it finds that he does not possess the qualifications agreed on by the parties*".

the parties be confirmed by the institution. It is perhaps not surprising therefore that the ICDR rules do not also contemplate the power of the institution to remove arbitrators *proprio motu*.

Statistics show that, removal of arbitrators in circumstances other than party challenge is uncommon[459]. Likewise, challenges are rarely successful and, more often than not, there is thus no need to proceed to the replacement of a challenged arbitrator[460]. Nonetheless, a decision to remove an arbitrator, whether in the context of a challenge or not, is an important one because of its potential impact on the outcome of the case[461]. As discussed previously, the choice of the individuals that sit on a tribunal can have a direct impact of the outcome of the case. Interestingly, as discussed in some detail in Chapter 4 below, the materiality of challenge decisions is underscored by the fact that such decisions have given rise, over the years, to proceedings in the domestic courts; be it when the challenge decision itself is the object of an "attempted appeal" before the national judge[462] or when the award of the tribunal is attacked at the enforcement stage[463].

[5] General Power of Interpretation of the Rules

Some sets of institutional rules contain a general provision which provides the institution with the power to interpret its own rules where they are ambiguous. This is

459. In 2010 for example, only 6 arbitrators were replaced in ICC arbitrations by the ICC court on its own initiative (i.e., outside of challenges) because the arbitrator had become unable to proceed with the arbitration. See Paula Hodges, Chris Parker, and David Ackebo, "International Chamber of Commerce (ICC)" in Karyl Nairn and Patrick Heneghan (eds), *Arbitration World: Institutional & Jurisdictional Comparisons* (4th Revised edn, Thomson Reuters 2012), The European Lawyer Reference 114. That year, 793 new Requests for Arbitration were filed with the ICC Court. See "Website of the ICC's International Court of Arbitration, http://www.iccwbo.org/about-icc/organisation/dispute-resolution-services/icc-international-court-of-arbitration" In the same sense, Hofbauer, Burkart, and Tari, "Survey on Scrutiny of Arbitral Institutions" 25.
460. An old study of challenges at the ICC between 1983 and 1989 showed that 82.1% of challenges were rejected. Study cited by the then General Counsel of the ICC, Guillermo Aguilar Alvarez. Aguilar Alvarez, "The Challenge of Arbitrators" 205. For the SCC, see Larsson and Magnusson, "Recent Practice of the Arbitration Institute of the Stockholm Chamber of Commerce: Prima Facie Jurisdiction and Challenges of Arbitrators" 48.
461. Aguilar Alvarez, "The Challenge of Arbitrators" 205. Talking of the disruptive character of challenges on the proceedings, Aguilar Alvarez notes the essential role played by institutions to guarantee the effectiveness of the system.
462. J. Y. Art, "Challenge of Arbitrators: Is an Institutional Decision Final?" (1986) 2 Arbitration International, Kluwer Law International 261-265. Examples of cases filed before the French and Swiss courts in France include *inter alia*: "Raffineries de Pétrole d'Homs et de Banias v Chambre de Commerce Internationale", Cour d'Appel de Paris 1985; "Société Opinter France v. S.A.R.L. Dacomex", Cour de Cassation, 2 Ch. civ. 1987; "Arab Republic of Egypt v Westland Helicopters Ltd.", Swiss Federal Tribunal 1984. These cases are discussed in Chapter 3 below.
463. Allegations of bias of the decision maker may give rise to arguments against enforcement under several prongs of Article V of the New York Convention, including, for example, Article V(1)(b) (party was unable to present his case); Article V(1)(d) (composition of the tribunal or procedure not in accordance with the agreement of the parties or the law of the country where the arbitration took place); and Article V(2)(b) (public policy). See the discussions of the relevance of institutional decisions at the enforcement stage under Article 5 of the New York convention in Chapter 5 below (under *"Proposition 3: Materiality of institutional decisions"*).

the case of the CIETAC rules, for example, which provide: "[t]*hese Rules shall be interpreted by CIETAC*"[464]. Occasionally, institutional rules will specify that the power of interpretation belongs both to the arbitral tribunal and to the institution. The ICDR rules for instance provide: "[t]*he tribunal shall interpret and apply these Rules insofar as they relate to its powers and duties. The administrator shall interpret and apply all other Rules*"[465]. In most cases institutional rules remain silent on the subject of interpretation[466].

When this is the case, however, it is difficult to imagine that an institution would have no authority to interpret its own rules. It would appear, indeed, that some measure of discretionary power in the interpretation of the rules is necessary for the institution to be able to discharge its functions. In particular, any power of the institution which entails some decision-making seems to imply, as a corollary, the power to interpret the terms of the rules and apply them to the circumstances of the case. For instance, deciding any applications for consolidation or for joinder, or determining challenges to arbitrators, appear necessarily to require the ability to decide what the requirements of the rules for joinder, consolidation or the removal of arbitrators are; and how such requirements apply to the facts of the case[467]. The contrary would lead to deadlocks whenever the parties disagree between themselves, or whenever one party disagrees with the institution on the interpretation of a particular provision.

464. Article 83 CIETAC rules (2015). In this respect, Michael Moser considers that CIETAC itself is thereby "*vested with powers which are normally reserved to the arbitral tribunal*". Michael J. Moser, "CIETAC Arbitration: A Success Story?" (1998) 15 Journal of International Arbitration, Kluwer Law International 27, 31. A similar approach is taken by the BAC rules at Article 65 of the Rules (2008).
465. Article 39 of the ICDR rules (2014). See also Article 3 HKIAC rules (2013). Because of their permanent nature, institutions are arguably better placed than tribunals to collect knowledge as to prior interpretations of their rules. This raises the question of the benefit of leaving interpretation issues to arbitral tribunals only. In practice, where tribunals are called upon to pass a judgment on the meaning of a provision of the rules, it is not uncommon that they would seek the views of the institution itself. In this respect, the permanent nature of institutions raises a number of questions including that of whether there is such a thing as "precedents" in the interpretation of the rules. If so, should such precedents be made widely available to users?
466. Examples of institutional rules that are silent include *inter alia*: the LCIA rules (1998 and 2014); SIAC rules (2013); Swiss rules (2012); SCC rules (2010); ICAC rules (2010). It should be noted that if the SIAC rules are silent it is the practice of SIAC to publish "Practice Notes" which aim at clarifying of SIAC applies its own rules among other things. In a similar vein, DIAC is working on an "*internal policy document on the basis of a select body of precedent awards to ensure consistent decision-making in the application of the provisions of the DIAC Rules over time*". This policy document "[...] *may be made accessible to the public for better guidance on the application of the DIAC Rules in due course*". Blanke and Abi Habib, "Arbitration in Dubai: A Basic Primer" 220.
467. This second task may be more accurately described as "construction" of the rules, rather than "interpretation". Black's Law dictionary defines "interpretation" as the term used for the explanation of the true meaning of a written document or statement. On the other hand, one definition of "construction" given by Black's Law Dictionary is the application of obscure or ambiguous terms or provisions in a statute, written instrument, or oral agreement to a case. "Black's Law Dictionary, 2nd Online Edition, available at http://thelawdictionary.org, Accessed 15 February 2016".

On one view, the parties' agreement to "institutional arbitration", which in the sense assigned to it in Chapter 1 implies a consent to confer on the institution some authority in the implementation of the rules, encompasses an agreement to submit to the authority of the institution to interpret its own rules. This is, it seems, the view taken by Tilia Maria de Hancock, for whom the role of the institution under the ICC rules (which are silent on interpretation) does include the "*interpretation of the rules of the Court*"[468]. This, incidentally, is consistent with the position taken by the French courts in the *Société Appareils Dragon* case[469].

In this case (which is discussed in more detail elsewhere below[470]), the company "Appareils Dragons" contested before the Court of Appeal of Paris the decision of the ICC to prolong the six-month period for the issue of the arbitral award[471], and on that basis was asking for the annulment of the arbitral award. One argument of the applicant was that the ICC was an agent of the parties ("*mandataire des parties*") and that therefore it was bound by a duty to inform the parties of the fact that the Chairman of the tribunal had applied to the ICC for a prolongation of the six-month period. A second argument was that the institution was under a duty to provide a reasoned decision (to extend the period). The Court of Appeal rejected the request of Appareils Dragon. Appareils Dragon then appealed to the Cour de Cassation[472] asking it to quash the decision of the Court of Appeal. Here again the applicant argued that: (1) the ICC was an agent of the parties and that therefore it had a duty of information, and (2) the finding of the Court of Appeal that the ICC had no duty to provide a reasoned decision, was not compatible with the nature of the ICC rules of arbitration. The French Cour de Cassation rejected the applicant's demand both as to the alleged requirements of information and of reasoned decision. What is interesting for present purposes is that, the court's decision appeared based on the grounds that the ICC had discretion in the interpretation of its own arbitration rules (une "*interpretation souveraine*") in order to decide not to inform the parties regarding the application for a prolongation; discretion which does not appear expressly in the rules[473].

468. de Hancock, "The ICC Court of Arbitration: The Institution and its Procedures" 26. In the same sense, a former Secretary General of the ICC explains that the ICC Secretariat routinely helps tribunals "*understand*" the rules (which seems to mean understand how the ICC would like the tribunal to apply the rules): "*In general terms, the Secretariat is a source of information for parties and arbitrators in respect of matters related to the understanding of the ICC Arbitration Rules and the way they operate. It does so either through direct exchanges with the parties or the arbitrators, or through notes and other documents issued by the Secretariat with the approval of the ICC Court* [...]" Horacio Grigera Naón, "The Role of the Secretariat of the International Court of Arbitration" (1997) The New 1998 ICC Rules of Arbitration - ICC Bulletin Special Supplement, 19.
469. "Société Appareils Dragon, Cour d'Appel de Paris, 22 June 1982 (Revue de l'Arbitrage, 1982, at p. 91)", p., Cour d'Appel de Paris 1982; "Société Appareils Dragon, Cour de Cassation, 2ieme Chambre Civile, 8 June 1983 (Revue de l'Arbitrage, 1987, at p. 309)".
470. Chapter 3 ("*The Traditional Representations of the Role of Institutions: A Critical Evaluation*"), section §3.02[A][2] ("*Origins of the Representation*").
471. Provided for in what was then Article 18 of the ICC rules, now Article 30.
472. France's highest court for civil and commercial matters.
473. See "Société Appareils Dragon, Cour d'Appel de Paris, 22 June 1982 (Revue de l'Arbitrage, 1982, at p. 91)"; and "Société Appareils Dragon, Cour de Cassation, 2ieme Chambre Civile, 8 June 1983 (Revue de l'Arbitrage, 1987, at p. 309)".

The prospect that arbitral institutions may have some inherent powers of interpretation raises a number of questions: What is the extent of this power of interpretation? Can the institution's own interpretation of a provision prevail over a conflicting interpretation shared by all the parties? Post-constitution of the tribunal these difficulties do not disappear. To the contrary, they only seem to gain an extra layer of complexity where the arbitral tribunal's interpretation differs from the institution's and the parties'. Questions that arise at that stage include for example: If the rules are silent, do both the institution and the tribunal have power to interpret the rules? In case of conflict which interpretation prevails[474]? Answering the above questions is beyond the scope of this part of the book, which only aims at giving an overview of the functions of institutions. These questions, however, are the object of detailed discussions in Chapter 4 (which discusses the traditional theoretical representations of the role of institutions). For present purposes it suffices to note that a power of interpretation is inherent to the notion of institutional arbitration, as defined in Chapter 1.

[6] General Supervision Role

Certain arbitral institutions exercise a general monitoring role over the proceedings, including after the tribunal has been constituted. This ensures, *inter alia*, that the tribunal and the parties are proceeding as expeditiously as possible and that the procedure is in keeping with due process[475]. This general supervisory role is sometimes described as a benefit of institutional arbitration. In the words of Professor Fouchard, for example:

> [t]*he success of institutional arbitration has a very simple reason: the efficiency that the supervision of the proceedings by an experienced permanent institution seems to offer. The institution can prevent any delay or paralysis of the proceedings that might arise as a result of the bad faith or negligence of a party or an arbitrator* (Translation by the author)[476].

474. In this respect, it is interesting to note that the HKIAC rules actually address the issue of conflict with the tribunal: *"HKIAC shall have the power to interpret all provisions of these Rules. The arbitral tribunal shall interpret the Rules insofar as they relate to its powers and duties hereunder. In the event of any inconsistency between such interpretation and any interpretation by HKIAC, the arbitral tribunal's interpretation shall prevail"*. Article 3 HKIAC rules (2013). The HKIAC rules however are unique in this respect. Other institutional rules do not address the issue of overlap.

475. The ASA survey of institutional arbitration claims that 73% of institutions have a time-control procedure in place (statistic based on a sample of twenty-two institutions). Hofbauer, Burkart, and Tari, "Survey on Scrutiny of Arbitral Institutions" 25.

476. In the original language: *"Son succès tient notamment à une raison fort simple: l'efficacité que semble assurer à l'arbitrage ainsi 'administré' l'intervention d'un organisme permanent et expérimenté. Celui-ci peut, à tout instant, empêcher que la procédure soit paralysée ou retardée par la mauvaise volonté ou la négligence d'une partie ou d'un arbitre"*. Fouchard, "Les Institutions Permanentes d'Arbitrage Devant le Juge Etatique (A Propos d'une Jurisprudence Récente)" 226. In the same sense, see also Aaron, "International Arbitration III: Choosing an Arbitration Institution and a Set of Rules" 306; Blackaby, Partasides, Hunter, and Redfern, *Redfern and Hunter on International Arbitration* 55; and Smit, "Future of International Commercial Arbitration" 15.

Many institutions state that they exercise a degree of monitoring over the proceedings including, for example, the ICC, LCIA, ICDR, ICSID, the Swiss Chambers, SIAC, the CAS, JAMS, WIPO, the Milan Chamber, the CRCICA, CEPANI, NAI, ACICA, KCAB, VIAC, BCICAC, CAMEX, the DIA, the Croatian Chamber of Economy, the PCC (Warsaw)[477]. In the ICC's own words, the functions of the ICC Court include: "*Monitoring the arbitral process from the filing of the request for arbitration to the notification of the final award to ensure that it proceeds in accordance with the Rules and with the required commitment to diligence and efficiency*"[478].

The extent to which an institution monitors the proceedings post-appointment varies greatly from one institution to another[479]. In fact, "post-appointment supervision" is arguably the area where the sharpest differences can be seen in terms of the degree of interference of the institutions with the proceedings. As discussed elsewhere[480], the diversity of practices between institutions as to the extent of this monitoring role has led some commentators to distinguish between "*supervised*" institutional arbitration form "*un-supervised*" institutional arbitration[481]. What varies is not only the extent to which the institution "keeps an eye" on the proceedings (i.e., some institutions read all correspondence exchanged between the parties[482] while some others only look at key submissions, procedural orders or awards)[483]. It extends also to the frequency of the intervention and the types of situations where the

477. Information based on the institutions' responses to the questionnaires sent out by the author.
478. "Website of the ICC's International Court of Arbitration, http://www.iccwbo.org/about-icc/organisation/dispute-resolution-services/icc-international-court-of-arbitration" under Home > About ICC > Organisation > Functions of the ICC International Court of Arbitration.
479. For Hofbauer, Burkart, and Tari, "*The supervision by the arbitral institutions over the proceedings may differ from institution to institution as well as the level of quality control exercised by these institutions*". Hofbauer, Burkart, and Tari, "Survey on Scrutiny of Arbitral Institutions" 2.
480. See section §3.04[B] of the present Chapter ("*Diversity of Institutional Interventionism Expressed as a Spectrum/Continuum*").
481. See Thompson, "Building an Arbitration and Mediation Centre: From International Foundations to Domestic Rooftops': The Establishment of the British Columbia International Commercial Arbitration Centre" 202-203. Gerold Hermann, "Power of Arbitrators to Determine Procedures under the UNCITRAL Model Law" in Albert Jan van den Berg (ed), *Planning Efficient Arbitration Proceedings: The Law Applicable in International Arbitration* vol. 7 (Kluwer Law International 1996) 39, 42. Blackaby, Partasides, Hunter, and Redfern, *Redfern and Hunter on International Arbitration* 54, at footnote 180.
482. For example, the LCIA. Although, according to Adrian Winstanley, "[the LCIA] *endeavours to intervene only as and when necessary, which will depend to some extent upon the relative sophistication and experience of the parties, their lawyers and the tribunal*". Winstanley, "Review of the London Court of International Arbitration" 3. In a different ball game, the Secretariat of ICSID follows the cases even more closely, with each Counsel being allocated only half a dozen cases. By contrast, Counsels at LCIA Secretariat are allocated up to sixty or so cases. The difference is explained by the fact that ICSID Counsels are often appointed as secretaries to the tribunals. Their unusually intense involvement in the monitoring of the proceedings includes serving as the official channel for the transmission of written submissions and evidence between the parties and the tribunals and keeping minutes of hearings. See Lucy Reed, Jan Paulsson, and Nigel Blackaby, *Guide to ICSID Arbitration* (2nd edn, Kluwer Law International 2011) 9. It may also include organizing a preliminary conference with the parties under Rule 21 of the ICSID Arbitration Rules.
483. For example, the CRCICA. Information provided by the institution in its response to our questionnaire.

institution will decide to intervene[484]. The nature of the "intervention"[485] also varies. Some institutions prefer merely to draw a tribunal's attention to the relevant provisions of the rules, while some others may go as far as "*inviting*" or even "*requesting*" a tribunal or parties to adopt a course of action[486]. Overall, however, it appears that "[m]*ost institutions have procedures in places for guiding arbitrators and parties through the arbitral proceedings, set time-limits for certain procedural steps and remind the arbitral tribunal as well as the parties of running deadlines*"[487].

In some rare instances, the staff of the institution participates in meetings, conference calls or hearings alongside the arbitral tribunal. Case-handlers at the ICDR for instance may arrange a preliminary conference with the parties at the beginning of the proceedings to explain some aspects of the ICDR rules[488]. In a different genre, ICSID counsels are often appointed secretaries to the tribunals, thereby gaining a much deeper involvement in the proceedings than case-handlers at most commercial arbitration institutions[489]. In those institutions which share the heritage of the soviet chambers of trade[490], it is customary for the case handlers to attend, as "*reporters*", not only hearings but also deliberations of the tribunal, of which they sometimes even take minutes with a view to facilitating the scrutiny of the award at a later stage[491].

Here again, lack of detailed provisions in institutional rules as to the extent of the institution's role in respect of supervision may raise difficulties in practice. In particular, this raises the question of whether, and if so when, an institution can require a tribunal and/or the parties to adopt of certain course of action. For a former Secretary General of the ICC:

484. Hofbauer, Burkart, and Tari, "Survey on Scrutiny of Arbitral Institutions" 24.
Some institutions like WIPO will intervene mostly to ensure that the proceedings progress expeditiously (without delay). Others like CRCICA will intervene to ensure that equality between the parties is respected. Information provided by the institution in its response to our questionnaire.
485. As previously indicated (in this Chapter's Abstract), The term "*intervention*", is used in this book as a generic term to describe any action that may be taken by an arbitral institution in respect of proceedings administered by it. Such intervention may be decisional in nature (e.g., extension of deadline, seat, consolidation, language etc.), or non-decisional (e.g., advice to a tribunal as to how the rules function, drawing the tribunal's attention as to a problem, logistical support etc.). In the context of the present discussions of the monitoring role of institutions, intervention refers more specifically to an institution's "contribution" or "involvement" which was not solicited by the parties and/or the arbitral tribunal which aim at keeping the arbitral procedure in line with the institution's expectations.
486. The Milan Chamber of Commerce for example states that its supervisory role involves "*competence over all matters relating to the administration of arbitral proceedings*" including "[issuing] *all orders relating thereto*" in such matters as independence and impartiality of arbitrators, the respect of due process, on time and costs of the proceedings. Information provided by the institution in its response to our questionnaire.
487. Hofbauer, Burkart, and Tari, "Survey on Scrutiny of Arbitral Institutions" 25.
488. Appel, "International Centre for Dispute Resolution (ICDR)" 83.
489. Reed, Paulsson, and Blackaby, *Guide to ICSID Arbitration* 9.
490. Like ICAC or CIETAC.
491. Chen, "International Law Reporter" 336; Ivan Zykin, "Procedural Aspects of the Activities of Institutional Arbitration Bodies" in Kaj Hobér and others (eds), *Between East and West: Essays in Honour of Ulf Franke* (Juris 2010) 606.

> [...] *the ICC Court's Statutes provide that the Court's function is "to ensure the application of the* [ICC] *rules". This clearly implies some obligation to ensure that arbitrators conduct the proceedings in accordance with those rules. But the rules' lack of specificity with regard to so many matters leaves the arbitrators with considerable freedom and power. In the absence of a clear breach by an arbitrator of a provision of the Rules, therefore, the ICC has generally been reluctant to interfere with the arbitrator's conduct of the case or to second guess the fairness or suitability of a particular procedural decision*[492].

The impact that an institution's general supervisory role may have on the proceedings, depends on the scope of the supervision. The more interventionist the institution is, the more this supervision may be said to restrict the tribunal's autonomy in deciding the case. Of course, interventions[493] made in the context of the institution's general supervisory role do not normally concern the merits of the dispute[494]. Institutional intervention may nonetheless prove significant in practice. In one case, for example, the institution's intervention aimed at clarifying the identities of the parties to the arbitration where both the tribunal and the parties had been inconsistent on the matter. In this case the parties had entered into a Master Agreement setting out the basic terms and conditions under which the claimant would provide various services to the respondent. The Master Agreement did not require the claimant to perform any services until the respondent had issued a "Work Release". Various disputes having arisen under separate Work Releases, the claimant commenced an arbitration in accordance with the clause contained in the Master Agreement. The difficulty was that, on the respondent's side, the different Work Releases had been entered into by many different entities of the same group of companies, so that it was difficult to identify the "right" respondent. The claimant therefore filed a Request for Arbitration naming, as respondents, as many companies of the group as it could, "casting its net" as broadly as possible. Surprisingly perhaps, counsel for the "respondents" did not raise any jurisdictional objection in the Response to the Request for Arbitration in respect of any of the entities named as respondents by the claimant. In fact, counsel for the respondents – apparently inadvertently – even listed as respondents additional entities of the group. In subsequent submissions (i.e., statement of claim and statement of defence) both sides added yet other entities as "respondents". To add a layer of complexity, the tribunal itself, in its procedural orders and other communications, referred inconsistently to the "respondents". The end result was that it was unclear who the parties to the arbitration were. In order to avoid having an arbitral award

492. Schwartz, "The Role of the Arbitral Institution in the New Millennium" 324-325.
493. As indicated above, in the context of the present discussions of the monitoring role of institutions, the term "intervention" means one that aims at keeping the arbitral procedure in line with the institution's expectations.
494. As explained in Chapter 5 below (under *"Proposition 2: Ancillary nature of the role of the institution"*), a common feature observed across all institutions studied for this book is that the entirety of the power to decide the merits of the dispute rests with the arbitral tribunals (to the exclusion of arbitral institutions).

issued in respect of ill-identified parties[495], the institution invited, on multiple occasions, the parties and of the tribunal to clarify the identities of the parties to the arbitration. Ultimately, and after several protracted meetings and conference calls between members of the institution's secretariat and the tribunal, the institution managed to convince the tribunal to obtain written confirmation from both sides as to the precise identities of the parties to the arbitration[496]. After that, the tribunal and the parties proceeded with the arbitration, and an award was issued (and ultimately enforced) in respect of the "correct" parties. Though this scenario is presumably rare, it nonetheless illustrates the fact that institutions will occasionally forcefully "advocate" with a tribunal the "correct" course of action – a course of action which may then ultimately be followed by the arbitral tribunal.

The persuasiveness of institutions should not be underestimated. One may wonder for instance whether arbitrators do not have an incentive to proceed in a manner consistent with the expectations of the institution if they wish to be reappointed by it[497]. In addition, the threat of "Sanctions" by institutions when an arbitrator fails to discharge his duties appears to be a potentially persuasive tool to assist institutions in the exercise of their supervisory roles. Such sanctions can include, for example, the replacement of an arbitrator[498] or a reduction in the arbitrator's fees[499]. The use of sanctions, or at least their threat, appears not to be infrequent in practice. Only one-third of the institutions consulted by the ASA in their survey do not provide for sanctions when an arbitrator is performing poorly[500].

Overall, therefore, the general monitoring role exercised by certain institutions may occasionally impact the manner in which proceedings are conducted by the arbitral tribunal. As explained above, this general supervisory role constitutes one of the perceived benefits of institutional arbitration[501].

495. Which might have rendered the award unenforceable under Article V of the New York Convention.
496. And to record the name of such parties by way of a procedural order.
497. In particular for arbitrators who are relying on institutional appointments for their livelihood.
498. Many institutions have the power to remove an arbitrator in the absence of a challenge made by a party. See, for example, Article 15.2 ICC rules (2012); Article 10 LCIA rules (1998 and 2014); Article 33.1 CIETAC rules (2015); Article 14.3 SIAC rules; Article 11 HKIAC rules (2013); Article 12 Swiss rules (2012); Article 16 SCC rules (2010); Article R35 CAS code (2013); Article 19 ICAC rules (2010); Article 32 WIPO rules (2002); Article 20 Milan Chamber rules (2010); Article 19 ACICA rules (2016). As noted by Voser, the precise circumstances which can give rise to removal of arbitrators vary from institution to institution, but one ground is the arbitrator's failure to comply with the applicable institutional rules. Voser, "Removal, Resignation, Dismissal and Replacement of Arbitrators" 87.
499. The ASA survey indicates that only 23% of institutions provide for a reduction of the arbitrators' fees in case of poor performance. Hofbauer, Burkart, and Tari, "Survey on Scrutiny of Arbitral Institutions" 26.
500. Hofbauer, Burkart, and Tari, "Survey on Scrutiny of Arbitral Institutions" 25.
501. Fouchard, "Les Institutions Permanentes d'Arbitrage Devant le Juge Etatique (A Propos d'une Jurisprudence Récente)" 226; Aaron, "International Arbitration III: Choosing an Arbitration Institution and a Set of Rules" 306; Blackaby, Partasides, Hunter, and Redfern, *Redfern and Hunter on International Arbitration* 55; and Smit, "Future of International Commercial Arbitration" 15.

[C] The Award and Post-award Phase

[1] Scrutiny of Draft Awards

At the end of an arbitration, in the absence of amicable settlement, the tribunal issues an award. In order to ensure that the award adequately deals with the parties' claims and to improve its enforceability[502], a number of arbitration rules require the tribunal to provide the institution's secretariat with a copy of the award in draft form for review. This review is what is referred to as "scrutiny" of the award.

Contrary to a commonly held belief[503], scrutiny is not a peculiarity found only in the ICC rules. A review of the rules and practices of many institutions indicate that the institutions that claim not to review at least the form of draft awards prior to their being issued to the parties are a minority. Such minority institutions include *inter alia* the CEPANI, the CRCICA, the BCICAC, the FCC (Helsinki), and the Arbitration Centre at the Chamber of Commerce of Caracas (Cámara de Caracas)[504]. On the other hand, a number of institutional rules, other than those of the ICC, contain express provisions on scrutiny. This is the case for instance of CIETAC, BAC, SIAC, ICAC, the CAS, JAMS, CAMEX, KIAC, CAMP and DIA[505]. In addition, some other institutions review (more or less extensively) draft awards despite their rules being silent on the subject. This is the case, for example, of the ICDR, whose "*staff review every award for completeness as to*

502. Horacio Grigera Naón, "The Powers of the ICC International Court of Arbitration vis-a-vis Parties and Arbitrators" *Arbitration in the Next Decade – ICC Bulletin Special Supplement* (International Chamber of Commerce 1999) 70. In the same sense see de Hancock, "The ICC Court of Arbitration: The Institution and its Procedures" 37; Gaillard and Savage, *Fouchard, Gaillard, Goldman on International Commercial Arbitration* para. 1375.
503. See, for example, Kassis: *"It has been stated, rightly, that the procedure whereby a draft award is examined and approved by an organ other than the tribunal is unique"*. Translation by the author. In the original language: *"Il a été constaté avec raison que cette procédure d'examen et d'approbation préalable d'un projet de sentence arbitrale par un organe autre que le tribunal arbitral est unique"*. Kassis, *Réflexions sur le Règlement d'Arbitrage de la Chambre de Commerce Internationale: les Déviations de l'Arbitrage Institutionnel* 66.
504. According to the information offered by these institutions in response to the questionnaires sent out by the author.
505. Article 51 CIETAC rules (2015); Article 28.2 SIAC rules (2013); Article 42 ICAC rules (2010); Articles R46 (ordinary arbitrations) and R59 (Appeals) of the CAS code (2013); Article 32.3 JAMS rules (2011); Article 34.1 CAMEX rules (2009); Article 27 CAMP rules (2014); Article 28 DIA rules (2013). Interestingly, the rules of the Court of Arbitration at the Bulgarian Chamber of Commerce and Industry contemplate scrutiny but only when the arbitrators are not on the panel of the institution. This "selective" scrutiny is to be conducted by a "*committee of three arbitrators*" whose task is to check whether the award *"corresponds to the formal provisions of the Law on International Commercial Arbitration (LICA) and to the Rules of the Court of Arbitration"*. The findings of this committee is binding on the tribunal. See Article 37 of the rules of the Court of Arbitration at the Bulgarian Chamber of Commerce and Industry (1993).

form"[506]. The same is true of the LCIA[507], the Swiss Institution[508] but also the NAI, the KCAB, the VIAC, the DIS[509].

The extent of the review varies from one institution to the next. On one side of the spectrum one finds WIPO, which rules merely contemplate that "[t]*he Tribunal may consult the Center with regard to matters of form, particularly to ensure the enforceability of the award*"[510]. On the other side of the spectrum one finds the ICC which is empowered to impose modifications as to the form of the award, and also to suggest changes to its substance[511]. At the ICC, the proportion of institutional awards modified as a result of scrutiny is not insignificant. In 2012, only 2% of all awards issued at the ICC were not the object of any suggestions of modifications[512]. In between lies a number of institutions. Some, for instance, may make non-binding suggestions as to both form and merits[513]. Others may draw the tribunal's attention to any provision of

506. Appel, "International Centre for Dispute Resolution (ICDR)" 84. Appel specifies: "*The most typical issues identified on review concern the calculation of costs. Senior staff also satisfy themselves that the requirements of the New York Convention have been met and that all claims are addressed*". In the same sense, see Hoellering: "[e]*ven though the administrator's role vis-a-vis the tribunal during the proceedings may be limited, it is the administrator who communicates the award to the parties. This does not imply AAA scrutiny of the substance of the award, but does include a review for matters of form*". Hoellering, "AAA Administration of International Arbitration Proceedings" 62.
507. Winstanley, "Review of the London Court of International Arbitration" 6.
508. As explained by Georg von Segesser: "[...] *in practice, Article (4) enables the Court to also draw the attention of the arbitral tribunal to any obvious issues to other aspects of the arbitral award*". Georg von Segesser, Alexander Jolles, and Sonja Stark-Traber, "Swiss Rules of International Arbitration" in Karyl Nairn and Patrick Heneghan (eds), *Arbitration World: Institutional & Jurisdictional Comparisons* (4th Revised edn, Thomson Reuters 2012), The European Lawyer Reference 194.
509. Information based on the institutions' respective responses to the questionnaire sent out by the author.
510. Article 62(e) of the WIPO rules (2002).
511. Article 33 of the ICC rules (2012) reads: *"Before signing any award, the arbitral tribunal shall submit it in draft form to the Court. The Court may lay down modifications as to the form of the award and, without affecting the arbitral tribunal's liberty of decision, may also draw its attention to points of substance. No award shall be rendered by the arbitral tribunal until it has been approved by the Court as to its form"*.

    Modifications on the form are mandatory. If the tribunal refuses to include the in the award, the award will not be approved by the ICC Court and the Secretariat will therefore not communicate it to the parties. See Grigera Naón, "The Powers of the ICC International Court of Arbitration vis-a-vis Parties and Arbitrators" 70. In effect, prior to scrutiny a draft award is not an award under the rules. See Born, *International Commercial Arbitration* 2352; Loquin, "La Sentence Arbitrale: L'Examen du Projet de Sentence par l'Institution et la Sentence au Deuxième Degré - Réflexions sur la Nature et la Validité de l'Intervention de l'Institution Arbitrale sur la Sentence" 428.
512. International Chamber of Commerce, "2012 Statistical Report" 15. Similarly, for the period 2008-2012, Simon Greenberg indicates that the ICC Court approved a total of 1,809 draft awards and decided not to approve 139 awards (for a total number of awards of 1,948 awards), which means that a "not insignificant" 7% of awards failed to meet the approval of the Court. Simon Greenberg, "Arbitral Award Scrutiny under Scrutiny" in Philipp Habegger and others (eds), *Arbitral Institutions Under Scrutiny* (JurisNet 2013), ASA Special Series No. 40, 89. For older statistics (1997) see Grigera Naón, "The Powers of the ICC International Court of Arbitration vis-a-vis Parties and Arbitrators" 70.
513. Article 28 SIAC rules (2013); Article 32.3 JAMS rules (2011).

the rules with which the draft award does not comply[514]. When institutional rules contain no express provisions as to scrutiny, the review process tends to be less extensive, with the institution often only drawing to the tribunal's attention the more important errors of form[515].

The impact of the institutions' review of draft awards is not insignificant[516]. When the institution suggests or imposes a change (whether on form or substance) which then finds its way into the award, the institution effectively directly affects the drafting of the tribunal's decision[517]. Naturally insofar as the tribunal has the power to reject a change on the substance proposed by the institution, the tribunal's decision seems prima facie to remain immune from any outside interference[518]. But, the line between what constitutes "form" and "substance" respectively is at times difficult to identify[519]. The ICC takes an extensive interpretation of what constitutes matters of form (for which the institution can impose a modification to the award). Grigera Naón, for example, explains that "form" includes not only compliance with formal requirements, errors of a mathematical, computational or clerical nature, but also internal inconsistencies in the award, absence of reasons, or of adequate reasons, and decisions *ultra* or *infra petita*[520]. Jason Fry similarly recognizes that the role of the ICC in scrutinizing draft awards goes as far as identifying "*flawed legal reasoning and procedural errors*", which by definition means that, if the recommended corrections are accepted by the tribunal, they will impact the outcome of the case[521]. In one extreme example, the case-handlers at the Beijing Arbitration Commission will point to the

514. Article 30.4 Milan rules (2010).
515. Marie Öhrström for example indicates in respect of the SCC that it "[...] *does not have any service equivalent to the ICCs 'scrutiny of award' but if the SCC Secretariat identifies any obvious miscalculations or similar it usually notifies the tribunal*". Öhrström, "SCC Rules" 847. Interestingly, in order to avoid the recurrence of certain mistakes as to form, the SCC has issued a model award included in its guidelines to arbitrators.
516. Especially when scrutiny concerns the merits of the case, as discussed below.
517. In the sense that the phrasing of the decision will be different from what it would have been in the absence of recommendations. Greenberg, "Arbitral Award Scrutiny under Scrutiny" 105.
518. For Loquin: "*The institution's organ does not intervene on the content of the award. Scrutiny is by nature incapable of reforming the decision*" (Translation by the Author). In the original language: "*L'organe de l'institution d'arbitrage n'intervient pas directement sur le contenu de la sentence. Le contrôle préalable n'a pas la nature d'un pouvoir de réformation de la sentence*". Loquin, "La Sentence Arbitrale: L'Examen du Projet de Sentence par l'Institution et la Sentence au Deuxième Degré – Réflexions sur la Nature et la Validité de l'Intervention de l'Institution Arbitrale sur la Sentence" 434.
519. Greenberg, "Arbitral Award Scrutiny under Scrutiny" 93; Loquin, "La Sentence Arbitrale: L'Examen du Projet de Sentence par l'Institution et la Sentence au Deuxième Degré – Réflexions sur la Nature et la Validité de l'Intervention de l'Institution Arbitrale sur la Sentence" 436.
520. Grigera Naón, "The Powers of the ICC International Court of Arbitration vis-a-vis Parties and Arbitrators" 70.

Simon Greenberg usefully distinguishes between matters of form, matters that are "*quasi substantive*" and matters that are "*usually substantive*". He seems to indicate that, depending on the circumstances, such questions as "*whether the reasoning in the award is consistent with the parties' pleadings or whether the rationale for the decisions could surprise the parties (iura novit curia)*" or even "*whether the reasoning is sufficient*" would not necessarily be substantive. Greenberg, "Arbitral Award Scrutiny under Scrutiny" 99.
521. Fry, "ICC International Court of Arbitration" 14.

attention of the arbitrators' inconsistencies between the decision set out in the draft award and previous decisions rendered in similar cases, thereby "*actually influencing decisions on the merits*"[522]. Incidentally, for questions of substance (where institutions may at most suggest, rather than impose, modifications), one may wonder whether the views expressed by an institution cannot be very persuasive, in particular for less experienced arbitrators or arbitrators who are relying on institutional appointments for their livelihood.

In short, the scrutiny of draft awards is a function which has the potential to affect the process significantly[523]. For Simon Greenberg, "[a]*ward scrutiny goes to the core of the question of the extent to which an administering institution can – or should- intervene with arbitral proceedings*"[524].

[2] Issue of Awards and Assistance with Enforcement

Worth mentioning briefly is the role assumed by institutions in respect of the issue of awards. A number of institutional rules indeed provide that when the tribunal has signed its award, the award shall be sent to the administrator for onward transmission to the parties[525]. In fact the opposite is relatively rare[526]. The requirement that all awards be sent out by the administrator rather than the tribunal appears to serve both legal and practical purposes. From a legal point of view, proper notification of the award is fundamental to preserve its enforceability. There is therefore an incentive for institutions to want to make sure that awards rendered under their auspices are served properly[527]. From a practical point of view, institutional awards are frequently issued as bound printed documents bearing the seal or stamp of the institution. It is thus necessary for the award to pass through the hands of the institution for these formalities to be completed. Furthermore, requiring that the administrator issue any award also allows the institution to ensure that an award is not issued where the costs of the arbitration have not yet been paid in full by the parties[528]. In addition and more

522. Chen, "International Law Reporter" 327. Fuyong Chen is the Deputy Secretary General of BAC.
523. In the words of Simon Greenberg, in some cases "*the Court's comments can result in significant changes to the award*". Greenberg, "Arbitral Award Scrutiny under Scrutiny" 101.
524. Greenberg, "Arbitral Award Scrutiny under Scrutiny" 89.
525. Article 34.1 ICC rules (2012); Article 26.7 LCIA rules (2014); Article 30.4 ICDR rules (2014); Article 28.6 SIAC rules (2013); Article 37.8 DIAC rules (2007); Article 32.4 JAMS rules (2011).
526. The SCC and the Swiss Institution may be mentioned in this respect. Article 36(4) of the SCC rules (2010) and Article 32.6 of the Swiss rules (2012) both contemplate that arbitral tribunal deliver a copy of the award to the parties and to the institution.
527. In this respect it is worth mentioning the suggestion made by Hans van Houtte that institutions be officially listed in domestic statutes as agencies habilitated to "serve" awards onto parties: "*Why should institutions such as the Secretariat of the International Court of Arbitration of the ICC, for instance, for the purposes of Regulation 1348/2000 not be assimilated to the Greffe of a French court, at present recognised by France as another 'transmitting agency'?*". Hans van Houtte, "The Delivery of Awards to the Parties" (2005) 21 Arbitration International, Kluwer Law International 177, 184.
528. As envisaged expressly by Article 34.1 of the ICC rules (2012), and Article 26.7 of the LCIA rules (2014) for instance.

importantly perhaps, it is a last-minute opportunity for the institution to cast an eye on the award before it is issued to the parties. In other words, a requirement that any award be issued by the institution fulfils a "quality control" purpose, notably for those institutions' which rules do not expressly contemplate scrutiny of draft awards.

Some institutions assist parties with any queries that they may have at the enforcement stage. An example is when an institution is asked to provide additional certified copies of an award. More problematic perhaps is when an institution is asked to issue an official document confirming the bona fides of a particular arbitration in the context of enforcement proceedings[529]. Assistance at the enforcement stage cannot be said to impact the outcome of a case as it takes place post-deliberation. Nonetheless this potentially raises an issue as to equality of treatment of the parties because this assistance benefits the party seeking to enforce the award (the winning party) to the detriment of the losing party. Be that as it may, it is now not unusual for the law of the country where the institution is based to confer on the local institution some official role in respect of enforcement proceedings. This is the case, for example, in Singapore where SIAC is, by law, empowered to certify and authenticate awards as may be required for enforcement purposes[530].

§3.04 DIFFERENT LEVELS OF INSTITUTIONAL INVOLVEMENT EXPRESSED AS A CONTINUUM: THE SPECTRAL REPRESENTATION OF INSTITUTIONAL ARBITRATION

[A] Why a Continuum?

The first three sections of this Chapter 3 established that the extent to which institutions intervene in the proceedings they administer (i.e., the "level of institutional involvement" or "degree of interventionism[531]") varies significantly. In the words of Michel Gaudet:

> [...] *institutional arbitration implies a more or less pronounced administration of the procedure by the institution. Here again, the responsibilities of the institution vary considerably depending on the sets of rules* [...] (Translation by the author)[532].

529. This is a role expressly considered by Article 36 of the VIAC rules (2006).
530. See section 19C of the Singapore International Arbitration Act 1994 as amended which contemplates that the government names, by ministerial order, institutions habilitated to certify and authenticate awards.
531. The term interventionism is used here in a neutral, non-pejorative, sense.
532. In the original language: "[...] *l'arbitrage institutionnel implique une administration plus ou moins poussée de la procédure arbitrale par l'organisation. Là encore, l'objet et la responsabilité de l'organisation variant considérablement selon le Règlement* [...]". Gaudet, "La Coopération des Juridictions Etatiques à l'Arbitrage Institutionnel" 102. In the same sense see the foreword to the ASA Special Series supplement on institutions: "*There are, however, significant differences between various arbitral institutions with regard to the scope as well as the level of administrative assistance and services provided*". Hofbauer, Burkart, and Tari, "Survey on Scrutiny of Arbitral Institutions" 2.

As stated above, the varying levels to which institutions intervene in the proceedings they administer have led some authors to distinguish, within institutional arbitration, between "supervised" and "un-supervised" arbitration. For Craig, Park and Paulsson:

> [s]*upervised arbitration is a special type of institutional arbitration* [...] *designed to reduce the supervisory role of national courts by creating an autonomous supervisory capacity within the arbitral institution*[533].

Along the same lines, Redfern and Hunter differentiate between "*wholly administered*" or "*semi-administered*" institutional arbitration[534]. Interestingly, in a different iteration of the same idea, Gerold Herman, instead of sub-dividing institutional arbitration in the supervised and unsupervised categories, describes "arbitration" in general as comprising three distinct forms: "*ad hoc*", "*administered*" and "*supervised*", thereby implicitly suggesting that there is as much difference between ad hoc and unsupervised arbitrations, as there may be between unsupervised and supervised ones[535].

Yet, distinguishing between two or three "forms" or "categories" of arbitrations does not adequately reflect the sheer diversity of degrees to which institutions are involved in the proceedings they administer[536]. The reality of institutional arbitration comprises such an array of different degrees of institutional involvement that the phenomenon of institutional arbitration is more adequately accounted for by a continuum/spectrum than by rigid categories such as "supervised" or "unsupervised" arbitration. An attempt has been made in the pages below to place the major institutions alongside continua depending on their degree of involvement in the proceedings.

The idea of comparing the level of involvement of one institution with one or more other institutions is not entirely new. The ICC having for long set the standard for arbitral institutions, it is not surprising that a number of authors, when describing the approach to case administration taken by other lesser known institutions, have used the ICC as a point of reference. For example, Simon Greenberg (then former deputy Secretary General of ACICA but not yet of the ICC) once observed: "*ACICA's role in supervising arbitration proceedings is moderate. ACICA arbitration is not 'highly supervised' as is, for example, ICC Arbitration*"[537]. Similar observations have been

533. Craig, Park, and Paulsson, *International Chamber of Commerce Arbitration* 40-41. In the same sense see, Thompson, "Building an Arbitration and Mediation Centre: From International Foundations to Domestic Rooftops': The Establishment of the British Columbia International Commercial Arbitration Centre" 202-203.
534. Blackaby, Partasides, Hunter, and Redfern, *Redfern and Hunter on International Arbitration* 54, at footnote 180.
535. Hermann, "Power of Arbitrators to Determine Procedures under the UNCITRAL Model Law" 42.
536. As the overview of institutions' activities in Chapter 3 above indicates.
537. Greenberg, "ACICA's New International Arbitration Rules" 190.

made over time in respect of the Swiss Institution[538], SIAC[539], the LCIA[540], the SCC, HKIAC and CIETAC[541].

What is more novel is using a spectrum/continuum to illustrate visually the varying degrees of interventionism which the notion of institutional arbitration comprises. For the purposes of building the continua, the level of a given institution's involvement may be assessed both in terms of the *"frequency"* of the intervention, and in terms of the *"extent of the power"* conferred to the institution for each issue.

By "frequency", I mean the number of issues which, pursuant to the institutional rules, fall within the scope of the institution's mandate (e.g., deciding on the seat, language, joinder, consolidation, challenges, scrutiny, etc.).

By "extent of the power conferred", I mean both:

(1) how much discretion is given to the institution (e.g., Is the discretion to exercise a certain power curtailed by a legal threshold set out in the rules[542]? Can the relevant power be exercised *proprio motu*?); and
(2) the "force" of the resulting institutional decision (e.g., Has the institution authority to impose a decision over the objections of both parties? Over the tribunal?).

The two continua below seek to reflect both the frequency and extent of institutions' level of intervention in the proceedings they administer.

538. Tobias Zuberbühler, Klaus Muller, and Philipp A. Habegger, "Introduction to the Swiss Rules" in Tobias Zuberbühler and Klaus Muller (eds), *Swiss Rules of International Arbitration: Commentary* (Kluwer Law International 2005) 8. In the words of another author: "[...] a 'lighter' administration compared to other institutional arbitration rules. Even though the 2012 revision of the Swiss Rules has strengthened the role of the Swiss Chambers' Arbitration Institution by vesting the Court with additional powers, the 2012 Swiss Rules still provide for a leaner administration of the arbitral proceedings than other institutional arbitration rules, giving the parties and the arbitral tribunal the necessary flexibility to tailor the arbitral proceedings to their needs". von Segesser, Jolles, and Stark-Traber, "Swiss Rules of International Arbitration" 195. Likewise, for another general statements that the Swiss rules offer a light-touch supervision see Habegger, "The Revised Swiss Rules of International Arbitration: An Overview of the Major Changes" 307.
539. For SIAC see Born, "[w]hile the SIAC rules now use terminology similar to that of the ICC International Court of Arbitration, the SIAC Court does not exercise the more involved review function of its ICC counterpart". Gary B. Born, "New Rules at the Singapore International Arbitration Centre", 14 May 2013.
540. For the LCIA see Sir Michael Kerr, "London Court of International Arbitration" in Albert Jan van den Berg (ed), *Planning Efficient Arbitration Proceedings: The Law Applicable in International Arbitration* vol. 7 (Kluwer Law International 1996) 213, 213-220.
541. For the CIETAC, SCC and HKIAC: Song, "The New CIETAC Arbitration Rules of 2012" 313-314.
542. See above by way of example the thresholds set in certain institutional rules for the institution to be able to consolidate proceedings; or the threshold for making a decision as to which set of arbitration rules apply to a particular case (e.g., expedited arbitration or regular arbitration).

[B] Caveat: Limitations of the Spectral Representation of Institutional Arbitration

For a number of reasons which will be discussed shortly, attempting to place institutions alongside a continuum depending on the extent of their involvement in the proceedings is challenging and entails a measure of arbitrariness. In light of these difficulties, it is important to stress that this attempt to place institutions alongside a continuum is made for illustrative purposes only. It aims at illustrating "visually" the diverse reality which the notion of institutional arbitration covers in practice. This "visual representation" is useful because it helps understand more fully the limitations of some of the theoretical representations of the functions, or role, of institutions in the institutional arbitration process discussed at Chapter 4 below (and in particular the dichotomic representations of the role of institutions).

In this respect, a first difficulty relates to the fact that the level of interventionism of one institution compared to others, varies depending on the *phase* of the proceedings. Some institutional rules appear interventionist in the phase that precedes the appointment of the tribunal, but much less so post-appointment. Therefore institutions are paced below on not one but two different "continua" for two different phases of the proceedings: (1) the initial phase of the proceedings (from the filing of a Request to the constitution of the tribunal); and (2) the proceedings proper (from the constitution of the tribunal to the issue of the final award).

Second, attempting to place institutions alongside a continuum depending on the extent of their involvement is difficult because there is, sometimes, a difference between what an institution's rules expressly provide, and what the institution does in actual practice. This will be the case whenever a set of institutional rules entrusts an institution with a particular power but the institution rarely utilize that power in actual fact. To take only one example, pursuant to the LCIA rules, when the relevant arbitration agreement is silent as to party nominations, it is for the LCIA Court to select all arbitrators[543]. In practice, however, the LCIA will be reluctant to exercise its power to select all arbitrators whenever there is an indication that the parties might wish and be able to agree on a mechanism for nominations. The institution will go to great length to ensure that the parties are given an opportunity to agree on a mechanism for party nominations. The LCIA's practice in this respect contrasts with what a literal interpretation of the rules would suggest: i.e., that the task of selecting arbitrators is to be exercised by the institution. Conversely, some institutions may intervene in a manner which is not expressly contemplated by their rules. An example is the informal scrutiny of draft awards which takes place at a number of institutions, despite the rules of these

543. See Article 5.5 of the LCIA rules (1998): "*The LCIA Court alone is empowered to appoint arbitrators*" and Article 7.1: "*If the parties have agreed that any arbitrator is to be appointed by one or more of them or by any third person, that agreement shall be treated as an agreement to nominate an arbitrator for all purposes. Such nominee may only be appointed by the LCIA Court as arbitrator subject to his prior compliance with Article 5.3. The LCIA Court may refuse to appoint any such nominee if it determines that he is not suitable or independent or impartial*".

institutions being silent on the subject[544]. When building the continuum, therefore, the question arises as to whether one should look only at what institutional rules expressly provide, or also at what the actual practices of institutions are. Obviously, unearthing the actual practices of institutions is more intricate than assessing the extent of institutional powers expressly provided for under a set of institutional rules. Occasionally, information as to how institutional practices deviate from the relevant rules may be found in the literature, in particular that produced by staff/former staff of the institutions[545]. It remains difficult, nonetheless, to assess precisely where, and to what extent, the actual practice of a particular institution differs from its rules. For this reason the spectra/continua below emphasize the role of institutions under their rules.

A third difficulty relates to the fact that not all decisions made by institutions have the same overall significance for the proceedings. The "materiality" of any institution's action, in the sense of its potential to affect the outcome of the proceedings, varies. For example, a final decision on jurisdiction rendered by CIETAC, or a decision on the seat of the arbitration made by the LCIA (under the 1998 LCIA rules), are perhaps likely to have a greater impact than a decision by the ICC Court to extend a deadline to file an Answer to the Request for Arbitration. In addition, to complicate things further, the materiality of any given institutional decision such as, for instance, a decision on the seat of an arbitration, may well vary from one arbitration to another.

A fourth difficulty results from the fact that the level of interventionism of any given institution does not depend exclusively on the extent to which certain powers are conferred to it. There are indeed instances in which, whilst the applicable rules do not grant any discretionary powers to an institution in respect of a particular issue (e.g., seat, language, number of arbitrators, etc.), the rules themselves "regulate" that issue directly, so that party autonomy ends up being as constricted as if the institution had made a discretionary decision on the same issue. For example, when the ICAC rules provide that, regardless of any agreement between the parties, the seat of ICAC arbitrations shall be Moscow[546], the rules do not directly grant to the institution any power to determine the seat, but the rules nevertheless limit party autonomy. In such a case, is it really correct to say that ICAC is less interventionist than say, the LCIA (which 1998 rules gives it the authority to select a seat other than London when the circumstances justify it)? Arguably, the direct regulation of a particular issue by the provisions of a set of institutional rules, restricts party autonomy just as much as any discretionary powers granted to the institution in respect of the same issue. The continuum below takes account of both forms of interventionism, i.e., as a result of discretionary powers, and by operation of the rules.

544. For example, the Swiss Institution, the ICDR and the LCIA. See the discussions above, in Chapter 3, in the section on scrutiny.

545. See, for example, the article of the ICC's former Deputy Secretary General, Simon Greenberg, on the actual practice of scrutiny. "*In assessing award scrutiny the real question is not what is contained in a brief provision like Article 33 of the ICC Rules, but how the provision is applied and how the process works internally*". Greenberg, "Arbitral Award Scrutiny under Scrutiny" 96.

546. Article 22 of the ICAC rules (2010). See also R28 of the CAS code (2013).

[C] First Continuum: From the Filing of a Request for Arbitration to the Constitution of the Tribunal

The initial phase of the proceedings, that is to say the phase starting with the filing of a Request for Arbitration and ending with the constitution of a tribunal, is the phase during which arbitral institutions are most implicated[547]. The actions taken by institutions at that stage concern *inter alia* determining the applicable rules, the extension of certain deadlines, jurisdictional objections, interim measures applications, the language and the seat of the arbitration, the consolidation of proceedings, the joinder of third parties, and, of course, the appointment of arbitrators. On the next page is a table which sets out the powers (as expressly provided for under the rules) of some major institutions in respect of these issues. This offers a visual representation of the diversity that characterizes the discretion which arbitral institutions exercise in the pre-appointment phase. On the following page is the actual continuum, on which some major institutions are placed depending on their level of interventionism.

547. Schlaepfer, "The Role of the Institution at the Commencement of the Proceedings" 56.

Table 3.1 Visual Representation of Institutional Powers (Pre-Appointment Phase) The table below is based on the version of the relevant arbitration rules in force at 8 January 2016.

	Final Decision on Jurisdiction	*Prima Facie Decision on Juris-diction*	*Decision on Applicable Rules*	*Extension of Deadlines*	*Interim Measures*	*Decision on Language*	*Decision on Seat*	*Consolidation (Other Than with All Parties' Agreement)*	*Joinder (Other Than Will All Parties' Agreement)*	*Number of Arbitrators (in the Absence of Agreement of the Parties)*	*Default Power to Select All Arbitrators (i.e., No "Right to Nominate" Provided in the Rules)*	*Confirmation of Arbitrators (i.e., Power to Reject a Nominee) or Appointment from a Closed List*
ICC		•		•			•	•	•	•		•
ICDR		•	•				•		•	•	•	
LCIA		•		•		•		•		•	•	•
SIAC		•	•	•						•		•
HKIAC		•		•				•		•		•
SCC		•		•			•	•		•		•
Swiss Inst.		•	•	•			•	•		•		•
JAMS			•	•			•	•		•		
Milan		•		•			•			•		•
CRCICA		•		•						•		•
WIPO		•		•			•	•		•		•
CAS				•	•	•		•	•	•		•
ICAC		•		•						•	[548]	•
CMAC	•		•	•			•					•

548. Default power to select chair and sole arbitrator.

	Final Decision on Jurisdiction	*Prima Facie Decision on Juris-diction*	*Decision on Applicable Rules*	*Extension of Deadlines*	*Interim Measures*	*Decision on Language*	*Decision on Seat*	*Consolidation (Other Than with All Parties' Agreement)*	*Joinder (Other Than Will All Parties' Agreement)*	*Number of Arbitrators (in the Absence of Agreement of the Parties)*	*Default Power to Select All Arbitrators (i.e., No "Right to Nominate" Provided in the Rules)*	*Confirmation of Arbitrators (i.e., Power to Reject a Nominee) or Appointment from a Closed List*
CIETAC	•	•		•		•	•	•			•	•
ACICA		•		•				•		•	•	•

Legend: In the table above, a [•] indicates that the relevant institution is primarily responsible for the issue at stake.

Note: The extent of an institution's power, and the conditions in which it may be exercised, varies from institution to institution. Therefore, where two institutions are marked in the table above as being responsible for a particular issue, it is not implied that the scope of the institution's power in this respect is identical for both institutions.

An absence of [•] may occasionally reflect the fact that the issue at stake (e.g., language, seat) is directly fixed by the rules themselves (i.e., with no measure of discretion given either to the tribunal or the institution).

Figure 3.1 Continuum of Institutional Powers (Pre-appointment Phase)

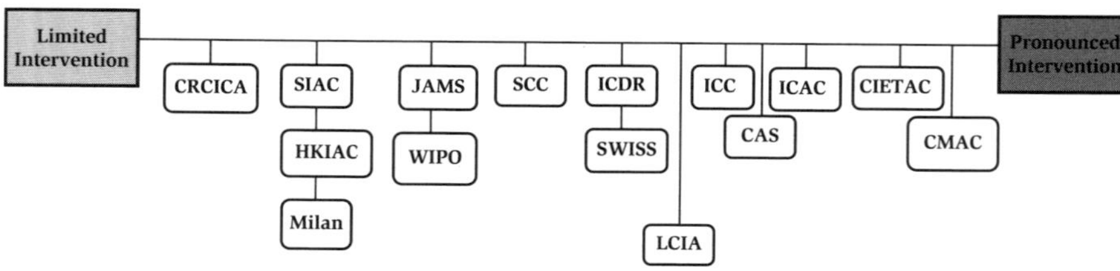

[D] Second Continuum: From the Constitution of the Tribunal to the Award

As previously stated, the second phase of the proceedings, which extends from the constitution of the tribunal to the award, is characterized by a degree of diversity in the level of intervention of institutions. The role of institutions at that stage concern *inter alia* the approval of terms of reference, challenges to and removal of arbitrators, the monitoring of the proceedings, the treatment of costs, and the scrutiny of awards. On the next page is a table which sets out the institutional powers of some major institutions for that second phase. On the following page is the actual continuum, on which the institutions are placed depending on their level of interventionism.

Table 3.2 Visual Representation of Institutional Powers (Post-Appointment Phase)

	Power to Direct Deposits (Throughout the Proceedings)	Power to Suspend Proceedings or Treat Claim as Withdrawn (for Non-payment)	Power to Decide Quantum of Costs of Arbitrators and Institution	Power to Decide Costs of Legal Representation	Power to Apportion Costs	Express Power to Interpret the Rules	Active Supervision Role (Monitoring of Correspondence Post Appointment)	Power to Remove Arbitrators in Case of Challenge	Power to Remove Arbitrators Other Than for Challenge	Scrutiny: Power to Impose Changes as to Form	Issue of Award Required to Be Made by Institution
ICC	•	•	•				•	•	•	•	•
ICDR	•	•				•		•	•		•
LCIA	•	•	•				•	•	•		•
SIAC	•	•	•		•			•	•	•	•
HKIAC	•					•		•	•		
SCC	•	•	•					•	•		
Swiss Inst.								•	•		
JAMS		•						•	•		•
Milan	•	•	•				•	•	•		•
CRCICA	•	•						•	•		
WIPO	•	•	•					•	•		•
CAS	•	•	•				•	•	•	•	
ICAC	•	•	•		•		•	•	•		•
CMAC		•					•	•			
CIETAC		•				•	•	•	•		
ACICA	•							•			

The table above is based on the version of the relevant arbitration rules in force at 8 January 2016.

Legend: In the table above, a [•] indicates that the relevant institution is primarily responsible for the issue at stake.

Note: The extent of an institution's discretion, and the conditions in which it may be exercised, varies from institution to institution. Therefore, where two institutions are marked in the table above as being responsible for a particular issue, it is not implied that the scope of the institution's discretion in this respect is identical for both institutions.

An absence of [•] may occasionally reflect the fact that the issue at stake (e.g., language, seat) is directly fixed by the rules themselves (i.e., with no measure of discretion given either to the tribunal or the institution).

Figure 3.2 Continuum of Institutional Powers (Post-Appointment Phase)

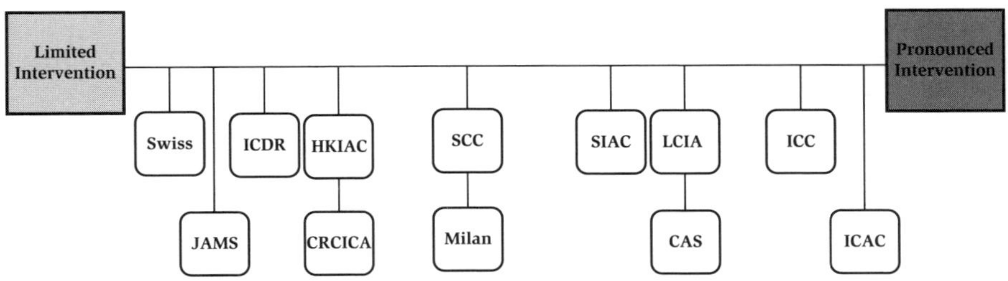

§3.05 CHAPTER CONCLUSIONS

This chapter provided an overview of the activities undertaken by institutions. This overview illustrated the diversity that characterizes the notion of institutional arbitration. This diversity concerns not only the "mechanics" provided for by institutional rules in respect of appointments, challenges or decisions on costs, etc. but also the role attributed to the institutions in the proceedings they administer. In particular huge variations may be seen in the level of involvement of the institutions in the proceedings they administer. This chapter illustrates that institutional arbitration is anything but a monolithic notion. Ultimately, the aim of this chapter was to provide the background information necessary to comprehend fully the limits of the traditional theoretical representations of the "functions", or "role", of arbitral institutions which are discussed in the following chapter (Chapter 4).

CHAPTER 4

The Traditional Representations of the Role of Institutions: A Critical Evaluation

§4.01 CHAPTER INTRODUCTION

In this book, the expression "representations of the functions of institutions" means the depictions, or mental images, of the role exercised by arbitral institutions in the institutional arbitration process[548] – a representation being the manner in which someone describes something (in our case how scholars, practitioners and judges describe the role of arbitral institutions). Insofar as these representations comprise a set of abstract principles which are intended to explain the role of arbitral institutions, they can be said to constitute "theories" or "theoretical representations" of the role of arbitral institutions[549].

The difficulty in identifying and extracting from the literature theoretical representations of the functions of arbitral institutions is that, under the pen of many authors, these representations take the form of unconscious assumptions as to the role of institutions in the arbitral process more often than of fully articulated theories[550].

548. The expression "theoretical representation" is borrowed from the seminal work of Professor Emmanuel Gaillard, *Legal Theory of International Arbitration* (Martinus Nijhoff Publishers 2010) 13.

549. See in this sense the definition of "theory" in "Oxford English Dictionary, Online Edition, available at http://www.oxforddictionaries.com, Accessed 14 March 2014"; "Merriam-Webster Dictionary, Online Edition, available at http://www.merriam-webster.com/dictionary, Accessed 14 March 2014." Of course, legal theories are not necessarily explanatory; they can also have a justificatory or a reformist aim. See Hanoch Dagan and Roy Kreitner, "The Character of Legal Theory" (2011) 96 Cornell Law Review 671, 685.

550. As Professor Gaillard explains this is also true of the more general subject of the "theories of international arbitration": *"The systematisation of the various representations of international arbitration is all the more difficult in that, being mental representations, they are by definition rarely articulated as such and only appear implicitly, often in relation to technical issues, in the legal thinking of arbitration experts."* Emmanuel Gaillard, *Legal Theory of International Arbitration* (Martinus Nijhoff Publishers 2010) 13.

The traditional definitions of "institutional arbitration" and of "arbitral institutions" examined in the first chapter of this book rarely if ever attempt to articulate the precise role of arbitral institutions in the arbitral process and the nature of that role. Often, also, a single author oscillates between different representations. Be that as it may, one may infer two main representations of the role of arbitral institutions from a review of literature on institutional arbitration.

According to the first representation, while institutions are occasionally called upon to make decisions, such decisions are immaterial because, contrary to the decisions rendered by an arbitral tribunal, they are considered to be "administrative" (i.e., "non-jurisdictional"), whatever these terms may mean. The first representation has been heavily influenced by French case law. According to the second (more marginal) representation, which can be seen as an unfortunate extension, or exaggeration, of the first one, arbitral institutions are seen as mere purveyors of logistical services with no decision-making power at all.

Whether the role of institutions is considered "non-decisional" (under the second representation) or "decisional but non-jurisdictional" (under the first representation), a key consequence is that requirements of due process are considered not to apply to the measures taken by arbitral institutions. This chapter demonstrates that while these representations may be useful, they fail to withstand close scrutiny, and do not reflect the diverse reality of institutional arbitration. For these purposes, this chapter discusses the two traditional representations of the functions of institutions consecutively. Each section contains a short overview of the representation, followed by an analysis of its limitations.

§4.02 FIRST REPRESENTATION: AN OCCASIONAL PARTICIPANT IN THE ADJUDICATIVE PROCESS WHICH DECISIONS ARE SOMEHOW IMMATERIAL

[A] Presentation of the Representation

[1] Short Overview

In this first representation, arbitral institutions are depicted as an administrator[551] with an incidental and occasional decision-making power[552], but which power is ultimately immaterial. In other words, measures taken by arbitral institutions in respect of the proceedings they administer "do not matter" from the point of view of the overall adjudication of the dispute. These measures do not bear any significance in respect of the determination of the dispute being referred to arbitration. For example, some

551. The term administrator occasionally used by the proponents of the first representation is not clear. As will be seen below, the term seems to be employed to denote, in general terms, that the role of institutions is extraneous to the adjudication of disputes: Institutions provide administrative, non-adjudicatory, services.

552. As discussed below, some proponents of the first representation seem to acknowledge that certain measures rendered by arbitral institutions in the course of the proceedings they supervise constitute decisions (i.e., certain measures are decisional in nature).

authors argue (in the context of the ICC): "[the institution] *does not take any substantive decisions as to who wins or loses ICC arbitrations. The Court also does not take decisions about timetable and procedure to be adopted in the arbitration. All such decisions are for the arbitral tribunal and the parties –exclusively*"[553].

In this first representation, the nature of the measures taken by institutions are said to differ from those rendered by arbitral tribunals. Measures taken by institutions, so the theory goes, are of an "*administrative*" nature whereas those of arbitral tribunals are "*jurisdictional*"[554]. Another more nuanced iteration of the first representation would consist of saying that, while decisions of institutions are in all instances administrative, the decisions of arbitral tribunals may either be administrative or jurisdictional depending on the type of decision concerned. By and large, however, this second, more nuanced, iteration remains very uncommon in the literature.

According to a leading German author (referring to the DIS and other institutions):

> *It is very important to understand that the DIS is not the arbitral tribunal. The task of the DIS and its Secretariat is not jurisdictional, but purely administrative. The powers and functions of the DIS and of its Secretariat are limited to the administration of the arbitral proceedings under the DIS Arbitration Rules. The same applies to other arbitral institutions, even if they are more involved in the administration of arbitrations conducted under their rules than the DIS and its Secretariat*[555].

As discussed below, this difference in the nature of the decisions rendered by arbitral institutions and arbitral tribunals is considered to be determinative of the legal regime applicable to such decisions. Qualifying arbitral institutions' decisions as "administrative" or "non-jurisdictional" means that institutions are not bound by all the due process requirements that apply to arbitrators[556]. This first representation, which effectively minimizes the role of arbitral institutions, aims at "liberating" them from the rigours of the due process requirements applicable to the decisions of arbitrators[557].

---

553. Hodges, Parker, and Ackebo, "International Chamber of Commerce (ICC)" 103.
554. For Eric Loquin for example: *"The intervention of the organ of the institution cannot be qualified of jurisdictional"* (Translation by the author). In the original language: *"L'intervention de l'organe de l'institution d'arbitrage ne peut être qualifiée de juridictionnelle.* Loquin, "La Sentence Arbitrale: L'Examen du Projet de Sentence par l'Institution et la Sentence au Deuxième Degré – Réflexions sur la Nature et la Validité de l'Intervention de l'Institution Arbitrale sur la Sentence" 451.
555. Klaus Peter Berger, *Private Dispute Resolution in International Business: Negotiation, Mediation, Arbitration (Third Edition)* (Kluwer Law International 2015) 362-363.
556. See Paulsson, "Vicarious Hypochondria and Institutional Arbitration" 248; Fouchard, "Les Institutions Permanentes d'Arbitrage Devant le Juge Etatique (A Propos d'une Jurisprudence Récente)" 240; Gaudet, "La Coopération des Juridictions Etatiques à l'Arbitrage Institutionnel" 109; Hautot, "Les Pouvoirs de la Cour d'Arbitrage de la C.C.I. de Décider ou Non d'Organiser l'Arbitrage" 19. The legal grounds for this assumption are not clear. See the discussions of the French courts decisions on the matter in section §4.02[B] below (*"Critical analysis of the first representation: Rejection of the 'administrative' vs. 'jurisdictional' dichotomy"*).
557. As discussed in Chapter 5 below (*"A realistic representation of the role of institutions: Arbitral institutions as ancillary participants in the adjudicative process"*) this view minimizes the role

This first representation of the functions of arbitral institutions finds echo in the ICC arbitration rules. Even if the ICC arbitration rules do not go as far as referring expressly to the "non-jurisdictional" or "administrative" character of the institution's actions, in ICC parlance, the institution is considered to administer the proceedings and not to participate in the adjudicative mission. Article 1(2) of the ICC rules famously provides:

> [t]*he Court does not itself resolve disputes. It administers the resolution of disputes by arbitral tribunals, in accordance with the Rules of Arbitration of the ICC* [...].

This idea that the ICC does not itself resolve disputes also appears in other official ICC materials. For example, the section of the ICC's Website introducing the Court's services in respect of arbitration explains:

> [t]*he Court provides parties with a flexible and neutral setting for dispute resolution. It offers confidentiality and extraordinary freedom for parties to choose the framework for how and where they want to resolve their dispute.* While the dispute itself is resolved by independent arbitrators, the Court supervises the process *from beginning to end, increasing the quality of the process and enforceability of the awards* (Emphasis added)[558].

This idea that the ICC's activities do not participate to the adjudication of the arbitrations conducted under its auspices has permeated the literature and, in the first place, the abundant external commentaries on the ICC rules. As early as the 1980s for instance, one author was writing:

> *The Court is not a judicial court, nor does the Court itself arbitrate disputes.* [...] *Broadly speaking, the Court offers the international business community the services of an administrative agency that provides institutional "supervision" of the arbitration of business disputes*[559].

More recently a former ICC Secretary General, noted:

> [t]*he ICC Court* [...], *does not itself settle disputes. Its main function is to ensure the application of the ICC Arbitration Rules, with the assistance of its Secretariat. As a result, the parties to an ICC arbitration are not heard by the ICC Court, nor do arbitral proceedings take place before the ICC Court*[560].

Likewise, a former ICC Counsel and General Counsel explained:

> [a]*s an institution, the ICC will only provide administrative services, but will not itself decide the dispute submitted to arbitration. It is rather the Arbitral Tribunal*

---

of institutions because it negates their influence on the outcome of the proceedings, and rather presumes their role as being merely facilitative.

558. "Website of the ICC's International Court of Arbitration, http://www.iccwbo.org/about-icc/organisation/dispute-resolution-services/icc-international-court-of-arbitration" http://www.iccwbo.org/products-and-services/arbitration-and-adr/arbitration.
The same idea may be found in introductory material of the SCC on their website ("*The SCC does not itself decide disputes*"). See http://www.sccinstitute.com/skiljeforfarande-2.aspx.
559. de Hancock, "The ICC Court of Arbitration: The Institution and its Procedures" 23.
560. Grigera Naon, "The Role of the Secretariat of the International Court of Arbitration" 18-19.

> *constituted specifically for each dispute under the ICC Rules* [...] *that will alone have the power and the responsibility of deciding the parties' dispute*[561].

Because of the formidable influence which the ICC has had on the development of international arbitration and arbitral institutions globally, it is not surprising that the idea then extended beyond the ICC, and was embraced by other institutions. Article 29 of the LCIA Rules of 1998 for example provided that:

> [t]*he decisions of the LCIA Court with respect to all matters relating to the arbitration shall be conclusive and binding upon the parties and the Arbitral Tribunal. Such decisions are to be treated as* administrative *in nature and the LCIA Court shall not be required to give any reasons*[562] (emphasis added).

This wording first appeared in the 1985 rules[563], the previous (and much shorter) edition of the LCIA rules being silent on the subject[564]. The most recent version of the LCIA rules (2014) continue to reflect the idea that the institution does not participate in the adjudication of the disputes referred to it, albeit in a more nuanced manner:

> *The determinations of the LCIA Court with respect to all matters relating to the arbitration shall be conclusive and binding upon the parties and the Arbitral Tribunal, unless otherwise directed by the LCIA Court. Save for reasoned decisions on arbitral challenges under Article 10, such determinations are to be treated as administrative in nature; and the LCIA Court shall not be required to give reasons for any such determination.*[565] (emphasis added).

While this new wording suggests that the LCIA Rules recognize implicitly that a decision of the LCIA Court on challenges to an arbitrator may not be "administrative" in nature, it continues to lend support to the notion that decisions may be characterized as either administrative or jurisdictional (and that the bulk of an institution's decisions will fall outside of the adjudication of the disputes it administers).

In a similar vein, while the ICDR rules do not qualify the centre's decisions in general terms as administrative, the schedule of fees talks of the institution "*administratively*" dismissing a claim in case of non-payment of an advance on costs[566]. Likewise, when the institution makes a negative prima facie decision on jurisdiction, in the event of an arbitration clause not referring expressly to either the AAA or the ICDR and the parties not agreeing to the application of the ICDR rules, the institution

561. Bühler and Jarvin, "The Arbitration Rules of the International Chamber of Commerce (ICC)" 1131. Other authors include for example Grierson and Van Hooft. See Grierson and Van Hooft, *Arbitrating Under the 2012 ICC Rules. An Introductory User's Guide* 44-45.
562. Article 29.1 LCIA rules (1998).
563. Article 3.9 of the LCIA rules (1985) provided: which provided *"The decision of the Court with respect to all matters referred to in this Article shall be final. Such decisions are deemed to be administrative in nature, and the Court shall not be required to give reasons for them."*
564. LCIA rules (1981).
565. Article 29.1 LCIA rules (2014).
566. *"If a Proceed Fee is not submitted within ninety (90) days of the filing of the Claimant's Demand for Arbitration, the ICDR will administratively close the file and notify all parties."* Administrative Fee Schedule, p. 1.

"*administratively*" closes the file[567]. More tellingly perhaps, in recent court proceedings in which the institution was named as a party, the AAA sought to qualify its own decision to remove an arbitrator as an "*administrative decision*"[568].

Today, this first representation has become the predominant representation of the role of arbitral institutions. It is expressed in one way or another under the pen of some of the leading experts in the field. While it is not possible to list them all here, they include *inter alios*, Fouchard, Gaillard & Goldman[569]; Jason Fry[570]; Horacio Grigera-Naon[571]; Yves Derains & Eric Schwartz[572]; Jean-Louis Delvolvé, Jean Rouche, & Gerald Pointon[573]; Klaus Peter Berger[574], Eric Loquin[575]; Guillermo Aguilar-Alvarez[576]; Jarvin & Buhler[577]; Isabelle Hautot[578]; Calvin Chan[579]; Professor Thomas Clay[580], Redfern & Hunter,[581] Patrick Scholdstrom[582], Paula Hodges, Chris Parker & David Ackebo[583],

567. "[...] *where the ICDR is unable to obtain the agreement of the parties to have the ICDR administer the arbitration, the ICDR will administratively close the case and will not proceed with the administration of the arbitration.*" Administrative Fee Schedule, p. 4.
568. "Adam Technologies International S.A. de C.V v. Sutherland Global Services, Incorporated, United States Court of Appeals, Fifth Circuit, 5 September 2013." The qualification was not confirmed by the court. In this case, the applicant was asking for the appointment of an arbitrator to replace the one appointed by the ICDR following a successful challenge to the original arbitrator. The applicant was arguing *inter alia* that the removal by the ICDR of the previous arbitrator was procedurally faulty because the other party had failed to make a timely challenge under Article 8 of the ICDR Rules, and that the procedure followed by the ICDR to appoint a replacement arbitrator was in breach of the rules because Articles 6 and 10 of the ICDR Rules required that one of the parties make a written request to the ICDR before such an appointment be made.
569. Gaillard and Savage, *Fouchard, Gaillard, Goldman on International Commercial Arbitration* 603. Specific instances of references by these authors to the first representation are cited in the relevant subsections below.
570. Fry, "ICC International Court of Arbitration" 2. Again, specific citations appear in the relevant subsections below.
571. Grigera Naon, "The Powers of the ICC International Court of Arbitration vis-a-vis Parties and Arbitrators" 358. See below for specific citations.
572. Derains and Schwartz, *A Guide to the New ICC Rules of Arbitration* 185. See below for specific citations.
573. Jean-Louis Delvolvé, Jean Rouche, and Gerald H Pointon, *French Arbitration Law and Practice* (2nd edn, Wolters Kluwer 2009) 87. See below for specific citations.
574. Klaus Peter Berger, *Private Dispute Resolution in International Business: Negotiation, Mediation, Arbitration (Third Edition)* (Kluwer Law International 2015) 362-363.
575. Loquin, "La Sentence Arbitrale: L'Examen du Projet de Sentence par l'Institution et la Sentence au Deuxième Degré – Réflexions sur la Nature et la Validité de l'Intervention de l'Institution Arbitrale sur la Sentence" 451. See below for specific citations.
576. Aguilar Alvarez, "The Challenge of Arbitrators" 207. See below for specific citations.
577. Michael Bühler and Sigvard Jarvin, "The Arbitration Rules of the International Chamber of Commerce (ICC)" in Frank-Bernd Weigand (ed), *Practitioner's Handbook on International Commercial Arbitration* (Oxford University Press 2009) 1154. See below for specific citations.
578. Hautot, "Les Pouvoirs de la Cour d'Arbitrage de la C.C.I. de Décider ou Non d'Organiser l'Arbitrage" 26-27. See below for specific citations.
579. Chan, "Of Arbitral Institutions and Provisional Determinations on Jurisdiction, Global Gold Case" 412-413. See below for specific citations.
580. Clay, *L'arbitre* para. 1053. See below for specific citations.
581. Blackaby, Partasides, Hunter, and Redfern, *Redfern and Hunter on International Arbitration* 43.
582. Scholdstrom, "Contractual Relations in Institutional Arbitration" 456.
583. Hodges, Parker, and Ackebo, "International Chamber of Commerce (ICC)" 103. See below for specific citations.

Stephen Bond, Nicole Duclos, Miguel Lopez Forastier and Jeremy Wilson[584], and Cristiana I. Stoica[585].

[2] Rationale behind the Representation: The Non-applicability of Due Process Requirements, and the Necessity to Preserve the Effectiveness of Institutional Arbitration

Whether or not the first representation of the decisions of institutions as non-jurisdictional is consistent with the reality of institutional arbitration, it is undeniable that this representation plays a useful function. As explained by Professor Fouchard:

> [...] *it is the whole legal regime applicable to the decisions taken by the institutions in the administration of each arbitration which ensues from the qualification* [of administrative/non-jurisdictional] (Translation by the author)[586].

By qualifying the decisions of arbitral institutions as administrative/non-jurisdictional one establishes the inapplicability of certain due process requirements to these institutional decisions. As Isabelle Hautot explains:

> [...] *first, the mechanisms for the judicial review of arbitral awards are not available against decisions rendered by arbitral decisions; and second, fundamental due process requirements –such as adversarial process, respect of the rights of the defence, and the requirement of reasoned decisions– do not have to be followed by arbitral institutions for their decisions to be legally valid* (Translation by the Author)[587].

The argument is that imposing the same due process requirements to institutions as are imposed on arbitrators[588] would render the institutional arbitration process overly burdensome. If every decision rendered by an arbitral institution had to be

584. Stephen Bond, Nicole Duclos, Miguel Lopez Forastier and Jeremy Wilson, "International Chamber of Commerce (ICC)", in K Nairn and P Heneghan (eds), *Arbitration World,* (Sweet & Maxcwell 2015) 105.
585. Cristiana I. Stoica, "Institutional Arbitration in Romania" in Crenguta Leaua and Flavius-Antoniu Baias (eds), *Arbitration in Romania: A Practitioner's Guide,* (Kluwer Law International 2016), Chapter 5 – §5.01.
586. In the original language: "*C'est en réalité tout le régime juridique des décisions prises par ces organes dans l'administration de chaque arbitrage qui va découler de leur qualification: aussi bien leurs conditions de régularité que les recours auxquels elles sont exposées.*" Fouchard, "Les Institutions Permanentes d'Arbitrage Devant le Juge Etatique (A Propos d'une Jurisprudence Récente)" 240. See also Gaudet, "La Coopération des Juridictions Etatiques à l'Arbitrage Institutionnel" 109.
587. In the original language: "[...] *d'une part, les recours prévus à l'encontre des sentences arbitrales sont irrecevables à l'encontre des décisions des institutions d'Arbitrage; d'autre part, les conditions fondamentales de régularité du procès – respect du contradictoire, respect des droits de la défense, motivation de la décision – ne sont pas nécessaires à la prise par les Institutions d'une décision valable*". Hautot, "Les Pouvoirs de la Cour d'Arbitrage de la C.C.I. de Décider ou Non d'Organiser l'Arbitrage" 19.
588. Where the requirements applicable to the arbitrators come from is, itself, the object of interesting debates. Theoretically they could result from legal requirements of the law of the seat of the arbitration, or as requirements of the laws of each of the places of enforcement or of a transnational arbitral order.

preceded by an exchange of submissions between the parties, or had to be accompanied by detailed reasons, this would lead to a slowing down of the institutional process (which in the context of the current complaints about delay and costs in arbitration appears inconceivable). For example Aguilar-Alvarez argues:

> *By refusing to allow that decisions taken by the ICC Court of Arbitration acting in application of Rules chosen mutually by the parties are judicial in character, the courts have certainly taken into account the "disastrous" consequences of such a classification: namely, the obligation to organise a hearing before rendering a reasoned award subject to enforcement but also to control by the courts*[589].

More importantly perhaps finding that extensive due process requirements are applicable to the decisions of institutions would open the door to the risk of strategic manoeuvres by some respondents who might attempt to stall the arbitral process. For Jan Paulsson "[u]*nscrupulous defendants would find a cornucopia of impediments to the arbitral process, and insist on endless complicated proceedings before the arbitral institution itself*"[590]. After all, the benefits for a disgruntled party could be potentially enormous. For example, imposing a possibility of review of institutional decisions for breach of due process would first add an additional layer of review to what is otherwise available: Institutional decisions could presumably be reviewed by a domestic judge not only in the course of enforcement proceedings for the arbitrators' award, but also in the context of an action against the institutional decision itself when the arbitration proceedings are still pending. In addition, this additional recourse would not be constrained by the limited grounds of Article V of the New York Convention (as institutional decisions do not constitute awards).

Imposing the same due process requirements on institutions as are applicable to arbitrators might, in turn, require institutions to alter the manner in which they function. For Jan Paulsson:

> *Arbitral institutions would have to react by operating in a more formal and cumbersome manner. [...] Bodies such as the ICC or LCIA Courts – or any of the other mentioned above – could no longer function as they do today. [...] If every decision to be taken by these institutions were to be subject to a full adversarial process, the result would be either that the time-period for arbitrations would be vastly extended, or that the membership of the supervising organ would be entirely replaced by career bureaucrats or "institutional magistrates." Institutional arbitration would either become greatly more expensive (and thus more inaccessible to Third World litigants) or simply go out of business*[591].

Ultimately, requiring of arbitral institutions that they abide by the same due process requirements as arbitral tribunals could potentially be disastrous. In the words of Professor Fouchard:

> *One can imagine the multiplication of applications for annulment of awards, the paralysing effect for existing arbitration proceedings, and the heaviness which*

589. Aguilar Alvarez, "The Challenge of Arbitrators" 16.
590. Paulsson, "Vicarious Hypochondria and Institutional Arbitration" 248.
591. Paulsson, "Vicarious Hypochondria and Institutional Arbitration" 248.

would therefore characterise institutional decision-making [...] (Translation by the Author)[592].

In sum, the first representation of the role of institutions serves an important function. This function is to preserve the effectiveness of the arbitral system in its institutional form.

[3] Origins and Historical Development of the First Representation

The precise origins of the representation are difficult to pinpoint. Under French law, arbitral institutions are prohibited from acting as arbitrators. In 1980, a new Article 1451 of the French code of civil procedure was adopted which prevented arbitral institutions from "deciding disputes" themselves. Fouchard, Gaillard and Goldman explain that the French New Code of Civil Procedure "*sought to limit the role of arbitral institutions in French domestic law, by prohibiting the appointment of an entity or organisation as an arbitrator and by favoring the direct appointment of arbitrators by the parties, even in institutional arbitration*"[593]. It is thus tempting to see the practice of describing the ICC's role as purely administrative, as the result of French law's prohibition against institutions acting as arbitrators (this practice would have been integrated in the ICC rules because of the institution's headquarters are located on French soil[594]). However, until the prohibition was introduced in 1980, French law did permit the appointment of entities ("*corps constitués*") as arbitrator[595]. The description of the ICC as a non-adjudicating entity, on the other hand, is something which predates 1980[596]. It does not appear therefore that this first representation of the role of institutions is rooted in the French law's limitation of the role of "corps constitués".

It would also be an exaggeration to single out the wording contained at Article 1(2) of the ICC rules as the original source of the first representation of the role of institutions. As explained below, in reality, the notion that the actions of any arbitral institution are necessarily administrative/non-jurisdictional in nature is one which

592. In the original language: "*De telles conséquences seraient désastreuses. On imagine la multiplication des recours en annulation, la paralysie en résultant pour les instances arbitrales en cours et la lourdeur qui s'attacherait désormais à la prise de ces décisions institutionnelle* [...]" Fouchard, "Les Institutions Permanentes d'Arbitrage Devant le Juge Etatique (A Propos d'une Jurisprudence Récente)" 244.
593. Gaillard and Savage, *Fouchard, Gaillard, Goldman on International Commercial Arbitration* 32. On the same, see Fouchard, "Les Institutions Permanentes d'Arbitrage Devant le Juge Etatique (A Propos d'une Jurisprudence Récente)" 242-243.
594. Whilst they are not entirely clear, it seems that Derains and Schwartz associate the provision of the ICC rules stating that the institution does not itself decide disputes, with the legal prohibition under French law against institutions acting as arbitrators. See Derains and Schwartz, *A Guide to the New ICC Rules of Arbitration* 18.
595. Clay, *L'arbitre* 379. Interestingly, Clay (citing J-F Poudret) also explains that examples of cases where the mission to arbitrate was entrusted to entities as opposed to individuals may be found throughout the Middle Ages in France. See the original article of Poudret: Jean-François Poudret, "Deux Aspects de l'Arbitrage Dans les Pays Romands au Moyen Age: L'Arbitrabilité et le Juge-Arbitre" (1999) 1999 Revue de l'Arbitrage 3, 14.
596. It may be found for instance in the 1975 rules of the institution which were already providing that "[t]*he Court of Arbitration does not itself settle disputes*".

materialized over three decades as a result of a series of decisions rendered by the French courts in relation to challenges made against various decisions rendered by two arbitral institutions (the ICC and the Chambre Arbitrale de Paris (CAP)) in the course of proceedings administered by them. However, because some of the later French decisions relied heavily upon the statement of the ICC rules that the institution "*does not itself resolve disputes*" one may say that the formulation of the ICC rules has had some influence on the development of the first representation.

The nature of the decisions of institutions and tribunals respectively is not a topic which had captured the interest of commentators before the question arose in the French courts. In fact, to this day, very few commentators have looked into the subject other than in the context of a discussion of the French decisions on the matter. Naturally, the abundance of French decisions on the nature of institutional decisions, itself, is purely coincidental in the sense that it is the consequence of the presence of the ICC's headquarters in France. Whenever, as discussed below, disgruntled parties to ICC arbitration proceedings attempted to obtain the annulment of decisions rendered by the institution (often for purely tactical reasons), they did so by initiating proceedings against the ICC itself, and for these purposes filed their claims in the French courts on the basis that the ICC's headquarters are located in Paris.

This abundance of cases is in sharp contrast with the dearth of decisions on the matter in the other leading jurisdictions such as the United States, Switzerland or England, and it is certainly no exaggeration to state that the manner in which the role of arbitral institutions is most commonly portrayed around the world today is intrinsically linked to French "case law". So much so that it is not possible fully to understand the question of the theoretical representations of the role of arbitral institutions without examining the French courts' decisions in some detail. Such decisions (which until now had not been translated into English) are therefore the object of a somewhat detailed analysis below. From that analysis it transpires that the first representation of the role of arbitral institutions is one which developed incrementally over a period of almost thirty years with each successive decision of the French courts – and which then permeated into the literature.

[a] *The* Société Appareils Dragon *Case*

The first case in which the French courts had to examine the nature of the decisions rendered by an institution appears to be the case of Société Appareils Dragon[597].

597. "Société Appareils Dragon, Cour d'Appel de Paris, 22 June 1982 (Revue de l'Arbitrage, 1982, at p. 91)"; "Société Appareils Dragon, Cour de Cassation, 2ieme Chambre Civile, 8 June 1983 (Revue de l'Arbitrage, 1987, at p. 309)."

As previously noted, the decisions rendered by the French courts are generally significantly shorter than those rendered by the courts of some common law jurisdictions (in part because French courts do not refer to previous decisions) and their paragraphs are not numbered. The Cour de cassation decision in the Appareils Dragon case occupies no more than two pages. For these reasons, commentators do not normally refer to specific paragraph numbers when discussing French decisions. Accordingly, references to French decisions in this book omit paragraph numbers.

Interestingly the case did not receive a lot of attention when first decided in the early 1980s. It was only towards the end of that decade, after other cases had been decided, that this first decision received the interest it deserved.

The case arises out of an ICC arbitration between two companies, "Appareils Dragon" and "Construimport". "Appareils Dragon" contested the validity of the decision of the ICC to prolong the six-month period for the issue of the award (provided for at the then Article 18 of the ICC rules[598]), and on that basis asked for the annulment of the award. One of the arguments raised by Appareils Dragon[599] was that the institution had failed to comply with an alleged duty to provide reasons for its decision to extend the six-month period. The French courts having rejected Appareils Dragon's application in first instance and on appeal, Appareils Dragon petitioned the Cour de Cassation[600]. The applicant was arguing that the finding of the Court of Appeal that the ICC had no duty to provide a reasoned decision was *"incompatible with the nature of the ICC rules of arbitration"*[601].

In what is a very short decision[602], the Cour de Cassation rejected the applicant's petition[603]. For these purposes[604], the Court observed that the ICC was not an arbitrator and consequently its decision to prolong the six-month period was not "jurisdictional":

> [...] *the Court of Arbitration, itself lacking the quality of arbitrator, was not bound to provide reasons for its decision of prolongation, which did not have a jurisdictional character* (Translation by the Author)[605].

598. Now Article 30 of the ICC rules (2012). Article 30 reads in relevant part: *"The time limit within which the arbitral tribunal must render its final award is six months. Such time limit shall start to run from the date of the last signature by the arbitral tribunal or by the parties of the Terms of Reference or, in the case of application of Article 23(3), the date of the notification to the arbitral tribunal by the Secretariat of the approval of the Terms of Reference by the Court.* [...] *The Court may extend the time limit pursuant to a reasoned request from the arbitral tribunal or on its own initiative if it decides it is necessary to do so."*
599. Another argument raised by Société Appareils Dragon was that the ICC was an agent of the parties (*"mandataire des parties"*, under French law) and that, therefore, as agent, it was bound by a duty of information towards the parties (as principals); duty which the ICC was said to have breached when it failed to inform the parties of the fact that the Chairman of the Tribunal had applied to the ICC for a prolongation of the six-month period for the issue of the award.
600. France's highest judicial authority for civil and criminal matters.
601. In the original language, *"l'Arrêt aurait dénaturé le règlement"*. In parallel, the applicant was also arguing that the ICC was an agent of the parties and that therefore it had a duty of information, which it had failed to discharge.
602. Excluding the paragraphs setting out the background of the case and the argument of the applicant, the analytical part of the decision is limited to a single paragraph.
603. The court rejected both the applications as to the alleged requirement of information and as to the one of a reasoned decision.
604. It also considered that: (1) the institution had discretion to interpret its own rules (the term used by the court in the original language was *"une interpretation souveraine"*); and that (2) the parties had agreed to abide by such rules, and the rules did not contemplate reasoned decisions. This latter point seemed to indicate, *a contrario*, that the court would have quashed a decision of the ICC taken in violation of its rules.
605. In the original language, *"la Cour d'arbitrage, qui n'avait pas elle-même la qualité d'arbitre, n'était pas tenue de motiver sa décision de prorogation qui ne présentait pas de caractère juridictionnel"*.

By this short statement, the court signified that a distinction had to be drawn between the nature of the decisions rendered by the ICC and those of an arbitral tribunal. Decisions of institutions were not jurisdictional, whereas decisions of arbitrators were. As a consequence, decisions of an institution did not need to be reasoned.

The wording above also suggested that, in order to find that the ICC's decision was non-jurisdictional, the court had applied what may be referred to as an organic criterion[606]: i.e., one relating to the person of the decision-maker rather than the decision itself. The court indeed suggested that the so-called non-jurisdictional character of the decision of the ICC derived from the fact that the ICC itself did not have the "*quality of arbitrator*". Regrettably, the court stopped short of explaining why the arbitral institution did not have the quality of arbitrator or, for that matter, why it was this quality of arbitrator which should be determinative of the so-called jurisdictional character of a decision.

In the silence of this decision, one might therefore wonder whether, in a distant past, the distinction between the so-called jurisdictional and administrative functions does not find echo in the dichotomy existing within French administrative law between the "administrative" and "jurisdictional" roles of certain governmental entities. From the French revolution onwards and throughout the nineteenth century, the progressive establishment in France of a court system for "administrative law"[607] alongside the existing "civil law" court system[608], resulted in the necessity to distinguish, within the functions exercised by governmental entities, those activities which constituted "administration" and those which pertained the resolution of disputes between the administration and its subjects ("jurisdictional" functions)[609].

More immediately, however, this "jurisdictional vs. non-jurisdictional" dichotomy seems to be inspired by the distinction entertained in French civil procedure between the "jurisdictional decisions" and the "measures of judicial administration" which a judge may take under French law[610]. The notion of measure of judicial administration is not defined by French law but it has appeared since 1971 in several articles of the code of civil procedure[611]. A measure of judicial administration is a decision made by a French magistrate relating to the administration of a particular matter, or to the running of a particular court. For example, decisions to postpone a

606. In the sense that the determinative criterion relates to the person of the decision-maker (i.e., the decisional organ), rather than, for example, the subject matter of the decision (i.e., material criterion), its purpose (i.e., functional criterion).

607. The jurisdiction of the administrative courts in France is limited to of matters involving the application of French administrative law, i.e., a branch of French law governing the relationship between the French administration and its subjects.

608. These private law courts ("Juridictions de l'ordre judiciaire") are the courts with general competence to hear matters relating *inter alia* to contracts law, torts, commercial law, family law, employment law, criminal law etc.

609. Pierre Tifine, Droit Administratif Français, Second edition, Éditions juridiques Franco-Allemandes, 2014, Chapter 2.

610. In French "acte de nature juridictionnelle" *v.* "mesure d'administration judiciaire".

611. See Articles 109, 126-3, 129-6, 368, 393, 499, 537, 836, 847-4, 879, 1224, 1237, 1384 of the Code od Civil Procedure.

hearing, to allocate a certain magistrate to a case, or even to consolidate two sets of proceedings, are all measures of judicial administration under French law. What characterizes the regime of these measures is that they are not appealable[612], that they can be freely modified by the authority that has issued them, and that they do not require that their recipients be given an opportunity to present their case[613]. The flip side of the coin, is that under the jurisprudence of the Court de Cassation, a measure which "*affects the rights or the obligations*" of one of the parties may not receive the qualification of "measure of judicial administration", and therefore remains appealable[614]. This last point, however, is where the parallel between the measures of judicial administration of a French magistrate and the decisions of an arbitral institutions, stops. According to the decision in *Société Appareils Dragon*, it is indeed the lack of quality of arbitrator of the ICC which conferred on its decision its non-jurisdictional nature, whereas for the measures of judicial administration of the French magistrates, it is the fact that they do not affect the rights and obligations of the parties. As we shall see, later decisions relied on alternative grounds to deny to arbitral institutions' decisions a jurisdictional character. However, the fact that such decisions do not affect the rights and obligations of the parties was never one such ground.

Be that as it may, with this decision, the first block of what would become the main theoretical representation of the role of arbitral institutions was laid down: the decisions rendered by the ICC and those of an arbitral tribunal are, somehow, of a different nature, and only those of a tribunal are jurisdictional.

[b] *The* Société Techni Import Professionnel *Case*

The holding of *Société Appareils Dragon* was confirmed shortly after by the French courts in a second case[615] which bears much resemblance to the first one, not just from a factual point of view, but also in terms of the reasoning of the court.

In this case, just like in *Société Appareils Dragon*, the applicant (Société Techni Import Professionnel) was contesting a decision by the ICC Court to prolong the six-month period for the issue of an award. Before the Court of Appeal of Paris, grounds invoked by the applicant, included *inter alia* that the multiple prolongations by the ICC of the six-month period were invalid because they were made "*automatically*" and

612. Because they are not covered by the principle of "autorité de la chose jugée".
613. Cedric Tahri, Procedure Civile, Breal (2007), p. 47.
614. Cass. soc. 24 mai 1995 n°92-10483, Bull. civ. V, n°168, RTDciv. 1995. 958, obs. R. Perrot. Bulletin 1995 V N° 168 p. 122.
615. "Société Techni-Import Professionnel v Société Electro Scientific Industries, Cour d'Appel de Paris, 17 May 1983 (Revue de l'Arbitrage, 1987, at p. 309)". This dispute arises out of a contract between an American company named Electro Scientific Industries and (ESI) and Techni Import Professionnel for the exclusive distribution by Techni Import of the products of ESI in various European countries and in particular in the Eastern European market. After the termination of the contract by Techni Import, ESI initiated ICC arbitration proceedings. The sole arbitrator having rendered an award for damages in favour of ESI, an exequatur decision was then entered into by the tribunal of first instance in Paris on 11 September 1982.

"*without prior adversarial debates*". According to the applicant, such prior adversarial debates were required by what was then Article 18 of the ICC rules which provided that the extension of the six-month period should remain "*exceptional*". The court rejected the application in short order, holding that: "[...] *as the Arbitration Court of the ICC is not a jurisdictional organ, it does not have to provide with its decisions any reasons, reasons which are not required by its rules of arbitration* [...]" (Translation by the Author)[616].

This confirmed that the ICC Court's decisions were not considered "jurisdictional"[617] and that consequently they did not need to be reasoned. The decision also followed the position previously adopted by the Cour de Cassation in the *Société Appareils Dragon case*, in that the lack of jurisdictional nature of the ICC's decision was seen to result from an organic criterion being the lack of jurisdictional quality of the decision-maker ("*the ICC is not a jurisdictional organ*"). And just like in the *Société Appareils Dragon* case, the court did not investigate (as it would presumably do for a measure of judicial administration taken by a magistrate) whether the decision in question "*affected the rights or obligations*" of the parties.

Ultimately, the French court fell short of explaining what precise difference between arbitral institutions and tribunals justified treating the decisions of the latter as jurisdictional and the ones of the former as administrative[618]. Be that as it may, this second decision can be said to cement the basic principle laid in *Société Appareils Dragon:* namely that the decisions rendered by the ICC and those of an arbitral tribunal were, somehow, of a different nature and that only those of a tribunal were jurisdictional.

[c] *The* Syrian Refineries *Case*

This matter[619], which was decided in first instance a mere ten month after the *Société Techni Import decision*, is interesting for two reasons. First, the type of measure taken by the ICC which was the object of a challenge was different. In this case the applicant requested the annulment of a decision by the ICC to revoke the appointment of an

616. In the original language, "*Considérant que la Cour d'arbitrage de la C.C.I., n'étant pas un organe juridictionnel, n'a pas à donner à ses décisions une motivation qui ne lui est pas imposée par son Règlement*".
617. Whatever this may mean to the court.
618. Interestingly, the statement that the obligation of providing reasoned decisions was "*not required by* [the ICC] *rules of arbitration*", implies that if the rules had required reasoning then a decision devoid of reasons would not have been valid. This in turn seems to indicate that compliance with the arbitration rules may be a condition of validity of the decisions of an institution. This seems to indicate that the court might accept to review, and as the case may be invalidate, decisions of institutions which are made in violation of such rules.
619. "Raffineries de Pétrole d'Homs et de Banias v Chambre de Commerce Internationale, Tribunal de Grande Instance, 28 March 1984 (Revue de l'Arbitrage, 1985, at p. 141)"; "Raffineries de Pétrole d'Homs et de Banias v Chambre de Commerce Internationale, Cour d'Appel de Paris, 15 May 1985 (Revue de l'Arbitrage, 1985, at p. 141)".

arbitrator following a successful party challenge[620]. Second, and more importantly, while the courts confirmed the jurisdictional versus administrative dichotomy established in previous decisions, the court seemed to rely on alternative justifications for this dichotomy.

Perhaps because of the decisions in *Société Techni Import* and the *Société Appareils Dragon* the applicant argued among other things[621] that the decision of the ICC was in reality of a *"jurisdictional nature"* and that, as such, under the French Code of Civil Procedure, the Court should have followed *"due process requirements"*[622] and permitted *"an adversarial procedure"*[623]. These requirements, the applicants argued, constituted *"public policy principles"*[624].

The tribunal rejected the request for annulment. While the judge's decision was unclear in parts[625], it reaffirmed the non-jurisdictional character of the ICC's challenge decision, qualifying it of a decision which merely aimed at *"policing the arbitration proceedings"*[626]. The court stated, in relevant part, that:

---

620. The case arises out of an ICC arbitration amongst, on the one hand, two para-Statal Syrian refineries and, on the other, Inexpétrole (a Swiss company) and Interexport (a Yugoslavian company), concerning a contract for the provision of oil. In the course of the proceedings, Inexpétrole and Interexport challenged the arbitrator appointed jointly by the Syrian refineries –challenge which was upheld by the ICC Court. The Syrian parties having unsuccessfully sought to have the ICC reconsider its decision on the challenge, they decided to initiate legal proceedings against the ICC before the French tribunal of first instance. In these proceedings, they were seeking: (1) the annulment of the ICC Court's decision removing the arbitrator, (2) a declaration that any subsequent nominations of a replacement arbitrator made by the ICC would be null and void, and (3) damages in the amount of 1 French Franc because of the loss allegedly suffered as a result of the ICC's challenge decision; decision which the applicant was stating had been taken *"illegally and with undue haste"* (Translation by the author). In the original language: "[une décision de récusation] *prise de façon illégale et intempestive*".
621. The applicants also argued that, as the challenge decision of the ICC Court was not accompanied by reasons and as the grounds for upholding the challenge were not communicated to the arbitrator, it was impossible to confirm that the ICC had complied with the applicable due process requirements. Incidentally, the applicants were arguing that the substance of the challenge decision of the ICC was ill-founded.
622. In French, *"les principes directeurs du procès"*.
623. In French, *"et notamment le principe du contradictoire"*.
624. On the other side, the ICC was arguing, *inter alia*, that the applicants' arguments were inconsistent with the mission of the ICC in respect of the decision of challenges – mission which was purely administrative. In addition, the ICC was arguing that the applicants were unduly seeking from the French judge a judicial review of the ICC's decision in a manner contemplated neither by the parties' agreement, nor by French law.
625. The judge introduced some uncertainty as to the extent to which due process requirements were applicable to the ICC's decision when deciding the challenge when it stated, in passing: "[i]*t suffices that, prior to the decision being made, the parties' comments, claims and arguments were sought and received by the Secretary General of the Arbitration Court for this decision to bear res judicata effect* [...]." Translation by the author. In the original language: *"Qu'il suffit que les explications des parties, leurs griefs et argumentations respectif, aient été provoqués et recueillis au préalable par le Secrétariat général de la Cour d'arbitrage pour qu'une autorité suffisante de chose décidée soit reconnue à un ace de police de l'instance arbitrale* [...]." Further the court, also noted that the ICC had not failed to notify the decision to the parties, implying perhaps that notification was, in itself, a requirement, or more likely, that notification of the decision which accepted the request for removal of the arbitrator was sufficient reasoning.
626. In the original language: *"un acte de police de l'instance arbitrale"*.

> [The ICC's challenge decision] *remains distinct from, or external to, the exercise of the powers to judge and decide the dispute, and consequently such measure does not call for the application of the same mandatory due process requirements* [as would apply to an arbitrator's decision][627].

The basis for the first instance decision[628] is not immediately evident (because the decision does not articulate the precise legal grounds on which it is based). Nonetheless, the decision may be said to differ from previous ones insofar as the type of criteria applied to distinguish the activities of the institution from those of the arbitrators. In previous decisions, the French courts had considered that the lack of jurisdictional character of institutional decisions resulted from the lack of jurisdictional character of the decision-maker (organic criterion). Here the judge appeared to consider that the non-jurisdictional character of the decisions stemmed from the fact that they fell outside the mission of deciding the dispute (the "*exercise of the powers to judge and decide the dispute*"). This new emphasis placed on a so-called adjudicative mission (rather than the person of the decision-maker) suggests that the non-applicability of due process requirements pertained more directly to the decision itself, than to the status of the decision-maker.

These hesitations as to the rationale for maintaining a distinction between the decisions of an institution and those of a tribunal are interesting. The consistency in the finding that decisions of institutions are not jurisdictional indeed contrasts neatly with the changing explanations given by the French courts in support of such a finding. These hesitations seem to proceed from a (laudable) desire on the part of the French the courts to safeguard, "*coûte que coûte*", the effectiveness of institutional arbitration by maintaining the actions of arbitral institutions outside the jurisdictional realm so as to avoid the applicability of due process requirements to such decisions – which as

627. In the original language: "[...] *une décision sur un incident de récusation ou de remplacement d'un arbitre reste extérieure à l'exercice du pouvoir de juger et de trancher un différend et ne saurait relever des mêmes règles impératives.*"
Interestingly, the tribunal also noted that it did not matter that the decision was not reasoned because this was what the parties had agreed to by submitting their dispute to the ICC rules. In the original language: "*il importe peu que les motifs de droit, de fait ou d'opportunité ayant déterminé cet acte n'ait pas été communiqués aux parties, puisque celles-ci l'ont voulu expressément* [...]."
628. This judgment was then confirmed by the Court of Appeal of Paris. "Raffineries de Pétrole d'Homs et de Banias v Chambre de Commerce Internationale, Cour d'Appel de Paris, 15 May 1985 (Revue de l'Arbitrage, 1985, at p. 141)."
Regrettably, the appeal decision avoids addressing the jurisdictional or administrative character of the decision of the ICC altogether. The court found that the ICC Court's decision was, in fact, reasoned because the ICC court had notified the parties that it was accepting the application and therefore the underlying arguments of Inexpétrole and Interexport. By finding that the decision was sufficiently reasoned, the Court of Appeal could then avoid passing judgment the nature of the decision of the institution: "[the Syrian refineries' application] *must be rejected, without there being any necessity to assess whether the decision presents a jurisdictional character, or to examine the other arguments proposed* [...]." Translation by the author. In the original language: "*Que par contre leur demande tendant à l'annulation de la décision de la Cour d'arbitrage ne peut qu'être déclarée irrecevable sans qu'il y ait lieu ni de rechercher si une telle décision présente ou non un caractère juridictionnel, ni d'examiner les autres moyens proposés* [...]."

explained elsewhere above would potentially open the system to the risk of dilatory tactics and abuse of process.

[d] The Opinter v. Dacomex *Case*

The *Opinter v. Dacomex* case[629] was considered by the Court of Appeals of Paris two years after the first instance decision in the *Syrian Refineries* case[630]. This decision offers the most detailed reasoning on the subject of the nature of institutional decisions and is therefore worthy of somewhat more thorough analysis.

The case concerned an ICC arbitration, which Dacomex had initiated against Opinter in respect of performance of contracts for the sale and transportation of some construction materials from Romania to the Middle East. In the course of the arbitration Opinter had challenged the Chairman of the Tribunal. The challenge had been rejected by the ICC and the Tribunal continued with the arbitration, making an award for damages against Opinter. Opinter then initiated court proceedings in France to obtain the annulment the arbitral award on the basis of the ICC Court's challenge decision.

Opinter argued a breach of *"public policy"*[631]. It argued first that the ICC decision rejecting the challenge violated the due process requirements of the French code of civil procedure (*"principes directeurs du procès"*), which are mandatory for arbitrators[632], because the ICC decision was not reasoned. It also argued that the ICC decision breached the right of the defendant to assert its claims (*"droits de la défense"*) because, in the context of the challenge proceedings, Opinter had allegedly not been given an opportunity fully to present its case. As a result, Opinter argued that the award should be annulled. In response, the ICC argued *inter alia* that the decision strictly complied with the terms of its rules; and that the challenge decision *"did not constitute a decision of a jurisdictional nature, which as such would be subject to the procedural requirements invoked by Opinter, but a mere decision aiming at policing the arbitration proceedings"* (Translation by the author)[633].

The Court of Appeal of Paris[634] rejected Opinter's application. It considered that the obligation of providing reasoned decisions applied only to *"jurisdictional acts, emanating from persons or organisms entrusted with a function having a jurisdictional*

629. "Société Opinter France v S.A.R.L. Dacomex, Cour d'Appel de Paris, 15 January 1985 (Revue de l'Arbitrage, 1986, at p. 87)"; and "Société Opinter France v. S.A.R.L. Dacomex, Cour de Cassation, 2 Ch. civ., 7 October 1987 (Revue de l'Arbitrage, 1987, at p. 479)."
630. But a few months before the appeals decision in the Syrian refineries case. That decision however, as previously stated, avoids addressing the jurisdictional or administrative character of the decision of the ICC altogether.
631. In French a *"violation de règles d'ordre publique"*.
632. Contained in the then Article 1460 of the NCPC.
633. In the original language: "[la décision] *ne constitue pas une décision de nature juridictionnelle – qui serait, comme telle, soumise aux règles de procédure invoquées par la société Opinter – mais une simple décision de police de l'instance arbitrale.*"
634. In a different Chamber from that which would decide the appeal in the Syrian Refineries case a few month later.

nature" (Translation by the author)[635]. Like in previous decisions[636], therefore, it implied that the jurisdictional nature of the "*act*" derived from the jurisdictional function of the decision-maker (i.e., the organic criteria)[637]. As in previous decision, however, the court failed to explain what it meant by "jurisdictional function".

What is novel, however, is the emphasis placed by the court on the then Article 2 of the ICC Rules[638]. This article provided that the ICC "[did] *not itself decide disputes*" and that its decisions on challenges were final and left entirely to the discretion of the ICC[639]. From these institutional provisions the court deduced that the institution "*itself lack[ed] the 'quality of arbitrator', and [was] only responsible with organising the arbitration*"[640]. In turn, the court deduced from this, that the ICC's "*powers*" and any "*decisions*" made in the application of such powers lacked any jurisdictional character[641]. In other words it was the terms of the ICC rules that conferred a so-called

635. In the original language: "*Considérant que l'obligation de donner des motifs ne s'applique, en matière de décisions de justice, qu'aux actes à caractère juridictionnel, émanant de personnes ou d'organismes investis de fonctions de nature juridictionnelle. Considérant qu'à cet égard, il apparaît que la décision critiquée, prise par la Cour d'arbitrage* [...] *pour rejeter la demande de récusation d'un arbitre, n'émane pas d'un organisme juridictionnel – à qui s'imposeraient les principes directeurs du procès auxquels renvoie, pour l'arbitrage, l'article 1460 du N.C.P.C., et ne constitue pas une décision de caractère juridictionnel, soumise à l'obligation de motivation.*"
636. Société Appareils Dragon and Société Techni Import.
637. Less relevant for present purposes but equally interesting is the fact that, just like in the *Techni Import* case, the court's decision also seems to be based on the ground that the ICC decisions were made in compliance with the provisions of the ICC rules. The reference to the rules seems to imply that compliance by the institution with the rules constitutes a condition of validity of the challenge decision. This indicates that the court could accept to review the consistency of the ICC decisions with its own rules and as the case may be declare them invalid.
638. Article 1(2) of the current (2012) edition of the ICC rules.
639. The decision took also note of Article 16 of the Statutes of the ICC, providing that the reasons of the ICC decisions' are not communicated to the parties.
640. The question of whether the French court is correct that the ICC rules (in their entirety) confer no jurisdictional power on the ICC is debatable, and it is the object of detailed discussion later in this chapter. What is important for present purposes is that the French court deduces from the terms of the ICC rules the lack of jurisdictional power and function on behalf of the institution, which in turn results in the decision of the institution not being jurisdictional.
641. Translation by the author. In the original language: "*Considérant dès lors, que la Cour d'arbitrage n'a pas elle-même la qualité d'arbitre, et qu'elle est seulement chargée d'organiser l'arbitrage, notamment par la nomination des arbitres; que ces pouvoirs n'ont pas le caractère juridictionnel, pas plus que les décisions qui en sont l'expression.*"

    Unfortunately, the Court of Appeal decision also introduces some ambiguity as to the rationale underlying its holding. The court indeed notes that in the present case the ICC's decision "*does not emanate from a jurisdictional organ –to which the due process requirements of Article 1460 of the N.C.P.C. would apply-* and *does not constitute a decision having a jurisdictional character, to which the obligation of a reasoned decision would apply*"). (Emphasis added) (Translation by the author). By making this statement the appeal decision seems to imply that different due process requirements apply depending on whether it is the decision itself, or the decision-maker's function, that are jurisdictional. The court seems to consider that the "*principes directeurs du procès*" apply when the decision-maker is a jurisdictional organ, but that the requirement of a reasoned decision applies when the nature of the decision itself is jurisdictional. This ambiguity is certainly unfortunate. However the general impression that one gets from considering the decision in this entirety is that the court does consider that the non-jurisdictional nature of a decision derives from the non-jurisdictional character to the institution's role, and that non-jurisdictional role in turn resulted in the non-jurisdictional nature of the institution's decisions (and therefore in the non-applicability of due process requirement).

This decision of the Court of Appeal of Paris was then affirmed by the Cour de Cassation. In this final decision, the Cour de Cassation confirmed both the Court of Appeals' decision and the underlying reasoning. The Cour de Cassation's decision emphasized the facts that: (1) the ICC, having only been retained by the parties to "*organise the proceedings*", it was not fulfilling a "*jurisdictional function*", and therefore (2) the decision of the ICC did not qualify as an arbitral "*award*"[642]. The Cour de Cassation, like the lower court, grounded its conclusion on the parties' agreement to use the ICC rules. Their agreement, according to the French Supreme Court, had for effect to limit the role of the institution to that of an organizer, which had no jurisdictional function because the ICC rules did not confer any jurisdictional powers on the ICC. It was only as a consequence of the ICC rules that the institution's decisions were not capable of being reviewed as such by the French judge. The Cour de Cassation thus applied an organic criterion. The non-jurisdictional nature of the decision of the ICC Court resulted from the fact that the parties had agreed that the ICC should *not* have the same jurisdictional status as arbitrators (organic criteria). While the court still failed to offer a precise explanation as to what "jurisdictional" functions or powers could be and how they might differ from "administrative" ones, it did indicate that it was the parties' agreement (by their choice of the relevant institutional rules) which conferred a so-called non-jurisdictional character to the decision-maker (and in turn to its decisions). The Court's reasoning thus implied that, should arbitration rules confer jurisdictional powers to an institution, then the decisions of that institution could be "jurisdictional".

Again, the hesitations as to the theoretical rationale for distinguishing institutional measures from those of a tribunal are arguably illustrative of the courts' attempts to safeguard institutional arbitration from a perceived risk of abuse of process. Ultimately, this decision, with its new emphasis on the parties' agreement as the source of the non-jurisdictional character of institutions' decisions, constituted a new step in the incremental crystallization of the theoretical representation of institutions as mere administrators.

[e] The SCPA *Case*

Around the same time as the *Opinter* case[643], the Court of Appeal of Paris[644], was given, with the *SCPA* case, an opportunity to confirm the principle that certain due process requirements did not apply to measures taken by arbitral institutions.

non-jurisdictional function of the decision-maker, and that the inapplicability of all due process requirements result from the non-jurisdictional character of a decision.

642. "Société Opinter France v. S.A.R.L. Dacomex, Cour de Cassation, 2 Ch. civ., 7 October 1987 (Revue de l'Arbitrage, 1987, at p. 479)."
643. Decided after the appeal decision in *Opinter* but before the confirmation of the decision by the Cour de Cassation.
644. "Société Commerciale de Produits Agricoles (S.C.P.A.) v Société Coopérative de la Roche Clermault, Cour d'Appel de Paris, 29 November 1985 (Revue de l'Arbitrage, 1987, at p. 335)."

In the case at hand, a company named SCPA was seeking the annulment of an arbitral award on the basis that the decision of the Chambre Arbitrale de Paris to apply its emergency rules of procedure was taken in violation of some mandatory due process requirements[645]. The Court rejected SCPA's application in the following terms:

> *It transpires from the rules of arbitration* [...] *that the choice of the emergency procedure* [...] *lies in the powers to organise the arbitration, such powers being exercised prior to the actual proceedings at a time when there can be no requirement of adversarial process or of reasoned decision* [...]. Translation by the Author[646].

The decision offered a slightly different basis from previous decisions, without it being clear whether this constituted an evolution in the grounds for the court's decision or merely an alternative expression of pre-existing grounds. Like in the *Syrian Refineries* case the judge found that the institutional decision fell outside a so-called adjudicative mission, and like in the *Opinter decision*, the judge looked at the parties' agreement (i.e., the institutional rules chosen). But here the judge did not find that the parties' agreement conferred a non-jurisdictional character on the decision-maker (a lack of quality of arbitrator). Rather it found that the parties had agreed that the relevant decision of the institution fell outside the scope of the adjudicative mission[647].

The court also found that, by operation of the parties' agreement, the timing of the CAP's decision prevented the applicability of due process requirements, because the decision intervened before the adjudicative phase had commenced. The court's reasoning implied that no decision made before the beginning of this supposed

645. By way of further background, the Claimant in the arbitration, a company named "Société Coopérative de la Roche Clermault", had initiated in October 1984 proceedings against the "Société Commerciale de Produits Agricoles" (SCPA) for breaches of a contract for the provision of wheat. The Claimant had requested from the president of the CAP, pursuant to Article 34 of the CAP rules of arbitration, that the arbitration be conducted under the emergency procedure. The president acceded to this request and a tribunal rendered an award in December 1984. The losing party (SCPA) sought the annulment of the arbitral award before the Tribunal de Grande Instance of Paris, on the grounds *inter alia* that the expedited procedure was in violation of principles of due process. The applicant was arguing *inter alia* that the CAP had failed to provide reasons in relation to its decision to apply the emergency rules; decision which had for effect to deprive the parties of the availability of the appeal procedure that is otherwise available under the CAP rules. In the original language: "[La CAP] *aurait méconnu le principe de la contradiction et violé une règle d'ordre public, en appliquant ainsi une procédure privant les parties du double degré de juridiction normalement applicable devant la Chambre arbitrale de Paris, sans débat contradictoire préalable, ni motivation de sa décision.*"

646. In the original language: "*Considérant qu'ainsi, il ressort du Règlement de la Chambre arbitrale – qui constitue la loi des parties en vertu de la référence expresse qui y est faite dans la clause compromissoire qu'elles ont souscrites – que le choix de la procédure d'urgence est laissé à l'appréciation du Président de cet organisme, au vu des éléments présentés par le demandeur, et relève des pouvoirs d'organisation de l'arbitrage s'exerçant préalablement à l'instance elle-même, dans une phase préparatoire d'administration, qui n'exige, en tant que telle, ni débat contradictoire ni décision motivée.*"

647. Incidentally, the court also draws a parallel with the procedure of "*assignation a jour fixe*" before the French courts, which does not require an adversarial procedure. That procedure is one by which a party can request on an emergency basis the hearing of the merits of its case before the French judge. The request that a case be heard on an expedited basis can be made ex parte and the decision to grant the expedited procedure does not have to be reasoned.

adjudicative phase was capable of being subject to the due process requirements applicable to arbitrators.

The correctness of the courts decisions in this respect is considered elsewhere below but what should be retained from this decision[648] is the new emphasis of the French judge on the notion of "adjudicative mission", and the continued reliance on the parties' agreement as the foundation of the non-jurisdictional nature of institutional decisions. As such, this decision can be said to have further cemented the theoretical representation of institutions as mere administrators.

[f] The REDEC *and* Pharaon *Case*

This case[649] concerned an attempt to obtain a judicial review by the French court of a prima facie decision of the ICC on jurisdiction[650]. While the decision is that of a lower court, and while it was rendered in the context of an emergency procedure ("*en référé*"), the reasoning of the court constitutes a significant progression towards the crystallization of the first theoretical representation of the functions of arbitral institutions for reasons explained below.

648. Incidentally, SCPA was seeking a suspension of the court proceedings before the TGI pending a decision of the administrative tribunal of Paris before which it had started a separate procedure in which it was requesting a "declaration of illegality" of Article 34 of the arbitration rules of the CAP. SCPA was arguing that the rules of arbitration constituted, for the purposes of French administrative law, an "administrative act" (i.e., type of measure capable of being declared void only by the French administrative courts). SCPA's argument (based on the applicable test in French administrative law) was that the CAP arbitration rules contained general provisions emanating from a body empowered with exorbitant public powers ("*prérogatives de puissance publique*") used in the context of a mission aiming to support the States' judicial activities. The tribunal rejected the notion that the arbitration rules could be qualified of administrative act. Its decision is based on the grounds that: (1) the CAP is a private entity (not created by the state), (2) that the institution was only acting on the basis of a private contract between the parties (not an empowerment by the State), (3) that the institution was not rendering a decision on behalf of the French People and (4) that the institution's mission is not one of *"public service"*: In the original language: *"La Chambre arbitrale de Paris, organisme constitué sous l'égide de l'Union des Syndicats professionnels, ne tient ses pouvoirs de trancher les litiges que de la convention des parties; les tribunaux arbitraux qu'elle constitue ne prononcent pas leurs décisions au nom du Peuple français et n'exercent aucune mission de service public.*" Cited by Fouchard in Fouchard, "Les Institutions Permanentes d'Arbitrage Devant le Juge Etatique (A Propos d'une Jurisprudence Récente)" 230.
649. "Société REDEC et M. Pharaon v Société Uzinexport Import et Chambre de Commerce Internationale, Tribunal de Grande Instance de Paris (Ref.), 13 July 1988 (Revue de l'Arbitrage, 1989, at p. 97)."
650. An (unsuccessful) attempt had been made in an earlier case to contest a decision by the ICC on prima facie jurisdiction. In that earlier case, however, the court had stopped short of qualifying the decision of the ICC as non-jurisdictional. See "Société Československa Obchodní Banka A.S.,Cour de Cassation, 19 May 1987 (Revue de l'Arbitrage, 1987, at p. 367)", p., Cour de Cassation 1987. For a more recent decision rejecting a review of the ICC's prima facie decision which also falls short of qualifying the decision of the ICC of non-jurisdictional/administrative, see "Société ABC International v Chambre de Commerce International, Tribunal de Grande Instance (Ref.), 25 November 2010 (Revue de l'Arbitrage, 2011, at p. 991)"; and "Société ABC International v Chambre de Commerce International, Cour d'Appel de Paris, 27 October 2011 (Revue de l'Arbitrage 2011, at p. 991)."

The case arose out of an ICC arbitration commenced by a Romanian company, "Uzinexport Import" in relation to the construction of a cement factory in Pakistan. The claimant had initiated the arbitration proceedings against four respondents, "Attock Cement Cie", "Attock Cement Pakistan Ltd", Mr Ghaith Pharaon and "Société REDEC". The first two respondents were signatories of the contract which had given rise to the dispute and which contained the relevant arbitration clause. Mr Pharaon had signed the contract, but only as president of the Board of Directors of the first respondent. REDEC was merely the guarantor of the second respondent in respect of the payment of a loan (i.e., not the contract under which the arbitration was arising). REDEC and Pharaon raised jurisdictional objections, which were rejected by the ICC on a prima facie basis. As a result the arbitration had to proceed, with any outstanding jurisdictional objections being for the arbitral tribunal to decide later on. REDEC and Pharaon sought from the French judge the annulment of the prima facie decision of the ICC[651].

The court, rejected the application, holding as follows:

> *By deciding prima facie to let a third party participate in the constitution of an arbitral tribunal, the Arbitration Court of the ICC is not rendering a* decision of a jurisdictional nature, which decision would otherwise fall within the exclusive competence of the arbitrator, *but prescribes a measure of administrative nature, aimed at finalising the constitution of the tribunal pursuant to the arbitration rules* (emphasis added)[652].

This decision is interesting for two reasons. First, from a semantic point of view, while earlier decisions had qualified institutional decisions of "*non-jurisdictional*", this was the first time that the French courts used the term "*administrative*" to describe a measure taken by an arbitral institution. Second, and much more importantly, by contrast to previous decisions which had been cautious to limit the scope of their findings to certain types of institutional decisions (e.g., challenges to arbitrators, or extensions of deadlines) or to one particular institution (e.g., the ICC or the CAP), the courts here make a sweeping generalization: all institutional decisions are necessarily administrative (regardless of the institutional rules concerned). When the courts state that "*the ICC is not rendering a decision of a jurisdictional nature, which decision would otherwise fall within the exclusive competence of the arbitrator*", they find a principle applicable across the board that all jurisdictional decisions are necessarily of the competence of the tribunal, and that all decisions of an institution must be administrative. This newly found principle is that there ought to be a "unity of the jurisdictional mission" (i.e., that the adjudicative mission is somehow indivisible).

In other words, building upon the general idea, already expressed in previous decisions, that the institutions and arbitrators exercise different missions (jurisdictional versus administrative), the court here goes one step further and finds that the

651. The ICC then reconsidered its decision in respect of Mr Pharaon so that the proceedings before the Tribunal de Grande Instance only continued with REDEC as applicant.
652. Translation by the author. In the original language: "*En décidant prima facie de faire intervenir à la constitution d'un tribunal arbitral une personne alléguant sa qualité de tiers à la convention d'arbitrage, la Cour d'arbitrage de la C.C.I. ne rend pas une décision juridictionnelle, laquelle relève de la seule compétence de l'arbitre, mais prescrit une mesure de nature administrative, destinée, en application de son Règlement, à parfaire la constitution du tribunal arbitral.*"

jurisdictional mission is of the exclusive competence of the arbitrators and that, consequently, institutions shall not "*interfere*" with the adjudication of the dispute which belongs exclusively to arbitrators[653].

Regrettably, the basis for this sweeping finding is not clear because the court does not identify the source of this alleged principle of unity of the adjudicative mission. Again, the correctness of the judge's reasoning will be discussed later in this Chapter but what matters here is that this decision takes a significant step towards cementing the first representation of the role of institutions by positing that, as a matter of principle, there is an exclusive competence of arbitral tribunals to make decisions of a jurisdictional nature, and consequently any decision made by any arbitral institution must necessarily be administrative. As explained elsewhere below, this sweeping generalization then found its way into the literature (despite the fact that it did not really find strong support in further decisions of the French courts).

[g] *The* Cubic Defense System *Case*[654]

This case concerns decisions by the ICC Court to extend the six-month period for issue of the final award. This case was decided ten years after REDEC Pharaon[655] and the other cases discussed above. The relevant statements made by the judge in this case were made *obiter* as the courts examined the nature of institutional decisions only incidentally[656]. This being said, because this matter reached France's highest court, and because the decisions were more detailed than previous ones on the subject, they received a lot of attention in the literature[657].

The case arose out of an ICC arbitration between the Ministry of Defence of Iran, as claimant, and a US company named Cubic, as respondent. The arbitration concerned two contracts for the provision and installation of a system for the training of Iranian Air Force pilots signed in the late 1980s. Approximately five years into what

653. If occasional references to some "*adjudicative mission*" may be traced back to decisions from the 1980s it is in these decisions that the courts establish for the first time that the "*adjudicative mission*" is by principle indivisible and that it must fall entirely with the arbitrators. For examples of early references to an "*adjudicative mission*" see: "Société Replor v SARL Ploemeloise de Financement de Participations and Others, Cour d'Appel de Paris, 12 January 1988 (Revue de l'Arbitrage, 1988, at p. 691)"; "Chambre Arbitrale de Paris, Sociétés Carfa Trade Group et Omnium de Travaux v Republique de Guinee, Cour d'Appel de Paris (1re Ch. A), 4 May 1988 (Revue de l'Arbitrage, 1988, at p. 656)." See also an indirect reference to the "*power to judge*" in "Raffineries de Pétrole d'Homs et de Banias v Chambre de Commerce Internationale, Cour d'Appel de Paris, 15 May 1985 (Revue de l'Arbitrage, 1985, at p. 141)".

654. "Société Cubic Defense Systems Inc. v Chambre de Commerce Internationale, Cour d'Appel de Paris, 15 September 1998 (Revue de l'Arbitrage, 1999, at p. 103)"; "Société Cubic Defense Systems Inc. v Chambre de Commerce Internationale, Tribunal de Grande Instance de Paris, 21 May 1997"; "Société Cubic Defense Systems Inc. v Chambre de Commerce Internationale, Cour de Cassation, 1ere Chambre Civile, 20 February 2001 (Revue de l'Arbitrage 2001, at p. 511)."

655. In particular that there should be a "unity of the adjudicative mission"; that the adjudicative mission may not be shared between the arbitrators and the institution but must in its entirety be exercised by the arbitral tribunal.

656. As explained below.

657. Another reason was certainly the unusually harsh criticism levelled by Cubic against the ICC, which seemed to have captured the attention of the arbitration community.

had been protracted arbitral proceedings (and therefore after multiple extensions by the ICC Court of the six-month period for the issue of the final award) Cubic initiated proceedings against the ICC before the French courts. The action aimed at obtaining the annulment of the so-called arbitration contract between Cubic and the ICC (i.e., the contract, distinct from the parties' arbitration agreement, under which the ICC was providing its services).

The claims made by the applicant are too numerous to be presented here exhaustively[658]. The main claims were that the ICC Court had refused to re-qualify an order of the arbitral tribunal as an award (which would have been subject to the ICC's scrutiny); that it had wrongly rejected a challenge to an arbitrator made by Cubic; that it had failed to control the duration of the proceedings, and more generally that it had been "*powerless and inactive in the face the faults of the arbitral tribunal so that it was justified to terminate its mission*"[659]. The ICC was denying all claims.

In first instance, the court rejected Cubic's application. While it did not focus on the nature of the decisions rendered by the ICC as this question was not at the heart of the matter (which instead concerned the contractual relationship between the ICC and the parties), the court made a number of statements, which are relevant to the representation of the functions of arbitral institutions. For instance, it stated:

> "[the ICC] *does not decide itself disputes but organises and supervises the arbitrations in accordance with the ICC rules";*
>
> "[...] *in exchange for the parties' agreement to be bound by the arbitration rules, the ICC commits to abide by the provisions of the said rules and to administer the arbitral proceedings* without intervening in the adjudication function which is devolved to the arbitrators"*;*
>
> "[Cubic] *knew, in particular from the documentation sent to it by the ICC describing clearly the procedure that the* international Court of arbitration has a non-jurisdictional role, limited to the organisation and the policing of the arbitration proceedings, *role which* does not allow it to interfere with the powers of the arbitrators"[660] (emphasis added).

---

658. First the applicant was arguing that it had been duped by the ICC into believing that it had to accept the jurisdiction of the institution. In effect, Cubic was arguing that the ICC's first letter to the parties notifying the receipt of the Request for Arbitration should have advised them that they did not have to accept to arbitrate under the ICC rules (this was because the arbitration clause seemed to provide for ad hoc arbitration).

    Second, Cubic was arguing (in rather convoluted terms) that the contract was null *ab initio* for "*lack of cause*" of Cubic's obligations ("*lack of cause*" in French law serves a purpose similar to the notion of consideration in the Common law). In essence, Cubic was arguing here that the tasks performed by the ICC in the administration of the case were so limited that they constituted a derisory consideration for the obligations of Cubic and that, as such, the contractual relationship between the respondent and the institution had to be declared inexistent by the judge. In this respect, Cubic was arguing that the ICC had been misleading in "*guaranteeing*" its efficiency and its competence in the administration of arbitral proceedings.

659. In the original language: "[...] *son impuissance et son inaction face aux fautes du tribunal arbitral justifient qu'il soit mis fin à sa mission.*"

660. Translation by the author. In the original language: "*Attendu que cet organisme, qui ne tranche pas lui-même les différends, mais organise et supervise les arbitrages effectués en vertu des règlements de la CCI* [...]"*;* "*Attendu qu'en contrepartie de l'adhésion des parties au*

Consistently with previous decisions, the tribunal declared that institutions and arbitrators exercise different missions (jurisdictional versus administrative), and that institution should not "*interfere*" with the decision-making of arbitrators who have competence over the adjudication of the dispute. The wording of the decision suggest that the fact that the adjudicative mission is reserved to the arbitrators results from the terms of the ICC rules, rather than form a supposed principle of general application that the adjudicative mission is somehow indivisible.

The first instance decision in *Cubic* was then confirmed by the Court of Appeal of Paris. Again, if the appeals decision did not focus on the legal qualification of the decision rendered by the ICC, it did contain a number of interesting statements. In particular the Court of Appeal did not make its own the sweeping conclusions of the *REDEC & Pharaon* tribunal previously that any decisions rendered by an institution must be external to the adjudicative mission – conclusion which entails the inapplicability of due process requirements to the decisions of arbitral institutions as a matter of principle. Instead the Court of Appeal emphasized that the parties had agreed to the rules of the ICC and could not therefore complain about the mission that such rules attribute to the institution and the tribunal respectively[661]. In fact, the Court of Appeal seemed to contemplate the applicability of due process requirements to the decisions of the ICC when it stated:

> *If it is true that the international arbitration court must in all circumstances be particularly prudent and act in an equitable manner* [...], *it has not been shown that the court has failed to comply with this obligation*[662].

Cubic then petitioned the Cour de Cassation[663]. Before France's highest court, Cubic argued that its contract with the ICC was illicit because it was in breach of international public policy as the ICC rules allowed undue interference by the institution in the adjudicative mission of the tribunal, in particular at the scrutiny stage. The court rejected the argument of Cubic. In the words of the Cour de Cassation:

> [...] *the* [lower judges] *noted that* the rules of arbitration of the ICC ensure the distinction *between the function of organisation of the arbitration, in particular though the "international court of arbitration", and* the jurisdictional function, left entirely to the arbitrators, the "court" having no jurisdictional power at all. [...] *in this respect the Court of Appeal has correctly judged that the scrutiny of draft awards*

règlement de l'institution, celle-ci s'engage à se conformer aux dispositions de ce règlement et à accomplir, sans s'immiscer dans la fonction de juger dévolue aux arbitres, les actes de gestion de l'instance arbitrale qui y sont définies";"[...] *qu'elle savait, en effet, notamment par la documentation qui lui avait été transmise décrivant très clairement les règles de la procédure d'arbitrage sous l'égide de la CCI que la Cour internationale d'arbitrage a une rôle non juridictionnel, limité à l'organisation et à la police de l'instance arbitrale, qui ne l'autorise pas à empiéter sur les pouvoirs des arbitres* [...]."

661. In the original language: "*que par suite les parties ne sauraient critiquer la délimitation de la fonction juridictionnelle du tribunal qui en résulte ni le rôle qu'elles ont, par leur convention, confié à la* [cour de la CCI]."
662. In the original language: "*Que s'il est vrai que la CIA doit faire preuve en toutes circonstances d'une prudence particulière et œuvrer avec équité à la réalisation de son objet, il n'est pas démontré qu'elle ait manqué à cette obligation.*"
663. "Société Cubic Defense Systems Inc. v Chambre de Commerce Internationale, Cour de Cassation, 1ere Chambre Civile, 20 February 2001 (Revue de l'Arbitrage 2001, at p. 511)."

implies no undue interference in the jurisdictional mission of the arbitrator, but merely aims at guaranteeing the effectiveness of the arbitration proceedings (emphasis added)[664].

The Cour de Cassation offers a confirmation at the highest level of the *"jurisdictional" versus "administrative"* dichotomy; and of the finding that, in ICC arbitration, the adjudicative mission is reserved in its entirety to the arbitrators by operation of the ICC rules (rather than because of a supposed principle of unity/indivisibility of the adjudicative mission). As such, the case further cements the idea of the ICC as an entity devoid of any jurisdictional powers.

[h] *The* Guinea v. CAP *Case*

For the sake of exhaustiveness, it should be noted that one French decision recognized expressly a so-called jurisdictional character to a decision of an arbitral institution. This is the decision of the Tribunal de Grande Instance de Paris of 23 June 1988, rendered in the context of the disputes opposing the Republic of Guinea and the Chambre Arbitrale de Paris[665]. The background of the case is complex but, for present purposes, it may be summed up as follows: the Republic of Guinea had entered into three separate but related contracts for the construction of 3,000 homes in Guinea. Disputes arose between Guinea under all three contracts and the CAP was entrusted with the administration of two arbitrations. These two arbitrations gave rise to some serious incidents as a result of which Guinea initiated a number of proceedings against the CAP itself in the French courts. Of relevance to us[666] are the proceedings in which Guinea

664. Translation by the author. In the original language: "[...] *les juges du fond ont relevé que le règlement d'arbitrage de la CCI assurait la distinction entre la fonction d'organisation de l'arbitrage, notamment par l'intermédiaire de la 'Cour internationale d'arbitrage', et la fonction juridictionnelle, laissée aux seuls arbitres, la 'Cour' n'ayant aucun pouvoir juridictionnel; qu'à cet égard, la Cour d'appel a exactement retenu que la communication du projet de sentence à la Cour internationale d'arbitrage n'emportait aucune ingérence dans la mission juridictionnelle de l'arbitre, mais avait seulement pour but d'assurer l'efficacité de l'arbitrage.*"

665. The decisions rendered in the *Guinea v. Chambre Arbitral de Paris saga* are noteworthy for a number of reasons. One such reason is that they shaped the legal regime applicable to the relationship between institutions and parties under French law. See, for example, "République de Guinée v Chambre Arbitrale de Paris et autres, Tribunal de Grande Instance de Paris, 28 January 1987 (Revue de l'Arbitrage, 1987, p. 371)", where the court qualifies the relationship as a "contract". The court indeed that this contract encompasses *"an obligation on the part of all parties to comply with the terms of the institution's arbitration rules"*. In the original language: "[...] *il s'est créé entre eux des liens contractuels imposant aux parties l'obligation de se conformer au Règlement* [...]." This in turn means that any breach of the rules will render the institution liable; a conclusion shared by Fouchard. See Fouchard, "Les Institutions Permanentes d'Arbitrage Devant le Juge Etatique (A Propos d'une Jurisprudence Récente)" 254.

666. Other related decisions are also interesting though less directly relevant to us. See, for example, "République de Guinée v Chambre Arbitrale de Paris et autres, Tribunal de Grande Instance de Paris, 28 January 1987 (Revue de l'Arbitrage, 1987, p. 371)" and "Chambre Arbitrale de Paris, Sociétés Carfa Trade Group et Omnium de Travaux v Republique de Guinee, Cour d'Appel de Paris (1re Ch. A), 4 May 1988 (Revue de l'Arbitrage, 1988, at p. 656)". These related decisions concern requests for the annulment of an arbitration agreement (on the grounds of error on the person of the centre, a point quickly rejected by the court) and for the rescinding of the "contract" between the parties and the institution which provides for the organization of

was challenging the appointment of two arbitrators, respectively President and Vice-President of the CAP, on the ground that the very disputes between the CAP and Guinea threatened the impartiality and independence of the arbitrators due to their relationship with the arbitral institution. The decision of the Tribunal de Grande Instance[667] rendered on 23 June 1988[668] recognizes that challenge decisions rendered by an institution have a so-called jurisdictional character:

> *In respect of challenges to arbitrators, if the decision forms part of the adjudicative function insofar as it aims at deciding a dispute concerning the person of the arbitrator rather than the dispute itself, this decision concerns essentially the organisation of the arbitration and more specifically the constitution of the arbitral tribunal* [...]. *Even though the determination of an objection to the person of the arbitrator, like any jurisdictional decision, must comply with fundamental due process principles and with the rights of the defence, the State judge has does not possess an exclusive and mandatory jurisdiction to hear challenges even for domestic arbitration proceedings* (Translation by the Author)[669].

The importance of this decision is not to be overstated. First, this decision rendered by a lower court remains isolated and now appears inconsistent with the more recent decisions of the Cour de Cassation. No other decision has shed any doubt on the now well-established (if erroneous[670]) notion that institutions do not participate to the adjudicative mission. Second, while the tribunal in this case qualifies the

---

the arbitration by the CAP. Here Guinea was relying on the ground that the CAP had committed serious breaches of its contractual obligations including the failure by the CAP to consult the arbitrator nominated by Guinea on certain questions of procedure whilst consulting the other arbitrators; and the fact that the Secretary General of the CAP had helped one party in a previous case with the drafting of submissions, in breach of his duty of neutrality. Guinea was ultimately unsuccessful on this request. The Appeal decision nonetheless presents some interest for us insofar as the court reaffirms the distinction between the respective roles of the institution and the arbitrator. "[from the appointment of the tribunal onward the arbitrators] *were fully vested with adjudicative powers. The prerogatives resulting from these powers, which have their own autonomous legitimacy, must be exercised in total independence, as is required of any judge, without any interference from the organ that has appointed the tribunal; organ which has lost all power to intervene*" (Translation by the author). In the original language: "[les juges arbitraux se trouvaient] *pleinement investis du pouvoir de juger; Que l'exercice des prérogatives attachées à ce pouvoir – qui relève d'une légitimité propre et autonome – doit être assuré de façon totalement indépendante, comme il sied à tout juge, sans aucune interférence avec l'organisme qui a mis en place le tribunal arbitral et qui, de ce fait, a perdu tout pouvoir d'action* [...]."

667. This is a lower court decision but one which was not appealed.
668. "République de Guinée v Mm. R. et O., Tribunal de Grande Instance, 23 June 1988 (Revue de l'Arbitrage, 1988, at p. 657)", p., Tribunal de Grande Instance de Paris 1988.
669. "République de Guinée v Mm. R. et O., Tribunal de Grande Instance, 23 June 1988 (Revue de l'Arbitrage, 1988, at p. 657)." *In the original language: "En matière de récusation d'un arbitre, si la décision participe de la fonction de juger dès lors qu'elle a pour objet de trancher un différend concernant la personne de l'arbitre et non le litige lui-même, cet acte relève essentiellement de la mise en œuvre des opérations d'arbitrage et plus spécifiquement de la constitution du tribunal arbitral* [...]. *Même si l'appréciation d'une contestation élevée à l'encontre de la personne de l'arbitre impose, comme pour toute décision juridictionnelle, le respect des principes essentiels de la contradiction et des droits de la défense, il n'a pas été attribué aux juridictions étatiques une compétence exclusive et dérogatoire de la volonté des parties pour connaître de toute demande de récusation, même en matière interne.*"
670. See the proposed representation of the role of institutions offered in Chapter 5 below.

challenge decision of jurisdictional, it concludes that, unlike awards made by arbitrators, such a challenge decision may not be subject to judicial review. Therefore, the basic position is not fundamentally altered: decisions of institutions are kept distinct from that of arbitrators[671].

[i] Recent Decisions

Since the decision in *Cubic Defense Systems,* French "case law" on the matter has been remarkably stable. In 2002, in "*Société Lear v. Chambre de Commerce Internationale*", the courts reaffirmed the principle that the ICC's scrutiny of draft awards does not interfere with a so-called jurisdictional mission of the arbitrator[672]. Likewise, in 2007 and 2009, the Tribunal de Grande Instance and the Court of Appeal of Paris respectively confirmed, in the *Société SNF* case[673] both the validity of the *"jurisdictional" v. "administrative"* dichotomy, and the fact that the scrutiny provisions of the ICC rules do not encroach on the jurisdictional function which the ICC rules reserve to the arbitrators. In 2009[674], in the *Trioplast* case, the Cour de Cassation confirmed again the *"jurisdictional" versus "administrative"* dichotomy, in a manner which suggested that such a dichotomy was grounded on the ICC rules[675]. In 2012, the Tribunal de Grande

671. On this point, see Paulsson, "Vicarious Hypochondria and Institutional Arbitration" 241.
672. Because the ICC can only prescribe changes over matters of form, its powers do not infringe on the arbitrators' "liberty of decision". "Société Lear v Chambre de Commerce Internationale, Tribunal de Grande Instance de Paris, 22 May 2002 (Revue de l'Arbitrage, 2002, at p. 785)."
673. "Société SNF v Chambre de Commerce Internationale, Tribunal de Grande Instance de Paris, 10 October 2007 (Revue de l'Arbitrage, 2007, at p. 847)"; "Société SNF v Chambre de Commerce Internationale, Cour d'Appel de Paris, 22 January 2009 (Revue de l'Arbitrage, 2009, at p. 233)."
674. "Mr X v Trioplast AB, Cour de Cassation, 1iere Chambre Civile, 11 mars 2009 (decision available on www.KluwerArbitration.com; Contribution by the ITA Board of Reporters)."
675. This dispute arose out of a contract under which Mr X was appointed as sole agent for a Swedish company named Trioplast AB to distribute the company's products on the French territory. Mr X commenced ICC arbitration proceedings for alleged wrongful termination of the contract by Trioplast, which concluded with an arbitral award being made in favour of Trioplast. Mr X thereafter sought the annulment of the award before the French courts. The Court of Appeal of Paris having rejected the appeal against the first instance decision denying the set-aside application, the matter was appealed to the Cour de Cassation. One of the grounds raised before France's highest court was that the decision of the Court of Appeal was made by a chamber comprising, as one of the judges, a former Secretary General of the ICC. The applicant was arguing that the appeal decision was thus rendered in breach of Article 6(1) of the Convention for the Protection of Human Rights and Fundamental Freedoms (4 November 1950), which provides the right to a fair and public hearing by an independent and impartial tribunal established by law. Article 6(1) reads in relevant part: *"In the determination of his civil rights and obligations or of any criminal charge against him, everyone is entitled to a fair and public hearing within a reasonable time by an independent and impartial tribunal established by law."* The court rejected the application. In so doing, the Court held that: *"the international court of arbitration, of which Mr Z had been the Secretary General, exercises only functions relating to the organisation of the arbitral proceedings; it has no jurisdictional powers and does not intervene in the jurisdictional mission of the arbitrators so that the impartiality of Mr Z cannot legitimately be questioned* [...]." Translation by the author. In the original language: *"Mais attendu que la Cour internationale d'arbitrage dont M. Z... a été le secrétaire général exerce seulement des fonctions d'organisation de l'arbitrage, n'a aucun pouvoir juridictionnel et n'intervient pas dans la mission juridictionnelle des arbitres, de sorte que l'impartialité de M. Z... ne peut être légitimement suspectée; que le moyen n'est pas fondé."*

Instance de Paris confirmed the position that the activities of the ICC (including the decisions on challenges or the constitution of a tribunal) are administrative in nature, and that only those of the Tribunal may be jurisdictional[676].

Interestingly, recent case law does not lend much support to the idea that there is a principle of general application requiring the unity/indivisibility of the adjudicative mission (as was found in *Redec Pharaon*). Instead, to justify the *"administrative" versus "jurisdictional"* dichotomy, recent decisions seem to rely on the terms of the arbitration rules agreed by the parties (which state that the institution does not decide disputes). Likewise, recent decisions do not really support the idea that all decisions of arbitrators are necessarily jurisdictional. Instead they leave room for a finding that certain decisions of arbitrators may in reality be administrative. Despite that, the broad assumption that, across the board, the decisions of arbitral institutions are administrative whereas those of arbitrators are jurisdictional permeated the literature[677], beyond the confines of French law and of the rules of the ICC or the CAP[678], such that it even appears occasionally in arbitral awards[679].

This representation of the role of institutions can now be said to be the most prevalent representation. In a commentary of the *Cubic Defence* case for example one author claims for instance:

> [...] *One can simply note that between the arbitrator and the arbitration centre, the roles are perfectly distributed: the arbitrator judges and the centre organises* [...]

676. S.A. Fairplus Holding and S.A. La Valaisanne Holding v Chambre de Commerce Internationale, Tribunal de Grande Instance de Paris, 19 December 2012.
Other cases decided in the same sense include: "Société Replor v SARL Ploemeloise de Financement de Participations and Others, Cour d'Appel de Paris, 12 January 1988 (Revue de l'Arbitrage, 1988, at p. 691)" (the "mission" of the ICC is distinct from the mission of the arbitrator); and "Société ABC International v Chambre de Commerce International, Tribunal de Grande Instance (Ref.), 25 November 2010 (Revue de l'Arbitrage, 2011, at p. 991)" (general statement that the TGI cannot decide "appeals" against decisions of the ICC).
677. See in particular Loquin, "La Sentence Arbitrale: L'Examen du Projet de Sentence par l'Institution et la Sentence au Deuxième Degré – Réflexions sur la Nature et la Validité de l'Intervention de l'Institution Arbitrale sur la Sentence" 451; Chan, "Of Arbitral Institutions and Provisional Determinations on Jurisdiction, Global Gold Case" 412-413; Charles Jarrosson, "L'instance Arbitrale: le Rôle Respectif de l'Institution, de l'Arbitre et des Parties dans l'Instance Arbitrale" (1990) 1990 Revue de l'Arbitrage 381-394; Bühler and Jarvin, "The Arbitration Rules of the International Chamber of Commerce (ICC)" 1131; Klaus Peter Berger, *Private Dispute Resolution in International Business: Negotiation, Mediation, Arbitration (Third Edition)* (Kluwer Law International 2015) 363.
678. For a statement that the decisions of the Swiss institution are administrative, see Habegger, "The Revised Swiss Rules of International Arbitration: An Overview of the Major Changes" 273. For the rules of VIAC: Franz T. Schwarz and Christian W. Konrad, *The Vienna Rules: A Commentary on International Arbitration in Austria* (Kluwer Law International 2009) 108. For the DIS see Klaus Peter Berger, *Private Dispute Resolution in International Business: Negotiation, Mediation, Arbitration (Third Edition)* (Kluwer Law International 2015) 363. For the CAS see Despina Mavromati and Matthieu Reeb, *The Code of the Court of Arbitration for Sport: Commentary, Cases and Materials* (Kluwer Law International 2015) 381.
679. *State Joint Stock Company (Uzbekistan) v. State agency (India), Final Award*, ICC Case No. 14667, 2011 in Albert Jan van den Berg (ed.), *Yearbook Commercial Arbitration 2015*, 40 (Kluwer Law International 2015) 60; *Buyer (Nigeria), v. Seller (US)*, Partial Final Award, ICC Case No. 15652, 2010 in Albert Jan van den Berg (ed.), *Yearbook Commercial Arbitration 2015*, 40 (Kluwer Law International; 2015) 178.

> *case law enounces unanimously since 1982 that the role of arbitration centres is confined, to use the consecrated expression, to organising and policing the arbitration proceedings*[680].

Similarly, another author's referred to the:

> "now well-established distinction *between the functions of organisation of the proceedings and the jurisdictional functions of the arbitrator*", or, of the:
>
> "golden rule *according to which the arbitration centre organises and polices the proceedings whereas the tribunal decides the dispute between the parties*" (emphasis added)[681].

Ultimately, this conventional representation of the role of arbitral institutions can be summed up as follows. Arbitral institutions are mere administrators, with occasional decision-making power, but which decision-making power falls outside the adjudicative mission and consequently does not call for the application of the due process requirements applicable to arbitrators. To be more precise, this representation can be decomposed in three constitutive elements as follows:

(a) There is a distinction between the measures taken by institutions and by arbitrators: the former are considered as administrative, whereas the latter are jurisdictional.

(b) Measures taken by institutions do not participate in the adjudicative mission of the arbitral tribunal. The mission is reserved in its entirety to the arbitral tribunal.

(c) Because all decisions of all arbitral institutions (including decisions on challenges to arbitrators, decisions to extend certain deadlines, prima facie decisions on jurisdiction, and measures taken in the context of the scrutiny of awards) are considered as non-jurisdictional, due process requirements applicable to arbitrators do not apply to institutional decisions, in particular:
   - There can be no right of parties to be heard by the institution prior to it making its decision and, more generally, no right for an adversarial process.
   - There is no need for institutional decisions to be reasoned.
   - Procedurally, the means of recourse available against arbitral awards are unavailable against institutional decisions.

---

680. Translation by the author. In the original language: "[...] *on peut simplement relever qu'entre l'arbitre et le centre d'arbitrage les rôles sont parfaitement distribués: l'arbitre juge et le centre organise* [...] *la jurisprudence énonce à l'unisson depuis 1982 que le rôle du centre d'arbitrage se résume, selon la formule consacrée, à 'organiser et maintenir la police de l'instance arbitrale'*." Clay, "Commentary of the 'Cubic Defense System' Decision (Cour de Cassation, 20 February 2001)" 518.

681. Christophe Tse, "Mais Jusqu'Où Ira-t-On? Après les Arbitres et les Centres d'Arbitrage, On s'en Prend au Juge de l'Annulation, Note sous Cass. civ. 1iere, 11 mars 2009: Trioplast AB" [2009] Petites Affiches 20-22.

[B] Critical Analysis of the First Representation: Rejection of the "Administrative" versus "Jurisdictional" Dichotomy

It is argued that this first representation, which distinguishes between the so-called jurisdictional and administrative nature of decisions of arbitrators and institutions respectively, fails to withstand close scrutiny.

Over time, some have queried the reasoning offered by the French courts to justify the administrative versus jurisdictional dichotomy. For instance, whilst recognizing the practical utility of the representation, Isabelle Hautot notes that "*the fact that decisions of institutions are qualified simply as administrative is not satisfactory*"[682]. According to her, the arguments underlying the French decisions on the matter are indeed "*not devoid of criticism*"[683]. Likewise, Aguilar-Alvarez, whilst noting the uniformity of the French court decisions on the matter, notes that the so-called administrative nature of the decisions of the ICC raise "*theoretical difficulties*"[684]. In the same sense Professor Lalive, although emphasizing the practical relevance of the representation, affirmed that "*denying altogether a jurisdictional character to the activities of an arbitration centre is questionable from a theoretical point of view* [...]"[685]. Romain Dupeyré rightly notes that "*Questions arise as to the role of the institution in the administration of the proceedings. Despite the apportionment of responsibilities as defined by the arbitration rules of the institution, it is sometimes difficult to distinguish what falls within the jurisdictional action of the arbitral tribunal and what falls within the role of the arbitration centre*"[686]. In the same sense see also Professor Fouchard[687] or Michel Gaudet[688].

In fact, when some of the above authors find some level of support for the administrative versus jurisdictional dichotomy, it is primarily because of the practical

682. Translation by the author. In the original language: "*Qu'une telle décision soit qualifiée de simplement administrative n'est pas satisfaisant.*" Hautot, "Les Pouvoirs de la Cour d'Arbitrage de la C.C.I. de Décider ou Non d'Organiser l'Arbitrage" 26.

683. Translation by the author. In the original language: "[...] *les motifs de ces décisions ne sont pas exempts d'ambiguïtés*" Hautot, "Les Pouvoirs de la Cour d'Arbitrage de la C.C.I. de Décider ou Non d'Organiser l'Arbitrage" 19.

684. Aguilar Alvarez, "The Challenge of Arbitrators" 207.

685. Translation by the author. In the original language: "[...] *du point de vue théorique, il est discutable de refuser en bloc un caractère juridictionnel aux activités du centre d'arbitrage, mais non d'un point de vue pratique.*" Pierre Lalive, "Case commentary: Cour d'Appel de Paris 15 September 1988, Société Cubic Defense Systems v. CCI" (1999) 1999 Revue de l'Arbitrage 113, 119.

686. Translation by the author. In the original language: "*Il s'agit, dès lors, de s'interroger sur le rôle de l'institution dans l'administration de la procédure. Malgré la répartition des tâches telle que définie dans le règlement de l'institution, il est parfois difficile de distinguer ce qui relève de l'action juridictionnelle du tribunal arbitral et ce qui ressort du rôle du centre.*" Romain Dupeyré, "Les arbitres et centres d'arbitrage face à leurs responsabilités: le droit francais à son point d'équilibre", ASA Bulletin, (Kluwer Law International 2014, Volume 32 Issue 2) p. 279.

687. Fouchard, "Les Institutions Permanentes d'Arbitrage Devant le Juge Etatique (A Propos d'une Jurisprudence Récente)" 244.

688. Gaudet, "La Coopération des Juridictions Etatiques à l'Arbitrage Institutionnel" 109.

consequences that the dichotomy entails (i.e., non-applicability of due process requirements to the actions of institutions and the necessity to preserve the effectiveness of institutional arbitration). Professor Fouchard for instance notes that:

> *the quasi-unanimous case law on the matter must be approved, even if from a theoretical point of view its grounds are difficult to ascertain. Because, from a practical point of view, its usefulness is evident*[689].

It remains that what distinguishes decisions rendered by an institution from the ones rendered by an arbitral tribunal is not always obvious. The difficulty resides precisely in the fact that the relevant court decisions and commentaries have not articulated clearly the specific reasons for supporting the jurisdictional versus administrative dichotomy. As indicated above the French courts, in particular, have oscillated between organic criteria (i.e., the identity of the decision-maker renders the nature of the decisions different) and material ones (i.e., there is something about the types of decisions made by each that explains the difference). In more recent decisions, they have appeared to apply a combination of both (e.g., it is the "*missions*" of the tribunal and the institution that differ), so that different types of arguments are intertwined. Another difficulty is that certain arguments are raised only in respect of specific types of measures taken by institutions (challenge decisions, scrutiny, prima facie jurisdiction, etc.). A synthesis and an assessment of the main arguments that have been put forward in the literature to justify the administrative versus jurisdictional dichotomy is set out below.

[1] Rejection of the Arguments Based on Material Criteria

Several arguments based on a material criterion (i.e., relating to the type of decision being taken) have been raised to justify the administrative versus jurisdictional dichotomy. A first one is that the decisions of arbitral institutions lack finality. A second one relates to the timing of institutional decisions (such decisions being made before or after the proceedings proper). A third one is that institutional decisions do not decide between two conflicting positions. A final argument is that the subject matter or the aim of such decisions is merely organizational. It is argued that none of these arguments are satisfactory.

689. Translation by the author. In the original language: "*Cette jurisprudence quasi-unanime doit être approuvée, même si, d'un point de vue théorique, son fondement est difficile à dégager. Car, sur le terrain pratique, son opportunité est évidente.*" Fouchard, "Les Institutions Permanentes d'Arbitrage Devant le Juge Etatique (A Propos d'une Jurisprudence Récente)" 241. Elsewhere in the same article Professor Fouchard further explains: "*The theoretical discussions do not result in a perfectly clear solution: in essence, courts are justified to refuse the jurisdictional character to the decisions of arbitral institutions even if certain of these decisions are in fact jurisdictional.*" Translation by the author. In the original language: "*La discussion théorique n'aboutit pas, en définitive, à une conclusion parfaitement nette: pour l'essentiel, la jurisprudence a raison de refuser le caractère juridictionnel aux décisions des centres permanents d'arbitrage, bien que certaines puissent revêtir ce caractère.*" Fouchard, "Les Institutions Permanentes d'Arbitrage Devant le Juge Etatique (A Propos d'une Jurisprudence Récente)" 244. In the same sense, see also Hautot, "Les Pouvoirs de la Cour d'Arbitrage de la C.C.I. de Décider ou Non d'Organiser l'Arbitrage" 26.

[a] Argument Based on the Lack of Finality of the Institutional Decisions

A first line of argument to justify the administrative versus jurisdictional dichotomy, made primarily in relation to prima facie decisions on jurisdiction, is that the decisions rendered by arbitral institutions are allegedly provisional, whereas those of arbitral tribunals are final. This is because institutional decisions on prima facie jurisdiction are not binding and are subject to review by the arbitral tribunal once constituted. The essence of the argument is that because the decision of the institution does not resolve definitely the issue at stake, it is different from a decision of the arbitral tribunal. For one author[690] for example, commenting on a US District Court decision[691]:

> [...] *the ICC Court's prima facie decision is "provisional", and is not legally binding on the parties or the arbitrators. The ICC Court's decision in this regard does not resolve the issue of whether there is in fact a binding agreement to arbitrate.* [...] *This is evidenced by the fact that even if the ICC Court preliminarily decides that jurisdiction exists, an arbitral tribunal when constituted still retains the authority to decide, as arbiters of their own jurisdiction, that they have no jurisdiction over the entire dispute or one or more of the parties*[692].

Later, the same author adds:

> *The quintessential nature of such determinations on jurisdiction* [...] *is that such decisions are generally not binding on the arbitrators, who retain the power to rule on their own jurisdiction (subject to the final control of competent national courts*[693].

With all due respect to the author the argument is not convincing because institutional decisions are not always provisional (and often cannot be challenged). Certainly prima facie decisions on jurisdiction are not always provisional. A negative prima facie decision on jurisdiction is final. It is not subject to review by an arbitral

690. Chan, "Of Arbitral Institutions and Provisional Determinations on Jurisdiction, Global Gold Case" 412-413.
691. "Global Gold Mining, LLC v Robinson et. al., United States District Court, Southern District of New York, 6 February 2008 (533 F Supp 2d)." In this case, a claimant sued the ICC in New York asking for the ICC to be compelled to reverse its decision (made under the then Article 6.2 of the 1998 ICC rules) by which it had refused to include a non-signatory respondent (the ministry of energy of Armenia) as a party to the arbitration. The Court rejected the claimant's application.
   It should be noted, however, that the decision in question does not support the Calvin Chan's opinion. In fact the Court does not look to the alleged provisional character of prima facie decisions to find that such decisions are administrative in nature, and therefore to justify refusing to review such a decision. The Court rather rejects the application for review of the institution's prima facie decision on jurisdiction on procedural grounds: namely that the case should have been brought before the District Court as a *"motion to compel arbitration"* rather than as a motion *"to review the ICC's decision."* In this sense see, Albert Jan van den Berg, "Commentary of: US No. 636 Global Gold Mining LLC v Peter M Robinson et. al., US District Court, SDNY, 6 February 2008" in Albert Jan van den Berg (ed), *Yearbook Commercial Arbitration*, XXXIII (Kluwer Law International 2008) 1117-1124.
692. Chan, "Of Arbitral Institutions and Provisional Determinations on Jurisdiction, Global Gold Case" 412-413.
693. Chan, "Of Arbitral Institutions and Provisional Determinations on Jurisdiction, Global Gold Case" 412-413.

tribunal because, by definition, no tribunal can be constituted if the institution decides that it manifestly lacks jurisdiction[694]. The finality of negative prima facie jurisdiction decisions explains why parties sometimes argue these issues forcefully. As Jan Paulsson explains:

> *Article 7* [the then provision of the ICC rules on *prima facie* jurisdiction] *may – and in practice often does – give rise to very intense disputes between the parties, and such disputes are decided by the ICC Court when it applies Article 7. The stakes involved are often even more significant than those of a challenge action (because, unlike the latter, they put in doubt the very availability of the arbitral mechanism*[695].

Another difficulty with an argument based on finality is that, if the administrative/non-jurisdictional character of a decision depends on whether it is subject to review by the arbitrators, then it would mean that a positive finding on prima facie jurisdiction would be administrative (because it can be reviewed), but a negative finding on the same would be jurisdictional (because it would escape review by a tribunal). In other words, determining the exact same question would constitute either an administrative task or a jurisdictional one, depending on the answer given to that question. In turn, the issue of whether due process requirements were applicable in the first place would depend on whether the decision ultimately given was positive or negative. This does not appear to be a satisfactory criterion.

More fundamentally, there are decisions of arbitral tribunals which must have a jurisdictional character if that term is to have any substance[696], but which are nonetheless provisional and subject to review. A decision for provisional measures granted by the tribunal (e.g., order for security for costs), is by definition not final. It is subject to review by the tribunal itself. If the provisional nature of this decision entails that it is merely administrative, then it would follow that the tribunal would not be bound by due process requirements in making this decision on provisional measures, a conclusion which appears incongruous. Similarly, other decisions made by arbitrators may also be reviewed by a judge. For example, a tribunal's decision on jurisdiction

694. In this sense see Hautot: *"In addition, the refusal to organise an arbitration is final (subject to the uncertain and unlikely referral of the question of the validity of the arbitration agreement to a domestic court), whereas the acceptance* [of prima facie jurisdiction] *is always provisional, and is subject to the decision of the arbitrators on their own jurisdiction."* Translation by the author. In the original language: *"le refus de mettre en place l'arbitrage est au surplus définitif (sous réserve de l'incertaine et improbable saisine d'une juridiction étatique pour juger de la validité de la convention* [...]) *tandis que l'acceptation en est toujours provisoire, soumise à la décision des arbitres quant à leur propre compétence."* Hautot, "Les Pouvoirs de la Cour d'Arbitrage de la C.C.I. de Décider ou Non d'Organiser l'Arbitrage" 12-13.

695. Paulsson, "Vicarious Hypochondria and Institutional Arbitration" 243. It is true that when an institutional decision on prima facie jurisdiction is negative, it is difficult to see how that decision differs fundamentally from a negative decision on jurisdiction rendered by an arbitral tribunal. In this sense, one author notes: "[the] *decision is of a jurisdictional and not administrative nature; the presence of the adverb 'manifestly' does not change this qualification"*. Schlaepfer, "The Role of the Institution at the Commencement of the Proceedings" 58. Statement made in the context of prima facie decisions under the Swiss Rules.

696. Our view, as discussed in Chapter 5 below (under *"Proposition 4: The rejection of dichotomic approaches"*) is that the notion of jurisdictional measure (as distinguished from administrative ones) has no substance and must be rejected entirely.

is subject to the control of the domestic courts[697]. That fact alone cannot negate the jurisdictional nature of a tribunal's decision on jurisdiction, save as to empty the notion of *"jurisdictional decision"* of any relevant substance[698]. In sum, the final or provisional character of a decision is not, of its own, a satisfactory criterion to justify the jurisdictional versus administrative dichotomy.

[b] Argument Based on the Timing of Institutional Decisions

A second argument to justify the administrative versus jurisdictional dichotomy relates to the timing of the decisions rendered by institutions. Institutional decisions are rendered, so the argument goes, either before the constitution of the arbitral tribunal, or after the proceedings have been closed by the tribunal, there is no need for due process requirements to be followed.

This argument was made in particular in respect of the scrutiny of draft awards by the ICC Court. The idea being that, because the scrutiny process takes place *after* the closing of the proceedings, no adversarial debate can take place between the parties, therefore no due process can be required of the institution. In the words of one author:

> *"By nature, this question* [*i.e.* scrutiny] *escapes adversarial debates. It takes place after the debates, at a moment when they have been exhausted. The organ of the arbitral institution indeed intervenes during the deliberation phase, at a moment when no new applications may be made and no new arguments may be raised, as is required by article 1468 of the French New Code of Civil Procedure. The mission of supervision conferred to the institution is therefore purely contractual* [in the sense non-jurisdictional].[699]

---

697. At the very least at the enforcement stage under Article V of the New York convention.
698. As previously indicated, our view is that the notion of jurisdictional measure (as distinguished from administrative ones) has no substance and must be rejected entirely. See, Chapter 5 below (under "*Proposition 4: The rejection of dichotomic approaches*").
699. Translation by the author. In the original language: "*D'ailleurs, cette question échappe par nature au débat contradictoire. Elle se situe en aval de ce débat, à un moment où celui-ci est épuisé. L'organe de l'institution d'arbitrage intervient en effet dans la phase du délibéré, à un moment où aucune demande ne peut être formée ni aucun moyen soulevé, et cela conformément à l'article 1468 N.C.P.C. La mission de supervision confiée à l'institution est donc purement contractuelle.*" Loquin, "La Sentence Arbitrale: L'Examen du Projet de Sentence par l'Institution et la Sentence au Deuxième Degré – Réflexions sur la Nature et la Validité de l'Intervention de l'Institution Arbitrale sur la Sentence" 452. In the same sense see Grigera Naon, "The Powers of the ICC International Court of Arbitration vis-a-vis Parties and Arbitrators" 58.

    This position is intrinsically linked to the requirement of French law (at the time, Article 1468 of the French New Code of Civil Procedure) that the arbitral tribunal determines a date at which the proceedings are officially closed, and when the tribunal therefore starts its deliberation. Under French law, *"after that date, no new application can be made and no argument can be raised"*. The text of the then Article 1468 NCPC reads in French: "*L'arbitre fixe la date à laquelle l'affaire sera mise en délibéré. Après cette date, aucune demande ne peut être formée ni aucun moyen soulevé. Aucune observation ne peut être présentée ni aucune pièce produite, si ce n'est à la demande de l'arbitre.*" This article now corresponds to Article 1476 of the Code of Civil Procedure since the enactment of Decree n°2011-48 of 13 January 2011. The 2011 amendment does not materially affect the meaning of the provision for our purposes.

A similar argument was also retained by the French courts in relation to a decision by the CAP to apply its emergency arbitration rules in the *SCPA* case discussed above. Here the argument was that the decision took place *before* the proceedings proper. The court found as follows:

> *It transpires from the rules of arbitration of the CAP* [...] *that the choice of the emergency procedure is left to the discretion of the president* [...] *and that it lies in the powers to organise the arbitration, such powers being exercised prior to the actual proceedings at a time when there can be no requirement of adversarial process or of reasoned decision* [...][700].

The argument that looks to the timing of institutional decisions arguably suffers a number of flaws, chief amongst which is its circular character. In effect, the argument posits the impossibility of adversarial debates before or after the proceedings proper, and deduces from it the non-jurisdictional nature of institutional decisions. At the same time, however, the argument deduces from the non-jurisdictional nature of the decisions the fact that it is not necessary to follow due process, including organizing adversarial debates[701]. In other words, the argument consists of saying:

(a) Adversarial debates cannot take place before or after the proceedings proper.
(b) Therefore any institutional decisions made outside of the proceedings proper cannot be jurisdictional.
(c) Therefore no due process requirements need to apply to such institutional decisions, including the need to have adversarial debates.
(d) In sum: Because it is impossible (or, rather, inconvenient) to have adversarial debates, there should be no legal requirement for such adversarial debates!

Further, the argument that the non-jurisdictional nature of certain institutional decisions derives from their occurring pre-appointment or post-closure of the debates, negates the role of institutions in between. This appears to be factually incorrect. While it is true that the bulk of the work of arbitral institutions is performed pre-appointment, the rules of certain institutions nonetheless confer on such institutions some important

700. Translation by the author. In the original language: "*Considérant qu'ainsi, il ressort du Règlement de la Chambre arbitrale – qui constitue la loi des parties en vertu de la référence expresse qui y est faite dans la clause compromissoire qu'elles ont souscrites – que le choix de la procédure d'urgence est laissé à l'appréciation du Président de cet organisme, au vu des éléments présentés par le demandeur, et relève des pouvoirs d'organisation de l'arbitrage s'exerçant préalablement à l'instance elle-même, dans une phase préparatoire d'administration, qui n'exige, en tant que telle, ni débat contradictoire ni décision motivée.*" "Société Commerciale de Produits Agricoles (S.C.P.A.) v Société Coopérative de la Roche Clermault, Cour d'Appel de Paris, 29 November 1985 (Revue de l'Arbitrage, 1987, at p. 335)."

701. Loquin affirms: "*The contractual and non-jurisdictional nature of the intervention of the institution also has for consequence that it is not necessary to organise adversarial debates in the presence of the parties before the institution.*" Translation by the author. In the original language: "*La nature contractuelle et non juridictionnelle de l'intervention de l'institution a également pour conséquence que devant elle, il n'est pas nécessaire d'organiser un débat contradictoire en présence des parties.*" Loquin, "La Sentence Arbitrale: L'Examen du Projet de Sentence par l'Institution et la Sentence au Deuxième Degré – Réflexions sur la Nature et la Validité de l'Intervention de l'Institution Arbitrale sur la Sentence" 452.

functions post-appointment but pre-award. This is the case, for example, of the determination of a challenge to an arbitrator[702] or of a decision on the quantum of the arbitration costs (i.e., fees of the tribunal and of the institution)[703]. If one were to follow the argument to its logical conclusion, one would need to conclude that decisions rendered by institutions on challenges and cost, because of their timing, are jurisdictional and are therefore subject to the same due process requirements as those applicable to the arbitral tribunal; a conclusion which the argument aims to avoid in the first place. In sum, the timing of a decision is not a satisfactory criterion for the purposes of justifying the jurisdictional versus administrative dichotomy.

[c] Arguments That Institutional Decisions Do Not Decide between Two Conflicting Positions

It has been argued that the measures taken by arbitral institutions are non-jurisdictional because they do not decide between two conflicting positions. It is true that a number of activities of arbitral institutions like making logistical arrangements in advance of a hearing like booking a room, making catering arrangements, organizing video links, or issuing visa letters for witnesses, seem to be qualitatively different from decisions made by an arbitral tribunal in the course of the proceedings. Such institutional measures or activities do not participate in the overall adjudication of the dispute submitted to arbitration, and in that sense the argument does not seem illogical.

But it appears that the argument that measures rendered by arbitral institutions are not jurisdictional because they do not decide between two conflicting positions, extends to all institutional measures, including those that are decisional. Professor Fouchard for instance argued that:

> *For most institutional decisions, the lack of jurisdictional character is easily justified by the absence of disagreement: when it designates an arbitrator, chooses a procedural avenue, or fixes or extends deadlines, an institution is not confronted with any disagreement, it is not called upon to pass a judgement on conflicting arguments*[704].

702. As discussed in Chapter 3 above, the rules of a number of institutions confer on the institution itself the power to decide challenges. This is the case of the ICC, the LCIA, ICDR, CIETAC, SIAC, SCC, the CAS, ICAC WIPO, the Swiss rules, the Milan Chamber rules, the ACICA rules and the CAMEX rules to cite only a few. See Articles 14-15 ICC rules (2012); Article 10.3 LCIA rules (1998) and Article 10.6 LCIA rules (2014); Articles 8-9 ICDR rules (2009); Articles 30-31 CIETAC rules (2012) and Article 32(6) CIETAC rules (2015); Articles 11-13 SIAC rules (2013); Articles 9-11 Swiss rules (2012); Article 15 SCC rules (2010); Article R34 CAS Code (2013); Article 18 ICAC rules (2010); Articles 24-29 WIPO rules (2002); Article 19 Milan Chamber rules (2010); Article 14.4 ACICA rules (2011) and Article 18.4 ACICA rules (2016); and Article 17 CAMEX rules (2009).
703. Article 37 ICC rules (2012); Article 28.1 LCIA rules (1998); Article 32 SIAC rules (2013); Article 43.2 SCC rules (2010); Article R64.4 CAS code (2013); and Article 14 of ICAC rules (2010) and ICAC's Schedule of Arbitration Fees and Costs.
704. Translation by the author. In the original language: "*Pour la plupart d'entre elles, le rejet de la qualification juridictionnelle se justifie aisément par l'absence de tout litige: lorsqu'elle désigne un arbitre, choisit une voie procédurale, fixe ou proroge les délais de l'arbitrage, l'institution n'est saisie d'aucun différend, elle n'a pas à statuer entre des prétentions opposées.*" Fouchard,

Here the argument is that the sort of decision-making done by arbitral institutions is functionally different from that of arbitrators because institutional decisions are made in the absence of any disagreement between the parties; whereas an arbitral tribunal is confronted with two conflicting theses between which it must choose. This argument seems to be premised on the idea that institutions are requested to intervene only when one party fails to participate fully in the proceedings (e.g., default appointment of arbitrators, selection of default seat, etc.). A similar argument, expressed in the context of scrutiny, is that when the ICC imposes changes as to the form of a draft award, it does not take a jurisdictional measure because it does not adjudicate between two conflicting positions[705].

The argument, which distinguishes between the decisions of arbitrators and of institutions based on the presence or absence of conflicting theses, is not very convincing for two main reasons. First, occasionally, arbitrators themselves render decisions without being confronted with two conflicting theses. For instance, when a respondent is non-participating, and the tribunal proceeds to a decision on the merits (be it on liability or quantum), the tribunal is not confronted with two conflicting positions. The tribunal is in the presence of one position put forward by the claimant, and an absence of position for the other side. Yet in such a situation the arbitral tribunal's decision on the merits must be "jurisdictional" if this term is to have any meaning. In fact, where a party fails to participate in the proceedings, the arbitral tribunal should arguably take extra care to ensure that all due process requirements are followed, with a view to facilitating the enforcement of the award[706].

Second, some decisions rendered by institutions do, in fact, involve adjudicating between two conflicting positions. This is the case, for example, whenever an institution is determining a challenge to an arbitrator, or when it is making a prima facie decision on jurisdiction. In the first case, in the absence of an agreement of all parties to remove the challenged arbitrator, the institution has to choose between two conflicting demands, i.e., that the arbitrator be removed, or that the challenge be rejected. In the second case, the institution also has to opt for one of two incompatible positions, i.e., that the institution does or does not manifestly lack jurisdiction. In fact, it is common in practice for parties to make relatively detailed submissions as to the reasons of fact and law why an arbitrator should or should not be removed, or why an institution should or should not have prima facie jurisdiction. For Professor Fouchard:

"Les Institutions Permanentes d'Arbitrage Devant le Juge Etatique (A Propos d'une Jurisprudence Récente)" 242-243. In the same sense, see also Kassis, *Réflexions sur le Règlement d'Arbitrage de la Chambre de Commerce Internationale: les Déviations de l'Arbitrage Institutionnel* 39.

705. This is an argument raised by Eric Loquin. For him the ICC "*does not adjudicate between two conflicting positions having for object the formulation of the award.*" Translation by the author. In the original language: "*En effet, la Cour d'arbitrage ne tranche pas le litige.* [...] *Quant aux injonctions concernant la forme de la sentence, elles ne peuvent constituer une activité de nature juridictionnelle. Ce faisant, l'organe de l'institution d'arbitrage ne tranche pas entre deux prétentions antagonistes ayant pour objet les formulations de la sentence.*" Loquin, "La Sentence Arbitrale: L'Examen du Projet de Sentence par l'Institution et la Sentence au Deuxième Degré – Réflexions sur la Nature et la Validité de l'Intervention de l'Institution Arbitrale sur la Sentence" 451-452.

706. Waincymer, *Procedure and Evidence in International Arbitration* 487 et seq.

> [...] *when an institution decides that there is prima facie no arbitration agreement allowing it to intervene where the parties take conflicting views on this question, or when it decides favourably a challenge to an arbitrator against the objection of the arbitrator and the other party, one can argue that it is fulfilling a jurisdictional function. Should those decisions be taken by the President of the Tribunal de Grande Instance* [...], *it would undeniably constitute a jurisdictional decision because he would be adjudicating a dispute/disagreement*[707].

For these two reasons, the presence or absence of conflicting theses must also be rejected as a criterion to justify the jurisdictional versus administrative dichotomy.

[d] Arguments Based on the Alleged Organizational Character of Institutional Decisions

Another argument based on a material criterion is that the decisions rendered by institutions concern the organization of the proceedings, rather than the "decision of the dispute"[708]. This argument is similar, but not identical, to other arguments studied elsewhere below that institutional decisions fall outside the scope of the "*adjudicative mission*".

There are various iterations of the argument based on the so-called organizational character of the measures taken by arbitral institutions. A first one is focused on the *subject matter* of institutional measures – subject matter which would be to organize the proceedings, not to adjudicate the substance of the dispute. Examples of the first iteration of the organizational argument may be found in the *SCPA* decision when the court emphasizes the fact that the institutional decision concerned "*the powers to organise the arbitration*" rather than the power to decide the substance of the dispute[709]. Similarly, the first instance decision in the *Syrian Refineries* case, for example, insisted on the fact that the ICC's challenge decision "*remains distinct from, or external to, the exercise of the powers to judge and decide the dispute, and consequently such measure does not call for the application of the same mandatory due process requirements* [as would apply to an arbitrator's decision]"[710]. A second iteration of the organizational argument looks to the *purpose* of the decisions rather

707. Translation by the author. In the original language: "[...] *lorsqu'elle estime qu'il n'existe pas prima facie une convention d'arbitrage lui permettant d'intervenir, alors que les deux parties soutiennent sur cette question des positions contradictoires, ou lorsqu'elle fait droit à une demande de récusation d'un arbitre, malgré la protestation de celui-ci et de l'autre partie, on peut soutenir qu'elle remplit une fonction juridictionnelle; à sa place, en tout cas, le Président du Tribunal de grande instance* [...] *accomplirait incontestablement, lui, un acte juridictionnel, car il trancherait une contestation.*" Fouchard, "Les Institutions Permanentes d'Arbitrage Devant le Juge Etatique (A Propos d'une Jurisprudence Récente)" 242-243.
708. It is unclear whether in this argument the idea of deciding the dispute is to be understood as being limited to determining issues of substance or also of procedure.
709. "Société Commerciale de Produits Agricoles (S.C.P.A.) v Société Coopérative de la Roche Clermault, Cour d'Appel de Paris, 29 November 1985 (Revue de l'Arbitrage, 1987, at p. 335)."
710. In the original language: "[...] *une décision sur un incident de récusation ou de remplacement d'un arbitre reste extérieure à l'exercice du pouvoir de juger et de trancher un différend et ne saurait relever des mêmes règles impératives.*" "Raffineries de Pétrole d'Homs et de Banias v Chambre de Commerce Internationale, Tribunal de Grande Instance, 28 March 1984 (Revue de l'Arbitrage, 1985, at p. 141)."

than their subject matter; namely to assist the tribunal in its adjudicative mission. This second iteration of the organizational argument focuses on the "objective" of the decisions, that is to say their underlying motive. An example of this argument may be found in the *REDEC Pharaon* case where the court emphasized that the ICC's prima facie decision on jurisdiction was *"a measure of administrative nature, aimed at finalising the constitution of the tribunal pursuant to the arbitration rules"*[711]. In the literature, this iteration of the organizational argument is relayed by a leading arbitration lawyer:

> "[...] *such powers should be viewed from the uniform perspective of the case management function of arbitral institutions, which is* oriented in an undivided way towards *procuring* [...] *rapidity, cost efficiency and impartiality in the conduct of the proceedings and contributing to the effectiveness of the award, that is to say,* towards *enhancing the inherent quality of the arbitration* [...]"[712] (emphasis added).
>
> "[...] *such powers are strictly* targeted to *contributing to the general management of the case and are* not intended *to interfere or be exercised in a manner which would interfere with the freedom of the parties to fashion legal proceedings within the context permitted by the ICC Rules, nor with the rights and independence of judgement of arbitrators concerning, among other things, the conduct of the arbitration and the making of determinations or awards also within the context of the ICC Rules*"[713] (emphasis added).

With all due respect to the above author, neither iterations of the organizational argument appear very persuasive. First, at a somewhat superficial level, there are decisions that appear organizational in nature but which, nonetheless, would be readily recognized as requiring the applicability of some due process requirements. Decisions as to timetabling, bifurcation, or as to the presentation of evidence at a hearing, for example, can all be termed "organizational". On one view they do participate to the organization of the proceedings. Yet it would seem that parties would expect to be able to have adversarial debates on each of these issues before a decision is reached. This is because decisions on these matters are not insignificant. In essence, and as discussed later in this book, a first difficulty with the organizational argument, is that the materiality[714] of a particular decision (in particular its capacity to impact the outcome of a case) does not necessarily depend on whether the decision is organizational, procedural or substantive.

---

711. Translation by the author. In the original language: *"En décidant prima facie de faire intervenir à la constitution d'un tribunal arbitral une personne alléguant sa qualité de tiers à la convention d'arbitrage, la Cour d'arbitrage de la C.C.I. ne rend pas une décision juridictionnelle, laquelle relève de la seule compétence de l'arbitre, mais prescrit une mesure de nature administrative, destinée, en application de son Règlement, à parfaire la constitution du tribunal arbitral."* "Société REDEC et M. Pharaon v Société Uzinexport Import et Chambre de Commerce Internationale, Tribunal de Grande Instance de Paris (Ref.), 13 July 1988 (Revue de l'Arbitrage, 1989, at p. 97)."
712. Grigera Naon, "The Powers of the ICC International Court of Arbitration vis-a-vis Parties and Arbitrators" 56.
713. Grigera Naon, "The Powers of the ICC International Court of Arbitration vis-a-vis Parties and Arbitrators" 56.
714. In the sense significance.

More fundamentally, this argument assumes that all decisions of institutions share this organizational character. One may wonder whether this is really correct. When an arbitral institution fixes the costs of an arbitration in accordance with its rules[715], the institution does not really appear to facilitate the arbitration process. Rather it disposes of a discrete aspect of the dispute (albeit one that is arguably less important than merits or jurisdiction). Similarly, a small number of institutions are habilitated by their own rules to make decisions on applications for provisional measures. As previously indicated, this is the case under the rules of the Arbitration Court Attached to the Czech Chamber of Commerce[716]; under the procedural rules of the CAS[717]; under the rules of Italian Association for Arbitration[718], and under the rules of the Maritime Arbitration Commission at the Chamber of Commerce and Industry of the Russian Federation (MAC)[719]. This was also the case under the ICAC rules until their 2005 revision. Some other institutions are even habilitated to make decisions on jurisdiction – that is, final decisions on jurisdiction, not prima facie decisions. As previously mentioned, by operation of Article 6 of the CIETAC rules the power to decide jurisdictional objection lies with CIETAC. A similar solution may be found in the CMAC rules[720]. It is difficult to see how decisions on interim relief or on jurisdiction could be qualified of merely organizational. It appears that, in both instances, the institution disposes of a discrete element of the dispute more than it facilitates the arbitration process.

In light of the above, the criterion of the organizational nature of decisions does not seem adequate to support the administrative versus jurisdictional dichotomy. As such, it must be rejected.

715. See, for example, Article 37 ICC rules (2012); Article 28.1 LCIA rules (1998) and (2014); Article 32 SIAC rules (2013); Article 43.2 SCC rules (2010); Article R64.4 CAS code (2013); and Article 14 of ICAC rules (2010) and ICAC's Schedule of Arbitration Fees and Costs.
716. Section 13 of the rules of the Arbitration Court Attached to the Czech Chamber of Commerce for instance provides: *"If requested by one of the parties in urgent matters, after the statement of claim has been filed, but before the arbitral tribunal is constituted, the President of the Arbitration Court may provide for conservation of evidence in a manner corresponding to the nature of the evidence and take other suitable measures to this effect."*
717. Article R37 of the CAS Code (2013) provides, in relevant part: *"The President of the relevant Division, prior to the transfer of the file to the Panel, or thereafter, the Panel may, upon application by a party, make an order for provisional or conservatory measures."*
718. Article 8 of the rules of arbitration of the Associazione Italiana per l'Arbitrato (AIA) (2012) provides that, before the formation of the arbitral tribunal and in the presence of a request for arbitration validly filed with AIA, any party may apply to the Permanent Committee for any interim measures listed at 19. In the original language: *"Prima della costituzione del tribunale arbitra le ed in presenza di una domanda per arbitrato A.I.A., la parte che vi abbia interesse può rivolgere istanza al Comitato permanente d'intervento per l'a dozione dei provvedimenti d'urgenza previsti dall'art. 19."*
719. Article 3(4) of the arbitration rules of MAC (1994) provide: *"In cases subject to consideration by the MAC the Commission President may, at the request of a party, establish the amount and form of security for the claim, and, in particular, he may make a ruling to attach the other party's vessel or cargo in a Russian port."*
720. Article 4 of the CMAC rules (2004) provides that "[t]*he arbitration Commission has the power to decide on the existence, validity or an arbitration agreement and the jurisdiction over an arbitration case*".

[2] Rejection of the Arguments Based on Organic Criteria

Several arguments based on an organic criterion (i.e., relating to the person of the decision-maker) have been raised to justify the administrative versus jurisdictional dichotomy. A first one is that arbitral institutions are not arbitrators. A second, more elaborate, one is that the parties have agreed, by the arbitration rules they have chosen, to allocate all jurisdictional powers to the arbitral tribunal (and therefore none to the institution). A third, similar, argument is based on an alleged principle of indivisibility of the so-called adjudicative mission. As discussed below, all three arguments must be rejected.

[a] Argument That Institutions Are Not Arbitrators

A first argument which was raised early on in support of the jurisdictional versus administrative dichotomy was that institutions are not arbitrators. This argument applies an organic criterion in the sense that it centres on the person of the decision-maker rather than on the nature of its decisions. As indicated previously, this argument appears, for example, in the *Société Appareils Dragon* decision, where the court noted:

> [...] *the Court of Arbitration, itself lacking the quality of arbitrator, was not bound to provide reasons for its decision of prolongation, which did not have a jurisdictional character*[721].

A second decision in which this argument is upheld by the French courts is *Société Techni Import Professionnel*, which was published shortly after the decision in *Société Appareils Dragon*. Here the court held similarly that:

> [...] *as the Arbitration Court of the ICC is not a jurisdictional organ, it does not have to provide with its decisions any reasons, reasons which are not required by its rules of arbitration* [...][722].

As previously indicated, in both cases the court stops short of explaining further what this "quality of arbitrator" is, and why arbitral institutions lack this quality. The court also does not explain why this quality should be determinative of the jurisdictional character of a decision. In effect the reasoning of the court is simply that arbitrators and institutions, somehow, have different qualities and that therefore when

721. Translation by the author. In the original language: "*la Cour d'arbitrage, qui n'avait pas elle-même la qualité d'arbitre, n'était pas tenue de motiver sa décision de prorogation qui ne présentait pas de caractère juridictionnel.*" "Société Appareils Dragon, Cour de Cassation, 2ieme Chambre Civile, 8 June 1983 (Revue de l'Arbitrage, 1987, at p. 309)."

722. Translation by the author. In the original language: "*Considérant que la Cour d'arbitrage de la C.C.I., n'étant pas un organe juridictionnel, n'a pas à donner à ses décisions une motivation qui ne lui est pas imposée par son Règlement*" "*Considérant que la Cour d'arbitrage de la C.C.I., n'étant pas un organe juridictionnel, n'a pas à donner à ses décisions une motivation qui ne lui est pas imposée par son Règlement.*" "Société Techni-Import Professionnel v Société Electro Scientific Industries, Cour d'Appel de Paris, 17 May 1983 (Revue de l'Arbitrage, 1987, at p. 309)."

a decision is rendered by an institution it cannot be treated in the same manner as a decision originating from an arbitral tribunal.

A first difficulty with just stating that "*institutions are not arbitrators*" or are not "*jurisdictional organs*" is that many of the decisions that are made by institutions (in an institutional context) are decisions which would be made by an arbitral tribunal or by the domestic courts in an ad hoc arbitration. For instance, decisions on the seat or the language of an arbitration, or on consolidation, joinder or costs, are all decisions which could be made by an arbitral tribunal or a judge in an ad hoc context. Taken to its logical conclusion, the argument based on an organic criterion would mean that two decisions on the very same subject matter (e.g., seat, language, joinder, consolidation, costs, etc.) could be both jurisdictional or administrative depending on whether the decision is made in an ad hoc context (by a tribunal) or an institutional context (by an institution). The applicability of due process requirements would then depend exclusively on who has made the decision: an institution or a tribunal. This appears counterintuitive. In the words of Professor Fouchard:

> [...] *if one thinks that* [...] *these institutions exercise functions which, when they are devolved to a domestic court, are undeniably jurisdictional (for example the challenge to an arbitrator), any conclusion of the sort appears too hasty*[723].

If the argument appears "*hasty*" it is perhaps because it is counterintuitive to subordinate the applicability of due process requirements solely to the identity of the decision-maker. As will be argued in the final chapter of this book, the materiality of a decision (in the sense its capacity to impact the outcome of a case) should matter more than the identity of the decision-maker in determining to what extent due process requirements should be complied with.

A further difficulty is that the argument based on the identity of the decision-maker is premised on the idea that there is a certain uniformity as to the role conferred to arbitral institutions and to arbitrators. Saying that the measures taken by arbitral institutions cannot be jurisdictional because institutions are not arbitrators, presupposes a certain level of stability as to what arbitrators and institutions are. This stability or uniformity, however, is not confirmed in practice. As discussed throughout Chapter 3, different sets of arbitration rules contemplate a different split of responsibilities between the arbitrators and the institution. While in some instances, the rules will reserve very little competence to the institution (therefore entrusting almost all decisional powers to the tribunal), in other instances the rules will contemplate a more heavy involvement of the institution in the proceedings (therefore limiting somewhat the sphere of competence of the tribunal). As explained in Chapter 3, the reality of institutional arbitration is more aptly described by a continuum than by strict categories. On one side of the continuum (where the rules provide for a significant involvement of the institution), the overall task of deciding the dispute may appear to

723. Translation by the author. In the original language: "*Cependant, si l'on songe que* [...] *ces institutions exercent des fonctions qui, lorsqu'elles sont dévolues à un tribunal étatique, sont incontestablement juridictionnelles (par exemple la récusation d'un arbitre), toute réponse de ce type paraît trop abrupte.*" Fouchard, "Les Institutions Permanentes d'Arbitrage Devant le Juge Etatique (A Propos d'une Jurisprudence Récente)" 243.

be shared between the institution and the arbitral tribunal[724]. In this context, it appears rather parochial to believe that all institutional rules share the same outlook as to the respective functions of the institution and the arbitrators, so that in all instances the decisions of one and the other should be treated differently for due process purposes. In sum, relying solely on the identity of the decision-maker (institution or arbitrator) to justify the jurisdictional versus administrative dichotomy does not appear satisfactory.

[b] Argument That the Parties Have Agreed to Confer a Non-jurisdictional Function to the Institution

Another (related) argument is the one that the decisions of an arbitrator and those of an institution are different because the parties have so agreed. According to this argument the parties have agreed to the terms of a set of arbitration rules, which rules provide that the decisions of the institution are administrative and those of arbitrators are jurisdictional. By way of illustration, one learned author (taking the example of the ICC and the Franco Arab Chamber of Commerce) argues:

> [t]*he intervention of the organ of the institution cannot be qualified of jurisdictional. The arbitration rules of the institutions affirm this clearly. Article 2 of the ICC Rules provides that "The Court does not itself resolve disputes", Article 24-1 of the rules of arbitration of the Franco Arab Chamber of Commerce provide that the intervention of the Council in the scrutiny of draft awards shall not lead to it being "considered as exercising the role of arbitrator"*[725].

724. This is particularly clear in those (admittedly rare) instances where decisions on the merits are rendered by the arbitrators *"in the name of the institution"*. Fouchard cites the rules of arbitration of the Yugoslavia arbitration centre. Fouchard, "Les Institutions Permanentes d'Arbitrage Devant le Juge Etatique (A Propos d'une Jurisprudence Récente)" 242. This also appears true in those institutions where (final) decisions on jurisdiction are made by the institution itself, but where the institution can delegate such power to the arbitral tribunal. In such a context it does not appear correct to say that it is the "quality of arbitrator" which confers a jurisdictional character to certain decisions. In these institutions, the adjudicative mission quite simply does not derive from the quality of arbitrator.
725. Translation by the author. In the original language: *"L'intervention de l'organe de l'institution d'arbitrage ne peut être qualifiée de juridictionnelle. Les règlements des institutions l'affirment clairement. L'article 2 du Règlement de la Cour d'arbitrage de la C.C.I. dispose ainsi que "la Cour d'arbitrage ne tranche pas elle-même les différends", l'article 24-1 du Règlement d'arbitrage de la Chambre de commerce franco-arabe précise que l'intervention du Conseil dans le contrôle du contenu de la sentence ne peut conduire à "le considérer comme jouant le rôle d'arbitre"*. Loquin, "La Sentence Arbitrale: L'Examen du Projet de Sentence par l'Institution et la Sentence au Deuxième Degré – Réflexions sur la Nature et la Validité de l'Intervention de l'Institution Arbitrale sur la Sentence" 451. In the same sense see Fouchard: "[the qualification of the object of the mission of institutions as that of an organiser] *is conform both with the will of the parties and the institutions themselves, as expressed in their arbitration rules, and it is conform with the wish of the French legislator.*" Translation by the author. In the original language: "[...] *conforme à la fois à la volonté des parties et des institutions elles-mêmes, telle qu'elle est exprimée dans leurs règlements de procédure, et aux voeux du législateur français.*" Fouchard, "Les Institutions Permanentes d'Arbitrage Devant le Juge Etatique (A Propos d'une Jurisprudence Récente)" 247-248.

This argument may be said to be based on an organic criteria because it is attached to the status of the decision-maker, more than to the type of decision rendered. According to this argument, it is because a decision is made by an arbitrator rather than an institution that the decision is jurisdictional.

As previously indicated, this argument has been regularly relied upon by the French courts since the *Cubic Defence Systems* case. In *Cubic*, the Cour de Cassation noted that the lower court had correctly:

> [...] *observed that the ICC's arbitration rules maintained a distinction between the function of organizing the arbitration, notably through the intermediary of the Court of International Arbitration, and the adjudicative function, which has been left solely to the arbitrators, the "Court" having no adjudicative power* [...][726].

In the above cases, the French courts appeared particularly sensitive to the fact that the ICC rules contained an express provision that the ICC itself does not decide disputes[727].

Considering that the parties may entrust two entities (being the arbitral tribunal and the institution) with powers which, in one instance, are meant to be purely administrative, and in the other jurisdictional does not seem inherently problematic so long as the agreement of the parties (i.e., the institutional rules according to the argument) does indeed operate a distinction as to the legal nature of the actions of the institution and arbitral tribunal. The relevant question is therefore: Do the arbitration rules of the ICC or of other institutions really confer a different legal nature to the decisions of the institution and those of the tribunal? In this respect an express provision similar to the one of the ICC rules to the effect that the institution "does not itself resolve disputes"[728] would seem to offer the basis of a strong presumption that the rules indeed aim to operate a distinction as to the nature of the actions of the institution and the arbitral tribunal. But it is doubtful that such a provision, on its own, would suffice to establish the intention of the parties to entertain such a distinction if other provisions of the rules point to a different reality. As Professor Fouchard explains, a domestic judge, when asked to assess the legality of the actions of an institution, may re-qualify the measures of that institution, ascribing to them a legal nature different

726. Derains and Schwartz, *A Guide to the New ICC Rules of Arbitration* 18-19 citing the Cubic case: "Société Cubic Defense Systems Inc. v Chambre de Commerce Internationale, Cour de Cassation, 1ere Chambre Civile, 20 February 2001 (Revue de l'Arbitrage 2001, at p. 511)." The same argument was also mentioned by the French courts in the "Société Techni-Import Professionnel v Société Electro Scientific Industries, Cour d'Appel de Paris, 17 May 1983 (Revue de l'Arbitrage, 1987, at p. 309)".

727. At present the corresponding provision reads: *"The Court does not itself resolve disputes'. It administers the resolution of disputes by arbitral tribunals, in accordance with the Rules of Arbitration of the ICC."* Article 1(2) of the ICC rules (2012).

728. Article 1(2) of the ICC rules (2012).

from the one which the express terms of the arbitration rules sought to confer to it[729]. This viewpoint is also shared by Professor Loquin[730].

Interestingly, while Article 1(2) of the ICC rules states that the ICC *"does not decide disputes"*, the rest of the rules contain no less than fifteen instances in which the word *"decide"* (or a derivative thereof[731]) is used in conjunction with the role of the Court[732]. Incidentally, it is amusing to note that the ICC rules contain "only" fourteen instances in which the same word *"decide"* (or a derivative thereof) is used in conjunction with the role of the arbitral tribunal! This is not to suggest, of course, that the ICC Court's decisional powers are somehow more important than that of arbitral tribunals but one may argue that it puts in perspective the importance to be attached to the words contained in Article 1(2).

More generally, as demonstrated in Chapter 3 above, institutional arbitration is characterized in reality by a high level of diversity when it comes to the level of responsibilities conferred on the institutions in the proceedings they administer. In some instances, the involvement of the institutions in the proceedings is so extensive that it can be said that the parties have agreed a split of the overall task of deciding the dispute between the tribunal and the institution (albeit with the bulk of the decision-making powers being reserved to the tribunal)[733]. This is particularly evident when the parties have agreed to confer on the institution the power to decide all jurisdictional objections[734], or to determine applications for interim measures[735]. This is also the case where, more commonly, the institution is given powers in regards to decision on the

729. In the original language: *"Malgré la position du législateur, il reste possible qu'en pratique, des organes permanents d'arbitrage conservent ou s'arrogent certaines fonctions juridictionnelles: le juge n'est donc pas pour autant dispensé de qualifier, le cas échéant, telle décision institutionnelle."* Fouchard, "Les Institutions Permanentes d'Arbitrage Devant le Juge Etatique (A Propos d'une Jurisprudence Récente)" 243.
730. Loquin, "La Sentence Arbitrale: L'Examen du Projet de Sentence par l'Institution et la Sentence au Deuxième Degré – Réflexions sur la Nature et la Validité de l'Intervention de l'Institution Arbitrale sur la Sentence" 451.
731. Like *"decided"* or *"decides."*
732. Examples include the statement at Article 6(4) that "[...] *the Court shall decide whether and to what extent the arbitration shall proceed"*. Another example may be found at Article 14 which provides that the *"Court shall decide on the admissibility and, at the same time, if necessary, on the merits of a challenge* [...]".
733. For instance, Christer Soderlund of Sweden, finds no difficulty is recognizing that some institutions exercise a *"quasi-judicial functions"* (he includes in these *prima facie* decisions on jurisdiction, appointment of arbitrators, and decisions on challenges). Christer Söderlund, "The Parties' Contract with the Arbitration Institution" in Kaj Hobér and others (eds), *Between East and West: Essays in Honour of Ulf Franke* (Juris 2010) 490-491. For Zykin, of Russia, one of the roles of institutions is to make decisions as to the procedure of the case. Zykin, "Procedural Aspects of the Activities of Institutional Arbitration Bodies" 607-609.
734. Article 6 of the CIETAC rules (2012) and (2015); Article 4 of the CMAC rules (2004).
735. Section 13 of the rules of the Arbitration Court Attached to the Czech Chamber of Commerce; Article 8 of the rules of arbitration of the Associazione Italiana per l'Arbitrato (AIA) (2012); Article 3(4) of the arbitration rules of MAC (1994).

seat of the arbitration[736], costs[737], consolidation[738], joinder[739], extension of deadlines[740], or challenges[741].

In light of the above, whenever the parties have opted for a set of institutional rules that provides for a high level of involvement of the institution, the jurisdictional versus administrative dichotomy is, in reality, inconsistent with the parties' intention. And the argument that the decisions of an arbitrator and those of an institution are different because the parties have so agreed is, in many cases, factually incorrect. If anything, an argument based on the intention of the parties will often support the idea that the parties have agreed to a system which contemplates an apportionment of the adjudicative mission.

[c] *Arguments Based on an Alleged "Unity of the Adjudicative Mission" of the Arbitrator*

A third (related) argument raised in support of the jurisdictional versus administrative dichotomy is that the decisions of institutions cannot be jurisdictional because they fall outside a so-called adjudicative mission. In arbitration, the adjudicative mission would fall exclusively to the arbitral tribunal (i.e., to say to the exclusion of arbitral institutions).

According to this argument, there is an overriding principle which mandates that, in any jurisdictional process (including arbitration), the adjudicative mission be conferred to a single person or body. In arbitration, that person or body would be the arbitral tribunal. Consequently, measures taken by an arbitral institution, even when decisional, would be incapable of participating to the "adjudicative mission". The argument is loosely based on a principle of "independence" or "liberty of decision" of the decision-maker. It is this independence or liberty of decision, so the argument goes, which would necessarily imply the "unity" of the adjudicative mission.

736. Article 18 ICC rules (2012); Article 39 WIPO rules (2002); Article 16 Swiss rules (2012); Article 14 JAMS rules (2011).
737. Article 37 ICC rules (2012); Article 28.1 LCIA rules (1998) and (2015); Article 32 SIAC rules (2013); Article 43.2 SCC rules (2010); Article R64.4 CAS code (2013); and Article 14 of ICAC rules (2010) and ICAC's Schedule of Arbitration Fees and Costs.
738. Article 10 ICC rules (2012); Article 13 CEPANI rules (2013); Article R39 CAS Code (2013).
739. Article 7 ICC rules (2012); Article 41 CAS Code (2013); Article 11 CEPANI rules (2013).
740. Article 5.2; Article 5.6; Article 23.2; Article 30.2; Article 38.2 ICC rules (2012); Article 2.5 of the SIAC rules (2013); Article R32 of the CAS Code (2013); Article 2.3 of the Swiss rules (2012); Article 3.3 of the "*Internal Rules of the Arbitration Center of Mexico*"; Article 32 Milan rules (2010); Article 41.2(f) HKIAC rules (2013); Article 3.4 ICDR rules (2009).
741. Articles 14-15 ICC rules (2012); Article 10.3 LCIA rules (1998) and Article 10.6 LCIA rules (2014); Articles 8-9 ICDR rules (2009) and Article 14(3) ICDR rules (2014); Articles 30-31 CIETAC rules (2012) and Article 32(6) of the CIETAC rules (2015); Articles 11-13 SIAC rules (2013); Articles 9-11 Swiss rules (2012); Article 15 SCC rules (2010); Article R34 CAS Code (2013); Article 18 ICAC rules (2010); Articles 24-29 WIPO rules (2002); Article 19 Milan Chamber rules (2010); Article 14.4 ACICA rules (2011) and Article 18.4 ACICA rules (2016); and Article 17 CAMEX rules (2009). The new LCIA Rules of 2014, in fact, admit that challenge to arbitrators is not an administrative function. Article 29.1 states "*Save for reasoned decisions on arbitral challenges under Article 10, such determinations are to be treated as administrative in nature; and the LCIA Court shall not be required to give reasons for any such determination.*"

This argument finds some echo in the French court decision of *REDEC Pharaon* discussed above. By way of reminder, a finding of *REDEC Pharaon* was that, as a matter of principle, "*jurisdictional decisions*" fall within the "*exclusive competence of the arbitrator*"[742]. This argument also finds some echo in the literature.

Various authors have argued that the adjudicative mission conferred to arbitrators must remain undivided; and that this should prevent institutions from taking jurisdictional decisions. As previously stated. Klaus Peter Berger has argued that that the tasks of all institutions are not jurisdictional but administrative and that no institution "*is allowed to or does in fact decide the dispute between the parties*"[743].

For Professor Loquin:

> "*It is certain that there can be no justice without the judge's independence, which implies the judge's liberty of decision*" [...] "*The principle of independence* [...] *forbids that the resolution of a dispute be affected by the intervention of a third party*"[744].

With great respect to these authors, one difficulty with this stance is that it is premised on the idea that there is a principle of unity of the adjudicative mission. It is because the adjudicative mission should not be shared that any institutional intervention must be merely administrative. It is not immediately clear, however, where the principle of unity of the adjudicative mission comes from. There is no indication in the French decisions as to the origin of the principle.

One author who did attempt to offer some explanation for this so-called principle of unity of the adjudicative mission is Professor Antoine Kassis. However, it should be noted immediately that Kassis' position is not in line with that of Professor Loquin (or of any other author for that matter). In short, these two authors found themselves at the beginning of the 1990s on the opposite sides of an interesting doctrinal dispute as to whether certain provisions of the ICC rules breached this so-called principle of the unity of the adjudicative mission. Professor Loquin's views (which in essence are consistent with the French court decisions studied above) were expressed as a

742. "*By deciding prima facie to let a third party participate in the constitution of an arbitral tribunal, the Arbitration Court of the ICC is not rendering a jurisdictional decision, which would fall within the exclusive competence of the arbitrator, but prescribes a measure of administrative nature, aimed at finalising the constitution of the tribunal pursuant to the arbitration rules.*" Translation by the author. In the original language: "*En décidant prima facie de faire intervenir à la constitution d'un tribunal arbitral une personne alléguant sa qualité de tiers à la convention d'arbitrage, la Cour d'arbitrage de la C.C.I. ne rend pas une décision juridictionnelle, laquelle relève de la seule compétence de l'arbitre, mais prescrit une mesure de nature administrative, destinée, en application de son Règlement, à parfaire la constitution du tribunal arbitral.*"
743. Klaus Peter Berger, *Private Dispute Resolution in International Business: Negotiation, Mediation, Arbitration (Third Edition)* (Kluwer Law International 2015) 363.
744. Translation by the author. In the original language: "*Il est certain qu'il n'est point de justice sans l'indépendance du juge, laquelle implique sa liberté de décision.*" [...] "*Le principe d'indépendance doit être compris dans son essence. Il interdit que la solution du litige soit affectée en raison de l'intervention du tiers.*" Loquin, "La Sentence Arbitrale: L'Examen du Projet de Sentence par l'Institution et la Sentence au Deuxième Degré – Réflexions sur la Nature et la Validité de l'Intervention de l'Institution Arbitrale sur la Sentence" 455-457. In the same sense, see Clay, *L'arbitre* para. 1053.

response to a publication by Professor Kassis[745]. Kassis was arguing that the ICC rules and practice were inconsistent with the alleged principle of unity of the adjudicative mission (because they were encroaching on the arbitrators' adjudicative mission), and that as a result any award rendered under the ICC rules was unenforceable. Professor Loquin's views were that, whilst there was a principle of unity of the adjudicative mission, the ICC rules were not in fact encroaching on the arbitrators' adjudicative mission.

Professor Kassis was in agreement that there was a principle of unity of the adjudicative mission in arbitration[746]. This necessarily required that arbitrators alone decide the disputes submitted to them[747]. However, instead of concluding (like Professor Loquin) that any institutional action must therefore be administrative, Kassis' conclusion was that: (1) any arbitral institution should refrain from intervening in the adjudicative process, and (2) if an institution does intervene in the adjudication of the dispute then this intervention is illicit. Kassis also viewed the arbitration rules of the ICC as being in breach of this principle of unity because they contemplate an intervention of the institution in the adjudicative process[748]. For example, requirements that the ICC approve Terms of Reference[749], that it decides challenges[750], and that it scrutinizes awards[751], all allegedly breached this principle of unity of the adjudicative mission[752].

745. Kassis, *Réflexions sur le Réglement d'Arbitrage de la Chambre de Commerce Internationale: les Déviations de l'Arbitrage Institutionnel.* A summary of the book was then published in English Kassis Kassis, "The Questionable Validity of Arbitration and Awards under the Rules of the International Chamber of Commerce."

746. *"The arbitral process is essentially jurisdictional, i.e. the process of adjudicating and deciding issues as in the judiciary. The arbitrator is a private judge, but still a judge, who takes decisions to settle disputes, as does a state judge. In this capacity, he is considered to have a power not shared by others."* Kassis, "The Questionable Validity of Arbitration and Awards under the Rules of the International Chamber of Commerce" 87.

747. *"A judicial (jurisdictional) process is the settlement of disputes by a judge, public or private, either alone or as member of a panel. The judge, or panel, should decide alone, in the sense that the function should not be shared by anyone or exposed to interference from any source or in any way."* Kassis, "The Questionable Validity of Arbitration and Awards under the Rules of the International Chamber of Commerce" 90.

748. *"The provisions of the ICC rules on scrutiny for example would constitute a "major defect which is self-evident"* Translation by the author. In the original language: *"un vice majeur évident"*. A defect which is *"as inadmissible as it is fatal for arbitration"* (*"aussi inadmissible que fatal pour l'arbitrage"*). Kassis, *Réflexions sur le Règlement d'Arbitrage de la Chambre de Commerce Internationale: les Déviations de l'Arbitrage Institutionnel* 6.

749. Now under Article 23(3) of the ICC rules (2012). Approval is only required when one party does not sign the Terms of Reference.

750. Now under Article 14(3) of the ICC rules (2012).

751. Now Article 33 of the ICC rules (2012).

752. *"The problem is that the validity of the arbitration process and of the award is questionable and might be considered in jeopardy, because these powers* [*i.e.* to scrutinize awards, decide challenges and approve terms of reference] *imply a direct and serious interference by the Court in the jurisdictional power and mission of the arbitrators to decide the issue and settle the dispute."* Kassis, "The Questionable Validity of Arbitration and Awards under the Rules of the International Chamber of Commerce" 82. See also generally: Kassis, *Réflexions sur le Règlement d'Arbitrage de la Chambre de Commerce Internationale: les Déviations de l'Arbitrage Institutionnel.*

Because, for Kassis, this alleged principle was a mandatory one[753], any award rendered under the ICC rules would necessarily be unenforceable. The overall conclusion reached by Kassis was that the ICC rules constituted a "*perversion*" (in the original language "*une deviation*") of the institutional arbitration process[754]. This "*perversion*", Kassis predicted, would necessarily lead to the demise of the entire ICC arbitration system[755]!

Leaving aside the fact that the ominous predictions of Professor Kassis were in fact contradicted by the ensuing period of exponential growth at the ICC, the origin of this principle of unity of the adjudicative mission is not clear. According to Kassis, this alleged principle would derive from the requirement of independence, and would not only be a principle of French arbitration law, but would also be a basic principle of every legal system[756]:

> [there] *exists a fundamental principle inherent to all justice, according to which the jurisdictional power shall not be alienated and shall not be shared. If one is a judge (sole judge or a tribunal) one must judge alone.* (Translation by the author)[757].

Any outside intervention would therefore necessarily threaten the independence of the decision-maker. In the context of scrutiny of arbitral awards, for example, Kassis argues:

> "[...] *it seems indisputable that the institutional obligation for an arbitrator to seek approval of his draft award by an outsider, as to the form, as a condition for finally rendering it, combined with his obligation to comply with the injunctions of that outsider in this respect, is a complete denial of his liberty of decision and a flagrant alienation of his independence*"[758].

---

753. Kassis, *Réflexions sur le Règlement d'Arbitrage de la Chambre de Commerce Internationale: les Déviations de l'Arbitrage Institutionnel* 6.
754. This is the title of Kassis' 1988 book: Kassis, *Réflexions sur le Règlement d'Arbitrage de la Chambre de Commerce Internationale: les Déviations de l'Arbitrage Institutionnel* 6. Jan Paulsson translates the term "*déviation*" by "*waywardness*". See Paulsson, "Vicarious Hypochondria and Institutional Arbitration."
755. "[...] *national courts* [...] *will sooner or later discover these defects and draw the conclusions that impose themselves as to the fate of arbitral awards.* [The provision on scrutiny] *on its own, if it is maintained, will one day inexorably lead* the [ICC] *system to its downfall*" (Translation by the author). Or elsewhere: "*ICC arbitration is not arbitration, awards rendered in accordance with the ICC rules are not arbitral awards, and are therefore incapable of being enforced in any domestic legal order.*" (Translation by the author) In the original language: "*L'arbitrage de la CCI n'est pas un arbitrage, la sentence rendue selon son Règlement n'est pas une sentence arbitrale et n'est donc susceptible d'être reconnue et exécutée dans aucun ordre juridique.*" Kassis, *Réflexions sur le Règlement d'Arbitrage de la Chambre de Commerce Internationale: les Déviations de l'Arbitrage Institutionnel* 81.
756. In the original language: "*un* [principe] *de base de tout droit judiciaire privé*". Kassis, *Réflexions sur le Règlement d'Arbitrage de la Chambre de Commerce Internationale: les Déviations de l'Arbitrage Institutionnel* 6.
757. In the original language: "*C'est qu'il existe un principe fondamental inhérent à toute justice, selon lequel le pouvoir juridictionnel ne s'aliène pas et ne se partage pas. Si on est juge – juge unique ou collège-, on juge soi-même et on juge seul.*" Kassis, *Réflexions sur le Règlement d'Arbitrage de la Chambre de Commerce Internationale: les Déviations de l'Arbitrage Institutionnel* 110.
758. Kassis, "The Questionable Validity of Arbitration and Awards under the Rules of the International Chamber of Commerce" 89.

> [...]
>
> *"His independence is eliminated by the sole fact that he is institutionally obliged to submit the draft award, reflecting his intimate and ultimate conviction to an outsider, thus seeking assessment and criticism which may lead to amendment or reversal"*[759].

A first difficulty with this idea is that the independence of the arbitrator is not the same as the independence of a judge. While for a domestic judge independence might arguably mean independence from any outside influences, in the context of international arbitration, independence is understood to mean independence vis-à-vis the parties and their counsel, not vis-à-vis the institution under the auspices of which the proceedings are conducted. In this sense, Karel Daele defines the independent arbitrator as "[...] *one who has no close relationship with a party in the arbitration or its counsel, be it of a financial, professional or personal nature*"[760]. This is also what the IBA Guidelines illustrate: "*Every arbitrator shall be impartial and independent of the parties*". The guidelines contain no requirement of independence in relation to the administering institution[761]. In essence, the problem with Kassis' assumption is that, for it to work in the context of international arbitration it would need institutional intervention to be placed on the same plane as the influence by a party or its counsel on the decision of an arbitrator, which is questionable. A sharing of the tasks between a tribunal and the institution, as may be contemplated by the arbitration rules chosen by the parties, poses no problem of independence so long as the institution itself remains independent from the parties (and their counsel)[762]. As Jan Paulsson argues:

> [t]*here is no apparent reason why parties, when agreeing to institutional arbitration, could not accept that there should be a division of tasks. In other words, even if one were to admit that the ICC Court overrules arbitrators' decisions on points of substance – which is far from proved in Réflexions, and which does not in fact correspond to reality – there seems to be no fundamental concept of justice that would deny the legitimacy of such a process*[763].

A second and more fundamental problem is that the alleged principle of unity of the adjudicative mission is at odds with the reality of institutional arbitration. As discussed in Chapter 3 above, some sets of institutional rules do contemplate a division of the overall task of deciding the dispute between the arbitrators and the institutions (albeit with the arbitrators being entrusted with the bulk of the adjudicative mission).

759. Kassis, "The Questionable Validity of Arbitration and Awards under the Rules of the International Chamber of Commerce" 89-90.
760. Karel Daele, *Challenge and Disqualification of Arbitrators in International Arbitration* (Kluwer Law International 2012) 279-280. See also William W. Park, "Rectitude in International Arbitration" (2011) 27 Arbitration International, Kluwer Law International 473, 477.
761. General Principle no. 1 provides: *"Every arbitrator shall be impartial and independent of the parties at the time of accepting an appointment to serve and shall remain so during the entire arbitration proceeding until the final award has been rendered or the proceeding has otherwise finally terminated."* "IBA Guidelines on Conflicts of Interest in International Arbitration, Approved on 22 May 2004 by the Council of the International Bar Association" (2004).
762. At this stage however it is not common practice for arbitration rules to impose requirements of independence and impartiality on to its staff or the members of its deciding organs.
763. Paulsson, "Vicarious Hypochondria and Institutional Arbitration" 231.

And this sharing of responsibilities does not seem to have caused any problem insofar as the enforcement of arbitral awards is concerned. While Kassis mentions one case of the Turkish Supreme Court from the 1970s where an ICC award was refused enforcement because the court found that the scrutiny process was contrary to Turkish public policy[764], this case no longer appears to be good law in Turkey and remains isolated[765]. Further, a brief review of case law of the leading jurisdictions for arbitration (other than France) shows no support for the idea that there is a universal principle requiring the unity of the adjudicative mission.

In the United States for instance decisions which have extended the arbitrators' immunity to arbitral institutions have done so on the premise that the actions of institutions form an integral part of the overall adjudicative mission[766]. In the *Austern v. Chicago Board Options Exchange* case[767], for instance, the courts recognized immunity to the organization administering the arbitration in the following terms[768]:

> *"extension of arbitral immunity to encompass boards that sponsor arbitration is a natural and necessary product of the policies underlying arbitral immunity".*

764. "Keban judgement, Supreme Court of Turkey, 10 March 1976 (excerpt quoted in Arbitration, Vol. 46, 1980, p. 241)." In this case, a French company and a Turkish para-Statal entity had concluded a contract for the construction of the so-called Keban Dam Project. The contract gave rise to an ICC arbitration. The award which resulted could not be enforced in Turkey because the courts found that the scrutiny process was contrary to Turkish public policy.
765. See Derains and Schwartz, *A Guide to the New ICC Rules of Arbitration* 315. According to one author, over time the approach of Turkish courts towards ICC arbitration has changed so that *"ICC awards are being enforced in Turkey"*. Bayata Canyaş Aslı, "Enforcement of Foreign Arbitral Awards in Turkey. Further Steps Towards a More Arbitration-Friendly Approach" (2013) 31 ASA Bulletin, Kluwer Law International 537, 553. This author cites the following authority: Sup. Court, 15. Chamber, Case No. E. 1996/3249, K. 1996/5584, T. 25.10.1996: www.kazanci.com (12 July 2012).
766. "International Medical Group vs. American Arbitration Association, United States Court of Appeals, Seventh Circuit, 3 December 2002 (312 F.3d 833)"; "Encyclopaedia Universalis S.A. v. Encyclopaedia Britannica Inc., United States Court of Appeals, Second Circuit, 31 March 2005 (403 F.3d 85)"; "Hawkins v. National Association of Securities Dealers Inc., United States Court of Appeals, Fifth Circuit, 23 June 1998 (149 F.3d 330)"; "Olson v. National Association of Securities Dealers, United States Court of Appeals, Eighth Circuit, 7 June 1996 (85 F.3d 381)."
767. "Austern v. Chicago Board Options Exchange, United States Court of Appeals, Second Circuit, 15 March 1990 (898 F.2d 882)."
768. By way of background, S. Ezra and Esther Austern (a couple resident in Israel) had entered into a contract with Fried Trading Company, an options trading partnership. As Fried was a member of the Chicago Board Options Exchange (CBOE), the contract contained a clause providing for arbitration under the rules of the CBOE. The rules of the CBOE contemplated that (1) the tribunal be composed of five arbitrators *"a majority of whom shall not be from the securities industry"* and (2) *"notice of the time and place for the initial hearing* [...] *be given at least eight (8) business days prior to the date fixed for the hearing* [...]". Fried commenced an arbitration against the Austerns, who decided not to participate in the proceedings. An award was rendered in favour of the claimant, who sought to enforce it in the US courts. Austerns successfully obtained the setting aside of the award on the basis that the institution (the CBOE) had appointed a tribunal comprising a majority of individuals from the securities market and had failed to notify them of the hearing in breach of the rules. Subsequently, the Austerns initiated proceedings the CBOE before the US District Court for the Southern District of New York, to recover the costs incurred in the set aside proceedings. The district court decided that the CBOE, *"as the organisation sponsoring the arbitration"* was *"shielded from civil liability under the doctrine of arbitral immunity"*. The decision was confirmed in appeal by the US Court of Appeals for the Second Circuit on 15 March 1990.

> [...]
> "*semantically* categorizing the challenged acts as 'ministerial' or 'administrative', as opposed to 'discretionary', in large part misses the mark, *since the scope of arbitral immunity is 'defined by the functions it protects and serves'*"[769] (emphasis added).

In Switzerland, the High Court of the Canton of Zürich has expressly recognized the possibility that the parties may agree to a division of tasks between the arbitrators and the institution:

> *According to the terms of Article 21 of the Rules of Arbitration* [on scrutiny of awards], *the Court of Arbitration is juxtaposed with the arbitral tribunal and must be consulted by the latter before it renders its award.* The fact that the parties may provide for such cooperation – or more exactly submit to rules which provide for it – must be recognized *in the same way as the possibility of providing for an appeal before an appellate arbitral tribunal* (emphasis added)[770].

At the Federal level, no decisions touching on institutional decisions have acknowledged the existence of a so-called principle of unity of the adjudicative mission. To the contrary, the Swiss Supreme Court has on occasions[771] accepted to review decisions rendered by arbitral institutions precisely because of the great impact that such institutional decisions can have on the overall adjudication of the case[772]. For

769. Citing Forrester, 484 U.S. at 227, 108 S.Ct. at 544. The court found also that "[...] *the acts complained of here* [....] *were not only performed directly in connection with the CBOE's management of contractually agreed upon arbitration, but, we believe, were sufficiently associated with the adjudicative phase of the arbitration to justify immunity*". See also Chan: "*U.S. courts have held that administrative decision-making process of arbitral institutions, like judicial courts, are functionally comparable and engenders the same need for independent judgment, free from the threat of lawsuits.*" Chan, "Of Arbitral Institutions and Provisional Determinations on Jurisdiction, Global Gold Case" 422. In the same sense see Hans van Houtte and Bridie McAsey, "The Liability of Arbitrators and Arbitral Institutions" in Philipp Habegger and others (eds), *Arbitral Institutions under Scrutiny* (JurisNet 2013), ASA Special Series No. 40 160.
770. "Decision of the High Court of the Canton of Zürich, 29 June 1979."
771. For a commentary as to the inconsistency of Swiss case law see Matthias Scherer, "Decisions of Private Bodies and Institutions Cannot Be Challenged under Article 190 PIL Act – Really?" (2004) 32 ASA Bulletin, Kluwer Law International 102-107. It is unclear whether decisions of arbitral institutions are reviewable by the Swiss courts independently of the arbitral award. Some judgments have indicated that decisions of "*private bodies*" (in the sense arbitral institutions) could not be reviewed on their own and that any challenge of such institutional decisions had to be made in the context of a challenge to the award. "Decision of the Swiss Federal Tribunal, Ref. No. 4A-644/2009, 13 April 2010 (Bulletin de l'ASA, 2011, at p. 107)." Recent decisions however indicate that some institutional decisions can in fact be challenged directly, without it being very clear what the criteria is for an institutional decision to be reviewable. "Decision of the Swiss Federal Tribunal, Ref. No. 4A-282/2013, 13 November 2013 (Bulletin de l'ASA, 2014, at p. 89)." Whatever the position is, the Swiss courts do not recognize the so-called principle of unity of the adjudicative mission. When they have refused to review institutional decisions pending issue of the final award it is on the basis that such decisions do not constitute awards made by arbitrators. Scherer, "Decisions of Private Bodies and Institutions cannot be Challenged under Art. 190 PIL Act – Really?" 106.
772. Which implicitly acknowledges the relevance of institutional decisions in the overall adjudicative process.

instance, in 2008[773], the Swiss Supreme Court accepted to review a decision of the CAS to treat an appeal as withdrawn for failure of the appellant to lodge the required advance on cost. The Supreme Court did so on the ground that the CAS decision was effectively a final decision on admissibility (by treating the appeal as withdrawn, the institution had irrevocably rejected the appeal). This decision implies that the measure taken by CAS was more than some mere administrative decision falling outside the scope of the adjudicative mission. At the same time, the importance of the CAS decision in the overall adjudication of the dispute was not in itself considered to encroach on the adjudicative mission of the appeal tribunal[774].

In Germany, the idea that institutions participate in the overall adjudication of the disputes also transpires, implicitly, in the decision of the Supreme Court in the "Berlin arbitration clauses" saga[775]. In that case, the question before the Federal Court of Justice was whether "old" arbitration clauses referring to the extinct Berlin Foreign Trade Chamber[776] continued to be valid after it was dismantled (following the German reunification), and its activities transferred to a newly established private entity named "Berlin Arbitration Court"[777]. The Federal Court of Justice held that such clauses had become null and void under the then German Code of Civil Procedure[778]. The decision was based on section 1033 no. 1 of that Code, pursuant to which an arbitration agreement becomes invalid if an arbitrator who was named in the agreement becomes

773. "Decision of the Swiss Federal Tribunal, Ref. No. 4A-600/2008, 20 February 2009 (Bulletin de l'ASA, 2009, at p. 568)." The dispute arises out of a claim made by a football club to FIFA against the club's former manager/coach. The club was claiming EUR 400,000 from the coach for early termination of his employment contract. A decision having been made in favour of the club, the coach lodged an appeal before the CAS. The CAS directed the parties to lodge an advance on cost, which the coach did not pay on time. The CAS decided to treat the appeal as withdrawn in accordance with its rules, and declared the proceedings closed. The appellant challenged the CAS decision before the Swiss Supreme Court. For a discussion of the case see Laurence Burger, "Sports Arbitration and Due Process, Kluwer Arbitration Blog, http://kluwerarbitrationblog.com/blog/2011/03/02/sports/arbitration-and-due-process, accessed 2/03/2014", 2 March 2011.

774. In the original language: "*Son prononcé s'apparente à une décision d'irrecevabilité qui clôt l'affaire pour un motif tiré des règles de la procédure. Qu'il émane du Président suppléant de la Chambre arbitrale d'appel plutôt que d'une Formation arbitrale, laquelle n'était du reste pas encore constituée, n'empêche pas qu'il s'agit bien d'une décision susceptible de recours au Tribunal fédéral.*" "Decision of the Swiss Federal Tribunal, Ref. No. 4A-600/2008, 20 February 2009 (Bulletin de l'ASA, 2009, at p. 568)", at para. 2.3.

775. "Federal Court of Justice Decision, 20 January 1994, Ref. no. III ZR 143/92."

776. This chamber of trade was established in 1954 in the German Democratic Republic (East Germany) and was administering East-West trading disputes. Uzelac, "Succession of Arbitral Institutions" 80.

777. Known in German as "Shiedsgericht Berlin". Kirchner and Marriott, "International Arbitration in the Aftermath of Socialism – The Example of the Berlin Court of Arbitration" 9-10.

778. According to the court: "*When the parties to an arbitration agreement have, by selecting the specific organization to carry out the arbitration* [...] *conced*[ed] *to that organization significant influence on the composition of the tribunal* [...], *then* [...] *the liquidation of this institution results in the arbitration agreement becoming null and void. The legal status granted by means of the arbitration agreement to the institution called upon to constitute the arbitral tribunal is not transferable to another organization without agreement of the contracting parties.*" Translation by the DIS. Decision cited in Uzelac, "Succession of Arbitral Institutions" 82.

incapacitated[779]. The court applied this provision by analogy on the basis that it found the disappearance of an institution to be comparable to the death or incapacity of a named arbitrator. The rationale being that, because of the importance of the functions conferred by the parties to the arbitral institution, a change in the identity of the institution affects the parties' overall bargain and thus invalidates the parties' arbitration agreement. In other words, the decision reflected an understanding that the arbitral institution forms an important part of the adjudicative process chosen by the parties.

A third problem with the thesis of Professor Kassis is that, when one looks outside the realm of arbitration, examples abound of judicial decision-making processes in which the adjudicative mission is divided in one way or another. Institutional arbitration is far from the only dispute resolution system in which the decision-making process is split and the existence of a universal principle of unity of the adjudicative mission is therefore highly doubtful. In criminal procedure for example, it is common for the decision-making process to be split between a judge (who may decide on sentencing) and a jury (deciding on liability). In a different vein, judicial processes in which a decision is made by one judicial organ on the basis of the persuasive opinion of a third party is not uncommon. This is the case at the European Court of Justice where decisions of the Court are heavily influenced by the Opinions of the Advocates General[780]. This is also the case of decisions made by a State court in the United Sates that would follow the advisory opinion issued by an Attorney General[781]. Similarly, the WTO's legal officers play a significant role in framing and deciding substantive and procedural issues for the benefit of the WTO Panel[782]. There is in fact a whole area of legal scholarship dedicated to analysing judicial decision-making through the prism of collective action[783]. Ironically, some scholars have even argued that collegiality between judges is desirable because its has a beneficial effect on the quality of judicial work product[784].

779. To be more precise if the arbitrator named in the clause dies, becomes unavailable, refuses to act, or causes of unduly delays.
780. Laure, Clément-Wilz. "The Advocate General: A Key Actor of the Court of Justice of the European Union" (2011) 14(1) Cambridge Yearbook of European Legal Studies 587-613.
781. Dee Ashley Akers, "The Advisory Opinion Function of the Attorney General" (1949-1950) 38(4) Kentucky Law Journal 561-598; Peter E. Jr. Heiser, "The Opinion Writing Function of Attorneys General" (1982) 18(1) Idaho Law Review 9-42.
782. According to the Joint Report of the International Commercial Disputes Committee and the Committee on Arbitration of the New York City Bar Association on Tribunal Secretaries: *"[...] a legal officer typically has the following responsibilities: (a) to choose the panelists [...]; (b) to prepare a summary of factual and legal issues to be addressed by the parties, which summary normally is discussed at the panel's first internal meeting; (c) to survey relevant case law for the panel members; (d) to prepare a set of questions from the panel to the parties' experts or the parties themselves; (e) to draft the award and participate in internal meetings between the panel members; and (f) to participate in the hearings (without directly addressing questions to the parties)"*. Joint Report of the International Commercial Disputes Committee and the Committee on Arbitration of the New York City Bar Association, "Secretaries to International Arbitral Tribunals" (2006) 17 American Review of International Arbitration 581.
783. See, for example, Walter Murphy, "Courts as Small Groups" (June 1966) 79(8) Harvard Law Review 1565-1572.
784. Harry T. Edwards, "The Effects of Collegiality on Judicial Decision Making" (May, 2003) 151(5) University of Pennsylvania Law Review 1639-1690.

Kassis' position is particularly difficult to understand considering that the author himself admits finding no difficulty with a dispute being resolved "collectively" by a panel of arbitrators or judges[785]. Likewise, the author finds no difficulty in a French Court of Appeal making a decision on the basis of mandatory instructions from the Cour de Cassation[786].

In sum, the argument that, by principle, the adjudicative mission cannot be shared or divided, whether raised with a view to finding that ICC awards are unenforceable (as for Kassis), or to deny any jurisdictional character to the decisions of institutions (as for Loquin or Berger) is not very convincing. There appears to be no basis for this alleged principle of unity of the adjudicative mission and it is inconsistent with the reality of institutional arbitration and of dispute resolution in general.

[C] Conclusions on the First Representation

None of the arguments raised to support the notion that the decisions rendered by arbitral institutions and by arbitral tribunals are qualitatively different appear convincing.

In fine, if the jurisdictional versus administrative dichotomy fails to convince, it is perhaps simply because it "does not ring true"[787]. The idea that there should, somehow, be a difference of nature between the decisions rendered by an institution and those of a tribunal is a construct that reflects the theoretical representation of the institutions as mere administrators. This representation, insofar as it is at odds with the complex reality of institutional arbitration, is much like a myth or fable[788]:

- like any myth or fable, the representation is an inaccurate, distorted, depiction of reality; but
- like any myth or fable it nonetheless serves an important social function – the function in this case being to liberate institutional action from the rigid due

785. As previously cited, Kassis affirms: "*If one is a judge (sole judge or a tribunal) one must judge alone.*" In the original language: "*Si on est juge – juge unique ou collège-, on juge soi-même et on juge seul*". Kassis, *Réflexions sur le Règlement d'Arbitrage de la Chambre de Commerce Internationale: les Déviations de l'Arbitrage Institutionnel* 110.
786. Kassis, "The Questionable Validity of Arbitration and Awards under the Rules of the International Chamber of Commerce" 97. In the French legal system, a Court of Appeal decision can be appealed on a question of law to the court of cassation. If the court of cassation annuls the Court of Appeal's judgment, the matter is remanded to a Court of Appeal for reconsideration; the Court of Appeal new decision can itself be appealed before the court of cassation. However, in that case, if the court of cassation annuls again the Court of Appeal's decision, then the matter is referred to a Court of Appeal one final time and that court is bound to comply with the judgment of the court of cassation. In such a case, therefore, the Court of Appeal last seized of the matter must decide on the basis of mandatory instructions from the court of cassation.
787. On the limitation of dichotomic or binary reasoning in legal thinking (in the context of a discussion of the limitations of adversarial systems), see Carrie Menkel-Meadow, "The Trouble with the Adversary System in a Postmodern, Multicultural World" (1996) 38 William and Mary Law Review 5, 30.
788. On the functions served by myths, see Joseph Campbell, *Creative Mythology (The Masks of God)* (Souvenir Press 2011).

process requirements that applies to arbitrators so as to preserve its effectiveness.

§4.03 SECOND REPRESENTATION: A MERE PURVEYOR OF LOGISTICAL SERVICES WITH NO DECISION-MAKING POWER AT ALL

[A] Presentation of the Representation

According to the second representation, institutions are mere purveyors of logistical services; which role consists of providing the arbitrators and the parties with clerical support, but excludes any "decision-making"[789]. For example, the definition of "institutional arbitration" given by Halsbury's Laws reads:

> *"Institutional arbitration" or "administered arbitration" refers to the settlement of disputes by arbitration procedures administered by a standing international body, such as the Permanent Court of Arbitration, and the International Centre for the Settlement of Investment Disputes. The standing body does not itself decide the dispute: it acts as the secretariat for arbitral tribunals established on an ad hoc basis under its auspices*[790].

At a superficial level, the first representation discussed above (at least in some of its iterations) appears similar to the second representation discussed in this part of Chapter 4. The idea, discussed above, that the actions of an institution are considered non-jurisdictional because there must be a unity of the adjudicative mission (and this mission has been conferred in its entirety to the arbitral tribunal), finds some resonance in the idea that institutional measures are devoid of any decisional character. However, while the two ideas are partly overlapping, they are not identical. In the first case, one says that institutional measures (whether decisional or not) fall outside the adjudicative mission. In the second case, one says that the nature of the activities of institutions is non-decisional (i.e., that the measures taken by institutions do not constitute decision-making). The difference is that, under the first representation, an institutional measure can be decisional but still fall outside the adjudication of the dispute. One example would be a decision on a challenge to an arbitrator. If its decisional character is evident, it would not participate to the adjudication of the overall dispute.

It should be noted that authors who make use of the second representation of the role of institutions, often oscillate between that second representation and the first one, sometimes within the same article. In that sense, the second representation seems like a mere "step-up" from the first representation – a step-up which results from an

789. A detailed definition of "decision-making" is offered in section §4.03[B] below ("*Critical analysis of the representation: Institutions do have a measure of decision-making power*"). For present purposes, and as explained in this book' introduction, it means the task of making decisions, in the sense binding determinations. It is not limited to determinations on the merits of a dispute but also includes determinations on jurisdiction and procedure.

790. Halsbury's Laws of England, "Institutional Arbitration" in *Halsbury's Laws of England Volume 61 (International Relations Law)* (5th edn, LexisNexis Butterworths 2010) 494.

over-simplification of the idea (in our view, erroneous in the first place) that the adjudicative mission is indivisible. The reasoning of those authors who take an occasional a leap from the first representation to the second one appears to be the following: The adjudicative mission is entirely with the arbitral tribunal. In that sense, institutions do not decide disputes. If institutions do not decide disputes, then in turn one must be able to say that the activities of institutions do not constitute decision-making.

Authors who have occasionally leaped to the second representation include Klaus Lionnet. Lionnet negates any decision-making on the part of institutions. In an extreme iteration of this second representation, Lionnet in fact negates *any independent action* on the part of institutions, be it decisional or otherwise. Lionnet indeed argues that[791], when administering proceedings, institutions are, in all respects, acting as mere agents of the parties, rather than in their own names and on their own behalves. In particular, when making appointments, Lionnet argues, "[t]*he arbitration institution appoints the arbitrators in the name of the parties and therefore not in its capacity as an arbitration institution*"[792]. This is because according to Lionnet:

> *[a]n arbitration institution, acts as a representative of the parties, with two powers of attorney, one from the defaulting party and another from the other party, which were given implicitly by both parties when choosing the appointing authority*[793].

More recently, another German author has taken a similar view (although it must be said that this author oscillates between the first and second representation):

> *Neither the DIS nor the ICC International Court of Arbitration, nor any other arbitral institution is allowed to or does in fact decide the dispute between the parties. Their only task is to serve as an administrative intermediary between the parties and the arbitral tribunal.* Even the prima facie examination of the arbitration agreement by the arbitral institution does not lead to a "decision" *of the parties' dispute as to whether the tribunal has jurisdiction*[794].

In a different category altogether, while rightly recognizing the leading role played by institutions in the drafting of arbitration rules and at the appointment stage, Professor Jarrosson appears to describe the role of the institution in respect of the "proceedings proper"[795] as one being devoid of any decisional character. For him, the role of institutions is thus limited to "*organising the proceedings*". The role of institutions is "*not to arbitrate disputes themselves*", because "*arbitration is a matter for*

791. In the context of a discussion of the arbitrator's contract with the parties under German law mostly.
792. Klaus Lionnet, "The Arbitrator's Contract" (1999) 15 Arbitration International, Kluwer Law International 161, 168.
793. Lionnet, "The Arbitrator's Contract" 166.
794. Klaus Peter Berger, *Private Dispute Resolution in International Business: Negotiation, Mediation, Arbitration (Third Edition)* (Kluwer Law International 2015) 363.
795. The term used in the original language is "*L'instance elle-même*". Jarrosson, "L'instance Arbitrale: le Rôle Respectif de l'Institution, de l'Arbitre et des Parties dans l'Instance Arbitrale" 30-31.

the arbitrators" (Translation by the author)[796]. Elegantly using a theatre play as a metaphor for institutional arbitration proceedings, Professor Jarrosson first compares institutions to theatre prompts whose job is to cue the actors (being the arbitrators) whenever they forget their lines[797]. When evoking the supervision functions of institutions (during the proceedings proper), Professor Jarrosson then compares institutions to a theatre's "line producer", whose job is to ensure that the conditions are in place for the play to run smoothly but without intervening in the artistic direction of the production – the artistic direction of the play being, we take it, the decision of the dispute[798].

This second representation, which portrays institutional arbitration as a system in which the parties have agreed to confer the entirety of the decision-making power to an arbitral tribunal, whilst retaining concomitantly the services of some administrative agency in a non-decisional capacity, has the virtue of simplicity. It certainly captures the idea that, in institutional arbitration, the principal decision-maker remains, by and large, the arbitral tribunal, not the institution. Incidentally, this representation may also serve to reassure users that the involvement of an arbitration centre alongside the traditional participants to an arbitration (i.e., the parties and the tribunal) does not alter fundamentally the private/non-judicial nature of the process: In institutional arbitration, just like in ad hoc arbitration, the dispute is not decided by a "permanent court". In sum, this second representation simplifies the complex reality of institutional arbitration in a way that makes it easily comprehensible to outsiders.

[B] Critical Analysis of the Representation: Institutions Do Have a Measure of Decision-Making Power

Needless to say, this second representation of the role of institutions remains relatively marginal. The majority of commentators who represent institutions in a manner consistent with the first representation often acknowledge some measure of "decision-making"[799] on the part of institutions, even if they consider it to be distinct from the sort of decision-making performed by arbitrators (administrative versus jurisdictional

796. In the original language, [noting the absence of intervention of institutions in the proceedings post-appointment] "*En effet cela montre que les centres d'arbitrage ont respecté leur rôle qui est celui d'organiser l'arbitrage et qu'ils n'ont pas été tentés d'arbitrer eux-mêmes* [...].*L'arbitrage est l'affaire de l'arbitre* [...]." Jarrosson, "L'instance Arbitrale: le Rôle Respectif de l'Institution, de l'Arbitre et des Parties dans l'Instance Arbitrale" 31.

797. In the original language: "[les arbitres] *sont seuls à pouvoir être investis d'un pouvoir juridictionnel, l'effacement du centre est dans la logique des choses. Cela n'empêche pas le centre de prendre la place du souffleur vers lequel les arbitres se tournent discrètement lorsqu'ils rencontrent une difficulté dans l'interprétation de leur rôle*". Jarrosson, "L'instance Arbitrale: le Rôle Respectif de l'Institution, de l'Arbitre et des Parties dans l'Instance Arbitrale" 33.

798. In the original language: "[La supervision de l'instance] *est un point commun à la totalité des règlements: elle est l'affaire du centre qui vérifie que le cadre fixé par le règlement est respecté par les arbitres.* [...] *Le centre est ici régisseur, il vérifie le bon agencement des décors*". Jarrosson, "L'instance Arbitrale: le Rôle Respectif de l'Institution, de l'Arbitre et des Parties dans l'Instance Arbitrale" 36.

799. A detailed definition of decision-making is offered later in this section below.

dichotomy discussed above). For Derains and Schwartz for instance (in respect of the ICC):

> *The Court's decision-making role is nonetheless generally regarded by those close to the ICC as vital to the ICC arbitral system. Thus, there has historically been widespread resistance within both the Court and the ICC Commission on Arbitration to any suggestion of either restricting the Court's powers or delegating its decision-making responsibilities to the Court's Secretariat.*[800]

Likewise, Grigera-Naon, also recognizes:

> [...] *the ICC arbitration system, since its very inception, should probably be considered as the one vesting the arbitral institution with more controlling powers in the arbitral process and its outcome than any other and, from that standpoint, as the one providing the institution with the most far-reaching decisional powers binding on the parties and the arbitral panel regarding the conduct and outcome of the arbitration proceedings governed by its rules.*[801]

The same is true of Bühler and Jarvin, who readily recognize the decisional nature of the ICC's activities:

> *When the ICC Court decides* [...] *it exercises the authority entrusted to it by the parties to take, in a given situation, a decision pursuant to its Rules, on behalf of those parties.* [...] *These decisions are all administrative in nature, as has been confirmed the French Supreme Court in the Cubic case, and the ICC Court is not required to provide reasons for its decisions*[802].

This is not surprising because, as previously stated, while Article 1(2) states that the ICC "*does not decide disputes*", the rest of the rules contain no less than fifteen instances in which the word "*decide*" (or a derivative thereof[803]) is used in conjunction with the role of the Court[804]. On the other hand, the ICC rules contain only fourteen instances in which the same word "*decide*" (or a derivative thereof) is used in conjunction with the role of the arbitral tribunal.

More importantly the review of the activities of the leading institutions conducted at Chapter 3 above demonstrates beyond any doubt that institutions routinely engage in "decision-making". For present purposes decision-making is understood in an "inclusive" sense[805]. It is taken to mean the general task of making a binding

800. Derains and Schwartz, *A Guide to the New ICC Rules of Arbitration* 13.
801. Grigera Naon, "The Powers of the ICC International Court of Arbitration vis-a-vis Parties and Arbitrators" 56.
802. Bühler and Jarvin, "The Arbitration Rules of the International Chamber of Commerce (ICC)" 1154.
803. Like "*decided*" or "*decides*".
804. Examples include the statement at Article 6(4) that "[...] *the Court shall decide whether and to what extent the arbitration shall proceed*". Another example may be found at Article 14 which provides that the "*Court shall decide on the admissibility and, at the same time, if necessary, on the merits of a challenge* [...]".
805. There is no literature in the field of international arbitration discussing what decision-making is. One field where some research has been carried out as to the notion of decision-making is US administrative law, in which rule-making was distinguished from decision-making. See for

determination between two or more possible outcomes. In other words, decision-making as presently understood requires the combination of two elements being, first, a measure of discretion to select between alternative outcomes, and second, a binding effect[806]. The first element, "discretion", means a measure of freedom in exercising a choice. There is discretion, therefore, whenever the decision-maker is called upon to evaluate comparatively (i.e., to say to "weigh") different options. From a practical point of view, this is the case whenever a choice is made between different outcomes based on comments or arguments put forward by the parties. But this is also the case in the absence of any comments or arguments submitted by the parties whenever the decision-maker, of its own volition, balances different factors[807]. Naturally, such "factors" may consist of legal arguments (i.e., arguments based on legal norms) but they may also be factual/non-legal factors such as cost, time, or even risk (as to enforceability of the tribunal's award, as to liability etc.). The second element, "the binding effect", simply means here that a decision is not subject to the acceptance or refusal of its recipients. It is not a proposal open to a possible agreement of the parties (like, for example, the solution proposed in an "early case assessment" or in conciliation).

Arbitral institutions engage in "decision-making" as defined above whenever they fix the seat[808] or the language of an arbitration[809], or determine the costs of the

example Brice Clagett, "Informal Action–Adjudication–Rule Making: Some Recent Developments in Federal Administrative Law" (1971) 20 Duke Law Journal 51-88; William Mayton, "The Legislative Resolution of the Rulemaking Versus Adjudication Problem in Agency Lawmaking" (1980) 29 Duke Law Journal 103-135; David Shapiro, "The Choice of Rulemaking or Adjudication in the Development of Administrative Policy" (1965) 78 Harvard Law Review 921.

806. The two aspects of "choice" and "binding determination" appear in some authors' definition of adjudication (as distinguished from rule-making) in US administrative law. "[decision-making involves] *a choice between various policies and the simultaneous application of the chosen policy to the facts of a particular case*". An alternative definition given by the author is "[...] *an agency process for the formulation of an order* [that is to say] *a final disposition, whether affirmative, negative, injunctive or declaratory in form of an agency in a matter other than rule-making* [...]". Clagett, "Informal Action–Adjudication–Rule Making" 51. Some other authors define adjudication even more broadly as the application of rules to a particular case. For Owen Fiss: "*Adjudication is the process by which the values embodied in an authoritative legal text, such as the Constitution, are given concrete meaning and expression.*" Owen M. Fiss, "The Social and Political Foundations of Adjudication" (1982) 6 Law and Human Behavior 121, 121. Finally, another definition of adjudication distinguishes adjudication from other processes on the ground that adjudication "[...] *confers on the affected party a peculiar form of participation in the decision, that of presenting proofs and reasoned arguments for a decision in his favour*". Lon L. Fuller, "The Forms and Limits of Adjudication" (1978) 92 Harvard Law Review 353, 364.

807. That is why our definition of decision-making differs from the definition of adjudication of Lon Fuller cited above. See Fuller, "The Forms and Limits of Adjudication" 364.

808. As is the case under the ICC, WIPO, Swiss and JAMS Rules. Article 18 ICC rules (2012); Article 39 WIPO rules (2002), Article 16 Swiss rules (2012) Article 14 JAMS rules (2011). For a view supporting implicitly that selection of seat involves decision-making see: Fellas, "AAA/ICDR International Arbitration Rules" 482.

809. As is the case under the CAS rules and in some instances under the LCIA and CIETAC rules. See Article R29 of the CAS Code (2013); Article 71 CIETAC rules (2012) and Article 81 CIETAC Rules (2015); Article 17.2 LCIA rules (1998) and (2014).

arbitrations[810]. This is also the case when they determine a joinder application[811] or one for the consolidation of proceedings[812]. This is obviously also the case in the rare instances where some institutions decide an interim measure application[813] or a jurisdictional objection[814]. Quite clearly in each of these cases, the task performed by the institution requires that it select between multiple outcomes, balancing different factors. For example, as discussed in Chapter 3, Article 10 of the ICC rules contemplates that the ICC Court may order the consolidation of proceedings[815]. In doing so, Article 10 leaves to the institution a measure of discretion in deciding whether or not to consolidate proceedings by stating that the Court may "*take into account any circumstances it considers to be relevant, including whether one or more arbitrators have been confirmed or appointed in more than one of the arbitrations and, if so, whether the same or different persons have been confirmed or appointed*"[816]. Likewise, in some instances the decision-making performed by the institution is going to involve interpreting legal norms and applying such legal norms to factual situations. An obvious example is when the institution passes a judgment on a challenge made by one party against an arbitrator[817]. The task implies assessing whether the arbitrator concerned lacks independence and or impartiality, and this in turn implies determining the content of the requirements of independence and impartiality, and applying such requirements to the facts of the case[818]. Sometimes, the decision on the challenge will be made on the basis

810. Article 37 ICC rules (2012); Article 28.1 LCIA rules (1998) and (2014); Article 32 SIAC rules (2013); Article 43.2 SCC rules (2010); Article R64.4 CAS code (2013); and Article 14 of ICAC rules (2010) and ICAC's Schedule of Arbitration Fees and Costs.
811. As may be the case under the ICC, CAS or CEPANI rules. Article 7 ICC rules (2012); Article 41 CAS Code (2013) and Article 11 CEPANI rules (2013).
812. See, for example, Article 10 of the ICC rules (2012). See also Article 13 CEPANI rules (2013), and Article R39 of the CAS Code (2013).
813. Although this is rare, some institutional rules contemplate that interim measures may be granted by the institution itself. See section 13 of the rules of the Arbitration Court Attached to the Czech Chamber of Commerce; Article R37 of the CAS Code (2013) and Article 8 of the rules of arbitration of the Associazione Italiana per l'Arbitrato (AIA) (2012).
814. Article 6 CIETAC rules (2012) and (2015) and Article 4 of the CMAC rules (2004).
815. Article 10 reads in relevant part as follows: "*The Court may, at the request of a party, consolidate two or more arbitrations pending under the Rules into a single arbitration, where: a) the parties have agreed to consolidation; or b) all of the claims in the arbitrations are made under the same arbitration agreement; or c) where the claims in the arbitrations are made under more than one arbitration agreement, the arbitrations are between the same parties, the disputes in the arbitrations arise in connection with the same legal relationship, and the Court finds the arbitration agreements to be compatible.*" Article 10 ICC rules (2012).
816. Article 10 ICC rules (2012).
817. Articles 14-15 ICC rules (2012); Article 10.3 LCIA rules (1998) and Article 10.6 LCIA rules (2014); Articles 8-9 ICDR rules (2009) and Article 14(3) if the ICDR rules (2014); Articles 30-31 CIETAC rules (2012) and Article 32(6) of the CIETAC rules(2015); Articles 11-13 SIAC rules (2013); Articles 9-11 Swiss rules (2012); Article 15 SCC rules (2010); Article R34 CAS Code (2013); Article 18 ICAC rules (2010); Articles 24-29 WIPO rules (2002); Article 19 Milan Chamber rules (2010); Article 14.4 ACICA rules (2011) and Article 18.4 of the ACICA rules (2016); and Article 17 CAMEX rules (2009). On institutions looking to domestic case law when deciding challenges, see Park, "Rectitude in International Arbitration" 493.
818. In this sense see Aguilar Alvarez: "[...] *the ICC Rules and the parties who select them adopt a flexible approach by giving the Court of Arbitration authority to assess and decide on the challenge of arbitrators. The flexibility of this solution enables the Court to examine the various*

of submissions made by the parties[819]. In addition, most often the "decisions" made by institutions in respect of the above tasks (seat, language, joinder, consolidation, challenges, etc.) have a "binding character" in the sense that they are not open to acceptance or refusal by the parties[820]. A decision on a challenge, for instance, is most often final; the only option left for the parties being to refer to the matter to the courts[821].

But, in our view, an institution also engages in decision-making whenever it selects arbitrator in the absence of nomination by the parties, or whenever it confirms[822] or refuses to confirm an arbitrator nominated by a party[823]. The selection of an arbitrator, first, implies the exercise of discretion. In the words of Jason Fry (in the context of the ICC), "[w]*hen deciding this matter, the Court takes account of such factors as the amount in dispute, the characteristics and complexity of the dispute and the nature of the parties*"[824]. Likewise, discretion is exercised in deciding whether or not to confirm a party-nominee:

> *The Court will examine several factors when considering the confirmation of an arbitrator whose statement of independence has given rise to objections. In so doing,*

---

situations to fact and law likely to arise between parties and arbitrators of very varied nationalities." Aguilar Alvarez, "The Challenge of Arbitrators" 224-225.

819. See, for example, Article 14.3 ICC rules (2012); Article 15.3 SCC rules (2010); Article R34 CAS Code (2013); and Article 26 WIPO rules (2002).

820. For a general statement that the ICC's decisions are "binding" see Grigera Naon, "The Powers of the ICC International Court of Arbitration vis-a-vis Parties and Arbitrators" 58: *"The court or its Secretariat take or may take a number of binding decisions affecting the parties and the arbitrators at an early stage of the proceedings for the setting in motion of the arbitration, that is to say, for leading such proceedings to the point where the file shall be ready to be sent to an already – constituted arbitral panel for it to commence to perform its duties."*

821. As discussed in Chapter 3 above, though this is fortunately rare, some dis-satisfied parties have sometimes sought to "appeal" decisions of institutions on challenges before domestic courts. See Art, "Challenge of Arbitrators: Is an Institutional Decision Final?". Examples of cases filed before the French and Swiss courts in France include *inter alia*: "Raffineries de Pétrole d'Homs et de Banias v Chambre de Commerce Internationale", Cour d'Appel de Paris 1985; "Société Opinter France v. S.A.R.L. Dacomex", Cour de Cassation, 2 Ch. civ. 1987; "Arab Republic of Egypt v Westland Helicopters Ltd.", Swiss Federal Tribunal 1984. These cases are discussed in more detail in the second part of this Chapter 3.

822. As contemplated under the Article 13 ICC rules (2012); Article 5(5) of the LCIA rules (1998) and Article 5(7) of the LCIA rules (2014); Article 9 HKIAC rules (2013); Article 6.3 SIAC rules (2013) and Article 5(1) Swiss rules (2012).

823. As Jan Paulsson explains (in the context of his response to an author who had argued that scrutiny but not the appointment of arbitrators or the fixing deadlines implied a participation of the ICC in "decision" of the dispute: *"There is no explanation for the conclusion that the Court can decide controversies regarding the extension of deadlines or the appointment of arbitrators without being considered as engaged in the task of resolving disputes."* See Paulsson, "Vicarious Hypochondria and Institutional Arbitration" 243. The author in question is Antoine Kassis, whose article is discussed (critically) at length in the second part of this Chapter 3. See Kassis, "The Questionable Validity of Arbitration and Awards under the Rules of the International Chamber of Commerce."

In the same sense as Paulsson (implying that the appointment of arbitrators implies decision-making), see Bühler and Jarvin, "The Arbitration Rules of the International Chamber of Commerce (ICC)" 1154.

824. Fry, "ICC International Court of Arbitration" 5.

it will balance the important right of parties to participate in the constitution of the arbitral tribunal against the equally important requirement of having an impartial and independent arbitral tribunal[825].

Again, both decisions as to the selection of an arbitrator and as to the confirmation of a nominee are "binding" on the parties in the sense that they are not open to acceptance or refusal, the only option being to challenge the arbitrator concerned. Naturally, as discussed throughout Chapter 3 above, the amount of discretion conferred on an institution, and its capacity to impose a binding outcome on the parties in respect of each of the above tasks (selection of seat, language, appointment and challenges of arbitrators, etc.), varies from one set of institutional rules to the next. It remains, however, that "decisional" functions are routinely exercised by various institutions.

In light of this, it is perhaps unsurprising that the arbitral institutions which, like to the ICC, have opted to describe their role as a purely non-decisional one, remain rare. Materials produced by a number of institutions indeed indicate, at best, an ambivalent position towards the second representation of the role of institutions. The position of the SCC in this respect is interesting. Its website for instance states that "*the SCC does not itself decide disputes*".[826] This wording mirrors that of Appendix 1 to the SCC Rules (which used to form part of the SCC rules in previous versions)[827]. On the other hand, the SCC rules state clearly that the Board of the SCC makes "*decisions*" under the rules. For example, Article 9 (unambiguously entitled "*Decisions by the Board*") states:

When necessary the Board shall:

(i) decide *whether the SCC manifestly lacks jurisdiction over the dispute pursuant to Article 10 (i);*
(ii) decide *whether to consolidate cases pursuant to Article 11;*
(iii) decide *the number of arbitrators pursuant to Article 12;*
(iv) make any appointment of arbitrators pursuant to Article 13;
(v) decide *the seat of arbitration pursuant to Article 20; and*
(vi) determine *the Advance on Costs pursuant to Article 45.* (Emphasis added)

825. Fry, "ICC International Court of Arbitration" 6.
826. "Website of the SCC, http://www.sccinstitute.com."
827. It reads in relevant parts: "*Article 1: The Arbitration Institute of the Stockholm Chamber of Commerce (the 'SCC') is a body providing administrative services in relation to the settlement of disputes." Article 2: The SCC does not itself decide disputes. The function of the SCC is to: (i) administer domestic and international disputes in accordance with the SCC Rules and other procedures or rules agreed upon by the parties; and (ii) provide information concerning arbitration and mediation matters*". Apparently, this wording, introduced in the 1990s on the occasion of a revision of the rules, aimed to replace a more general statement that the SCC "*assist*[s] *in the settlement of domestic and international disputes*". This earlier wording was considered to give the wrong impression that the SCC decides disputes. Annette Magnusson and Patricia Shaughnessy, "The 2007 Arbitration Rules of the Arbitration Institute of the Stockholm Chamber Of Commerce" (2006) 2006 Stockholm International Arbitration Review 33, 36.

Similar wording appears on the SCC's website[828], and naturally found its way into the literature. For example, former Deputy Secretary General, Marie Öhrström, explains that making decisions is the very function of the Board:

> *The SCC Board's function is to make decisions regarding prima facie jurisdiction, the appointment of arbitrators, challenges to arbitrators, removal of arbitrators, advances on costs, and determining the arbitration costs. The SCC Board is very active.*[829]

If the SCC's stance on this first representation may be qualified of ambivalent, the position of other institutions is much less so. It is indeed not uncommon for the rules of institutions to contemplate expressly decision-making on the part of the institution. This is the case of organizations like the LCIA[830], or ICDR[831], which rules routinely talk of "*decisions*" made by organs of the institution. This is also the case of institutions such as SIAC[832] and HKIAC[833] which rules contain express provisions confirming the binding and final character of the "*decisions*" of the institution. But the decisional nature of the institutions' functions transpires even more clearly in the Swiss rules, which Article 2 ("*Powers of the Court*") states:

> *The Court shall render decisions as provided for under the Swiss Rules. It may delegate to one or more members or committees the power to make certain decisions pursuant to the present Internal Rules. The Court has all the necessary powers to fulfil such purpose.*[834]

Interestingly, the internal rules of the Swiss Institution acknowledge implicitly the existence of an internal "administrative case law" of the institution which confirms not only decision-making but also consistency in such decision-making. The internal rules of the Swiss Institution indeed contemplate expressly the possibility for the Court to establish a particular "practice": "*the Court may at such time define a common practice in order to ensure consistent and efficient administration of arbitration*

828. *"The functions of the SCC Board is to take decisions as required under the SCC Rules."* "Website of the SCC, http://www.sccinstitute.com."
829. Öhrström, "The Arbitration Institute of the Stockholm Chamber of Commerce (SCC)" 4.
830. Verbs used include *inter alia "decide", "determine"* or *"refuse"* or derivatives thereof. For the LCIA rules (1998) see: Article 5(4) (number of arbitrators), Article 7(1) (confirmation of nominee), Article 10 (removal of arbitrators), Article 11 (replacement of arbitrators), Article 16 (seat) and Article 17 (language).
831. Verbs used include *inter alia "decide", "determine"* or *"establish"* or derivatives thereof. For the ICDR rules (2009) see: Article 9 (challenges), Article 11 (replacement of arbitrators), Article 13 (seat), Article 32 (fee rates).
832. Article 36 of the SIAC rules (2013) provide: *"Subject to Rule 25.1, the decisions of the President, the Court and the Registrar with respect to all matters relating to an arbitration shall be conclusive and binding upon the parties and the Tribunal. The President, the Court and the Registrar shall not be required to provide reasons for such decisions."*
833. Article 3(2) of the HKIAC rules (2013) provide clearly: *"HKIAC has no obligation to give reasons for any* decision *it makes in respect of any arbitration commenced under these Rules. All* decisions *made by HKIAC under these Rules are final and, to the extent permitted by any applicable law, not subject to appeal."* (Emphasis added).
834. Article 2 of the Swiss rules (2012).

proceedings"[835]. Likewise, the internal rules require Chairs and Vice-Chairs to report to a plenary session of the Swiss Court if there is a change to the said practice[836].

On an extreme side of the spectrum one finds those institutions which trace their origins back to the old socialist chambers of trade. Their rules are often phrased in a manner that suggests that it is the institution in the first place which is entrusted with the mission of resolving of the dispute; a mission for which the institution then appoints an arbitral tribunal. Article 2 of the ICAC rules, for instance. provides that: "[t]*he ICAC shall settle disputes subject to an agreement in writing between the parties to refer a dispute that has arisen, or may arise, between them to the ICAC*"[837]. This notion that ICAC decides disputes is then replicated throughout the rules. One example is Article 9 which talks of the "*jurisdiction of the ICAC*", rather than that of the tribunal. More telling is Article 11 which deals with the situation where a claimant has failed to rectify defects in its Request for Arbitration[838]. This provision contemplates that "*the ICAC shall either make an arbitral award or rule to terminate the proceedings*"[839]. This "reversal" of the roles between the institution and the arbitral tribunal appears also clearly in the choice of law provisions at Article 26 of the ICAC rules, which state:

> [...] *ICAC shall settle disputes in accordance with the rules of law which the parties chosen to apply to the subject matter of the dispute* [...] *ICAC shall make decisions in accordance with the terms and conditions of the contract with reference to the trade usages applicable to the transactions.*[840]

[C] Conclusions on the Second Representation

It is clear that arbitral institutions routinely engage in decision-making in respect of the arbitrations they administer. The second representation of the role of institutions as

835. Fry, "ICC International Court of Arbitration" 6.
836. *"The Chairperson, the Vice-Chairpersons and the committees must report to the Court if they have encountered an issue of interpretation of any provision of the Swiss Rules or have rendered a decision inducing a change of practice in the administration of arbitration proceedings pending under the Swiss Rules."* Swiss Chambers' Arbitration Institution, "Internal Rules of the Arbitration Court of the Swiss Chambers' Arbitration Institution, available at: https://www.swissarbitration.org/sa/download/internal_rules_2012.pdf" (2012).
837. Article 2(2) of the ICAC rules (2005).
838. A "Statement of Claim" in ICAC parlance.
839. Article 11 of the ICAC rules (2005). Likewise, Article 23 states that "*the ICAC may conduct the arbitral proceedings in a different language*".
840. Article 26 of the ICAC rules (2005).
    Likewise, Article 2 of the CMAC rules provide that the Chinese institution *"independently and impartially resolves, by means of arbitration, marine, maritime, logistic disputes and other contractual or non-contractual disputes* [...]". Its Article 3 states that *"The Arbitration Commission takes cognizance of cases in accordance with an arbitration agreement between the parties* [...]".
    Likewise, Articles 1 and 4 of the CIETAC rules (2012) and (2015) talk of "*arbitration by CIETAC*". Likewise, as explained before Article 6 of the CIETAC rules contemplated that it is for CIETAC to make decisions on jurisdiction and that CIETAC may delegate that power to the tribunal.

mere administrators devoid of any decision-making power therefore appears at odds with the reality of institutional arbitration. This second representation of the role of institutions is not only at odds with the reality of institutional arbitration as it transpires from a review of institutions' activities but, in our view, it is also incompatible with the concept of institutional arbitration. In Chapter 1, we concluded that for there to be institutional arbitration it is necessary that the relevant arbitration rules reserve, to the institution, some "competence" in the implementation of the said rules. One may now take this conclusion further and state that the very essence of institutional arbitration implies a measure of decision-making on the part of the institution. Certainly, the rationale for users to opt for institutional arbitration seems to lie in the competence reserved to the institution – competence to resolve impasses through the exercise of decisional powers[841].

§4.04 CHAPTER CONCLUSIONS

This chapter looked into the manner in which institutions' role in the institutional arbitration process is conventionally depicted. A review of the literature permitted to identify two such representations of the functions of arbitral institutions.

Under one representation, measures taken by arbitral institutions have no decisional character whatsoever. This (admittedly rare) representation, which takes the form of an unconscious assumption more often than a fully articulated theory, was easily rejected. This is because it is blatantly incompatible with what the arbitration rules of numerous institutions contemplate, and with the practice of institutional arbitration.

Under the other representation, measures taken by institutions (whether decisional or not) are considered to be ultimately immaterial because such measures, contrary to those taken by arbitral tribunals, are allegedly administrative (i.e., non-jurisdictional). While this representation serves an important purpose, which is to justify that institutions are not bound by all the due process requirements that apply to arbitrators, it had to be rejected.

The practical significance of the theoretical representations of the functions of arbitral institutions should not be underestimated. Such theoretical representations have the potential of impacting, or constraining, actual court decisions. For example, for the French courts, it is the supposition that the role of institutions is non-adjudicative which entails that institutions' decisions must be qualified as "*administrative*" rather than "*jurisdictional*", which in turn justifies not requiring from institutions that they follow due process in discharging their duties. In this sense, these theoretical representations, which emerged from the observation of anecdotal evidence as to how institutional arbitration functions (and from a subsequent process of

841. In this sense see, for example, Mirèze, "Les Pouvoirs de l'Arbitre et de la Cour d'Arbitrage de la CCI relatifs à leur Compétence" 606.

abstraction), in turn inform/shape the decisions of judges. In sum, these theoretical representations both observe and influence their object[842].

The final chapter of this book attempts to offer a more realistic theoretical representation of the functions of institutions. In particular Chapter 5 attempts to identify a better basis for distinguishing which measures (institutional or otherwise) should be subject to due process requirements than the dichotomic approach adopted in the first representation.

842. On legal theories, informing judicial decisions: Anthony D'Amato, "The Effect of Legal Theories on Judicial Decisions" (1999) 74 Chicago-Kent Law Review 517-527. See also (implicitly) Lon Fuller, "The Case of the Speluncean Explorers" (1949) 62 Harvard Law Review 616-645.

CHAPTER 5

A Realistic Representation of the Role of Institutions: Arbitral Institutions as Ancillary Participants in the Adjudicative Process

§5.01 INTRODUCTION

The preceding chapter offered a critical evaluation of the traditional representations of the role of institutions in the arbitration process. According to one such representation, arbitral institutions are mere administrators of the arbitral proceedings with no decision-making power whatsoever. According to the other representation, whilst institutions are occasionally called upon to exercise some measure of decision-making, institutional decisions remain ultimately immaterial because they are, in nature, "administrative"/"non-jurisdictional". According to one iteration of this second representation, the administrative character of measures taken by arbitral institutions means that such measures (whether decisional in nature or not) do not participate to the overall "adjudication" of the dispute.

In this chapter, an attempt is made at offering a theoretical representation of the functions of institutions that is more compatible with the reality of institutional arbitration. Our proposed representation of the role of institutions is informed both by the limitations of the traditional representations identified in Chapter 4 above, and by our analysis of the activities of institutions set out at Chapter 3. It may be summed up by the following seven propositions.

> *Proposition no. 1*: In the course of the proceedings they administer, arbitral institutions are required to take various measures, many of which have a decisional character. In other words arbitral institutions regularly engage in "decision-making".

Proposition no. 2: In all arbitral institutions surveyed in this book, the bulk of the decision-making powers are reserved to the arbitral tribunal rather than to the institution. In particular, in all institutions surveyed, the entirety of the power to decide the merits of disputes falls to the arbitral tribunals. It is thus a truism to say that, in institutional arbitration, the principal decision-maker remains, by and large, the arbitral tribunal.

Proposition no. 3: Nonetheless, some of the measures taken by arbitral institutions may, from time to time, have an impact on the outcome of a case. In other words, some institutional decisions bear a certain level of "materiality". Overall, therefore, it is incorrect to state that the role of institutions remains extraneous to the adjudicative mission. It is more accurate to depict arbitral institutions as entities which participate, albeit in an ancillary capacity, in the overall adjudication of the arbitrations conducted under their auspices.

Proposition no. 4: The assumption that all institutional decisions are necessarily less material than those taken by the arbitrators is incorrect. The level of materiality of a given decision[843] is not primarily dependent on the identity of the decision-maker (i.e., to say on whether the decision is made by an arbitral tribunal or an institution). As a result, any dichotomic classification of decisions of the type advocated by the first representation (i.e., institutional decisions are "administrative" whereas arbitrators' decisions are "jurisdictional") is not satisfactory.

Proposition no. 5: If some institutional decisions bear a certain level of materiality, then it would appear that institutions should be expected to abide by "due process" when making such decisions[844]. The contrary proposition would be at odds both with the expectations of the users of the system and with the actual practice of institutions. On the other hand, it is clear that there is a danger in imposing overly stringent due process requirements on all institutional decisions (e.g., impeding the process, exposing the procedure to strategic manoeuvres, etc.).

Proposition no. 6: The rules and practices of arbitral institutions indicate that the aspects of due process which may be relevant to the activities of institutions include: (1) treating the parties equally; (2) ensuring the independence and impartiality of the institution from the parties; (3) giving the parties same opportunity to present their case ("adversarial process"); (4) providing reasons for some institutional decisions; and (5) providing the parties the possibility to appeal or otherwise seek judicial review of some institutional decisions.

Proposition no. 7: The level of materiality of a given decision (i.e., to say, its capacity to be outcome-determinative) appears to be a viable proxy for the

843. That is its capacity to impact the outcome of a case.
844. Due process is used in a broad sense. It is taken to mean in the present context an *"international minimum standard of procedural safeguards"*. Kurkela and Turunen, *Due Process in International Commercial Arbitration* 3-4.

purposes of determining to what extent certain due process standards should be followed.

These seven propositions are further discussed below. For convenience they are subdivided in two. Propositions one to four are discussed in section §5.02 below ("*The Substance of the Representation*"). Propositions five to seven are then examined under section §5.03 ("*The Consequences of the Representation*").

§5.02 SUBSTANCE OF THE REPRESENTATION

[A] Proposition 1: The Decisional Character of Certain Institutional Measures

As explained in the discussion of the second representation in Chapter 4 above, institutions routinely engage in decision-making. It appears that, the second representation, which portrays institutions as entities incapable of exercising any decisional powers, proceeds from an unfortunate expansion or exaggeration of the first representation. As previously discussed, the decisional character of certain measures taken by institutions is self-evident. It suffices to mention again by way of example the final determinations which some institutions are habilitated to make on such issues as the applicable set of arbitration rules[845], the seat of an arbitration[846], its language[847], the extension of deadlines[848], the joinder of third parties[849], the consolidation of proceedings[850], the confirmation[851] and removal of arbitrators[852], or the quantum of the costs

845. Article 5.1 and 5.2 of the SIAC rules (2013); Article 42(2) of the Swiss rules (2012) (discretion to choose between for traditional or expedited rules). Article 1 of the ICDR rules (2009) and Article 1(3) of the ICDR rules (2014) (discretion to choose between international or domestic rules).
846. Article 18 ICC rules (2012); Article 39 WIPO rules (2002); Article 16 of the Swiss rules (2012); Article 14 JAMS rules (2011). See also Article 13 of the ICDR rules (2009) and Article 17(1) of the ICDR rules (2014) (but here the decision is subject to review by the tribunal). See also Article 16.1 of the LCIA rules (1998) and Article 16.2 of the LCIA rules (2014); Article 7 CIETAC rules (2012) and Article 7(2) of the CIETAC rules (2015) and Article 4 of the Milan Chamber rules (2010), which all provide for a default seat whilst granting the institution the power to select another one.
847. Article R29 of the CAS Code (2013). Article 17.2 of the LCIA rules (1998) and Article 17.1 of the LCIA rules (2014) confers on the institution the power to decide the "initial language". The term indicates that the decision is subject to review by the tribunal once appointed. See also Article 71 of the CIETAC rules (2012) and Article 81 of the CIETAC rules (2015), although the default language is Chinese (unless decided by CIETAC).
848. Article 2.5 of the SIAC rules (2013); Article R32 of the CAS Code (2013); Article 2.3 of the Swiss rules (2012); Article 4(g) WIPO rules (2002); Article 3.3 of the "*Internal Rules of the Arbitration Center of Mexico*", at Annex I of the CAMEX rules (2009).
849. Article 7 ICC rules (2012); Article 41 CAS Code (2013); Article 11 CEPANI rules (2013).
850. Article 10 ICC rules (2012); Article 13 CEPANI rules (2013); Article R39 CAS Code (2013).
851. Article 13 ICC rules (2012); Article 5(5) of the LCIA rules (1998) and Article 5(6) LCIA rules (2014); Article 9 HKIAC rules (2013); Article 6.3 SIAC rules (2013) and Article 5(1) Swiss rules (2012).
852. Articles 14-15 ICC rules (2012); Article 10.3 LCIA rules (1998) and Article 10.6 LCIA rules (2015); Articles 8-9 ICDR rules (2009) and Article 14 ICDR rules (2014); Articles 30-31 CIETAC rules (2012) and Article 32(6) of the CIETAC rules (2015); Articles 11-13 SIAC rules (2013);

of an arbitration[853]. All such determinations require the exercise of discretion, that is to say a choice between two or more options or solutions. In our view, whenever these determinations are, by operation of the applicable arbitration rules, binding on the parties[854] they may be said to constitute "decisions".

[B] Proposition 2: Ancillary Nature of the Role of the Institution

Stating that some measures rendered by arbitral institutions are capable of assuming a decisional character does not, of course, signify that arbitrators and institutions share the decision-making powers equally. In institutional arbitration, the principal decision-maker remains, by and large, the arbitral tribunal; with arbitral institutions assuming at best an ancillary role. It is important to note that while, as discussed in Chapter 3 above, the level of interventionism of an institution in the proceedings varies greatly from one institution to the next[855], a common feature observed across all institutions studied is that the entirety of the power to decide the merits of the dispute falls to the arbitral tribunals. At most, under the rules of some of the former Soviet institutions, objections to jurisdiction will fall primarily to the institution rather than the tribunal to decide (i.e., in a final, not prima facie, manner)[856]. This, however, remains atypical. Similarly, some institutional rules contemplate that interim measures may be granted by the institution itself, rather than by the tribunal[857]. In any event, however, deciding the merits of disputes falls squarely within the remit of arbitral tribunals.

[C] Proposition 3: Materiality of Institutional Decisions

It is a euphemism to say that assessing the impact of a particular decision on the outcome of a case is difficult. This is not least because, in the context of dispute resolution, the very notion of "outcome" is difficult to apprehend. The notion of outcome cannot for instance be confined to the question of "*who wins vs. who loses*" because, in arbitration as in litigation, victory is often a matter of perception and

---

Articles 9-11 Swiss rules (2012); Article 15 SCC rules (2010); Article R34 CAS Code (2013); Article 18 ICAC rules (2010); Articles 24-29 WIPO rules (2002); Article 19 Milan Chamber rules (2010); Article 14.4 ACICA rules (2011) and Article 18.4 of the ACICA rules (2016); and Article 17 CAMEX rules (2009).

853. As previously defined, the term *"costs of the arbitration"* refers to the fees and expenses payable to the arbitrators and the administrative charges of the institution. Article 37 ICC rules (2012); Article 28.1 LCIA rules (1998) and (2014); Article 32 SIAC rules (2013); Article 43.2 SCC rules (2010); Article R64.4 CAS code (2013); and Article 14 of ICAC rules (2010) and ICAC's Schedule of Arbitration Fees and Costs.
854. That is, when they are not open to acceptance or rejection.
855. And in fact for a single institution it sometimes varies from one phase of the proceedings to another, e.g., pre-appointment of the tribunal and post-appointment.
856. Article 6 CIETAC rules (2012) and (2015); Article 4 CMAC rules (2004) provides that "[t]*he arbitration Commission has the power to decide on the existence, validity or an arbitration agreement and the jurisdiction over an arbitration case*".
857. See section 13 of the rules of the Arbitration Court Attached to the Czech Chamber of Commerce; Article R37 of the CAS Code (2013) and Article 8 of the rules of arbitration of the Associazione Italiana per l'Arbitrato (AIA) (2012).

relativity. A respondent condemned to pay damages by an arbitral tribunal may hold the belief that it has won, if the damages provided for in the award represent a fraction of the damages which the respondent in question was expecting to have to pay. Yet, in the same scenario, the claimant could very well hold the same belief that it has prevailed in the arbitration as the award establishes the liability of the other side and condemns it to pay damages. In other words, the notion of outcome in litigation or arbitration is not a black or white notion. At best, it is possible to say that the notion of outcome should encompass *the extent* to which one party has prevailed on the merits –that is to say the extent to which the award displays a preference to the position advocated by one side or the other. This, in turn, suggests that any decision – institutional or otherwise – which influences the substance of a decision on the merits can be said to bear an impact on the "outcome of the case". Our argument is that, in this context, some decisions of institutions have the capacity to be "outcome-determinative".

This opinion is not an isolated one. For example, former Secretary General of the International Court of Arbitration of the ICC, Eric Schwartz recognizes that:

> [a]*lthough the functions of an arbitral institution are generally characterised as administrative, some of an institution's decisions may have considerable impact on a case, such as whether to agree to administer an arbitration where the existence of an arbitration clause is uncertain, or to replace an arbitrator in the case of a challenge*[858].

Amusingly, the evident materiality of certain institutional measures has not gone unnoticed by those authors (cited in Chapter 4 above) who nonetheless argue that institutional decisions are merely administrative/non-jurisdictional. The contradiction between the facts that a decision may prove crucial for the outcome of a case, and that it cannot participate to the adjudication of the dispute, forces these authors to adopt a quasi-schizophrenic attitude. One author for instance finds simultaneously that:

> "[...] *the ICC arbitration system* [...] *should probably be considered as the one vesting the arbitral institution with more controlling powers in the arbitral process* and its outcome *than any other and, from that standpoint, as the one providing the institution with the most far-reaching decisional powers binding on the parties and the arbitral panel regarding the conduct and* outcome *of the arbitration proceedings governed by its rules*" (emphasis added); and

858. Schwartz, "The Role of the Arbitral Institution in the New Millennium" 325.
Other authors who recognize, in general terms, the importance of the decisions made by an institution include Jason Fry (another Secretary General of the ICC): *"At these* [monthly plenary] *meetings, the* [ICC] *Court makes decisions of particular importance, for which a special report may be prepared by one of its members"*. Fry, "ICC International Court of Arbitration" 2. See also Professor Grigera-Naon (a third former Secretary General of the ICC): *"It is in the nature of institutional arbitration that institutional arbitration rules provide the respective institution with a number of important powers they are required or may be called to exercise and on the basis of which certain decisions may be imposed both on the parties to the arbitration and on the arbitral tribunal"*. Grigera Naon, "The Powers of the ICC International Court of Arbitration vis-a-vis Parties and Arbitrators" 55. See also, Kee, "The Evolving Role of an Appointing Authority" 424.

"[...] *such powers should be viewed from the uniform perspective of the case management function of arbitral institutions* [...][859].

Another author having found, in rather emphatic terms, that institutional decisions "*radically*" and "*definitely*" lack jurisdictional character[860], concludes her article by underlining how significant such institutional decisions in fact are - calling on institutions' "*moral responsibility*" to proceed with caution when performing their duties[861].

The French courts also struggled[862] with the thought that no due process requirements could be found to apply to arbitral institutions. In one of the first instance decisions rendered in the *Guinea v. CAP* dispute[863] (discussed in Chapter 4 above) the French courts found that the contractual relationship[864] between the institution and the parties contained a number of obligations among which an obligation for the institution to put in place conditions which guarantee to the parties equal treatment, and which permits a normal and reasonable procedure respectful of the "*essential principles of neutrality and objectivity applicable to all judicial proceedings*" (Translation by the author)[865]. The courts went on the state that, if no due process obligation could bind the institutions themselves (as their functions are merely administrative), institutions nonetheless had a legal obligation to put in place conditions capable of guaranteeing an "*equitable trial*". For the French court it is in the institutions' "*vocation*" to ensure that due process is respected[866]. What this so-called "*vocation*" means as a matter of law is

859. Grigera Naon, "The Powers of the ICC International Court of Arbitration vis-a-vis Parties and Arbitrators" 55-56.
860. Hautot, "Les Pouvoirs de la Cour d'Arbitrage de la C.C.I. de Décider ou Non d'Organiser l'Arbitrage" 26.
861. Hautot, "Les Pouvoirs de la Cour d'Arbitrage de la C.C.I. de Décider ou Non d'Organiser l'Arbitrage" 30.
862. At least in some of their early decisions.
863. "République de Guinée v Chambre Arbitrale de Paris et autres, Tribunal de Grande Instance de Paris, 28 January 1987 (Revue de l'Arbitrage, 1987, p. 371)". By way of reminder the background of the case is as follows: A dispute arose out of a series of contracts entered into by the Republic of Guinea and four different parties, for the construction of 3,000 homes in the sub-Saharan State. Two of these contracts contained clauses which were found to refer to arbitration under the auspices of the Chambre Arbitrale de Paris (CAP), two cases were started before that institution. Incidents arose in the proceedings which led Guinea to initiate legal proceedings against the CAP with a view to obtaining *inter alia* the "revocation" of the contract between the parties and the institution for the organization of the arbitration on the grounds of breaches by the CAP of its contractual obligations.
864. That is, the so-called contract of services for the organization of proceedings.
865. In the original language: "[l'obligation de] *mettre en œuvre les instances arbitrales dans des conditions qui assurent à chacun une égalité de traitement, au cours d'une procédure conduite de façon normale et raisonnable, respectant les principes essentiels de la neutralité et l'objectivité, propres à toute instance juridictionnelle*". "République de Guinée v Chambre Arbitrale de Paris et autres, Tribunal de Grande Instance de Paris, 28 January 1987 (Revue de l'Arbitrage, 1987, p. 371)".
866. In the original language: "*Que si la finalité première de celles-ci reste la solution qui doit être donnée, par les seuls juges-arbitres, du différend substantiel volontairement déduit devant eux,* il entre dans la vocation de ce tiers *librement choisi par les parties d'organiser et de maintenir la police de l'instance arbitrale ainsi que* de prendre, *dans le respect de son Règlement,* les initiatives qui s'imposent pour donner à chacune des parties les garanties essentielles propres à assurer "un procès équitable" *au sens du droit interne et des articles 6 de la Convention de*

not very clear, and it is fair to say that the above citation illustrates the evident unease of the French judge in taking to its logical conclusion the idea that institutional decisions are merely administrative.

The *Pirelli* case offers a more recent illustration of the French Courts' ambivalence. As previously explained, in this case, the Court of Appeal of Paris annulled an arbitral award in which a respondent's counterclaim had been treated by the ICC as withdrawn in application of the then Article 30(2) of the 1998 ICC rules[867]. The rationale was that the respondent was in bankruptcy proceedings at the time of the ICC's decision, and therefore the possibility that it may at a later stage introduce a request for arbitration in respect of its counterclaims was purely "*theoretical*"[868]. The Court of Appeal's decision was annulled by the Cour de Cassation[869], but the annulment decision nonetheless maintained that the refusal by a tribunal to look at a counterclaim (for lack of payment of the deposit or otherwise) could constitute a breach of due process which would justify refusing the enforcement an award if the counterclaims are in fact "*indissociable from the main claims*"[870].

This "legal schizophrenia" was picked on by the late Professor Lalive[871] who noted the contradiction in institutions claiming simultaneously a quasi-judicial mission so as to justify their immunity, and a purely administrative mission so as to avoid being subject to due process. Drawing a parallel with a fable by Jean de la Fontaine[872], Professor Lalive compared arbitral institutions to the little bat which, in order to avoid being devoured by a weasel which had mistaken it for a mouse, argues that it is not a mouse but a bird ("*Just see the wings with which I fly!*"). But moments later, when the same little bat is caught by a second weasel which this time mistakes it for a tasty bird, the little bat, pointing to her fur and her absence of feathers, claims that it is in fact a mouse![873].

In fact a review of the activities of institutions such as the one conducted in Chapter 3, establishes quite clearly the capacity of institutions to impact the proceedings they administer. When an institutional decision disposes "finally" of a discrete aspect of the dispute, the impact of that decision is obvious. This is the case of decisions that may be rendered by certain institutions on the quantum of the costs of an

sauvegarde des droits de l'homme et 14 du Pacte de New York relatif aux droits civils et politiques" (Emphasis added). "République de Guinée v Chambre Arbitrale de Paris et autres, Tribunal de Grande Instance de Paris, 28 January 1987 (Revue de l'Arbitrage, 1987, p. 371)".

867. "Société Licensing Projects SL v Société Pirelli, Cour d'Appel de Paris, 17 November 2011".
868. See Kleiman and Pauly, "Award Annulled Due to Withdrawn Counterclaims Introduced by Insolvent Defendant".
869. "Société Licensing Projects SL v Société Pirelli, Cour de Cassation, 28 mars 2013".
870. That is to say, if they are set off claims rather than independent counterclaims. In this particular case, the Cour de Cassation found that the Court of Appeal of Paris had failed to establish that the counterclaims were indissociable from the main claims.
871. In his commentary of the *Cubic Defense Systems* case. Lalive, "Case commentary: Cour d'Appel de Paris 15 September 1988, Société Cubic Defense Systems v. CCI" 118.
872. Jean De la Fontaine, "The Bat and the Two Weasels" in *Recueil 1, Livre 2, Fable 5*, 1668.
873. *"I am a bird; And, if you doubt my word, Just see the wings with which I fly* [...] *Your eyesight strange conclusions gathers. What makes a bird, I pray? Its feathers"*.

arbitration for example[874]. Likewise, this is so in the (admittedly rare) case where an institution is habilitated to make a final decision on jurisdiction[875]. In both instances, the decision affects directly the outcome of a discrete aspect of the proceedings (albeit not the merits).

Sometimes, the materiality of an institutional decision comes from the fact, not that it disposes of a discrete issue directly, but that it is determinative of part of the legal framework applicable to the arbitration. This can be the case of a decision on the seat of the arbitration (whenever the seat is taken by the arbitral tribunal to be determinative of the *lex arbitri)*[876]. This is also the case of a decision on the set of arbitration rules applicable (i.e., expedited rules, small claims rules, international rules, etc.[877]). The choice of seat and of arbitration rules will impact the procedure of the arbitration, and therefore potentially its outcome.

Other institutional decisions are material because they have an impact on the make-up of the arbitral tribunal. Decisions like nominations of arbitrators, confirmation (or refusal of confirmation) of arbitrators, and decisions on challenges have an immediate or direct impact on the make-up of the panel. But, as argued in Chapter 3, other decisions like the choice of language or of the number of arbitrators[878] may also have an impact (indirect this time) on the make-up of the arbitral tribunal. In turn, the make-up of the tribunal influences how the tribunal will apprehend procedural and substantive decisions, and therefore on the manner in which the parties' will need to present their case[879]. As previously discussed, for many commentators the choice of arbitrators is one of the most important decisions made by a party in an arbitration[880].

874. In the sense, the fees of the tribunal and the institution. Article 37 ICC rules (2012); Article 28.1 LCIA rules (1998) and (2014); Article 32 SIAC rules (2013); Article 43.2 SCC rules (2010); Article R64.4 CAS code (2013); and Article 14 of ICAC rules (2010) and ICAC's Schedule of Arbitration Fees and Costs.

875. See above discussions of CIETAC and CMAC.

876. As indicated in Chapter 3, whenever the seat of the arbitration is taken by the arbitral tribunal to be determinative of the *lex arbitri*, a decision on the seat will have a direct impact, throughout the arbitration, on the manner in which the tribunal approaches decisions on procedure. See Fellas, "AAA/ICDR International Arbitration Rules" 482. See also in the same sense Sabater, "When Arbitration Begins Without a Seat" 443 and 458. See also, Blackaby, Partasides, Hunter, and Redfern, *Redfern and Hunter on International Arbitration* 317.

877. As indicated in Chapter 3, for Anne Veronique Schlaepfer a decision of the Swiss institution as to the application of the expedited rules "[...] *will have a significant impact on the organisation of the arbitration proceedings*". Schlaepfer, "The Role of the Institution at the Commencement of the Proceedings" 60.

878. See discussion in Chapter 3 about the different dynamics at play in the nomination process when there are one or three arbitrators, and therefore when nominations are made by the parties or the institution. Arguably, decisions on consolidation may indirectly have an impact on the make-up of the tribunal too. See discussions in Chapter 3 above in relation to the Dutco jurisprudence.

879. Arguing that that the make-up of an arbitral tribunal has the potential of affecting the outcome of the case: Gaillard and Pinsolle, "Advocacy in International Commercial Arbitration: France" 143; Beechey, "Advocacy in International Commercial Arbitration: England" 252; Seppälä, "Recommended Strategy For Getting The Right International Arbitral Tribunal" 1-2.

880. For Juliet Blanch, for instance, "[t]*he choice of arbitrator is one of the most important decisions a party can make in the course of the arbitration*". Blanch, "Appointment and Confirmation of Arbitrators" 65. In the same sense see, Bockstiegel, "Commercial and Investment Arbitration:

The "outcome" of arbitral proceedings should also be seen to include the enforceability of awards[881]. Surprisingly, the capacity of institutional decisions to influence the enforceability of awards has seldom attracted the attention of commentators[882]. This is curious considering that many of the grounds for refusing enforcement of an award under the New York Convention[883] could be raised in relation to actions taken by arbitral institutions. By way of example, Article V(1)(b) of the Convention provides that the recognition and enforcement of an award may be refused if the "*party against whom the award is invoked was not given proper notice of the appointment of the arbitrator or of the arbitration proceedings*"[884]. Under the rules of certain institutions, notice of the filing of a case[885], or of the constitution of the tribunal[886], are for the institution to provide, and one can imagine that an award could be refused enforcement on the basis of a failure by an institution to provide adequate notice.

Likewise, under Article V(1)(b) of the Convention, recognition and enforcement may be refused if the party against whom the award is invoked was "*unable to present his case*"[887]. Leaving aside the question of whether an award could be refused enforcement on the basis that an institution has failed to allow a party to present its case to the institution itself (i.e., in respect of some matter to be decided by the institution such as challenges, joinder, consolidation, etc.)[888], some institutional measures may effectively prevent a party from presenting its case to the arbitral

How Different are they Today?"; Waincymer, *Procedure and Evidence in International Arbitration* 275; Bishop, "Toward a Harmonized Approach to Advocacy in International Arbitration" 457-458.

881. Because there is little point in securing a favourable award, if the award is then incapable of being enforced.
882. For example, it is interesting to note that none of the commentaries to the *Dutco* decision (discussed below) noted the fact that it was an institutional measure (rather than one by a tribunal) which had jeopardized the award in that case.
883. "Convention on the Recognition and Enforcement of Foreign Arbitral Awards, ('New York Convention')".
884. The UCITRAL Model Law contains at Article 34 a similar provision for the setting aside of award.
885. Article 4(5) ICC rules (2012); Article 3(6) Swiss rules (2012); Article 7 VIAC rules (2013); Article 7(1) NAI rules (2010); Article 9 Milan rules (2010); Article 8 CAMEX rules (2009); and Article 13.2 CIETAC rules (2012) and 2015; In case of Summary procedure, the same obligation exists under Article 57 CIETAC rules (2015).
886. Notification of the constitution of the tribunal will often fall to the institution when the institution is required to confirm the appointment of arbitrators: Article 13 ICC rules (2012); Article 5(5) of the LCIA rules (1998) and Article 5.6 read with 5.9 LCIA rules (2014); Article 9 HKIAC rules (2013); Article 6.3 SIAC rules (2013) and Article 5(1) Swiss rules (2012).
887. The UNCITRAL Model Law contains at Article 34 a similar provision for the setting aside of award.
888. It is interesting to note that the New York Convention does not limit this requirement to presenting one's case to the tribunal. As we have seen in Chapter 3, the French courts have been reluctant to look into whether a party should be entitled to *"present its case"* to the institution itself in respect of matters that are for the institution to decide. Other courts have been less reluctant to do so. In the Netherlands, enforcement of an award was refused under the New York Convention because of an error by the ICAC presidium. See below the discussion of the "Goldtron Limited v. Media Most B.V., Rechtbank of Amterdam, 27 August 2002 (Yearbook Commercial Arbitration, 2003, at p. 814)". See also commentary of Steindl, "The Development of Due Process under the New York Convention" 272.

tribunal. This may be the case when an institution omits to transfer certain communications to a tribunal, or to a party, when the institution is "channelling communications".

But under Article V(1)(d) of the Convention, recognition and enforcement of an award may also be refused if the "*composition of the arbitral authority or the arbitral procedure was not in accordance with the agreement of the parties, or, failing such agreement, was not in accordance with the law of the country where the arbitration took place*"[889]. Here again, examples of scenarii where an institutional measure could negatively affect the enforceability of an award are not hard to find. If an institution appoints a tribunal in a manner that is inconsistent with the parties' agreement (including presumably the applicable arbitration rules) it may lead to a refusal to enforce the award. This happened, for example, in the *Encyclopaedia Universalis v. Encyclopaedia Britannica* case, where the US Court of Appeals for the Second Circuit confirmed the decision of the district court denying the application to confirm an award where the Chairman of the Tribunal had been selected in a manner inconsistent with the relevant arbitration clause[890]. Likewise, procedural decisions made by an institution that are inconsistent with the parties' agreement (including the agreed institutional rules) may render an award unenforceable. In the *Goldtron v. Media Most* case[891] the District Court of Amsterdam refused enforcement of an ICAC award on the ground *inter alia* that the institution had breached its own rules by finding that a challenge to an arbitrator was time-barred[892].

889. The UCITRAL Model Law contains at Article 34 a similar provision for the setting aside of award.

890. "Encyclopaedia Universalis S.A. v. Encyclopaedia Britannica Inc., United States Court of Appeals, Second Circuit, 31 March 2005 (403 F.3d 85)" In this case a party was seeking "*confirmation*" of a foreign award before the US courts. The other side was resisting enforcement on the ground that the composition of the tribunal did not conform to the parties' arbitration agreement. Under the relevant arbitration agreement it fell to the co-arbitrators to seek to agree on a Chairman; the default appointing authority in case of disagreement being the Luxembourg courts. The lack of conformity concerned the fact that the Chairman of the tribunal had been appointed by the default appointing authority in the absence of a disagreement between the co-arbitrators (as the two arbitrators had no in fact discussed the appointment at all). The US Court of Appeals for the Second Circuit confirmed the decision of the district court denying the application to confirm the award.

891. "Goldtron Limited v. Media Most B.V., Rechtbank of Amterdam, 27 August 2002 (Yearbook Commercial Arbitration, 2003, at p. 814)".

892. The background of this case is the following: The dispute arises out of a share purchase agreement under which Goldtron, a Singaporean company, sold shares in a Russian entity to Media Most (a company incorporated in the Netherlands). The contract price was to be paid in three instalments. After the first instalment was paid, Media Most started arbitration in order to have the contract varied, arguing that as a result of some alleged changed circumstances, the sum paid by Media Most under the first instalment was a reasonable contract price. The arbitration clause provided for arbitration at ICAC. A sole arbitrator, Mr Lev Nikolaevic Orlov, was appointed. In the course of the proceedings, Mr Orlov made an ex parte phone call to Media Most, wrongly assuming that he was talking to the other side (Goldtron). During this call, thinking that he was addressing Goldtron, Mr Orlov urged Media Most to file a counterclaim! A month later Goldtron did file a counterclaim. While the time limit under the rules of ICAC for filing such a counterclaim had passed, the arbitrator nonetheless accepted the counterclaim. Shortly thereafter Media Most challenged Mr Orlov. The ICAC Presidium rejected the challenge a few months later on the "formal ground" that the challenge was time barred under the ICAC rules on the basis that the challenge had not been raised within fifteen days of the phone call.

A violation by the institution of its own institutional rules may also lead to the award being set aside (as opposed to "refused enforcement"). Under section 68(2) of the English Arbitration Act, for example, an arbitral award may be set aside for serious irregularity arising out of a decision, not only of the arbitrators, but also of the institution[893].

Arguments may also be made under Article V(2) of the Convention that, because of some institutional measure taken in the course of the proceedings, the enforcement of an award would violate the public policy of the country where enforcement is sought. For example in the Dutco jurisprudence[894], it was a decision by the ICC Court to impose on the two respondents to make a joint nomination while the claimant was allowed to nominate "its" own arbitrator, which led to the annulment of the award. In this decision, the Cour de Cassation held that "*equality of the parties in the appointment of arbitrators* [was] *a matter of* public policy *which* [could] *be waived only after the disputes have arisen*" (emphasis added)[895]. The Dutco decision serves as a powerful illustration of the potential materiality of certain institutional interventions because of the drastic consequence that the institution's intervention in that instance ultimately bore in the proceedings.

By way of conclusion on this proposition no. 3, some institutional decisions have the capacity of being outcome-determinative. Overall, therefore, it is incorrect to state that the role of institutions remains extraneous to the adjudicative mission. Arbitral

---

Goldtron sought enforcement of the award in the Dutch courts. The Court of First Instance of Amsterdam found that the award could not be enforced because the arbitration's procedure was not in accordance with the parties' agreement on the basis that the ICAC Presidium had misapplied its own rules. According to the Dutch court, the fifteen-day time limit only started to run from the moment Media Most became certain that the arbitrator had entered into an ex parte communication with the other side. This is interesting because in this case the Dutch courts refused enforcement on the basis of an institutional decision -the decision not hear a challenge to an arbitrator. Incidentally, the court relied on the fact that the ICAC had failed to motivate its decision as required by the ICAC rules; and that the ICAC breached due process (right to present one's case) by not examining the substantive grounds of a challenge to an arbitrator which one party believed lacked impartiality.

893. As explained by Toby Landau: "[...] *in drawing up a closed list of (narrow) grounds upon which an award may be set aside or remitted,* [...] *the DAC included the following grounds, again expressly recognising the importance of arbitral institutions:* [Section] *68(2) Serious irregularity means an irregularity of one or more of the following kinds which the court considers has caused or will cause substantial injustice to the applicant: ... (e) any arbitral or other institution or person vested by the parties with powers in relation to the proceedings or the award exceeding its powers; ... (i) any irregularity in the conduct of the proceedings or in the award which is admitted by the tribunal or by any arbitral or other institution or person vested by the parties with powers in relation to the proceedings or the award.*" Landau, "The Effect of the New English Arbitration Act on Institutional Arbitration" 127.

894. The Dutco decision concerned annulment rather than enforcement proceedings.

895. Dr Stefan Kröll, "Siemens – Dutco Revisited? Balancing Party Autonomy and Equality of the Parties in the Appointment Process in Multiparty Cases | Kluwer Arbitration Blog", 15 October 2010. By way of reminder, in "Sociétés BKMI et Siemens v Société Dutco", Cour de Cassation 1992, the French *Cour de Cassation* annulled an ICC award where the two respondents had been refused the opportunity to make separate nominations (they had ultimately made a joint nomination but under protest) while the claimant was allowed to nominate "its" own arbitrator. The French Court held that the principle of equality of the parties in regards to party nominations was of public policy and that it could only be waived after the proceedings had started.

institutions are entities which participate in the overall adjudication of the arbitrations conducted under their auspices, albeit in an ancillary capacity.

[D] Proposition 4: The Rejection of Dichotomic Approaches

The level of materiality of a given decision[896] is not primarily dependent on the identity of the decision-maker (i.e., to say on whether the decision is made by an arbitral tribunal or an institution). To take just one example, one might argue that a decision rendered by an arbitral tribunal to grant a short extension of time for a party to comply with a document production request will bear less influence on the outcome of the proceedings than a decision by an institution on, say, the seat of the arbitration, its language, the constitution of the tribunal, the joinder of third parties or the decision to treat a claim as withdrawn for failure pay an advance on costs. If that is the case, then the binary/dichotomic approach of the first representation which simultaneously (1) negates any materiality to institutional decisions and (2) assume a constant materiality to arbitrators' decisions, must be rejected.

But beyond the fact that decisions of both institutions and tribunals may impact the outcome of a case, the "*administrative v. jurisdictional*" dichotomy must be rejected because it is not based on anything tangible. It is difficult to see any difference in the "fabric" of the decisions made by institutions and those made by arbitral tribunals which would justify treating them differently. This is particularly striking when considering that the same decisions can be taken by an arbitrator or by an institution depending on whether one finds itself in an ad hoc or an institutional context. As already indicated, a decision on language, seat, consolidation, joinder, etc. entrusted to an institution in institutional arbitration would otherwise fall to the arbitral tribunal or the domestic courts to decide in an ad hoc context[897].

§5.03 CONSEQUENCES OF THE REPRESENTATION

[A] Proposition 5: Desirability of the Application of Due Process by Institutions When They Participate in the Adjudicative Mission

There is a danger in subjecting all institutional decisions to overly stringent due process requirements. As discussed above in the context of the rationale underlying the first doctrinal representation of the role of institutions, one concern is that if every decision rendered by an arbitral institution had to be preceded by an exchange of submissions between the parties, or had to be accompanied by detailed reasons, this would slow the institutional process (which in the context of the current complaints about delay and costs in arbitration appears inconceivable). Another concern is that this would expose the process to the risk of strategic manoeuvres by some parties who might attempt to

896. That is, its capacity to impact the outcome of a case.
897. See Slate, expressing the view that under certain sets of rules, the institution is entrusted with functions that are otherwise reserved to arbitrators. Slate, "International Arbitration: Do Institutions Make a Difference?" 47.

stall the arbitral process[898]. This might in turn, require institutions to alter the manner in which they function by operating in a more formal and cumbersome manner[899]. Ultimately, overly stringent due process requirements imposed systematically could negatively affect the integrity and efficiency of the arbitral system in its institutional form[900].

This being said, if institutions occasionally participate in the adjudication of the disputes they administer, then it would appear that they should be expected to abide by some due process standards. In our view, this point can hardly be contested. If as demonstrated in this book, there is nothing in the fabric of decisions rendered by institutions that differentiate them from those of arbitrators, and if at the same time some institutional decisions are occasionally outcome-determinative, then due process should be of concern to arbitral institutions. This position is not isolated. For Jan Paulsson, for instance: "[...] *there is no question but that institutions should be held to fundamental standards of fair procedure* [...]"[901].

The contrary proposition would be at odds with the expectations of the users of the system. According to Paulsson: "*When parties entrust their dispute to an institution, the presumption should be that it respects its own rules as well as fundamental principles of due process*"[902]. In fact, according to Nassib Ziade (then Deputy Secretary General of ICSID), the legitimacy of institutions rests on the very fact that they are seen by the users as maintaining procedural fairness:

> *Institutions are entrusted with such important powers because they, and the solutions they offer, are perceived to be legitimate. And what does "legitimacy" mean here? It means to be procedurally fair and trustworthy, and increasingly this will require institutional transparency*[903].

The contrary proposition would also be at odds with the actual practice of institutions, which are keen to respect due process[904]. As Jan Paulsson explains: "[...]

898. Paulsson, "Vicarious Hypochondria and Institutional Arbitration" 248.
899. Paulsson, "Vicarious Hypochondria and Institutional Arbitration" 248.
900. Fouchard, "Les Institutions Permanentes d'Arbitrage Devant le Juge Etatique (A Propos d'une Jurisprudence Récente)" 244. In the same sense see also Aguilar Alvarez, "The Challenge of Arbitrators" 16.
901. Paulsson, "Vicarious Hypochondria and Institutional Arbitration" 249.
902. Paulsson, "Vicarious Hypochondria and Institutional Arbitration" 250. This is also the position taken by the Dutch courts in the *Goldtron v. Media Most* case discussed previously. "Goldtron Limited v. Media Most B.V., Rechtbank of Amterdam, 27 August 2002 (Yearbook Commercial Arbitration, 2003, at p. 814)" In that case, the Amsterdam Court of First Instance refused enforcement, under the New York Convention, of an ICAC award on the ground, *inter alia*, that the decision of the ICAC Presidium that a challenge to an arbitrator was time-barred breached due process (in the sense one's right to present its case). Other grounds included also that the procedure was not accordance with the parties' agreement (due to ICAC's misapplication of its arbitration rules).
903. Nassib G. Ziadé, "Reflections on the Role of Institutional Arbitration Between the Present and the Future" (2009) 25 Arbitration International, Kluwer Law International 427, 429.
904. See discussions further below on this point. For present purposes, it is interesting to note that the website of the AAA emphasizes how the institution strives to offer its services having regard to fairness and impartiality: "*Ultimately, the AAA aims to move cases through arbitration or mediation in a fair and impartial manner until completion*". "Website of AAA/ICDR, http://www.adr.org/". In a similar vein, the institution has adopted statements of principles

reputable institutions do not in fact claim the right to disregard the imperatives of natural justice or l'ordre public"[905].

It should be noted however that the above proposition does not concern the question of whether, as a matter of law, due process norms apply to the activities of institutions. The present proposition merely raises – *de lege ferenda* – the question of the "opportunity" or "desirability" of the application of due process standards. For present purposes therefore only a few elementary points will be made: First, from a substantive point of view, the notion of due process is a multifaceted one. The substantive norms which constitute the minimum standards of procedural safeguards that must be respected in the course of arbitration proceedings varies from one jurisdiction to another. Whilst the New York Convention has a certain harmonizing effect (by setting out common grounds for resisting enforcement), the terms of the Convention remain vague and leave much room for interpretation[906].

Second, one may wonder what the "sources" of these due process norms are. The answer to this question will greatly depend on one's take on the theory of arbitration. For some, the source of these due process norms could derive from the parties' arbitration agreement, or from the so-called contract that the parties and the institution are sometimes said to enter into for the institution to provide its services. Likewise, due process requirements could arguably arise out of the legal system within which the arbitration agreement or the so-called services contract are legally anchored (in this perspective both domestic statutes and international human rights instruments such as the European Convention on Human Rights may bear some relevance). On the other hand, one may argue that due process norms apply to arbitral institutions because they constitute principles of transnational arbitration law. Finally, another possibility is for the due process norms to be seen to arise, *a posteriori*, from the requirements of any legal order in which an attempt will be made to enforce the award. Prima facie, the last two theories (i.e., the transnational theory and the multi-local one) have our preference because they seem to be more in line with the reality of arbitration, and in particular the fact that, in practice, the impact of a violation of due process norms by an arbitral institution will find expression at the enforcement stage. Indeed, as we have seen domestic courts are often reluctant to review institutional decisions in the course of

applicable to its own staff, thereby formalizing the applicability of some of these due process norms. "*To further ensure the AAA's integrity, however, the Association also developed Standards of Ethics and Business Conduct for its staff, as well as a general Statement of Ethical Principles to expand on its core values as an organisation*". "Website of AAA/ICDR, http://www.adr.org/". For some domestic arbitration disputes (e.g., consumer debt collection disputes) the institution has a more formal "*Due Process protocol*". This protocol embodies principles applicable not just to the institution but also to the parties to consumer debt collection disputes. The protocol contains as a "*key provision*", being "*the necessity of independent administration*" (see the document entitled Consumer Debt Collection Due Process Protocol – Statement Of Principles, available on AAA's website). "Website of AAA/ICDR, http://www.adr.org/".

905. Paulsson, "Vicarious Hypochondria and Institutional Arbitration" 250.

906. In this sense, see Kurkela and Turunen, *Due Process in International Commercial Arbitration* 11-13. In the context of set aside proceedings (as opposed to enforcement), the degree of harmonization appears even more limited.

proceedings (even when a breach of due process is alleged), and prefer to limit such review to the enforcement stage.

As interesting as this may be, the question of the legal applicability of due process norms to the activities of institutions is of limited relevance for present purposes. What matters is that, because there is a risk on non-enforcement of awards should an institution fail to take into consideration due process requirements, arbitral institutions should be concerned to ensure that due process is respected. In other words, if one finds that institutions do participate to the overall adjudication of disputes, then there should be a strong incentive for them to comply with some basic notion of due process. On this point it is interesting to note that some institutional rules provide that the institution shall take steps to ensure that awards rendered under its auspices are enforceable[907].

[B] Proposition 6: Identification of the Aspects of Due Process That Are Relevant to the Activities of Arbitral Institutions

In our view, the aspects of "*due process*"[908], or fair procedure, which may be relevant to the activities of institutions include[909]: (1) guaranteeing the independence and impartiality of the institution from the parties; (2) treating the parties equally; (3) giving the parties same opportunity to present their case ("adversarial process"); (4) providing reasons for institutional decisions; and (5) providing an opportunity to appeal or otherwise seek judicial review of institutional decisions.

[1] Impartiality and Independence

The two requirements of independence and impartiality aim at protecting parties against decision-makers being "*influenced by factors other than those related to the merits of the case*"[910]. In the context of arbitration, the requirement of "*impartiality*" may be understood as the absence of bias towards one of the parties. As explained

907. See for example, Article 32.2 LCIA rules (1998) and (2014); Article 41 ICC rules (2012); Article 37.2 SIAC rules (2013); Article 47 of the SCC rules (2010); Article 44 CAMEX rules (2009); Article 43 DIAC rules (2007).

908. As previously indicated, in the present context due process is taken in a broad sense to mean an "*international minimum standard of procedural safeguards*". Kurkela and Turunen, *Due Process in International Commercial Arbitration* 3-4. Some authors restrict the notion to the opportunity of a party to present its case. See for example Steindl, "The Development of Due Process under the New York Convention"; Bernard Hanotiau and Olivier Caprasse, "Arbitrability, Due Process, and Public Policy Under Article V of the New York Convention: Belgian and French Perspectives" (2008) 25 Journal of International Arbitration 721-741. As explained below, we include in the notion different aspects which relate to the overall idea of the fair and equitable trial.

909. It should be noted that these requirements are no different from the ones that apply to tribunals. On the basis, as we have found above, that there is no tangible difference in the fabric of the decisions rendered by institutions and by arbitral tribunals, the aspects of due process which present some relevance for arbitrators will also be likely to present some relevance to institutions.

910. Daele, *Challenge and Disqualification of Arbitrators in International Arbitration* 367.

above[911], "*independence*" may be defined as the lack of close relationship between the decision-maker and the parties or their counsel[912]. Because institutions play an ancillary adjudicative role, imperatives of independence and impartiality are relevant to their activities. In the words of some Swiss authors:

> *It is accepted practice that potential arbitrators are asked to disclose any possible matter which could cause a conflict of interest and to confirm their availability.* [...] *What about the persons administering the cases on behalf of arbitral institutions? They may be asked to decide on the challenge of one or more arbitrators and appoint new arbitrators. How is it assured that these persons deciding on crucial aspects of an arbitral procedure are independent and follow the same standards of good governance that are required form the arbitral tribunals for the conduct of the arbitration proceedings?*[913]

Naturally, to the extent that institutions' adjudicative functions are more limited than that of arbitrators, the need to apply requirements of independence and impartiality is less pressing for institutions than for arbitrators. In practice, however, problems have been known to exist. An illustration may be found in the "scandal" of the NAF[914] consumer arbitration discussed previously, where NAF was said to have systematically favoured one category of users (companies) over another one (consumers)[915]. Of course, the risk is much lower when the institution conducts its activities on

911. In the context of the critical analysis of the foundations of Antoine Kassis' theory.
912. For Daele: an arbitrator lacking independence is "[...] *one who has no close relationship with a party in the arbitration or its counsel, be it of a financial, professional or personal nature*". Daele, *Challenge and Disqualification of Arbitrators in International Arbitration* 279-280. See also Park, "Rectitude in International Arbitration" 477.
913. Habegger, Hochstrasser, and Nater-Bass, *Arbitral Institutions Under Scrutiny* v. Similarly, expressing the view that institutions need to be independent in their scrutiny of draft awards, Eric Loquin states: *"This being said, in the exercise of their scrutiny powers, arbitral institutions has to guarantee to the parties an impartial examination of the draft award.* [...] *In particular, the organ of the institution in charge of examining the substance of the award must in its composition be independent from the parties. Any member of the organ who fails to meet such a requirement should abstain from participating"*. (Translation by the author). In the original language: "*En revanche, dans l'exercice de son pouvoir de surveillance de la sentence, l'institution d'arbitrage doit garantir aux parties un examen impartial de celle-ci.* [...] *En particulier, l'organe de l'institution d'arbitrage qui procède au contrôle du contenu de la sentence doit dans sa composition être en situation d'indépendance à l'égard des parties. Tout membre de l'organe qui ne répondrait pas à cette exigence doit s'abstenir de siéger*". Loquin, "La Sentence Arbitrale: L'Examen du Projet de Sentence par l'Institution et la Sentence au Deuxième Degré – Réflexions sur la Nature et la Validité de l'Intervention de l'Institution Arbitrale sur la Sentence" 454.
914. As previously indicated, the NAF is a for-profit arbitration institution established in 1986 which specialized in US domestic arbitrations and in particular consumer arbitration. When it ceased to administer consumer disputes, in 2009, NAF was claiming to be largest administrator of consumer disputes in the US. NAF, "Press Release: National Arbitration Forum to Cease Administering All Consumer Arbitrations in Response to Mounting Legal and Legislative Challenges, available at: http://www.adrforum.com/newsroom.aspx?&itemID=1528&news=3" (19 July 2009).
915. A number of law suits have been filed against the NAF including one in 2008, by the City of San Francisco on behalf of its citizens, and one in 2009 by the Minnesota Attorney General, in which the NAF was accused of unfairly favouring credit card companies in disputes with their customers. This led the NAF in 2009 to stop accepting cases relating to consumer debt collection claims.

a not-for-profit basis[916] but issues of independence and impartiality may also arise in connection with an institution's relationship, organic[917] or financial[918], with the government of the country where it is based.

In this context, it is not surprising that some arbitration rules address this issue of the independence and impartiality of the institution[919]. For instance, the members of the ICAS (CAS' International Council for Arbitration for Sport), when appointed, are required to sign a written undertaking to exercise their functions on a personal basis with total objectivity and independence[920]. Similarly, Article 3 of the Statutes of the Court of Arbitration of Madrid provides that the Court will act in full independence from the other organs of the chamber in the administration of proceedings[921].

Ultimately, institutions should, in my view, put in place internal processes apt to dispel perceptions of partiality or lack of independence. At the very least, institutions might wish to ensure that any members of their deciding organs who may have an interest in a case do not participate in decisions concerning that case. This may mean, for example, expressly requiring from members of the deciding organ that they routinely disclose to the other members of the deciding organ any potential conflict. A rare example of institution that has adopted specific rules on the matter is the Swiss Institution, which Court's internal rules provide that in case of conflict the member of the court concerned should (1) notify the Secretariat, (2) abstain from participating in decisions regarding the case in question, (3) be physically absent from meetings of the Court where the case is discussed, and (4) receive no documents concerning the case[922]. At present, however, my research shows that the approach of the Swiss Institution does not reflect a prevalent practice. In our view, a self-regulated approach, and one that is limited to internal disclosure[923], should suffice in most instances.

916. As previously indicated, the majority of institutions involved in the administration of international arbitration proceedings operate on a not-for-profit basis. This is the case, to mention only a few, of ICC, LCIA, ICDR, the Swiss Chamber's Arbitration Institution, the SCC, SIAC, HKIAC, CIETAC, CAS, CRCICA, DIS, KCAB, Milan Chamber of Arbitration, NAI, VIAC and WIPO (Information based on these institutions' responses to the questionnaires sent out by the author). One notable exception is JAMS International and the NAF, which are for-profit companies.

917. As discussed previously, some institutions have been established by governments, for example, the Chinese government established CIETAC and CMAC. Some other institutions' status is regulated by statutory instruments, for example ICAC or MAC in Russia.

918. As previously discussed, CIETAC is required to hand up its revenues to the Ministry of Finance and to make an annual budget for its expenditures which is submitted to the Ministry for approval. Moser and Jianlong, "CIETAC and its Work – An Interview with Vice Chairman Yu Jianlong" 557.

919. Generally speaking, as the ASA survey of arbitral institutions highlights, institutions are keen to "*emphasize their ability to carry out their functions in complete independence*". Hofbauer, Burkart, and Tari, "Survey on Scrutiny of Arbitral Institutions" 4.

920. Information based on the institution's responses to the questionnaires sent out by the author.

921. Article 3 of the Statutes of the Court of Arbitration of Madrid, Chamber of Commerce and Industry of Madrid (2008).

922. Article 9 of the Internal Rules of the court of the Swiss Institution.

923. Rather than disclosure to the parties.

[2] Equal Treatment of the Parties

Equality of treatment aims to ensure that one party is not favoured to the detriment of another; the rationale being that the notion of justice requires that a dispute be decided on its merits, not on the basis of the identity of the parties. Here again, if institutions are found to play an adjudicative role, imperatives of equality should be relevant to their activities[924].

In practice, illustrations of problems relating to unequal treatment of one party by an institution are not uncommon. The NAF scandal[925] and the *Guinea v. CAP* case[926] provide two good (if extreme) examples of preferential treatment being afforded to a party in breach of equality. In a different genre, the Dutco case offers another illustration[927]. By way of reminder, in this case, the French "Cour de Cassation" annulled an ICC award where the two respondents had been refused, by the institution, the opportunity to make separate nominations[928] while the claimant was allowed to nominate "its" own arbitrator. The French court held that the principle of equality of the parties in regards to party nominations was of public policy and that it could only be waived after the proceedings had started[929].

One aspect of the question of equality concerns ex parte communications between a party and the institution itself. It is not uncommon for a party to seek advice from the institution as to the application of its rules[930]. The challenge will be for the institution to ensure that its advice does not favour one side over the other. In this respect, a former Secretary General of the ICC explains:

> *An institution is obviously at liberty to provide general information about how proceedings are conducted under its auspices, as well as about arbitration law and practice. But once an arbitration is looming or has begun, the institution is required*

924. For Zykin because institutions are making procedural decisions they should treat the parties equally just like arbitrators. Zykin, "Procedural Aspects of the Activities of Institutional Arbitration Bodies" 609.
925. As discussed above NAF was said to have systematically favoured one category of users (companies) over another one (consumers) in their credit disputes/consumer arbitrations.
926. "République de Guinée v Chambre Arbitrale de Paris et autres, Tribunal de Grande Instance de Paris, 28 January 1987 (Revue de l'Arbitrage, 1987, p. 371)". The relevant aspect of these decisions concerns the request for the rescinding of the "contract" between the parties and the institution which provides for the organization of the arbitration by the CAP on the ground that the CAP had committed serious breaches of its contractual obligations including the fact that the Secretary General of the CAP had helped one party with the drafting of submissions, in breach of his duty of neutrality.
927. "Sociétés BKMI et Siemens v Société Dutco", Cour de Cassation 1992.
928. They had ultimately made a joint nomination but under protest.
929. That is to say not before the commencement of the proceedings by way of a general agreement to arbitrate under the ICC rules.
930. So much so that it is rare for arbitration rules to prohibit ex parte communications with the institution altogether. In this respect, Article 13.3 of the LCIA rules (1998) appears rather atypical in that it requires a party to copy all communications to the other side when writing to the Registrar thereby "officially" barring ex parte communications with the institution: *"Where any party sends to the Registrar any communication (including Written Statements and Documents under Article 15), it shall include a copy for each arbitrator; and it shall also send copies direct to all other parties and confirm to the Registrar in writing that it has done or is doing so".*

to be concerned about its neutrality as well as the appearance of neutrality, while at the same time providing such information and advice to the parties and arbitrators as they may reasonably expect[931].

The principle of equality of treatment is enshrined in the rules of certain number of institutions insofar as the decisions of arbitral *tribunals* are concerned[932]. It is more uncommon for such principle to be expressed in relation to the activities of the institution itself. The DIS rules offer an example of a set of rules which do not restrict the equality of treatment to arbitral tribunals. Article 26 provides that "*the parties shall be treated with equality*"[933] without stating that this requirement applies to arbitral tribunals only. Likewise, the ICAC rules which specify that:

[...] *the ICAC shall, while abiding by the provisions of the applicable law on international commercial arbitration, conduct the arbitration as it considered appropriate, and ensure that the parties are treated with equality and that each party is given a fair opportunity to protect his interests*[934].

In our view, the deciding organs of arbitral institutions should ensure that they treat parties equally. In this respect, incorporating the principle of equality of treatment in arbitration rules, not only in regards to the arbitrators but also for the institution, appears to be a good place to start. Systematic training of staff of the institutions' secretariat, and awareness-raising activities for new members of the institution's deciding organs could also prove valuable. At present, however, this approach is certainly not widespread in practice[935].

---

931. Schwartz, "The Role of the Arbitral Institution in the New Millennium" 323. One extreme example is the Secretariat of the BAC which offers extensive advice to parties pre-filing of their Request for Arbitration, which the BAC itself describes as "*a free case filing consultation service*". Fuyong Chen and Wei Sun, "Looking Beyond the Rules – An Analysing Insight into the Competitive Attractions of BAC" (Lexis Nexis Dispute Resolution Law Guide 2014) 6.
932. Article 13.1 of the HKIAC rules (2013) for instance states: "*Subject to these Rules, the arbitral tribunal shall adopt suitable procedures for the conduct of the arbitration in order to avoid unnecessary delay or expense, having regard to the complexity of the issues and the amount in dispute, and provided that such procedures ensure equal treatment of the parties and afford the parties a reasonable opportunity to present their case*". Similarly, Article 16 of the ICDR (2009) provides: "*Subject to these Rules, the tribunal may conduct the arbitration in whatever manner it considers appropriate, provided that the parties are treated with equality and that each party has the right to be heard and is given a fair opportunity to present its case.*"
933. Joerg Risse, "Commentary on the Arbitration Rules of the German Institution of Arbitration (DIS Rules), Article 26 (Due Process)" in Karl-Heinz Bockstiegel and others (eds), *Arbitration in Germany: The Model Law in Practice* (Kluwer Law International 2007).
934. Article 26 ICAC rules (2010). This is also the case of the UNCITRAL Model Law on International Arbitration which provides at Article 18: "*The parties shall be treated with equality and each party shall be given a full opportunity of presenting his case*", without their being a distinction between the roles of the institution and the tribunal.
935. A more problematic issue as to equality, which in our view cannot be addressed easily, is that of the systemic bias that institutional arbitration shows in favour of "*enforcement*". One might indeed wonder whether institutions' traditional pro-enforcement "stance" does not tend to favour claimants over respondents, at least whenever the respondents have raised no counterclaims in the proceedings. Clearly institutions have a vested interest in ensuring the enforceability of awards rendered under their auspices because this goes to their reputation ("*arbitral awards have the institution's last name*" Droulers, "Institutional Commercial Arbitration from the Inside" 144). Corrective actions taken by institutions in the context of their

[3] Adversarial Process

One may wonder whether the requirement that there be a measure of adversarial debates[936] before a decision is made forms part of the due process standards that institutions should be expected to uphold. Whenever the institution is to render a decision that may significantly impact the outcome of a case, the parties would appear to be entitled to expect to be given a meaningful opportunity to present their case to the institution itself, and as the case may be to respond to arguments presented by the other side.

It is not surprising, therefore, that various institutional rules contemplate consultations with the parties prior to certain decisions being made by the institution[937]. This is frequently the case in respect of challenges to arbitrators. Paragraphs 9 and 10 of the HKIAC Practice Note on Challenges for instance contemplate that:

> "[the non-challenging] *parties to the arbitration and the Challenged Arbitrator shall submit an Answer to the Notice of Challenge*" and that
>
> *"The challenging party shall thereafter be given, within such time as HKIAC shall direct, an opportunity to comment on the Answers to the Notice of Challenge* [...]"[938].

To the contrary, under its 1998 arbitration rules, the LCIA Court was permitted to make a decision on a challenge without having to seek the comments of the non-challenging party[939]. This, of course, was not the actual practice of the Court, which systematically sought the views of all parties[940]. The same is true of the LCIA Court's decisions on the expedited formation of a tribunal under Article 9A.2 of the LCIA

supervisory role will ultimately favour one side over the other. For example, when an institution reminds an arbitral tribunal that, because a respondent is no longer represented by its outside counsel communications should be sent to the respondent's own address rather than to that of its former counsel, is the institution not making a favour to the claimant? Likewise, when an institution brings to the attention of the tribunal an unusual requirement as to the form of arbitral awards at the seat of the arbitration, is the institution not helping the winning party? Overall, however, exception made of the issue of the pro-enforcement bias, it seems fair to say that institutions appear keen to treat the parties equally. In short, the principle of equal treatment can be said to be one which the users of the system can legitimately expect the institution to abide by, and it is one which institutions instinctively apply.

936. This principle is known as the *"principe de la contradiction"* ou *"droits de la défense"* in some civil law jurisdictions. Hanotiau and Caprasse, "Arbitrability, Due Process, and Public Policy Under Article V of the New York Convention: Belgian and French Perspectives" 727.

937. Article 26 of the ICAC rules of 2010 provides in general terms that: *"the ICAC shall* [...] *conduct the arbitration as it considered* [sic] *appropriate, and ensure that the parties are treated with equality and that each party is given a fair opportunity to protect his interests"*.

938. HKIAC Practice Note on the Challenge of an Arbitrator (2013), paras 9 and 10.

939. Article 10 of the LCIA rules (1998). Under the new 2014 rules, the LCIA must now give a reasonable opportunity to the non-challenging party to provide its views.

940. And in this context it is interesting to note that the then Article 10 required that the challenge application be copied to all parties. Similar provisions may be found in the 2009 ICDR rules. Under Article 9 of ICDR rules (2009), the institution is under no duty to seek the views of the non-challenging party, but the rules contemplate that challenge application be brought to all parties' attention prior to a decision being made. However, this position has been changed in the ICDR rules of 2014. As per Article 14.2, the Administrator is also under a duty to give the non-challenging party an opportunity to respond.

rules[941] where, if the rules require the application to be *"copied to all other parties"*, there is no requirement of consultation (even though it is the practice of the institution do so). Other areas which are likely to give rise to an expectation of consultation include among others decisions on the seat of an arbitration[942], on the applicable institutional rules[943], the appointment or replacement of arbitrators[944], or the consolidation of proceedings[945].

One difficulty with requiring that institutions give to the parties a meaningful opportunity to be heard in respect of decisions rendered by the institution itself, is that it creates a risk of abuse by unscrupulous parties and a general risk of delay. In our view, therefore, it would appear important to ensure that if a set of institutional rules contemplates "party consultations" in respect of certain institutional decisions, that the rules also *expressly* bestow the institution with a measure of discretion in this respect. It is suggested that the arbitration rules, should *expressly* empower the institution to decide whether submissions are to be made in respect of a given decision (e.g., challenge, consolidation, etc.), and if so how many. At present, most institutional rules approach this question haphazardly. A more systematic consideration of the issue would arguably be useful.

[4] Reasoning

Related to the idea of due process is the question of whether a decision-maker should offer reasons for its decisions. The rationale behind accompanying a decision with an account of its underlying reasons is to allow the decision's recipients to understand it, and also to establish that the decision was not arbitrary. Again, insofar as some institutional decisions have the potential to impact the outcome of cases, parties would be entitled to expect that such decisions be accompanied by reasons[946].

Providing reasons for certain institutional decisions raises a number of difficulties. A first difficulty is that reasoned decisions facilitate bad faith challenges of the award at the enforcement stage[947]. A second, more practical, difficulty is that the task of writing-up a decision is a time-consuming and resource-intensive one. A decision on an application for an extension of time may be easily accompanied by reasons because the issue at stake is unlikely to be very complex and therefore the reasons need not be

941. Article 9 LCIA rules (1998) and Article 9A.2 LCIA rules (2014).
942. In this sense see Sabater, "When Arbitration Begins Without a Seat" 458.
943. Article 5.2 of the SIAC rules (2013) for instance provides that the institution should consult the parties before deciding on the application of the emergency procedures. A similar provision may be found in Article 41.2 of the HKIAC rules (2013).
944. Article 6.4 of the ICDR rules (2009) required the administrator to seek the views of the parties before making a default appointment. A similar provision may be found at Article 12.4 ICDR rules (2014).
945. Article R39 CAS Code (2013); and Article 6 JAMS rules (2011).
946. In this sense, Nassib Ziadé argues: *"When institutions are called upon to decide on challenges to arbitrators, their decisions ought to be reasoned. This is particularly so when the issues presented are substantial in scope and complex in nature. Reasoned decisions will enhance public understanding of the process and foster expectations of good practices."* Ziadé, "Reflections on the Role of Institutional Arbitration Between the Present and the Future" 429.
947. It offers to the challenging party more *"material"* to support a challenge to the award.

detailed. It is in fact not uncommon for an institution to provide some limited explanations in the form of an email to the parties[948]. On the other hand, a decision on a challenge or on joinder or consolidation may be more problematical and may thus require more detailed explanations. Few institutions seem equipped to provide detailed reasons for their more complex decisions. Even a very sophisticated institution like the ICC, for instance, will struggle to implement the recent change to its policy[949] not to provide reasons for challenge decisions because the meetings of the ICC Court at which challenges are decided would not easily permit to identify the operative reasons for the decisions of the Court[950].

The institutional rules which expressly contemplate that institutional decisions be accompanied by reasons are rare[951]. In fact, what is more common is for the rules to state expressly that the institution is *not* required to provide reasons. One example may be found in the SIAC rules, for instance, which provide in relevant part that "[t]*he President, the Court and the Registrar shall not be required to provide reasons for such decisions*"[952]. This, however, does not mean that these institutions never provide reasons. Even when their rules expressly contemplate that the institution has no obligation to provide reasons for its decisions, it is the practice of certain institutions to offer some justifications for some of their decisions. This is the case of SIAC[953]. The LCIA was another institution which (under its previous sets of arbitration rules) famously provided reasons for its challenge decisions, in the absence of requirement for it to do so in its rules[954].

948. An example would be when a respondent to an ICC arbitration makes a request for extension of time for the filing of its Answer to the Request for Arbitration *after* the expiry of the thirty-day period of Article 5 of the ICC rules (2012). In such a case, in the absence of an agreement for the extension by the other side, the Secretariat would routinely reject the application. For these purposes, the ICC would inform the respondent that the "*reason*" for such a decision is the untimely character of the application and the lack of consent of the other side for the extension. In this respect one may say that the decision is accompanied by reasons.
949. The ICC announced on 8 October 2015 that it would provide reasons for challenge decisions. See http://www.iccwbo.org/News/Articles/2015/ICC-Court-to-communicate-reasons-as-a-new-service-to-users.
950. On the other hand, decisions of the ICAC Presidium are *"formalized in a document called minutes"*. Zykin, "Procedural Aspects of the Activities of Institutional Arbitration Bodies" 605.
951. An example of an institution which rules do so is CAS (Articles R34 for challenges, and R37 for provisional measures). R34 provides: *"The ICAS Board or ICAS shall give brief reasons for its decision and may decide to publish it"*.
952. Article 36.1 SIAC rules (2013). See also Article 13.4 CAMEX rules (2009), Article 43.2 ACICA rules (2011) and Article 48.2 ACICA rules (2016) which states *"ACICA shall not be required to give any reasons."*
953. As Hwang and Boo explain: "*There is no prescription by law or in the SIAC Rules that requires the giving of reasons for decisions on challenge. The Chairman of SIAC has however consistently given written decisions with reasons for his rulings.*" Hwang, Boo, and Han, "National Report for Singapore (2011)" 18.
This is also the case of the Milan Chamber, the DIA, VIAC, FCC (Finland). Institutions which do not offer reasons to their decisions include ICDR, JAMS, Swiss Chamber, Cámara de Caracas, KCAB, DIS, and BCICAC. Information based on the institutions' responses to the questionnaires sent out by the author.
954. Daele, *Challenge and Disqualification of Arbitrators in International Arbitration*. See however to the contrary the new Article 10.6 of the 2014 rules.

Overall, there seems to be room for more frequent use of reasoned decisions by arbitral institutions. Use of reasoned decisions appears particularly justified insofar as outcome-determinative decisions are concerned. On the other hand, leaving to the institutions a measure of discretion, under the relevant arbitration rules, in deciding whether reasons should be provided and, if so, what the extent of such reasons should be, would appear desirable. Institutions are well placed to assess, on a case-by-case basis, the need of accompanying their decisions by an account of the underlying reasons. As the legitimacy of arbitral institutions continues to be challenged, a more systematic and thought-through consideration by institutions of the issue may be warranted.

[5] Judicial Review of Institutional Decisions

Part of the rationale under the first representation of the role of institutions for qualifying institutional decisions as administrative was to ensure, as one author puts it, that "*the mechanisms for the judicial review of arbitral awards are not available against decisions rendered by arbitral decisions*"[955].

One may wonder whether the rejection of any dichotomic approaches should lead to the conclusion that those institutional decisions which are outcome-determinative should be open to review. As Paulsson puts it:

> [...] *parties to an international contract generally do prefer to avoid national authorities, and rather entrust the task of managing and policing their arbitrations to a neutral institution. The question then may arise whether, and to what extent, someone should police the police. Surely there ought to be some mechanism that could neutralise the decision of an institution which is found to be a sham (perhaps not an unthinkable thought in an age of proliferating institutions amongst which there may well be some whose institutional integrity and methods of governance are dubious). And even in the respect to well-known and reputable institutions, occasions may arise where a party feels impelled to test the legitimacy of a particular administrative decision*[956].

The problem again is that any such review process would necessarily increase the duration of institutional arbitrations[957]. It would also be open to a risk of abuse. In today's context, where concerns are increasingly being heard about the cost and duration of arbitration[958], one cannot overstate the potential for disruption that an overly extensive review of institutional decisions would create. In addition, finding that some of the more material institutional decisions should be open to review raises a number of difficult questions:

955. In the original language: "[...] *les recours prévus à l'encontre des sentences arbitrales sont irrecevables à l'encontre des décisions des institutions d'Arbitrage*". Hautot, "Les Pouvoirs de la Cour d'Arbitrage de la C.C.I. de Décider ou Non d'Organiser l'Arbitrage" 19. (Translation by the Author).
956. Paulsson, "Vicarious Hypochondria and Institutional Arbitration" 226.
957. If it were to take place while the proceedings are still pending.
958. Queen Mary, University of London, "Corporate Choices in International Arbitration: An Industry Approach".

- Should the review take place at the enforcement stage only, or while proceedings are still pending?
- By whom should this review be conducted, the enforcement judge, the arbitral tribunal or by an appeal's committee within the institution?
- Should the scope of the review be limited to allegations of due process violations or should it permit review of the wider merits of the institutional decision?

Despite the undeniable difficulties that a review of institutional decisions would raise, we would suggest that some measure of review is both desirable (in so far as outcome-determinative decisions are concerned) and achievable (provided that this review remains strictly constrained). Below is a rudimentary outline of an achievable review process. First, it goes without saying that not all institutional decisions need to be reviewable, but only those that are most likely to be outcome-determinative. Any review should ideally remain limited to alleged violations of due process and not extend to the wider merits of the institutional decisions. The institutional rules should expressly provide that any allegation of violation of due process should be raised first with the institution during the proceedings so that it may remedy it, if need be. Some "internal" review could be integrated in institutional rules. For example institutional decisions on the seat, language, joinder, consolidation, and applicable rules could be appealed to the arbitral tribunal once appointed[959]. For other questions, review by an internal institutional committee would, on the other hand, appear excessively cumbersome even for the more material decisions such as on challenges. If an alleged due process violation is not remedied internally during the proceedings, then any review of the institutional decision can, in my view, be exercised by the enforcement judge, after the proceedings are concluded[960]. It is indeed unclear that an institutional decision would ever reach a level of materiality sufficient to require that such decision be reviewed immediately (as opposed to alongside the tribunal's award)[961]. Finally, for enforcement actions, the existing framework of the New York Convention is to our

959. Interestingly this is occasionally contemplated by existing arbitration rules. Article 17 of the ICDR rules (2014) provides that the institution's decision on the seat of the arbitration is subject to later review by the tribunal.

960. Or as the case may be the interim award corresponding to the phase of the proceedings where the due process violation occurred has been issued.

961. This view is shared by Fouchard: *"This judicial control after the arbitration must be and must remain the normal way to control institutions and their activities. There are several reasons for this: – first such a control does not paralyse the proceedings, and if on occasion it is still subject to abuse and dilatory tactics, their consequences are less problematic than during the arbitration; – second, the enforcement judge is able to assess the arbitration in its entirety, that is to say both the work of the arbitrators and of the institution."* (Translation by the author).
In the original language: *"Ce contrôle judiciaire postérieur à l'instance arbitrale, et dont la sentence fait l'objet, doit être et doit rester – répétons-le – le contrôle normal de l'institution arbitrale et de son activité. Et cela, pour plusieurs raisons: – d'abord, il ne paralyse pas le déroulement de cette instance, et s'il reste, dans certains cas, l'occasion de manœuvres dilatoires, les conséquences en sont moins fâcheuses qu'en cours d'arbitrage; – ensuite, le juge est en mesure d'apprécier globalement l'œuvre arbitrale, celle des arbitres principalement, mais aussi les mesures institutionnelles qui l'ont organisée et encadrée".* Fouchard, "Les Institutions Permanentes d'Arbitrage Devant le Juge Etatique (A Propos d'une Jurisprudence Récente)" 269.

mind adequate as the convention does not limit the grounds of Article V to actions taken solely by arbitration tribunals[962]. In our submission, the approach outlined above would meet the requirement of expediency. It would also permit to avoid the undesirable approach of the supporters of the first representation whereby no due process standards whatsoever may be found to apply to the decisions of institutions[963].

[C] Proposition 7: Materiality of a Decision as a Viable Proxy for Determining to What Extent Due Process Should Be Complied With

The crux of this ultimate proposition is that looking at the level of materiality of a given decision (i.e., to say, its capacity to be outcome-determinative) appears to be a viable approach for the purposes of determining to what extent certain due process standards should be followed. The more a decision is likely to be outcome-determinative, the more pressing the need becomes for the decision-maker to apply due process (regardless of who the decision-maker is). This factor of materiality appears more adequate than a suppositious dichotomy between "administrative" and "jurisdictional" decisions.

This proposition is based on the premise that the application of due process is a question which cannot always be approached in a binary fashion, that is to say, in terms of "*whether or not*" the due process norm in question should apply. The application of certain due process norms is a question of degree. A prime example of this would be the requirement of "adversariality" (i.e., giving a party an opportunity to present its case before the institution makes a decision). Often, the controversial question will not so much be whether or not a party should be given an opportunity to provide its views on a particular issue, but how much of a consultation should be allowed by the institution. Namely, should there be more than one round of submissions[964]? In this regard, the materiality of a given decision seems a useful factor for determining the extent to which an opportunity must be given to a party to continue to assert its case. The more material a decision is for the outcome of a case, the more the

962. For set aside proceedings, the rules of certain jurisdictions already contemplate that institutional decisions may give rise to the annulment of an award. As previously explained, this is the case of section 68 of the English Arbitration Act (1996).
963. If certain decisions of arbitral institutions become subject to judicial review, then it may be desirable at the same time to "strengthen" arbitral institutions' defences against actions for liability that may be commenced against the institution. In other words, it may become necessary to provide qualified immunities to institutions.
964. What about an oral hearing? The author is aware of only two cases at the LCIA where a party obtained a hearing on a challenge to an arbitrator. See Thomas W. Walsh and Ruth Teitelbaum, "The LCIA Court Decisions on Challenges to Arbitrators: An Introduction", in William W. Park (ed.), *Arbitration International Special Edition on Arbitrator Challenges*, (Kluwer Law International 2011) 286: *"The parties may submit to the Divisions reasoned requests for an oral hearing, but, to date, only in two challenges, LCIA Reference No. UN7949 (December 3, 2007) and LCIA Reference No. LCIA Reference No. 3488 (July 11, 2007), has an oral hearing been held."*

    Another issue is that of whether institutions should base their decisions solely on points discussed or put for discussion to the parties? This, in our view, would be too extreme.

parties will have a legitimate claim to see their processual rights respected, and therefore the more strictly due process standards should be applied.

Another aspect of due process that is not adequately expressed in a binary fashion is the requirement for reasoned decisions. Again, the controversial question will often not be "*whether or not*" a decision should be accompanied by reasons, but "*how expansive*" the reasons should be. At present, an institution is more likely to provide some explanations for rather uncontroversial decisions (e.g., short extension of time), than for the more material and complex ones (e.g., challenges or removal of arbitrators). This is because it is more convenient for an institution to explain an uncontroversial decision than a problematical one. This, surely, cannot be satisfactory. Again, the materiality of a given decision seems a useful factor for determining the extent to which a given decision should be accompanied by reasons[965].

As indicated above, assessing the precise impact which a decision has on the outcome of a case is uneasy (even *ex post facto,* when the award has been rendered). What is suggested, however, is not for institutions to determine the precise materiality of each decision, but to "*factor-in*" their likely impact in deciding whether and to what extent the parties should be allowed to make additional submissions, receive reasoned decisions, etc.

Later on, the same factor of materiality may be used when domestic courts are asked to review whether an award should be refused enforcement or set aside. The less an institutional decision affected the outcome of the case, and the less the violation of due process alleged should justify refusing enforcement or setting aside the award. In this respect it should be noted that the English Arbitration Act (1996) contemplates a similar approach. Section 68(2) of the Act, which expressly refers to arbitral institutions, requires that for a serious irregularity to justify setting aside an award, the irregularity should have caused "*substantial injustice to the applicant*".

§5.04 CHAPTER CONCLUSIONS

This chapter offered a novel, and hopefully balanced, theoretical representation of the functions of arbitral institutions. According to this representation, arbitral institutions are ancillary participants in the adjudicative process which decisions, insofar as they may occasionally be outcome-determinative, should call upon the application of certain due process standards. Such standards could arguably include: (1) guaranteeing the independence and impartiality of the institution from the parties; (2) treating

965. One might also wonder whether the notion of equality is not also one of degree. At first glance, it seems that one party cannot be treated "*more equally*" in one situation than in another, but in reality some aspects of equality raise questions of degrees. As indicated above it may, for instance, be acceptable for an institution to engage in ex parte communications if the subject matter of the communication is trivial, or at least if it is unlikely to be outcome-determinative. An example would be answering by telephone a query about the number of copies of a Request for Arbitration that a party needs to file. On the other hand, a discussion about the threshold expressed in the applicable arbitration rules for a challenge to an arbitrator to succeed would appear too material to be discussed ex parte. Once again, the materiality of a given subject matter seems a useful factor for determining the extent to which a given decision should be accompanied by reasons.

the parties equally; (3) giving the parties same opportunity to present their case; (4) providing reasons for institutional decisions; and (5) providing an opportunity to appeal or otherwise seek judicial review of certain institutional decisions. Naturally, imposing overly stringent due process requirements could negatively affect the efficiency of institutional arbitration, but the balanced approach outlined in this chapter should adequately deal with this concern.

It is sometimes stated that when parties opt for institutional arbitration, they are making the choice of taking away some responsibilities from the domestic courts (and from the arbitrator in an ad hoc context) to entrust them to an arbitral institution[966]. In that sense, by choosing institutional arbitration, parties can be said to operate a transfer of part of the adjudicative mission to an arbitral institution. While, of course, the role of such institutions remains less significant than that of the arbitrators, it is hard to ignore the significance of the part played by such institutions in the overall adjudicative process.

An aspect of this question which, regrettably fell outside of the scope of this book, is the role played by permanent arbitral institutions in facilitating the settlement of disputes. When one considers that the vast majority of arbitrations are resolved by way of amicable settlements prior to the merits of the case being heard by any tribunal[967], at a stage where the institution is the parties' only interlocutor, it is fair to say that arbitral institutions appear more as *bone fide "organs of justice"* or *"custodians of the* [dispute resolution] *process"* than as mere purveyors of logistical services[968].

966. In the words of Aguilar Alvarez: "[...] *certain tasks vested in the courts are transferred to arbitral institutions. Parties wishing to exclude their disputes from State court jurisdiction altogether, aware of the delays and risks involved in drafting a 'self-sufficient' arbitration clause, have found that institutional arbitration provides a significant contribution to the legal security of their contract*". Aguilar Alvarez, "The Challenge of Arbitrators" 208.
967. According the 2008 PwC Queen Mary University international arbitration survey, "[a]*lmost three quarters of settlements occur before the hearing on the merits of the case*". Queen Mary, University of London, "Corporate Attitudes and Practices: Recognition and Enforcement of Foreign Awards" (2008) 7.
968. Paulsson, "Moral Hazard in International Dispute Resolution, Inaugural Lecture as Holder of the Michael R. Klein Distinguished Scholar Chair University of Miami School of Law on 29 April 2010" 19.

In the same sense, see Weber Stecher, commenting on the results of the ASA institutional survey, "*Arbitral institutions have far-reaching decision-power and are for that reason a significant element of the judiciary authority within the alternative dispute settlement procedure*". Weber-Stecher, "Principles of Good Governance and Organisation of Arbitral Institutions" 39.

CHAPTER 6
General Conclusions

The central question that this book proposed to investigate was: "*What is the role of arbitral institutions in the institutional arbitration process?*" The underlying motivation for undertaking this work rested on the paradox that despite the staggering success of institutional arbitration, there appeared to be little understanding of the exact functions of arbitral institutions. Conventional wisdom on the matter, which depicted institutions as mere administrators of the proceedings whose activities were entirely foreign to the adjudicative process, seemed at odds with reality.

This paradox is not only captivating theoretically but also significant in practice. After all theories, when widely shared, have the capacity to shape the very object which they aimed to describe[969]. In our case, the belief that arbitral institutions are adequately depicted as mere administrators, has the potential of impacting both the legal regime to which we subject the decisions rendered by such institutions, and the manner in which institutions ultimately discharge their duties.

In this context, the ultimate purpose of the book was to offer some clarity as to the role played by institutions in the proceedings they administer. With this goal in sight the book started in the first Chapter by offering a definition of the notion of "arbitral institution". For these purposes the notion of "institutional arbitration" had to be defined first. Having looked at the limitations of the approach which consists of defining institutional arbitration by distinguishing it from the neighbouring notions of "*ad hoc* arbitration" and "judicial dispute resolution", I offered a novel autonomous definition of institutional arbitration based on a cumulative list of essential characteristics.

The notion of arbitral institution having been ascertained in Chapter 1 and 2, Chapter 3 offered a synthetic overview of the activities undertaken by institutions. The aim of the second chapter was twofold. The first aim was to illustrate the diversity that exists in the role that institutions assume in respect of the proceedings they administer,

969. See the discussions on this point in the introduction to Chapter 3 above ("*The traditional representations of the role of institutions: A critical evaluation*").

in particular in terms of the level of discretion conferred upon institutions for the purposes of discharging their duties. Second, Chapter 3 served to provide the information required to understand the theoretical representations of the functions of arbitral institutions that have permeated both the literature and court decisions.

Chapter 4 identified, critically assessed and ultimately rejected the two traditional theoretical representations of the functions of institutions. According to one representation, arbitral institutions are mere administrators with no decision-making power whatsoever. According to the other representation, whilst institutions are occasionally called upon to exercise some measure of decision-making, institutional measures remain immaterial because they are "administrative"/"non-jurisdictional" in nature.

In Chapter 5, which to a large extent served as a synthesis of the previous three Chapters, I proposed a novel and more realistic representation of the functions of arbitral institutions. According to this representation, arbitral institutions were described as ancillary participants in the adjudicative process which decisions, insofar as they may occasionally be outcome-determinative, should call upon the application of due process or fair trial standards. Aspects of "due process" which are relevant to the activities of institution include the equal treatment of the parties; the independence and impartiality of the institution; the requirement of an adversarial process; the provision of reasoned decision; and the possibility for the parties to seek judicial review of institutional decisions. Recognizing, however, that overly stringent requirements could negatively affect the attractiveness of institutional arbitration, I suggested that the level of materiality of a given decision (understood in the sense, its capacity to be outcome-determinative) could often be used as a factor for determining the extent to which certain due process standards ought to be followed by arbitral institutions when they discharge their duties.

Of course, this book did not aim to dispose of all discussions on its subject matter. To the contrary, I would hope that, by clarifying the functions of arbitral institutions, the book might permit to re-invigorate an important debate. Many issues are left unresolved by my book, and these issues constitute as many opportunities for further research. For example, if the desirability of the application of some fair trial standards by institutions seems established, further enquiry could be made into the source of such standards. As alluded to in Chapter 5, could due process norms be said to derive from the parties' arbitration agreement, or from the so-called contract that the parties and the institution are sometimes said to enter into for the institution to provide its services? Could they arise out of the legal system within which the so-called services contract or the arbitration agreement are legally anchored. Could such norms apply to arbitral institutions because they constitute principles of transnational arbitration law? Or should they be seen to arise only, *a posteriori*, from the requirements of any domestic legal system in which an attempt will be made to enforce the award? Beyond the question of their source, further research could also be made into these norms' exact substance. What precise due process standards apply to institutions? What remedies are available when they are breached? These questions, as fascinating as they are, would deserve a book of their own.

In a sense, each of them illustrates the paradox highlighted above: *How can it be that a mechanism said to have been used since times immemorial*[970] *still provide such fertile ground for research on such fundamental aspects of its functioning?*

The answer may lie in the quote of Alfred Adler with which this book commenced: "*Man knows much more than he understands*".

970. See the account of the historical development of arbitration in the introductory Chapter of Clay, *L'arbitre*.

Appendix

Template of Questionnaire Sent Out to Arbitral Institutions

Instructions: Thank you for accepting to respond to this questionnaire. If your organisation applies different/separate sets of arbitration rules for domestic and international arbitrations, please answer the questions below for international arbitration only. When answering the questions, please point to relevant provisions of the applicable rules.	
STATUS AND FORM	
DATE CREATED	
CORPORATE FORM	
GOVERNMENT / PRIVATE ENTITY?	
FOR PROFIT / NOT FOR PROFIT?	
ARBITRATION RULES	
INTERNAL STRUCTURE	
ACTIVITIES	
PRIMA FACIE JURISDICTION	Does your institution have the power to make a *prima facie* decision on jurisdiction?
INTERIM RELIEF	Does your institution have the power to grant interim relief prior to the appointment of the arbitral tribunal?
SELECTION OF ARBITRATORS	Does your institution have the power to select arbitrators in default of party nominations?
CONFIRMATION OF TRIBUNAL	Does a tribunal need to be confirmed by the institution before it may proceed with arbitration?

NUMBER OF ARBITRATORS	Does your institution decide the number of arbitrators (in the absence of an agreement of the parties)? If not who does?
SEAT OF THE ARBITRATION	Does your institution decide the seat of the arbitration (in the absence of an agreement of the parties)? If not who does?
LANGUAGE	Does your institution decide the language of the arbitration (in the absence of an agreement of the parties)? If not who does?
CONSOLIDATION	Does your institution (as opposed to the arbitral tribunal) have the power to consolidate proceedings?
JOINDER	Does your institution (as opposed to the arbitral tribunal) have the power to join third parties?
CHALLENGES TO ARBITRATORS	Does your institution decide challenges to arbitrators? Does your institution have a general power to remove arbitrators in certain circumstances?
EXTENSION DEADLINES	Does your institution have a general power to extend deadlines under the arbitration rules?
PAYMENT OF ADVANCES	Does your institution order payment of advances (deposits) on account of the tribunal's fees and expenses?
TREATING CLAIM AS WITHDRAWN	Is your institution able to treat a claim as withdrawn in the event one party fails to lodge a deposit?
COSTS	Does your institution determine, or reviews, the quantum of the tribunal's fees at the end of the proceedings? If not, who does?
SCRUTINY	Does it review draft awards prior to the awards being issued to the parties?
REASONED DECISIONS	Does your institution ever give reasoned decisions? (for example, on challenges to arbitrators, on *prima facie* jurisdiction, etc.).
LOGISTICAL SUPPORT	Does your institution provide logistical support to the parties (e.g., hearing rooms, interpreters & Court reporters etc.).
CHANNEL OF COMMUNICATION	Does your institution act as the channel of communication between the parties and the Tribunal?
NOTIFYING RESPONDENT OF A REQUEST	Is your organisation responsible for notifying Respondent parties of the filing of a new Request for Arbitration?
HOLDING SECURITY FOR COSTS OR CLAIM	Does your institution accept to hold monies to the order of the Tribunal as security for a party's costs or for the claim?
SUPERVISION ROLE	To what extent does your institution "monitor" the proceedings after the constitution of the tribunal?

APPEAL	Do your arbitration rules provide for a form of appeal against arbitral awards?
AWARENESS RAISING	Does your organisation engage in awareness-raising, training or lobbying?
FORMAL ROLE UNDER LOCAL LAW	Is your institution entrusted by the local legislation with certain tasks? (*eg.* default appointing authority for *ad hoc* arbitrations seated in your jurisdiction; official arbitration centre for certain types of domestic disputes, certification of awards for enforcement, etc.)
EXCLUSION OF LIABILITY	Do the rules of your institution contain provisions to limit or exclude the liability of the institution?
RELATIONSHIP WITH ARBITRATORS	Would you say that there is a contractual relationship between the arbitrators appointed in proceedings conducted under the auspices of your institution and the institution itself?

Bibliography

Aaron S, "International Arbitration III: Choosing an Arbitration Institution and a Set of Rules" (1991) 108 South African Law Journal 306.

Abdel Raouf J, "New Rules of the Cairo Regional Centre for International Commercial Arbitration (CRCICA)" (2011) 3 International Journal of Arab Arbitration 7.

Aguilar Alvarez G, "The Challenge of Arbitrators" (1990) 6 Arbitration International, Kluwer Law International 203.

Alcántara JM, "An International Panel of Maritime Arbitrators?" (1994) 11 Journal of International Arbitration, Kluwer Law International 117.

Alley ER, "International Arbitration: The Alternative of the Stockholm Chamber of Commerce" (1988) 22 International Lawyer 837.

Amato AD, "The Effect of Legal Theories on Judicial Decisions" (1999) 74 Chicago-Kent Law Review 517.

Appel M, "International Centre for Dispute Resolution (ICDR)" in Karyl Nairn and Patrick Heneghan (eds), *Arbitration World: Institutional & Jurisdictional Comparisons* (4th Revised edition, Thomson Reuters 2012).

Arkin HL, "International Ad Hoc Arbitration: A Practical Alternative" (1987) 15 International Business Lawyer 5.

Art JY, "Challenge of Arbitrators: Is an Institutional Decision Final?" (1986) 2 Arbitration International, Kluwer Law International 261.

Aslı BC, "Enforcement of Foreign Arbitral Awards in Turkey. Further Steps Towards a More Arbitration-Friendly Approach" (2013) 31 ASA Bulletin, Kluwer Law International 537.

Bao C, "Hong Kong International Arbitration Centre" in J William Rowley (ed), *Arbitration World: Jurisdictional Comparisons* (4th Revised edn, Thomson Reuters 2012).

Bedjaoui M, "Challenge of Arbitrators" (1993) 6 Albert Jan van den Berg (ed), International Arbitration in a Changing World, Kluwer Law International 85.

Beechey J, "Advocacy in International Commercial Arbitration: England" in R Doak Bishop (ed), *The Art of Advocacy in International Arbitration* (1st edn, Juris 2004)

Beerbower JE, "International Arbitration: Can We Realise the Potential?" (2011) 27 Arbitration International, Kluwer Law International 75.

Bishop RD, "Toward a Harmonized Approach to Advocacy in International Arbitration" in R Doak Bishop (ed), *The Art of Advocacy in International Arbitration* (1st edn, Juris 2004).

Blackaby N and others, *Redfern and Hunter on International Arbitration* (5th edn, Oxford University Press 2009) <http://www.kluwerarbitration.com/document.aspx?id=Ch5-ipn26309&query=AND(content%3A%22institution%22,content%3A%22institutional%22)> accessed 10 May 2012.

"Black's Law Dictionary, 2nd Online Edition, Available at Http://thelawdictionary.org, Accessed 13 September 2013".

Blanch J, "Appointment and Confirmation of Arbitrators" in Philipp Habegger, Daniel Hochstrasser and Gabrielle Nater-Bass (eds), *Arbitral Institutions Under Scrutiny* (JurisNet 2013).

Blanke G and Abi Habib C, "Arbitration in Dubai: A Basic Primer" (2011) 2011 Christian Klausegger, Peter Klein, et al. (eds), Austrian Yearbook on International Arbitration 217.

Bockstiegel K-H, "Commercial and Investment Arbitration: How Different Are They Today?" (2012) 28 Arbitration International, Kluwer Law International 577.

Boo L, "Singapore International Arbitration Centre" in Loukas A Mistelis, Laurence Shore and Stavros Brekoulakis (eds), *The World Arbitration Reporter*, vol. 3 (Juris 2010).

Born G, *International Commercial Arbitration: Commentary and Materials* (2nd edn, Kluwer Law International 2001).

Born GB, *International Commercial Arbitration* (Kluwer Law International 2009; Second Edition 2014) <http://www.kluwerarbitration.com/CommonUI/book-toc.aspx?book=TOC-Born-2014> accessed 9 May 2012.

Born GB, "New Rules at the Singapore International Arbitration Centre" <http://kluwerarbitrationblog.com/blog/2013/05/14/new-rules-at-the-singapore-international-arbitration-centre/> accessed 17 May 2013.

Bredow J and Mulder I, "Commentary on the Arbitration Rules of the German Institution of Arbitration (DIS Rules), Introduction" in Karl-Heinz Bockstiegel, Dr Stefan Kröll and Patricia Nacimiento (eds), *Arbitration in Germany: The Model Law in Practice* (Kluwer Law International 2007).

Berger KP, Private Dispute Resolution in International Business: Negotiation, Mediation, Arbitration (3rd edn), (Kluwer Law International 2015) p. 363.

Bühler M and Jarvin S, "The Arbitration Rules of the International Chamber of Commerce (ICC)" in Frank-Bernd Weigand (ed), *Practitioner's Handbook on International Commercial Arbitration* (Oxford University Press 2009).

Bühler M and Webster TH, *Handbook of ICC Arbitration: Commentary, Precedents, Materials* (2nd edn, Thomson/Sweet & Maxwell 2008).

Buhring-Uhle C, Kirchhof L and Scherer G, *Arbitration and Mediation in International Business* (2nd Revised edn, Panel Publishers 2006).

Burger L, "Sports Arbitration and Due Process, Kluwer Arbitration Blog, http://kluwerarbitrationblog.com/blog/2011/03/02/sports/arbitration-and-Due-Process, Accessed 2/03/2014" <http://kluwerarbitrationblog.com/blog/2011/03/02/sports-arbitration-and-due-process/> accessed 2 May 2014.

Calvo Goller K, "The 2012 ICC Rules of Arbitration – An Accelerated Procedure and Substantial Changes" (2012) 29 Journal of International Arbitration, Kluwer Law International 323.

Calvo MA, "The Challenge of the ICC Arbitrators: Theory and Practice International" (1998) 15 Journal of International Arbitration, Kluwer Law International 63.

Campbell J, *Creative Mythology (The Masks of God)* (Souvenir Press 2011).

Capper P and Zagonek J, "Relevant Aspects of the English Legal System" in Julian DM Lew and others (eds), *Arbitration in England. Including Chapters on Scotland and the Republic of Ireland* (Kluwer Law International 2013).

Carabiber C, "L'Evolution de l'Arbitrage Commercial International", (1960) 99 Collected Courses of the Hague Academy of International Law, Martinus Nijhoff Publishers & Brill Academic.

Caron DD, "The Nature of the Iran-United States Claims Tribunal and the Evolving Structure of International Dispute Resolution" (1990) 84 American Journal of International Law 104.

Chan C, "Of Arbitral Institutions and Provisional Determinations on Jurisdiction, Global Gold Case" (2009) 25 Arbitration International, Kluwer Law International 403.

Chang WS, "CIETAC's Perspective on Arbitration and Conciliation Concerning China" (2005) 12 Albert Jan van den Berg (ed), New Horizons in International Commercial Arbitration and Beyond, Kluwer Law International 27.

Chen F, "Striving for Independence, Competence, and Fairness: A Case Study of the Beijing Arbitration Commission" (2007) 18 American Review of International Arbitration 313.

Chen F and Sun W, "Looking Beyond the Rules - An Analysing Insight into the Competitive Attractions of BAC".

Chiu J, "Consolidation of Arbitral Proceeding and International Arbitration" (1990) 7 Journal of International Arbitration, Kluwer Law International 53.

Clagett B, "Informal Action—Adjudication—Rule Making: Some Recent Developments in Federal Administrative Law" (1971) 20 Duke Law Journal 51.

Clay T, "Commentary of the "Cubic Defense System" Decision (Cour de Cassation, 20 February 2001)" (2001) 2001 Revue de l'Arbitrage 511.

Clay T, *L'arbitre* (Dalloz 2001).

"Convention on the Recognition and Enforcement of Foreign Arbitral Awards, ('New York Convention')".

Craig WL, Park WW and Paulsson J, *International Chamber of Commerce Arbitration* (3rd edn, Oceana Publications 2000).

Crookenden S, "Who Should Decide Arbitration Confidentiality Issues?" (2009) 25 Arbitration International, Kluwer Law International 603.

Daele K, *Challenge and Disqualification of Arbitrators in International Arbitration* (Kluwer Law International 2012).

Dagan H and Kreitner R, "The Character of Legal Theory" (2011) 96 Cornell Law Review 671.

de Hancock TM, "The ICC Court of Arbitration: The Institution and Its Procedures" (1984) 1 Journal of International Arbitration, Kluwer Law International 21.

Delvolvé J-L, Rouche J and Pointon GH, *French Arbitration Law and Practice* (2nd edn, Wolters Kluwer 2009).

Derains Y, "Synthesis (of the 1993 ICCA Congress in Bahrain)" (1993) 6 Albert Jan van den Berg (ed), International Arbitration in a Changing World, Kluwer Law International 239.

Derains Y and Schwartz EA, *A Guide to the New ICC Rules of Arbitration* (2nd edn, Kluwer Law International 2005).

Drahozal CR, "Arbitration by the Numbers: The State of Empirical Research on International Commercial Arbitration" (2006) 22 Arbitration International, Kluwer Law International 291.

Droulers D, "Institutional Commercial Arbitration from the Inside" in Kaj Hobér, Annette Magnusson and Marie Öhrström (eds), *Between East and West: Essays in Honour of Ulf Franke* (Juris 2010).

Dupeyré R, "Les arbitres et centres d'arbitrage face à leurs responsabilités: le droit français à son point d'équilibre", (2014) 32(2) ASA Bulletin, Kluwer Law International 265-285.

Emerson FD, "History of Arbitration Practice and Law" (1970) 19 Cleveland State Law Review 156.

Fellas J, "AAA/ICDR International Arbitration Rules" in Loukas A Mistelis (ed), *Concise International Arbitration* (Kluwer Law International 2010).

Fiss OM, "The Social and Political Foundations of Adjudication" (1982) 6 Law and Human Behavior 121.

Fouchard P, "Les Institutions Permanentes d'Arbitrage Devant Le Juge Etatique (A Propos D'une Jurisprudence Récente)" (1987) 1987 Revue de l'Arbitrage 225.

Fouchard P, "Relationships between the Arbitrator and the Parties and the Arbitral Institution", *The Status of the Arbitrator - ICC Bulletin Special Supplement* (International Chamber of Commerce 1995).

Friedland P and Yan B, "Negotiating and Drafting Arbitration Agreements with Chinese Parties: Special Considerations of Chinese Law and Practice" (2011) 28 Journal of International Arbitration, Kluwer Law International 467.

Fry JA, "ICC International Court of Arbitration" in Loukas A Mistelis, Laurence Shore and Stavros Brekoulakis (eds), *The World Arbitration Reporter*, vol. 3 (Juris 2010).

Fry JA, Greenberg S and Mazza F, *The Secretariat's Guide to ICC Arbitration* (ICC 2012).

Fuller L, "The Case of the Speluncean Explorers" (1949) 62 Harvard Law Review 616.

Fuller LL, "The Forms and Limits of Adjudication" (1978) 92 Harvard Law Review 353.

Gaillard E, *Legal Theory of International Arbitration* (Martinus Nijhoff Publishers 2010).

Gaillard E and Pinsolle E, "Advocacy in International Commercial Arbitration: France" in R Doak Bishop (ed), *The Art of Advocacy in International Arbitration* (1st edn, Juris 2004).

Gaillard E and Savage J (eds), *Fouchard, Gaillard, Goldman on International Commercial Arbitration* (Kluwer Law International 1999).

Gaudet M, "La Coopération Des Juridictions Etatiques à l'Arbitrage Institutionnel" (1988) 6 ASA Bulletin, Kluwer Law International 90.

Gelinas F, "Investment Tribunals and the Commercial Arbitration Model: Mixed Procedures and Creeping Institutionalization" in Mark Gehring and Marie-Claire Cordonier Segger (eds), *Sustainable Development in World Trade Law* (Kluwer Law International 2005) <http://papers.ssrn.com/sol3/papers.cfm?abstract_id=1336099> accessed 12 July 2012.

Gerbay R, "London Court of International Arbitration" in Loukas A Mistelis, Laurence Shore and Stavros Brekoulakis (eds), *The World Arbitration Reporter*, vol. 3 (Juris 2010).

Gerbay R, "The London Court of International Arbitration" in Julian DM Lew and others (eds), *Arbitration in England. Including Chapters on Scotland and the Republic of Ireland* (Kluwer Law International 2013).

Goldman B, "Les Conflits de Lois Dans l'Arbitrage International de Droit Privé", (1963) 109 Collected Courses of the Hague Academy of International Law, Martinus Nijhoff Publishers & Brill Academic 1963.

Gray W, "Is There a Growing International Arbitration Culture?" (1998) 8 Albert Jan van den Berg (ed), International Dispute Resolution: Towards an International Arbitration Culture, Kluwer Law International 23.

Greenberg S, "ACICA's New International Arbitration Rules" (2006) 23 Journal of International Arbitration, Kluwer Law International 189.

Greenberg S, "Arbitral Award Scrutiny under Scrutiny" in Philipp Habegger, Daniel Hochstrasser and Gabrielle Nater-Bass (eds), *Arbitral Institutions Under Scrutiny* (JurisNet 2013).

Grierson J and Van Hooft A, *Arbitrating Under the 2012 ICC Rules. An Introductory User's Guide* (Kluwer Law International 2012).

Grigera Naon H, "The Role of the Secretariat of the International Court of Arbitration", *The New 1998 ICC Rules of Arbitration - ICC Bulletin Special Supplement* (1997).

Grigera Naon H, "The Powers of the ICC International Court of Arbitration Vis-a-Vis Parties and Arbitrators", *Arbitration in the Next Decade - ICC Bulletin Special Supplement* (International Chamber of Commerce 1999).

Guillaume G, "The Future of International Judicial Institutions" (1995) 44 International & Comparative Law Quarterly 848.

Gusy MF, Hosking JM and Schwarz FT, *A Guide to the ICDR International Arbitration Rules* (Oxford University Press 2011).

Habegger P, Hochstrasser D and Nater-Bass G (eds), *Arbitral Institutions Under Scrutiny* (JurisNet 2013).

Habegger PA, "The Revised Swiss Rules of International Arbitration: An Overview of the Major Changes" (2012) 30 ASA Bulletin, Kluwer Law International 269.

Halsbury's Laws of England, "Institutional Arbitration", *Halsbury's Laws of England Volume 61 (International Relations Law)* (5th edn, LexisNexis Butterworths 2010).

Hanotiau B, *Complex Arbitrations: Multiparty, Mulicontract Multi-Issue and Class Actions* (Kluwer Law International 2006).

Hanotiau B, "International Arbitration in a Global Economy: The Challenges of the Future" (2011) 28 Journal of International Arbitration, Kluwer Law International 89.

Hanotiau B and Caprasse O, "Arbitrability, Due Process, and Public Policy Under Article V of the New York Convention: Belgian and French Perspectives" (2008) 25 Journal of International Arbitration 721.

Haridi S, Alrashid M and Bouhabib A, "The Cairo Regional Centre for International Commercial Arbitration (CRCICA) Newly Revised Arbitration Rules: Incorporating the New UNCITRAL Model Rules of 2010 and Expanding the Centre's Role as an Appointing Authority" (2011) 8 Transnational Dispute Management <http://www.transnational-dispute-management.com/article.asp?key=1711> accessed 8 May 2012.

Harris B, "London Maritime Arbitration" (2011) 77 Arbitration 116.

Hausmaninger C, "Rights and Obligations of the Arbitrator with Regard to the Parties and the Arbitral Institution – A Civil Law Viewpoint", *The Status of the Arbitrator - ICC Bulletin Special Supplement* (International Chamber of Commerce 1995).

Hautot I, "Les Pouvoirs de La Cour d'Arbitrage de La C.C.I. de Décider Ou Non d'Organiser l'Arbitrage" (1990) 8 ASA Bulletin, Kluwer Law International 12.

Heger S, "The International Commercial Arbitration Court at the Chamber of Commerce and Industry of the Russian Federation: A Short Overview and the New Arbitration Rules" (2008) 2008 Austrian Arbitration Yearbook 283.

Hermann G, "Power of Arbitrators to Determine Procedures under the UNCITRAL Model Law" (1996) 7 Albert Jan van den Berg (ed), Planning Efficient Arbitration Proceedings: The Law Applicable in International Arbitration, Kluwer Law International 39.

Hodges P, Parker C and Ackebo D, "International Chamber of Commerce (ICC)" in Karyl Nairn and Patrick Heneghan (eds), *Arbitration World: Institutional & Jurisdictional Comparisons* (4th Revised edn, Thomson Reuters 2012).

Hoellering MF, "AAA Administration of International Arbitration Proceedings" (1998) 13 ICSID Review 51.

Hofbauer S, Burkart M and Tari M, "Survey on Scrutiny of Arbitral Institutions" in Philipp Habegger, Daniel Hochstrasser and Gabrielle Nater-Bass (eds), *Arbitral Institutions Under Scrutiny* (JurisNet 2013).

Hong Kong International Arbitration Centre, "Annual Report 2012, Available at http://www.hkiac.org/images/stories/hkiac/2012_annual%20report.pdf" (2012).

Hong Kong International Arbitration Centre, "The 2013 HKIAC Administered Arbitration Rules Unveiled (Press Release)" <http://www.hkiac.org/index.php/en/news/479> accessed 25 June 2013.

Horvath G, "The Judicialization of International Arbitration: Does the Increasing Introduction of Litigation-Style Practices, Regulations, Norms and Structures into International Arbitration Risk a Denial of Justice in International Business Disputes? (Chapter 13)" in Stefan Michael Kröll and Loukas A. Mistelis (eds),

International Arbitration and International Commercial Law: Synergy, Convergence and Evolution (Kluwer Law International 2011) <http://www.kluwerarbitration.com/CommonUI/document.aspx?id=KLI-KA-1143517-n> accessed 1 May 2012.

Hunter JMH, "Arbitration Procedure in England: Past, Present and Future" (1985) 1 Arbitration International, Kluwer Law International 82.

Hunter JMH, "Dubai International Arbitration Centre (DIAC)" in Loukas A Mistelis, Laurence Shore and Stavros Brekoulakis (eds), *The World Arbitration Reporter*, vol. 3 (Juris 2010).

Hwang M, Boo L and Han Y, "National Report for Singapore (2011)" (2011) Supplement no. 64 Jan Paulsson (ed), International Handbook on Commercial Arbitration, Kluwer Law International 1.

"IBA Guidelines on Conflicts of Interest in International Arbitration, Approved on 22 May 2004 by the Council of the International Bar Association".

ICC, "Techniques for Controlling Time and Costs in Arbitration: Report from the ICC Commission on Arbitration" (2007) ICC document no. 843.

Idid SA, "Kuala Lumpur Regional Centre for Arbitration-Impact of the Old and New Arbitration Act" (2006) 2 Asian International Arbitration Journal, Kluwer Law International 97.

Indlekofer M, *International Arbitration and the Permanent Court of Arbitration* (Wolters Kluwer Law & Business 2013).

International Chamber of Commerce, "2012 Statistical Report" (2013) 24 ICC Bulletin 6.

Jarrosson C, "L'instance Arbitrale: le Rôle Respectif de l'Institution, de l'Arbitre et des Parties dans l'Instance Arbitrale" (1990) 1990 Revue de l'Arbitrage 381.

Jarvin S and Young B, "A New Arbitration Regime in Sweden - The Swedish Arbitration Act 1999 and the Rules of the Stockholm Chamber of Commerce" (1999) 16 Journal of International Arbitration, Kluwer Law International 89.

Kačevska I, "Latvia", *The European, Middle Eastern and African Arbitration Review* (Global Arbitration Review 2014) <http://globalarbitrationreview.com/reviews/58/sections/203/chapters/2286/latvia/> accessed 14 August 2014.

Kaplan N, "Arbitration in Hong Kong" (1986) 3 Journal of International Arbitration, Kluwer Law International 7.

Kaplan N, "HKIAC's Perspective on Arbitration and Conciliation Concerning China" (2005) 12 Albert Jan van den Berg (ed), New Horizons in International Commercial Arbitration and Beyond, Kluwer Law International 55.

Kassis A, *Réflexions sur le Règlement d'Arbitrage de la Chambre de Commerce Internationale: les Déviations de l'Arbitrage Institutionnel* (Librairie Générale de Droit et de Jurisprudence 1988).

Kassis A, "The Questionable Validity of Arbitration and Awards under the Rules of the International Chamber of Commerce" (1989) 6 Journal of International Arbitration, Kluwer Law International 79.

Kee C, "The Evolving Role of an Appointing Authority" in Stefan Michael Kröll and Loukas A. Mistelis (eds), *International Arbitration and International Commercial Law: Synergy, Convergence and Evolution* (Kluwer Law International 2011).

Kerr SM, "London Court of International Arbitration" (1996) 7 Albert Jan van den Berg (ed), Planning Efficient Arbitration Proceedings: The Law Applicable in International Arbitration, Kluwer Law International 213.

Khodykin R, "International Commercial Arbitration Court (ICAC) and Maritime Arbitration Commission (MAC) at the Russian Federation Chamber of Commerce and Industry" in Loukas A Mistelis, Laurence Shore and Stavros Brekoulakis (eds), *The World Arbitration Reporter*, vol. 3 (Juris 2010).

Kirby J, "Insigma Technology Co. Ltd v. Alstom Technology Ltd SIAC Can Administer Cases under the ICC Rules?" (2009) 25 Arbitration International, Kluwer Law International 319.

Kirchner J and Marriott AL, "International Arbitration in the Aftermath of Socialism - The Example of the Berlin Court of Arbitration" (1993) 10 Journal of International Arbitration, Kluwer Law International 5.

Kleiman E and Pauly C, "Award Annulled Due to Withdrawn Counterclaims Introduced by Insolvent Defendant".

Komarov AS, "Introduction to the Revision of the Rules of the International Commercial Arbitration Court at the Chamber of Commerce and Industry of the Russian Federation (ICAC)" Albert Jan van den Berg (ed), Yearbook Commercial Arbitration, XXXI (Kluwer Law International 2006) 456.

Kröll DS, "Siemens – Dutco Revisited? Balancing Party Autonomy and Equality of the Parties in the Appointment Process in Multiparty Cases | Kluwer Arbitration Blog" <http://kluwerarbitrationblog.com/blog/2010/10/15/siemens-%e2%80%93-dutco-revisited-balancing-party-autonomy-and-equality-of-the-parties-in-the-appointment-process-in-multiparty-cases/> accessed 27 January 2014.

Kun F, "Prospects of Foreign Arbitration Institutions Administering Arbitration in China" (2011) 28 Journal of International Arbitration, Kluwer Law International 343.

Kurkela M and Turunen S, *Due Process in International Commercial Arbitration* (2nd edn, Oxford University Press 2010).

la Fontaine J De, "The Bat and the Two Weasels", *Recueil 1, Livre 2, Fable 5* (1668).

Lalive P, "Problèmes Relatifs à l'Arbitrage International Commercial" (1967) 120 Collected Courses of the Hague Academy of International Law, Martinus Nijhoff Publishers & Brill Academic.

Lalive P, "Case Commentary: Cour d'Appel de Paris 15 September 1988, Société Cubic Defense Systems v. CCI" (1999) 1999 Revue de l'Arbitrage 113.

Landau T, "The Effect of the New English Arbitration Act on Institutional Arbitration" (1996) 13 Journal of International Arbitration, Kluwer Law International 113.

Larsson H and Magnusson A, "Recent Practice of the Arbitration Institute of the Stockholm Chamber of Commerce: Prima Facie Jurisdiction and Challenges of Arbitrators" (2004) 2004 Stockholm Arbitration Report 47.

Leahy ER and Bianchi CJ, "The Changing Face of International Arbitration" (2000) 17 Journal of International Arbitration, Kluwer Law International 19.

Levine JM, "Ancients and Moderns Reconsidered" (1981) 15 Eighteenth-Century Studies 72.

Lew JDM, Mistelis LA and Kröll DS, *Comparative International Commercial Arbitration* (Kluwer Law International 2003).

Lionnet K, "The Arbitrator's Contract" (1999) 15 Arbitration International, Kluwer Law International 161.

London Court of International Arbitration, "Registrar's Report (2012), Available at http://www.lcia.org/LCIA/reports.aspx" (2013) http://www.lcia.org/LCIA/reports.aspx.

Loquin E, "La Sentence Arbitrale: L'Examen Du Projet de Sentence Par l'Institution et La Sentence Au Deuxième Degré - Réflexions Sur La Nature et La Validité de l'Intervention de l'Institution Arbitrale Sur La Sentence" (1990) 1990 Revue de l'Arbitrage 427.

Magnusson A, "The Practice of the Arbitration Institute of the Stockholm Chamber of Commerce — An Inside View" (2001) 2001 Stockholm Arbitration Report 45.

Magnusson A and Shaughnessy P, "The 2007 Arbitration Rules of the Arbitration Institute of the Stockholm Chamber of Commerce" (2006) 2006 Stockholm International Arbitration Review 33.

Mangan M, "The Arbitrator and the Arbitration Procedure - Sports Arbitration: Citius Altius Fortius?" (2009) 2011 Christian Klausegger, Peter Klein, et al. (eds), Austrian Yearbook on International Arbitration 301.

Mayton W, "The Legislative Resolution of the Rulemaking Versus Adjudication Problem in Agency Lawmaking" (1980) 29 Duke Law Journal 103.

McLean DJ, "Toward a New International Dispute Resolution Paradigm: Assessing the Congruent Evolution of Globalization and International Arbitration" (2009) 30 University of Pennsylvania Journal of International Economic Law 1087.

Menkel-Meadow C, "The Trouble with the Adversary System in a Postmodern, Multicultural World" (1996) 38 William and Mary Law Review 5.

Merkin R, *Arbitration Law* (3rd edn, Informa 2004).

"Merriam-Webster Dictionary, Online Edition, Available at Http://www.merriam-Webster.com/dictionary, Accessed 14 March 2014".

Mirèze P, "Les Pouvoirs de l'Arbitre et de La Cour d'Arbitrage de La CCI Relatifs à Leur Compétence" 2006 Revue de l'Arbitrage 591.

Mistelis LA, "Reality Test: Current State of Affairs in Theory and Practice Relating to 'Lex Arbitri'" (2006) 2006 American Review of International Arbitration 155.

Mosak H and Maniacci M, *Primer of Adlerian Psychology: The Analytic - Behavioural - Cognitive Psychology of Alfred Adler* (Routledge 1999).

Moser M and Yeoh F, "Choosing an Arbitral Institution Arbitration" (2006) 2 The In-House Perspective 18.

Moser MJ, "CIETAC Arbitration: A Success Story?" (1998) 15 Journal of International Arbitration, Kluwer Law International 27.

Moser MJ and Jianlong Y, "CIETAC and Its Work — An Interview with Vice Chairman Yu Jianlong" (2007) 24 Journal of International Arbitration, Kluwer Law International 555.

NAF, "Press Release: National Arbitration Forum to Cease Administering All Consumer Arbitrations in Response to Mounting Legal and Legislative Challenges, Available at: http://www.adrforum.com/newsroom.aspx?&itemID = 1528&news = 3".

Najar J-C, "Inside Out: A User's Perspective on Challenges in International Arbitration" (2009) 25 Arbitration International, Kluwer Law International 515.

Nariman FS, "The Spirit of Arbitration - The Tenth Annual Goff Lecture" (2000) 16 Arbitration International, Kluwer Law International 261.

Nesbitt S, "London Court of International Arbitration (LCIA) Arbitration Rules, 1998" in Loukas A Mistelis (ed), *Concise International Arbitration* (Kluwer Law International 2010).

Öhrström M, "The Arbitration Institute of the Stockholm Chamber of Commerce (SCC)" in Loukas A Mistelis, Laurence Shore and Stavros Brekoulakis (eds), *The World Arbitration Reporter*, vol. 3 (Juris 2010).

Öhrström M, "SCC Rules" in Rolf A Schütze (ed), *Institutional Arbitration: Article-by-Article Commentary* (Beck; Hart; Nomos 2013).

"Oxford English Dictionary, Online Edition, Available at Http://www.oxforddiction aries.com, Accessed 14 March 2014".

Park WW, "Rectitude in International Arbitration" (2011) 27 Arbitration International, Kluwer Law International 473.

Parra AR, "ICSID and the Rise of Bilateral Investment Treaties: Will ICSID Be the Leading Arbitration Institution in the Early 21st Century?" (2000) 94 Proceedings of the 101st Annual Meeting (American Society of International Law) 41.

Paulsson J, "Introduction (to the First Volume of Arb. Int.)" (1985) 1 Arbitration International, Kluwer Law International 2.

Paulsson J, "Vicarious Hypochondria and Institutional Arbitration" (1990) 6 Arbitration International, Kluwer Law International 226.

Paulsson J, "Moral Hazard in International Dispute Resolution, Inaugural Lecture as Holder of the Michael R. Klein Distinguished Scholar Chair University of Miami School of Law on 29 April 2010" (2011) 8 Transnational Dispute Management (TDM).

Paulsson J and Rawding N (eds), *The Freshfields Guide to Arbitration Clauses in International Contracts* (3rd edn, Kluwer Law International 2010).

Pendell G, "The Rise and Rise of the Arbitration Institution" <http://kluwerarbitrationblog.com/blog/2011/11/30/the-rise-and-rise-of-the-arbitration-institution/> accessed 16 April 2012.

Pontavice E du, "Un Centre Spécialisé: La Chambre Arbitrale Maritime de Paris" (1990) 1990 Revue de l'Arbitrage 239.

Poudret J-F, "Deux Aspects de l'Arbitrage Dans Les Pays Romands Au Moyen Age: L'Arbitrabilité et Le Juge-Arbitre" (1999) 1999 Revue de l'Arbitrage 3.

Queen Mary, University of London, "Corporate Attitudes and Practices: Recognition and Enforcement of Foreign Awards" www.arbitrationonline.org/research.

Queen Mary, University of London, "Current and Preferred Practices in the Arbitral Process" www.arbitrationonline.org/research.

Queen Mary, University of London, "Corporate Choices in International Arbitration: An Industry Approach" www.arbitrationonline.org/research.

Rahman A, "An Insight Into The Application of Arbitral Theory: Arising Judicial Practice" (2011) 7 Asian International Arbitration Journal, Kluwer Law International 97.

Reed L, Paulsson J and Blackaby N, *Guide to ICSID Arbitration* (2nd edn, Kluwer Law International 2011).

"Report of the Working Group on Arbitration and Conciliation on the Work of Its Forty-Eighth Session (New York, 4-8 February 2008), UN Doc. A/CN.9/646".

Ridgway DA, "International Arbitration: The Next Growth Industry" (1999) 54 Dispute Resolution Journal 50.

Risse J, "Commentary on the Arbitration Rules of the German Institution of Arbitration (DIS Rules), Article 26 (Due Process)" in Karl-Heinz Bockstiegel, Dr Stefan Kröll and Patricia Nacimiento (eds), *Arbitration in Germany: The Model Law in Practice* (Kluwer Law International 2007).

Sabater A, "When Arbitration Begins Without a Seat" (2010) 27 Journal of International Arbitration, Kluwer Law International 443.

Sanders P, "Trends in the Field of International Commercial Arbitration", (1975) 145 Collected Courses of the Hague Academy of International Law, Martinus Nijhoff Publishers & Brill Academic.

Scherer M, "Decisions of Private Bodies and Institutions Cannot Be Challenged under Art. 190 PIL Act - Really?" (2004) 32 ASA Bulletin, Kluwer Law International 102.

Schlaepfer AV, "The Role of the Institution at the Commencement of the Proceedings" in Philipp Habegger, Daniel Hochstrasser and Gabrielle Nater-Bass (eds), *Arbitral Institutions Under Scrutiny* (JurisNet 2013).

Schlaepfer AV and Bartsch P, "Swiss Chambers" Court of Arbitration and Mediation (Swiss Chambers)" in Loukas A Mistelis, Laurence Shore and Stavros Brekoulakis (eds), *The World Arbitration Reporter*, vol. 3 (Juris 2010).

Schlaepfer AV and Petti AM, "Institutional versus Ad Hoc Arbitration" in Elliott Geisinger and Nathalie Voser (eds), *International Arbitration in Switzerland - A Handbook for Practitioners* (Kluwer Law International 2013).

Schneider A, "Not Quite a World Without Trials: Why International Dispute Resolution Is Increasingly Judicialized" (2006) 2006 Journal of Dispute Resolution 119.

Scholdstrom P, "Contractual Relations in Institutional Arbitration" in Kaj Hobér, Annette Magnusson and Marie Öhrström (eds), *Between East and West: Essays in Honour of Ulf Franke* (Juris, 2010).

Schwartz EA, "The Role of the Arbitral Institution in the New Millennium" (1999) 65 Arbitration 321.

Schwartz EA, "Is Procedure Really Neutral? The Seat: Does It Matter? (A Tale of More than Two Cities)", A Contribution by the ITA Board of Reporters' (2012) 6 Dispute Resolution International.

Schwarz FT and Konrad CW, *The Vienna Rules: A Commentary on International Arbitration in Austria* (Kluwer Law International 2009).

Segesser G von, Jolles A and Stark-Traber S, "Swiss Rules of International Arbitration" in Karyl Nairn and Patrick Heneghan (eds), *Arbitration World: Institutional & Jurisdictional Comparisons* (4th Revised edn, Thomson Reuters 2012).

Seppälä C, "Recommended Strategy for Getting the Right International Arbitral Tribunal: A Practitioner's View" (2009) 6 Transnational Dispute Management (TDM).

Shapiro D, "The Choice of Rulemaking or Adjudication in the Development of Administrative Policy" (1965) 78 Harvard Law Review 921.

Shaughnessy P, "Pre-Arbitral Urgent Relief: The New SCC Emergency Arbitrator Rules" (2010) 27 Journal of International Arbitration, Kluwer Law International 337.

Sheppard A, "Chapter 23 - English Arbitration Act" in Loukas A Mistelis (ed), *Concise International Arbitration* (Kluwer Law International 2010).

Sidklev J, "Arbitration Institute of the Stockholm Chamber of Commerce (SCC)" in Karyl Nairn and Patrick Heneghan (eds), *Arbitration World: Institutional & Jurisdictional Comparisons* (4th Revised edn, Thomson Reuters 2012).

Sinclair A, "ICSID Arbitration: How Long Does It Take?" (2009) 4 Global Arbitration Review.

Slate WK, "International Arbitration: Do Institutions Make a Difference?" (1996) 31 Wake Forest Law Review 41.

Smit H, "The Future of International Commercial Arbitration: A Single Transnational Institution" (1986) 25 Columbia Journal of Transnational Law 9.

Smith G, "Commentary on the New Singapore International Arbitration Centre Rules" (2010) 76 Arbitration 727.

Söderlund C, "The Parties' Contract with the Arbitration Institution" in Kaj Hobér, Annette Magnusson and Marie Öhrström (eds), *Between East and West: Essays in Honour of Ulf Franke* (Juris 2010).

Song L, "The New CIETAC Arbitration Rules of 2012" (2012) 29 Journal of International Arbitration, Kluwer Law International 299.

Steindl B, "The Development of Due Process under the New York Convention" (2008) 2008 Christian Klausegger, Peter Klein, et al. (eds), Austrian Yearbook on International Arbitration 255.

Stockholm Chamber of Commerce, "The SCC in Numbers – Statistics 2012, Available at http://www.offentligupphandling.se/?id=23696&newsid=44876".

Swiss Chambers' Arbitration Institution, "Internal Rules of the Arbitration Court of the Swiss Chambers' Arbitration Institution, Available at: https://www.swissarbitration.org/sa/download/internal_rules_2012.pdf" https://www.swissarbitration.org/sa/download/internal_rules_2012.pdf.

Szász I, "The Value of a Network of Arbitration Institutions" (1982) 1 Pieter Sanders (ed), New Trends in the Development of International Commercial Arbitration and the Role of Arbitral and Other Institutions, Kluwer Law International 26.

Thompson BJ, "Building an Arbitration and Mediation Centre: From International Foundations to Domestic Rooftops": The Establishment of the British Columbia International Commercial Arbitration Centre" (1988) 4 Pieter Sanders (ed), Arbitration in Settlement of International Commercial Disputes Involving the Far East and Arbitration in Combined Transportation, Kluwer Law International 189.

To CW, "Developments of the Hong Kong International Arbitration Centre" (2000) 28 International Business Lawyer 506.

Truttmann A and Segesser G von, "Swiss and Swiss-Based Arbitral Institutions" in Nathalie Voser and Elliott Geisinger (eds), *International Arbitration in Switzerland - A Handbook for Practitioners* (Kluwer Law International 2013).

Tschanz PY, "Advocacy in International Commercial Arbitration: Switzerland" in R Doak Bishop (ed), *The Art of Advocacy in International Arbitration* (1st edn, Juris 2004).

Tse C, "Mais Jusqu'Où Ira-T-On? Après Les Arbitres et Les Centres d'Arbitrage, On S'en Prend Au Juge de l'Annulation, Note Sous Cass. Civ. 1iere, 11 Mars 2009: Trioplast AB" [2009] Petites Affiches 20.

Uzelac A, "Succession of Arbitral Institutions" (1996) 3 Croatian Arbitration Yearbook 71.

van den Berg AJ, "CIETAC Amended Arbitration Rules 2000 Embrace the New Century" in Albert Jan van den Berg (ed), *Yearbook Commercial Arbitration*, XXVI (Kluwer Law International 2001) <http://www.kluwerarbitration.com/CommonUI/document.aspx?id=ipn22909> accessed 1 May 2012.

van den Berg AJ, "Commentary of: US No. 636 Global Gold Mining LLC v Peter M Robinson Et. Al., US District Court, SDNY, 6 February 2008" in Albert Jan van den Berg (ed), *Yearbook Commercial Arbitration*, XXXIII (Kluwer Law International 2008) 1117.

van Houtte H, "The Delivery of Awards to the Parties" (2005) 21 Arbitration International, Kluwer Law International 177.

van Houtte H and McAsey B, "The Liability of Arbitrators and Arbitral Institutions" in Philipp Habegger, Daniel Hochstrasser and Gabrielle Nater-Bass (eds), *Arbitral Institutions Under Scrutiny* (JurisNet 2013).

Veeder VV, "Strategic Management in Commencing an Arbitration" in Albert Jan van den Berg (ed), Arbitration Advocacy in Changing Times, vol. 15 (Kluwer Law International 2011) 27.

Vigras B, "The Role of Institutions in Arbitration" in Ronald Bernstein and Derek Wood (eds), *Handbook of Arbitration Practice* (2nd edn, Sweet & Maxwell in conjunction with the Chartered Institute of Arbitrators 1993).

Voser N, "Multi-Party Disputes and Joinder of Third Parties" in Albert Jan van den Berg (ed), *50 Years of the New York Convention: ICCA International Arbitration Conference in Dublin*, vol. 14 (Kluwer Law International 2009) 343.

Voser N, "Removal, Resignation, Dismissal and Replacement of Arbitrators" in Philipp Habegger, Daniel Hochstrasser and Gabrielle Nater-Bass (eds), *Arbitral Institutions Under Scrutiny* (JurisNet 2013).

Waincymer J, *Procedure and Evidence in International Arbitration* (Kluwer Law International 2012).

Weber-Stecher U, "Principles of Good Governance and Organisation of Arbitral Institutions" in Philipp Habegger, Daniel Hochstrasser and Gabrielle Nater-Bass (eds), *Arbitral Institutions Under Scrutiny* (JurisNet 2013).

Wilske S and Fox T, "The Global Competition for the "Best Place" for International Arbitration - Myth, Prejudice, and Reality Bits" [2009] Austrian Arbitration Yearbook 383.

Winstanley A, "Review of the London Court of International Arbitration" in Horacio A Grigera Naón and Paul E Mason (eds), *International Commercial Arbitration Practice: 21st Century Perspectives* (LexisNexis 2010).

Winstanley A, "Arbitral Appointments at the LCIA" (2013) 1 ABA Newsletter, Section of International Law, International Arbitration Committee 31.

Wunschheim C von and Kun F, "Arbitrating in China: The Rules of the Game - Practical Recommendations Concerning Arbitration in China" (2008) 26 ASA Bulletin, Kluwer Law International 35.

Xiaobing Xu and Wilson GD, "One Country, Two-International Commercial Arbitration-Systems" (2000) 17 Journal of International Arbitration, Kluwer Law International 47.

Yesilirmak A, *Provisional Measures in International Commercial Arbitration* (Kluwer Law International 2005).

Yesilirmak A, "Provisional Measures" in Loukas A Mistelis and Julian DM Lew (eds), *Pervasive Problems in International Arbitration* (Kluwer Law International 2006).

Yong Tong A, "SIAC: Arbitration in the New Millennium" [2000] Law Gazette (Singapore) http://www.lawgazette.com.sg/2000-1.

Yuryev S and Kantyrev, "Arbitration in Russia" in Torsten Loercher, Guy Pendell and Jeremy Wilson (eds), *CMS Guide to Arbitration* (4th edn, CMS Legal Services 2012) <http://www.lexology.com/library/detail.aspx?g=2eb32797-8ffb-433a-910d-8d84bc8f5c72> accessed 6 August 2013.

Zhou J, "Arbitration Agreements in China: Battles on Designation of Arbitral Institution and Ad Hoc Arbitration" (2006) 23 Journal of International Arbitration, Kluwer Law International 145.

Ziadé NG, "Reflections on the Role of Institutional Arbitration Between the Present and the Future" (2009) 25 Arbitration International, Kluwer Law International 427.

Zuberbühler T, Muller K and Habegger PA, "Introduction to the Swiss Rules" in Tobias Zuberbühler and Klaus Muller (eds), *Swiss Rules of International Arbitration: Commentary* (Kluwer Law International 2005).

Zykin I, "Procedural Aspects of the Activities of Institutional Arbitration Bodies" in Kaj Hobér, Annette Magnusson and Marie Öhrström (eds), *Between East and West: Essays in Honour of Ulf Franke* (Juris 2010).

Internet Sources

Website of Beijing Arbitration Commission, Http://www.bjac.org.cn/en (1 July 2013) <http://www.bjac.org.cn/en> accessed 9 April 2014.

Website of JAMS, Http://www.jamsadr.com (1 July 2013) <http://www.jamsadr.com> accessed 1 July 2013.

Website of the American Arbitration Association (AAA), Http://www.adr.org/aaa/faces/home (13 June 2013) <http://www.adr.org/aaa/faces/home> accessed 13 June 2013.

Website of the Arbitration Institute of the Stockholm Chamber of Commerce (SCC), Http://www.sccinstitute.com (16 June 2013) <http://www.sccinstitute.com> accessed 16 June 2013.

Website of the Australian Centre for International Commercial Arbitration (ACICA), Http://acica.org.au (17 July 2013) <http://acica.org.au> accessed 17 July 2013.

Website of the Belgian Centre for Arbitration and Mediation (CEPANI), Http://www.cepani.be (13 September 2013) <http://www.cepani.be> accessed 13 September 2013.

Website of the Cairo Regional Centre for International Commercial Arbitration (CRCICA), Http://www.crcica.org.eg (12 February 2013) <http://www.crcica.org.eg> accessed 2 February 2013.

Website of the China International Economic and Trade Arbitration Commission (CIETAC), Http://www.cietac.org (12 February 2013) <http://www.cietac.org> accessed 2 July 2013.

Website of the China Maritime Arbitration Commission (CMAC), Http://www.cmac-Sh.org/en/home.asp (1 July 2013) <http://www.cmac-sh.org/en/home.asp> accessed 2 July 2013.

Website of the Dubai International Arbitration Centre (DIAC), Http://www.diac.ae/idias (15 July 2013) <http://www.diac.ae/idias> accessed 31 July 2013.

Website of the Federation of Oils, Seeds and Fats Associations (FOSFA), Http://www.fosfa.org (15 February 2013) <http://www.fosfa.org> accessed 15 February 2013.

Website of the German Institution of Arbitration (DIS), Http://www.dis-Arb.de/scho/ (12 February 2013) <http://www.dis-arb.de/scho/> accessed 12 February 2013.

Website of the Government Communication Office of the Republic of Slovenia, Http://www.slovenia.si (4 September 2014) <http://www.slovenia.si> accessed 9 April 2014.

Website of the Hong Kong International Arbitration Centre (HKIAC), Http://www.hkiac.org (2 April 2013) <http://www.hkiac.org> accessed 2 February 2013.

Website of the ICC's International Court of Arbitration, Http://www.iccwbo.org/about-Icc/organization/dispute-Resolution-Services/icc-International-Court-of-Arbitration (2 April 2014) <http://www.iccwbo.org/about-icc/organization/dispute-resolution-services/icc-international-court-of-arbitration> accessed 2 April 2014.

Website of the International Centre for Settlement of Investment Disputes (ICSID), https://icsid.worldbank.org/ICSID (17 March 2014) <https://icsid.worldbank.org/ICSID/FrontServlet> accessed 17 March 2014.

Website of the International Commercial Arbitration Court at the Chamber of Commerce and Industry of the Russian Federation (ICAC), Http://www.tpprf-Mkac.ru/en (4 April 2014) <http://www.tpprf-mkac.ru/en/component/content/article/385-mkacmain> accessed 9 April 2014.

Website of the International Court of Justice (ICJ), Http://www.icj-Cij.org (21 March 2013) <http://www.icj-cij.org> accessed 21 March 2013.

Website of the International Tribunal for the Law of the Sea, Http://www.itlos.org (21 March 2013) <http://www.itlos.org> accessed 21 March 2013.

Website of the Internet Corporation for Assigned Names and Numbers (ICANN) (12 February 2013) <http://www.icann.org/en/help/dndr/udrp/providers> accessed 15 July 2013.

Website of the Kuala Lumpur Regional Centre for Arbitration, Http://www.klrca.org (21 July 2015).

Website of the London Court of International Arbitration (LCIA), Http://www.lcia.org (2 April 2014) <http://www.lcia.org> accessed 2 April 2014.

Website of the London Maritime Arbitrators Association (LMAA), Http://www.lmaa.org.uk (25 February 2013) <http://www.lmaa.org.uk> accessed 15 February 2013.

Website of the Maritime Arbitration Commission at the Chamber of Commerce and Industry of the Russian Federation (MAC), Http://www.tpprf-Arb.ru/en/mac (4 April 2014) <http://www.tpprf-arb.ru/en/mac> accessed 9 April 2014.

Website of the Permanent Court of Arbitration (PCA), Http://www.pca-Cpa.org (17 March 2014) <http://www.pca-cpa.org/> accessed 17 March 2014.

Website of the Singapore International Arbitration Centre (SIAC), Http://www.siac.org.sg (12 February 2013) <http://www.siac.org.sg> accessed 12 February 2013.

Website of the UN Compensation Commission (UNCC), Http://www.uncc.ch (15 February 2013) <http://www.uncc.ch> accessed 15 February 2013.

Website of the US-Iran Claims Tribunal, Http://www.iusct.net (15 February 2013) <http://www.iusct.net> accessed 15 February 2013.

Website of the World Intellectual Property Organization, Http://www.wipo.int/portal/index.html.en (17 July 2013) <http://www.wipo.int/portal/index.html.en> accessed 17 July 2013.

Table of Cases

Adam Technologies International SA de CV v. Sutherland Global Services, Incorporated, United States Court of Appeals, Fifth Circuit, 5 September 2013, **122**

Arab Republic of Egypt v. Westland Helicopters Ltd, Swiss Federal Tribunal, 16 May 1983 (Bulletin de l'ASA, 1984, at p 203) (1983) 1984 Bulletin de l'ASA 203 (Swiss Federal Tribunal), **92, 179**

Austern v. Chicago Board Options Exchange, United States Court of Appeals, Second Circuit, 15 March 1990 (898 F2d 882), **168**

Chambre Arbitrale de Paris, Sociétés Carfa Trade Group et Omnium de Travaux v. Republique de Guinee, Cour d'Appel de Paris (1re Ch A), 4 May 1988 (Revue de l'Arbitrage, 1988, at p. 656), **139, 142**

Decision of the High Court of the Canton of Zürich, 29 June 1979, **169**

Decision of the Swiss Federal Tribunal, Ref No 4A-282/2013, 13 November 2013 (Bulletin de l'ASA, 2014, at p. 89), **169**

Decision of the Swiss Federal Tribunal, Ref No 4A-600/2008, 20 February 2009 (Bulletin de l'ASA, 2009, at p. 568), **170**

Decision of the Swiss Federal Tribunal, Ref No 4A-644/2009, 13 April 2010 (Bulletin de l'ASA, 2011, at p. 107), **169**

Encyclopaedia Universalis SA v. Encyclopaedia Britannica Inc, United States Court of Appeals, Second Circuit, 31 March 2005 (403 F3d 85), **168, 194**

Federal Court of Justice Decision, 20 January 1994, Ref no III ZR 143/92, **170**

Global Gold Mining, LLC v. Robinson et al, United States District Court, Southern District of New York, 6 February 2008 (533 F Supp 2d), **149**

Goldtron Limited v. Media Most BV, Rechtbank of Amterdam, 27 August 2002 (Yearbook Commercial Arbitration, 2003, at p. 814), **193, 194, 197**

Hawkins v. National Association of Securities Dealers Inc, United States Court of Appeals, Fifth Circuit, 23 June 1998 (149 F3d 330), **168**

Insigma Technology Co Ltd v. Alstom Technology Ltd, Singapore Court of Appeal, 2 June 2009 (Singapore Law Report, 2009, 3, at p 24) (2009) [2009] 3 SLR(R) Singapore Law Report 936 (Singapore Court of Appeal), **49**

International Medical Group v. American Arbitration Association, United States Court of Appeals, Seventh Circuit, 3 December 2002 (312 F3d 833), **168**

Keban judgement, Supreme Court of Turkey, 10 March 1976 (excerpt quoted in Arbitration, Volume 46, 1980, p. 241), **168**

Mr X v. Trioplast AB, Cour de Cassation, 1iere Chambre Civile, 11 mars 2009 (decision available on www.KluwerArbitration.com; Contribution by the ITA Board of Reporters), **144**

Olson v. National Association of Securities Dealers, United States Court of Appeals, Eighth Circuit, 7 June 1996 (85 F3d 381), **168**

Raffineries de Pétrole d'Homs et de Banias v. Chambre de Commerce Internationale, Cour d'Appel de Paris, 15 May 1985 (Revue de l'Arbitrage, 1985, at p 141) (1985) 1985 Revue de l'Arbitrage 141 (Cour d'Appel de Paris), **92, 130, 132, 139, 179**

Raffineries de Pétrole d'Homs et de Banias v. Chambre de Commerce Internationale, Tribunal de Grande Instance, 28 March 1984 (Revue de l'Arbitrage, 1985, at p 141) (1984) 1985 Revue de l'Arbitrage 141 (Tribunal de Grande Instance de Paris), **130, 155**

République de Guinée v. Chambre Arbitrale de Paris et autres, Tribunal de Grande Instance de Paris, 28 January 1987 (Revue de l'Arbitrage, 1987, p. 371), **142, 190, 191, 202**

République de Guinée v. Mm R et O, Tribunal de Grande Instance, 23 June 1988 (Revue de l'Arbitrage, 1988, at p 657) (1988) 1988 Revue de l'Arbitrage 657 (Tribunal de Grande Instance de Paris), **143**

Société ABC International v. Chambre de Commerce International, Cour d'Appel de Paris, 27 October 2011 (Revue de l'Arbitrage 2011, at p. 991), **137**

Société ABC International v. Chambre de Commerce International, Tribunal de Grande Instance (Ref), 25 November 2010 (Revue de l'Arbitrage, 2011, at p. 991), **137, 145**

Société Appareils Dragon, Cour d'Appel de Paris, 22 June 1982 (Revue de l'Arbitrage, 1982, at p 91) (1982) 1982 Revue de l'Arbitrage 91 (Cour d'Appel de Paris), **94, 126**

Société Appareils Dragon, Cour de Cassation, 2ieme Chambre Civile, 8 June 1983 (Revue de l'Arbitrage, 1987, at p 309) (1983) 1987 Revue de l'Arbitrage 309 (Cour de Cassation, 2ieme Chambre Civile), **68, 94, 126, 158**

Société Československa Obchodní Banka AS,Cour de Cassation, 19 May 1987 (Revue de l'Arbitrage, 1987, at p 367) (1987) 1987 Revue de l'Arbitrage 367 (Cour de Cassation), **137**

Société Commerciale de Produits Agricoles (SCPA) v. Société Coopérative de la Roche Clermault, Cour d'Appel de Paris, 29 November 1985 (Revue de l'Arbitrage, 1987, at p. 335), **135, 152, 155**

Société Cubic Defense Systems Inc v. Chambre de Commerce Internationale, Cour d'Appel de Paris, 15 September 1998 (Revue de l'Arbitrage, 1999, at p. 103), **139, 147, 191**

Société Cubic Defense Systems Inc v. Chambre de Commerce Internationale, Cour de Cassation, 1ere Chambre Civile, 20 February 2001 (Revue de l'Arbitrage 2001, at p. 511), **139, 141, 161**

Société Cubic Defense Systems Inc v. Chambre de Commerce Internationale, Tribunal de Grande Instance de Paris, 21 May 1997, **139**

Société Lear v. Chambre de Commerce Internationale, Tribunal de Grande Instance de Paris, 22 May 2002 (Revue de l'Arbitrage, 2002, at p. 785), **144**

Société Licensing Projects SL v. Société Pirelli, Cour d'Appel de Paris, 17 November 2011, **88, 191**

Société Licensing Projects SL v. Société Pirelli, Cour de Cassation, 28 mars 2013, **89, 191**

Société Opinter France v. SARL Dacomex, Cour d'Appel de Paris, 15 January 1985 (Revue de l'Arbitrage, 1986, at p 87) (1985) 1986 Revue de l'Arbitrage 87 (Cour d'Appel de Paris), **133**

Société Opinter France v. SARL Dacomex, Cour de Cassation, 2 Ch civ, 7 October 1987 (Revue de l'Arbitrage, 1987, at p 479) (1987) 1987 Revue de l'Arbitrage 479 (Cour de Cassation, 2 Ch civ), **92, 133, 135, 179**

Société REDEC et M Pharaon v. Société Uzinexport Import et Chambre de Commerce Internationale, Tribunal de Grande Instance de Paris (Ref), 13 July 1988 (Revue de l'Arbitrage, 1989, at p. 97), **137, 156**

Société Replor v. SARL Ploemeloise de Financement de Participations and Others, Cour d'Appel de Paris, 12 January 1988 (Revue de l'Arbitrage, 1988, at p. 691), **139, 145**

Sociétés BKMI et Siemens v. Société Dutco (1992) 1992 Yearbook Commercial Arbitration 124 (Cour de Cassation), **77, 195, 202**

Société SNF v. Chambre de Commerce Internationale, Cour d'Appel de Paris, 22 January 2009 (Revue de l'Arbitrage, 2009, at p. 233), **144**

Société SNF v. Chambre de Commerce Internationale, Tribunal de Grande Instance de Paris, 10 October 2007 (Revue de l'Arbitrage, 2007, at p. 847), **144**

Société Techni-Import Professionnel v. Société Electro Scientific Industries, Cour d'Appel de Paris, 17 May 1983 (Revue de l'Arbitrage, 1987, at p 309) (1983) 1987 Revue de l'Arbitrage 309 (Cour d'Appel de Paris), **68, 129, 158, 161**

State Joint Stock Company (Uzbekistan) v. State agency (India), Final Award, ICC Case No. 14667, 2011 in Albert Jan van den Berg (ed), Yearbook Commercial Arbitration 2015 - Volume 40, (Kluwer Law International; 2015) p. 60, **145**

Buyer (Nigeria), v. Seller (US), Partial Final Award, ICC Case No. 15652, 2010 in Albert Jan van den Berg (ed), Yearbook Commercial Arbitration 2015 - Volume 40, (Kluwer Law International; 2015) p. 178, **145**

Table of Arbitration Rules Examined

Institution	*Title of Arbitration Rules & Year of Publication*
AAA/ICDR	International Arbitration Rules (2009 and 2014), **12, 14, 15, 21, 24–26, 30, 31, 37, 47, 56, 58–63, 65, 67, 70, 77, 81, 82–89, 91–93, 96, 97, 100, 101, 108, 110, 113, 121, 122, 153, 163, 177, 178, 181, 187, 192, 197, 198, 201, 203–206, 208**
ACICA	Arbitration Rules (2011 and 2016), **56, 61, 63, 65, 77, 81, 82, 85, 87, 89, 91, 96, 99, 105, 111, 113, 153, 163, 178, 188, 206**
BCICAC	International Commercial Arbitration Rules of Procedure (2000), **22, 77, 96, 100**
BAC	Beijing Arbitration Commission Arbitration Rules (2008 and 2015), **10, 27, 69, 93, 100, 103, 203**
Bulgarian Ch. of Com. and Ind.	Rules of the Court of Arbitration (1993), **3, 69, 90, 100**
CAMEX	Reglas de Arbitraje del CAM (2009), **60, 63, 66, 75, 84, 85, 89, 96, 100, 153, 163, 178, 187, 188, 193, 199, 206**
CAMP	Arbitration Rules (2012), **100**
CAS	Procedural Rules of the CAS (2013), **24, 56, 57, 63, 65, 66, 70, 72, 75, 77–79, 81, 83, 86, 88–91, 96, 100, 108, 110, 113, 145, 153, 157, 163, 170, 177–179, 187, 188, 192, 205, 206**
CEDRAC	Arbitration Rules (2012), **3, 9, 10, 22, 84**

Institution	*Title of Arbitration Rules & Year of Publication*
CEPANI	Arbitration Rules (2013), **61, 74, 75, 77, 78, 96, 100, 163, 178, 187**
CIETAC	Arbitration Rules (2012 and 2015), **26, 43, 48, 58–60, 63, 65, 69, 74, 77, 79, 81–85, 88– 93, 97, 99, 100, 106, 108, 111, 113, 153, 162, 163, 177, 178, 182, 187, 188, 193**
CRCICA	CRCICA Arbitration Rules (2011), **14, 20, 56, 57, 63, 69, 77, 82, 96, 100, 110–112**
DIA (Denmark)	Rules of Procedure (2013), **76, 79, 89, 91, 100**
DIAC	DIAC Arbitration Rules (2007), **10, 12, 22, 26, 57, 93, 103, 199**
DIS	DIS Arbitration Rules (1998), **14, 17, 21, 56, 57, 63, 74, 77, 79, 90, 119, 145, 170, 174, 203**
DIA	Rules of Arbitration Procedure of the Danish Institute of Arbitration (2013), **3, 76, 96, 100, 206**
ECAFE	ECAFE Rules of International Commercial Arbitration (1966), **15**
FCC	Rules of Arbitration of the Finland Chamber of Commerce (2013), **70, 81, 100**
FOSFA	Rules of Arbitrations and Appeals (2012), **7, 8, 18, 25**
GAFTA	Gafta Arbitration Rules (Rules no. 125) (2012), **7, 25**
HKIAC	HKIAC Administered Arbitration Rules (2013), **12, 24, 20, 22, 26, 31, 41, 42, 45, 57, 58, 60, 61, 63, 65, 67, 70, 75, 77–79, 81, 82, 85, 86, 88, 91, 93, 95, 99, 106, 110, 113, 163, 179, 181, 187, 193, 203–205**

Institution	*Title of Arbitration Rules & Year of Publication*
ICAC	Rules of the International Commercial Arbitration Court at the Russian Chamber of Commerce and Industry (2005and 2010), **10, 14, 22, 45, 48, 60, 65, 72, 73, 77, 78, 86–91, 93, 97, 99, 100, 108, 100, 113, 153, 157, 163, 178, 182, 188, 192, 194, 195, 197, 201, 203, 204, 206**
ICC	Rules of Arbitration of the International Chamber of Commerce (1975, 1988, 1998, 2012), **12, 25, 27, 30, 31, 32, 35–37, 39–43, 45, 47, 49, 50, 52, 53, 56, 58, 60, 61, 63, 64, 67–70, 72, 74–92, 94, 96, 98–110, 113, 119, 120, 121, 127–142, 144, 145, 147, 149–151, 153, 154, 156–158, 160–168, 172, 174, 176–180, 182, 187–193, 195, 199, 202, 206**
ICSID	Rules of Procedure for Arbitration Proceedings (Arbitration Rules), **82, 90, 96, 97**
ICSID	Rules of Procedure for the Institution of Conciliation and Arbitration Proceedings (Institution Rules), **60**
JAMS	JAMS International Arbitration Rules (2011), **3, 23, 56, 62, 64, 75–77, 82, 96, 100, 101, 103, 110, 113, 163, 177, 187, 205**
KCAB	Rules of International Arbitration (2011), **31, 56, 77, 96, 101**
KIAC	KIAC Arbitration Rules (2012), **84, 100**
LCIA	LCIA Arbitration Rules (1998 and 2014), **2, 3, 12, 14, 16, 19, 25, 26, 30, 31, 36, 37, 40–43, 45, 47, 50, 56–61, 63, 65–67, 70, 72–74, 77, 79–83, 85, 86, 88–91, 93, 96, 99, 101, 103, 106–108, 110, 113, 121, 124, 153, 157, 163, 177–179, 181, 187, 188, 192, 193, 199, 202, 204–206, 209**
LCIA India	LCIA India Arbitration Rules (2010), **3, 50, 81**

Institution	***Title of Arbitration Rules & Year of Publication***
LMAA	LMAA Terms (2006), **7, 8, 18**
MAC	Rules of the Maritime Arbitration Commission at the Chamber of Commerce and Industry of the Russian Federation (2006), **10, 22, 26, 48, 72, 73, 90, 157, 162, 201**
Milan Chamber	Arbitration Rules (2010), **3, 22, 56, 60, 63, 65, 70, 74, 77, 81, 89, 91, 96, 99, 153, 163, 178, 187, 188**
PCA	Arbitration Rules (2012), **19, 30, 84**
PCC	Rules of the Court of Arbitration at the Polish Chamber of Commerce in Warsaw (2007), **81, 82, 96**
SCC	Arbitration Rules of the Arbitration Institute of the Stockholm Chamber of Commerce (2010), **12, 19, 22, 31, 41, 45, 52, 56–58, 60–62, 67, 70–75, 79, 81–86, 88–93, 99, 102, 103, 106, 110, 113, 120, 153, 157, 163, 178–181, 188, 192, 199**
SIAC	Arbitration Rules of the Singapore International Arbitration Centre, 5th edition (2013), **14, 17, 31, 48, 49, 56, 58, 60–62, 65, 66, 70, 71, 74, 77, 79, 81–83, 86–91, 93, 96, 99–101, 103, 104, 106, 110, 113, 153, 157, 163, 178, 179, 181, 187, 188, 192, 193, 199, 205, 206**
Swiss Institution	Swiss Rules of International Arbitration (2012), **3, 22, 26, 45, 46, 48, 50, 51, 62, 70, 86, 101, 103, 106, 108, 145, 181, 192, 201**
UNCITRAL	Arbitration Rules (1976 and 2010), **13–17, 19, 40, 41, 60, 69, 80, 86, 96, 105, 193, 203**
VIAC	Rules of Arbitration and Conciliation (2006 and 2013), **56, 60, 74, 77, 85, 88, 96, 101, 104, 145, 193**

Institution	***Title of Arbitration Rules & Year of Publication***
WIPO	WIPO Arbitration Rules (2002), **24, 56, 58, 61, 63, 64, 66, 70, 77, 88–91, 96, 97, 99, 101, 110, 113, 153, 163, 177–179, 187, 188**
Croatian Chamber of Economy (Zagreb)	Rules of Arbitration of the Permanent Arbitration Court at the Croatian Chamber of Economy (Zagreb rules) (2002), **3, 96**

Index

A

Adjudicative mission
  indivisibility of, 142, 145, 158
  unity of, 139, 163–173
Adjudicative phase, 136, 137
Administered arbitration, 43, 44, 173
Administrative case law, 181
Administrative nature, 119, 138, 147, 156
Advances on arbitration costs. *See* Deposits
Adversarial process, 123, 124, 136, 146, 152, 186, 199, 204–205, 214
Annulment of award, 94, 124, 126, 127, 130, 131, 133, 136, 138, 140, 191, 195
Antoine Kassis, 164
Appointment
  arbitrators, 4, 63, 68, 78, 79, 91, 109, 125, 143, 180, 181, 193, 195
  decision-making, institutions, 174
  default, 7, 81, 154
  direct, 125
  by government, 23
  institutional, 103, 107
  issues, 59
  joint, 76
  LCIA rules, 12
  mechanisms, 42, 55
  party-appointment, 7
  post-appointment, 83–86, 89, 91, 96, 107, 113–115, 153
  pre-appointment, 109–112, 152
  process, 4, 27
  and replacement of arbitrators, 205
  revoke, ICC, 130
  SCC rules, 67
  stage, 174
  tribunal, 12, 66, 78, 84

B

Berlin Clause, 170

C

Caseload
  analysis, 25
  annual, 73
  ICC, 30, 31
  ICDR's, 25
  institutions, 34, 57, 69
  international commercial arbitration cases, 3
  limit, 34
  statistical information, 29
Challenges of arbitrators, 180
Channel of communication, 17
Collective decision-making, 93, 118, 125, 141, 146, 154, 171, 173–183, 185–188, 214
Confirmation of arbitrators, 82–83, 91, 110–111, 192
Consolidation
  applications, 93
  arbitration, 159, 163
  decision-making, 2, 4, 179
  dichotomic approaches, 196

institution, 59, 106, 193
institutional powers (pre-appointment phase), 110–111
and joinder (*see* Joinder)
proceedings, 73–77, 109, 178, 187, 205
Constitution of Tribunal. *See* Appointment
Continuum
description, 104–105
forms/categories, 105
frequency of intervention, 106
initial phase of the proceedings, 109
institutional powers (pre-appointment phase), 110–113, 115
level of involvement, institution, 105–106
limitations, spectral representation, 107–108
supervised and unsupervised categories, 105
tribunal award, 112
Costs
arbitration costs, 38, 40, 50, 86, 87, 153, 181
legal costs, 38, 62, 63

D

Deadlines
extension of (*see* Extension of deadlines)
parties, 97
Decision, 63–66, 68–71, 79–80, 118–183, 187–213
Decisional nature. *See* Decision
Decision-making
arbitrators, 141
incidental and occasional, 118, 146
institutional power, 93, 125, 154, 186
judicial, 171
logistical services
measure, institutions, 175–182
presentation of the representation, 173–175
measure of, 22, 185, 214
process, 171
sharing, 188
Delay
arbitral proceedings, 36
complaints, 124, 196
and cost, 45
institutional arbitration rules, 53
prevention, 95
risk, 205
undue, 91
unreasonable, 91
Deposits, 38, 86, 87, 113
Discretion/discretionary power
administrator's, 78
degree of, 61, 70, 90
extensive, 90
granting, 108
ICC, 134
institution, 63, 74, 76, 91, 106, 109
interpretation, 94
level of, 55, 214
measure of, 65, 68, 75, 76, 79, 93, 112, 177, 178, 205
power, 59, 60
Domestic arbitration, 4, 23, 25, 143
Due process
activities of arbitral institutions
adversarial process, 204–205
equal treatment of the parties, 202–203
impartiality and independence, 199–201
judicial review, institutional decisions, 207–209
reasoning, 205–207
application of, 214
breach of, 191
desirability of the application, 196–199
extent, 209–210
institutional decisions, 186
mandatory, 155
principle, 143
purposes, 160

requirements of, 118, 119, 123–125, 131–133, 135–137, 141, 146, 148, 150, 151, 153, 154, 156, 159, 183, 184, 211
standards, 3, 187, 210, 214
supervision, 95
vocation, 190

Dutco
decision, 195
equal treatment of the parties, 202
jurisprudence, 77, 195

E

Enforceability
awards, 3, 39, 77, 80, 101, 120, 177, 193, 194
draft awards, 100
proper notification of award, 103–104

Equal treatment of the parties, 190, 202–203, 214

Ex parte, 202

Expedited arbitration, 106

Extension of deadlines, 66–68, 109–111, 138, 146, 153, 163, 187

F

Fast track arbitration. *See* Expedited arbitration

Formation of Tribunal. *See* Appointment

Frequency of intervention, 96, 106

G

Growth (of institutional arbitration)
benefits
authority in the implementation of the rules, 37–38
confidentiality, 41–43
enforceability of the award, 39
logistical support, 35–36
lower costs, 39–40
pre-established arbitration rules, 36–37
treatment of costs, 38
development
number of institutions, 33–35
volume of cases referred to institutions, 29–33
institutionalization (*see* Institutionalization of arbitration)
popularity *vs.* legitimacy, 43–47

Guerrilla tactics. *See* Strategic manoeuvres

H

Hands-on/hands-off approach, 46

I

Immunity, 25, 149, 168, 191

Impartiality
and cost efficiency, 156
and independence, 83, 143, 178, 186, 199–201, 210, 214

Independence
arbitrators, 143, 156, 167
decision-maker, 166–167
guaranteeing, 199
and impartiality (*see* Impartiality)
lacks of, 178
principle of, 163, 164
requirement of, 166, 178
statement of, 179–180

Institutionalization
additional responsibilities for the institutions, 48
autonomy, 50
complexity of arbitration proceedings, 48–49
development
flexibility, 49
ICC arbitration rules, 47
institutionalization *vs.* judicialization, 51–53
intervention, 47
LCIA, 50
source, 49

Interim measures, 71, 73, 109–111, 162, 188
Interpretation of arbitration rules, 92–95
Interventionism/interventionist, 44, 85, 98, 104, 106–109, 112, 188

J

Joinder
  application, 178
  and consolidation, 49, 93, 163, 206
  institutional powers (pre-appointment phase), 110–111
  institutional rules, 59, 75, 106, 193
  third parties, 4, 77–79, 109, 187, 196
Judicialization
  arbitration, 47
  vs. institutionalization, 51–53
Judicial nature. *See* Jurisdictional nature
Judicial review
  arbitral awards, 123, 144
  institutional decisions, 186, 199, 207–209, 211, 214
  The REDEC and *Pharaon* case, 137
Jurisdiction (decisions on), 69, 71, 78, 108, 110, 111, 121, 149–151, 154, 156, 192
Jurisdictional nature
  decision, 138, 139, 151
  ICC, 131, 138
  lack of, 130
  Opinter vs. Dacomex case, 133, 134

L

Language
  arbitration, 16, 109, 196
  choice of, 192
  decisions, 2, 4, 63–64, 110–111, 179, 180, 196, 208
  institutions, 106, 108, 187
Legal theory, 117
Legitimacy
  administrative decision, 207
  immediate, 22
  institutionalization of arbitration, 49
  institutions, 197, 207
  process, 167
  vs. institutional arbitration, 43–46
Level of intervention. *See* Interventionism
Lex arbitri, 65, 192
Logistical support, 17, 18, 35–36, 40, 84–86

M

Materiality (of institutional decisions)
  administrative/non-jurisdictional, 189
  ancillary capacity, 195–196
  arbitral award, 191
  capacity of institutions, 191
  challenges, 92
  choice of language, 192
  costs of arbitration, 191–192
  due process obligation, 190
  enforceability of awards, 193
  level of, 186
  moral responsibility, 190
  New York Convention
    Art. V(1)(b), 193–194
    Art. V(2), 195
  notion of "outcome", 188–189
  number of arbitrators, 192
  parties equal treatment, 190
  potential, 89
  quasi-judicial mission, 191
  seat of arbitration, 108, 192
  set aside award, 195
  vocation, 190–191
Monitoring role, 95–99
Myth/Mythology, 172

N

New York convention, 61, 86, 124, 193, 198, 208
Number of arbitrators, 79–82, 108, 110–111, 181, 192

O

Organisational nature, 11, 20, 34, 43, 125, 140, 141, 143, 146
Outcome
arbitral proceedings, 55, 59, 63, 66, 108, 176–178, 193, 196
cases, 3, 77, 79, 82, 92, 102, 104, 156, 159, 186, 188, 196, 204, 209, 210
determinative (*see* Outcome-determinative)
institutional decisions, 188–190, 192
Outcome-determinative, 186, 195, 197, 207–210, 214

P

Prima facie decisions on jurisdiction, 60, 69–71, 146, 149

R

Reasoned decisions, 121, 123, 133, 205, 207, 210
Removal of arbitrator, 89–93, 112, 181, 187, 210
Reporters, 17, 35, 85, 97
Representation
continuum (*see* Continuum)
cost of legal, 39
process, 117
realistic
ancillary nature, institution, 188
desirability of the application of due process, 196–199
functions of arbitral institutions, 185, 214
identification, due process, 199–209
institutional measures, 187–188
materiality, institutional decisions, 188–196
rejection, dichotomic approaches, 196
viable approach, 209–210
theoretical, 55, 95
traditional
"administrative" *vs.* "jurisdictional" dichotomy, 147–152
decision-making, 118, 175–182
functions of arbitral institutions, 214
origins and historical development, 125–146
presentation of, 118–123, 173–175
rationale, 123–125
Right to be heard. *See* Adversarial process

S

Scrutiny
arbitral awards, 48, 97, 112, 146, 166, 169
close, 147
decision-making, 2, 151
draft awards, 16, 100–104, 160
ICC's, 140, 141, 144, 154
informal, 107
institutional powers, 113
institutional rules, 106
process, 151, 168
Seat
arbitration, 4, 16, 48, 64–66, 76, 108, 109, 163, 180, 187, 192, 196, 205
China-seated arbitrations, 42
confidentiality, 41
decision-making, 2, 106, 110, 111, 159, 177, 179, 180, 208
issues, 112
selection of, 154
Selection of arbitrators. *See* Appointment
Set aside of award. *See* Annulment of award
Small claims, 61, 192
Soviet heritage/USSR chambers of trade, 9, 26, 27

Spectral representation, 114–115
Spectrum, 8, 76, 101, 105, 106, 182. *See also* Level of intervention
Strategic manoeuvres, 124, 186, 196
Supervised arbitration. *See* Administered arbitration
Supervision
  active, 113
  general, 95–99
  institution, 15, 120, 175
  LCIA, 21
  mission of, 151
  proceedings, 38
Systemic bias, 203

T

Terms of reference
  approval of, 84, 112, 165
  finalization of, 67
Theoretical representation. *See* Representation

W

Withdrawal of claim, 87–89, 113, 170

1. Moshe Hirsch, *The Arbitration Mechanism of the International Center for the Settlement of Investment Disputes,* 1993 (ISBN 07-923-1993-1).
2. Aida B. Avanessian, *Iran-United States Claims Tribunal in Action,* 1993 (ISBN 18-533-3902-4).
3. Isaak I. Dore, *The UNCITRAL Framework for Arbitration in Contemporary Perspective,* 1993 (ISBN 18-533-3573-8).
4. Vesna Lazić, *Insolvency Proceedings and Commercial Arbitration,* 1998 (ISBN 90-411-1115-8).
5. Joachim Frick, *Arbitration in Complex International Contracts,* 2001 (ISBN 90-411-1662-1).
6. Katherine Lynch, *The Forces of Economic Globalization: Challenges to the Regime of International Commercial Arbitration,* 2003 (ISBN 90-411-1994-9).
7. Christoph Liebscher, *The Healthy Award: Challenge in International Commercial Arbitration,* 2003 (ISBN 90-411-2011-4).
8. Hamid G. Gharavi, *The International Effectiveness of the Annulment of an Arbitral Award,* 2003 (ISBN 90-411-1717-2).
9. Abdulhay Sayed, *Corruption in International Trade and Commercial Arbitration,* 2004 (ISBN 90-411-2236-2).
10. Gabrielle Kaufmann-Kohler & Thomas Schultz, *Online Dispute Resolution: Challenges for Contemporary Justice,* 2004 (ISBN 90-411-2318-0).
11. Christopher R. Drahozal & Richard W. Naimark (eds), *Towards a Science of International Arbitration: Collected Empirical Research,* 2005 (ISBN 90-411-2322-9).
12. Ali Yeşilirmak, *Provisional Measures in International Commercial Arbitration,* 2005 (ISBN 90-411-2353-9).
13. Christian Bühring-Uhle, *Arbitration and Mediation in International Business,* second revised edition, 2006 (ISBN 978-9-041-12256-8).
14. Bernard Hanotiau, *Complex Arbitrations: Multiparty, Multicontract, Multiissue and Class Actions,* 2006 (ISBN 978-9-041-12442-5).
15. Loukas A. Mistelis & Julian D.M. Lew (eds), *Pervasive Problems in International Arbitration,* 2006 (ISBN 978-9-041-12450-0).
16. Julian D.M. Lew & Loukas A. Mistelis (eds), *Arbitration Insights – Twenty Years of the Annual Lecture of the School of International Arbitration, Sponsored by Freshfields Bruckhaus Deringer,* 2006 (ISBN 978-9-041-12606-1).
17. Mark Kantor, *Valuation for Arbitration: Compensation Standards, Valuation Methods and Expert Evidence,* 2008 (ISBN 978-9-041-12735-8).
18. Christoph Brunner, *Force Majeure and Hardship under General Contract Principles: Exemption for Non-Performance in International Arbitration,* 2009 (ISBN 978-90-411-2792-1).

19. Loukas A. Mistelis & Stavros L. Brekoulakis (eds), *Arbitrability: International & Comparative Perspectives,* 2009 (ISBN 978-90-411-2730-3).
20. Sam Luttrell, *Bias Challenges in International Commercial Arbitration: The Need for a 'Real Danger' Test,* 2009 (ISBN 978-90-411-3191-1).
21. Monique Sasson, *Substantive Law in Investment Treaty Arbitration: The Unsettled Relationship between International Law and Municipal Law,* 2010 (ISBN 978-90-411-3223-9).
22. Ileana M. Smeureanu, *Confidentiality in International Commercial Arbitration,* 2011 (ISBN 978-90-411-3226-0).
23. Won Kidane, *China-Africa Dispute Settlement: The Law, Economics and Culture of Arbitration,* 2011 (ISBN 978-90-411-3674-9).
24. Karel Daele, *Challenge and Disqualification of Arbitrators in International Arbitration,* 2012 (ISBN 978-90-411-3799-9).
25. Crina Baltag, *The Energy Charter Treaty: The Notion of Investor,* 2012 (ISBN 978-90-411-3428-8).
26. Alexandra Diehl, *The Core Standard of International Investment Protection: Fair and Equitable Treatment,* 2012 (ISBN 978-90-411-3869-9).
27. Manuel Indlekofer, *International Arbitration and the Permanent Court of Arbitration,* 2013 (ISBN 978-90-411-4766-0).
28. Günther J. Horvath & Stephan Wilske (eds), *Guerrilla Tactics in International Arbitration,* 2013 (ISBN 978-90-411-4002-9).
29. Albert Badia, *Piercing the Veil of State Enterprises in International Arbitration,* 2014 (ISBN 978-90-411-5162-9).
30. Nadja Erk, *Parallel Proceedings in International Arbitration: A Comparative European Perspective,* 2014 (ISBN 978-90-411-5264-0).
31. Simon Vorburger, *International Arbitration and Cross-Border Insolvency: Comparative Perspectives,* 2014 (ISBN 978-90-411-5419-4).
32. Ahmad Ali Ghouri, *Interaction and Conflict of Treaties in Investment Arbitration,* 2015 (ISBN 978-90-411-5417-0).
33. Reto Marghitola, *Document Production in International Arbitration,* 2015 (ISBN 978-90-411-5159-9).
34. Alfonso Gómez-Acebo, *Party-Appointed Arbitrators in International Commercial Arbitration,* 2016 (ISBN 978-90-411-6671-5).
35. Jonas von Goeler, *Third-Party Funding in International Arbitration and Its Impact on Procedure,* 2016 (ISBN 978-90-411-5015-8).
36. Dean Lewis, *The Interpretation and Uniformity of the UNCITRAL Model Law on International Commercial Arbitration: Focusing on Australia, Hong Kong and Singapore,* 2016 (ISBN 978-90-411-6700-2).
37. Stavros Brekoulakis, Julian D.M. Lew & Loukas Mistelis (eds), *The Evolution and Future of International Arbitration,* 2016 (ISBN 978-90-411-7004-0).
38. Rémy Gerbay, *The Functions of Arbitral Institutions,* 2016 (ISBN 978-90-411-6217-5).